DOGVILLE
VS
HOLLYWOOD

BY JAKE HORSLEY

CONTENTS

DOGS
VS
HOLLYWOOD

BY JAKE HORSLEY

Published in Great Britain and the United States in 2005 by

MARION BOYARS PUBLISHERS LTD

24 Lacy Road
London SW15 1NL

www.marionboyars.co.uk

Distributed in Australia and New Zealand by
Peribo Pty Ltd
58 Beaumont Road
Kuring-gai, NSW 2080

Printed in 2005
10 9 8 7 6 5 4 3 2 1

A CIP catalogue record for this book is available from the British Library.
A CIP catalog record for this book is available from the Library of Congress.

ISBN 0-7145-3103-0
13 digit ISBN 9780-7145-3103-8

Set in Bembo 11 pt
Printed in England by Mackays of Chatham.

For the precious few who stay true to the Muse.
And for Valerie, my original Muse.

'There's a natural war in Hollywood between the businessmen and the artist. It's based on drives that may go deeper than politics or religion: on the need for status, and warring dreams.'
Pauline Kael

'There's a place where money grows
on trees. The only way to reach it's on your knees.'
David Byrne, 'Something Ain't Right'

INTRODUCTION: *Dogville*, Hollywood and the Rule of the Mediocracy

'I think very often people start off with very good intentions, especially artists, and then they themselves become more and more important, so that the cause they have been working for slips into the background, and sometimes they lose it completely. I think that's very often the case.'

Lars von Trier

Talking of creative integrity in Hollywood is akin to preaching chastity in a whorehouse. At best, it is bad manners, at worst, suicide. Either way, you are going to upset the punters. The whores, on the other hand – for which read 'filmmakers' – might well be open to conversion; but if so, then the whorehouse is clearly not the place to do it (there are pimps as well as punters to worry about). Lars von Trier was never going to go to Hollywood, either, and so Hollywood would just have to come to him. This it finally did, in the alluring and delicate form of Nicole Kidman.

But first, let us define what we mean by 'Hollywood'.

Any collective of individuals, be this a business or group enterprise, must by definition develop and serve an interest of its own. It must, therefore, develop an agenda outside of and eventually overruling that of the individuals who have formed the group. This is the will (if not intelligence) of the collective. To clarify this point, consider government institutions, religions, even a simple sports club or protest group.

When enough individuals are directed towards a single goal, they cease to function as individuals, and begin to operate as components within the structure and agenda which they have created. Thus, it may be seen how the medical community, for example, 'conspires' to keep people sick and therefore dependent on it, even though the number of corrupt physicians deliberately poisoning their patients must – we trust – be relatively few. Instead, they poison us with paranoia about disease and a slavish dependence on medicine, both of which increase our susceptibility to illness. Ditto our various governments, which conspire collectively, and in this case individually too, to keep the world in a state of chaos and thus in need of governing.

There is no special need to posit malevolence in such an agenda – although we can if we like – since it is really the most basic, and base, of all interests that is being served: that of self-preservation. When individuals group together to solve, or at least address, some problem, the purpose of that group thereby becomes dependent on the existence of the very problem it seeks to solve. And so, as it develops autonomy and becomes a group-agenda – and hence develops the will to self-preservation – it begins quite naturally to serve a function directly counter to its original aim, namely: the maintenance (and even aggravation) of 'the problem'. The 'solution', which was abstract to begin with, gets lost in the shuffle, and is eventually forgotten altogether. Which brings us to Hollywood.

The purpose of Hollywood is – I trust none will argue – to make movies. This goes without saying, just as the purpose of bees is to make honey, McDonald's to make 'Big Macs' and politicians to wage war. The other purpose of Hollywood, or rather the purpose which is perhaps less self-evident (though still elementary), is to entertain the public and make money by doing so – though not necessarily in this order.

It might be said that the primary purpose of Hollywood (namely, those individuals who run the studios and make the deals and, further down the food chain, the ones who make the movies) is to entertain the public, and that movies, once invented, seemed like a good way to do it. This would be credible enough in a Utopian society populated by individuals geared towards making people happy. Since we do not live in such a society (at least, the author doesn't), let us assume that, in actual fact, the primary purpose of Hollywood is, and has always been, to make money.

Entertaining the public with movies was decided upon as a viable way to achieve this. Yet Hollywood is not a factory. Its 'products' cannot be mass-produced by machines to be identical, and sold over and over again for as long as people consume them, eat them, wipe their butts with them or go jogging in them. No. Here is the difference: the purpose of Hollywood is three-pronged, then: to make money by making movies that entertain people – and make them 'happy'. Since this three-pronged purpose cannot really be broken down like this, there might eventually occur to the self-sustaining system of Hollywood the following puzzling dilemma: if people need or at least will pay money for movies that make them happy, then happy people do not need or at least won't pay for movies. In fact, the less happy people are, the more bored and frustrated with their lives, the more they will pay to escape their misery and flee into the temporary relief of movies.

Just as medicine that makes us sicker keeps the medical industry thriving, movies that insult our intelligence and frustrate our hopes, that leave us despondent and fed up, are, perhaps, better for the movie industry as a whole than movies that make people 'happy'. After all, there is no acceptable alternative to modern medicine or Hollywood movies. So people will keep going back for more anyway, in the hope of finding that elusive cure. It is not likely to ever occur to these people that their needs are being deliberately denied in order to be better exploited. That is a possibility too ghastly to consider. It verges on paranoia.

The Art of Revenge

'I'm afraid you've learned far too much already.'

Grace's father, *Dogville*

Lars von Trier has almost certainly considered this possibility, however. Dogme 95 (which von Trier invented in Denmark in 1995, along with three of his 'Dogme brothers') was described in the manifesto as a 'rescue action'. It took on the hue of a military operation such as only an aesthetic crisis might require. Since art (or rather artists, those honeymakers) thrive on crisis, it is immaterial, finally, whether the crisis really existed or whether it was invented by those who wished to counteract it – or if the act of counteracting itself created the crisis. The fact remains that creativity and complacency cannot co-exist. Ergo, crisis is necessary for inspiration to arise, and for novelty – new perspectives and experiences – to come about.

Since the crisis I describe and which Lars von Trier responded to is itself a crisis of inspiration, a lack of novelty, then the irrelevancy of attributing credit or blame for such a crisis quickly becomes evident. I mention von Trier simply to drop his name and so reassure the reader that he or she is indeed reading a book about film, and not a manifesto of terrorist activity – though it may be a call to aesthetic terrorism. My intent is merely to bring these words back to specifics, and out of the almost abstract realm into which they were beginning to stray. Not only Lars but many, perhaps all, artists and creators (in this case of movies), must also have, at one time or another, considered the possibility that moviemaking has become a function of a collective agenda, global in scale, and thus ceases to be, if indeed it ever was, the means of individual creative expression. That it has become instead a diabolic system dedicated to the exact opposite goals that it once swore, or was at least assumed, to uphold.

Of course Hollywood is not, nor was it ever, about making art. This is something that hardly needs to be said at all, and it is perhaps merely a show of naiveté and guilelessness to do so. But that Hollywood is not even about making decent entertainment, that it is in fact, and with all the evidence before us, about making worthless dreck and so selling popcorn and securing product placement advertising (which make more money than human admissions ever could), this may give us reason to pause and consider. Because if Hollywood movies no longer even entertain us, then what the hell are they good for?

Which brings us to *Dogville*. *Dogville* is not so much an attack on Hollywood as an attack on its public. That makes perfect sense. Lars von Trier is an activist filmmaker, militant and austere, perhaps the most austere filmmaker that ever was. He has an agenda all his own. He is not susceptible to temptation, he is not to be assimilated, ever, into any other agenda outside his own. His agenda is akin to that of the preacher who preaches chastity outside the whorehouse – not because he disapproves of it and certainly not to save souls, but because he finds it boring and tasteless, because all the delights of sex are now gone from it, now that it has been made so easily and cheaply available. Von Trier's puritanism is not self-righteous or hypocritical; he doesn't denounce sin and then sneak off and fantasize about it in private (or worse still, commend himself for his virtue). From limitation comes new possibilities for freedom; and in chastity are new levels, new intensities, of desire. It is for the enhancement of lust, then, that he preaches chastity.

When von Trier attacks (i.e. deliberately alienates) his audience with *Dogville*, he is doing it, or so I believe, not merely for the satisfaction of revenge upon audiences for acquiescing to decades of Hollywood crap, but also, perhaps more astutely, in order to send a message to other filmmakers, those whores longing secretly for the chaste life, maybe even to regain their lost virginity. The message is simple: look, it can be done. Fuck studios. Fuck rules of engagement or entertainment. Fuck the audience. Fuck art. Fuck commerce. Just do it.

With *Dogville*, Lars 'just did it', making a film that rendered irrelevant any questions as to whether you like it or hate it. *Dogville* exists beyond that. He has even made it boring, I believe deliberately, and made boredom part of its aesthetic (the boredom increases the film's power). He has made a 'masterpiece' (i.e. a film that achieves what it sets out to achieve) that is neither entertaining nor even that artistic, that may not even be terribly good, at least if we use ordinary criteria – that of drama, for example – to judge it. But it is a film that is precisely what it was meant to be. What it is, and was meant to be, is a polemic disguised as a movie and not even well-disguised, either. It is a fable that is only partially about human beings. Mostly it is about the conventions of melodrama and the trappings, the follies and foibles, of movies. Ironic then, that US critics and ordinary viewers chose to see it, huffily, as an indictment of their country – a country von Trier has never visited and says he never will, partly due to a phobia of flying. In fact, *Dogville* is a much narrower (and broader) attack, aimed not at the USA but at one small, disproportionately influential corner of it: Hollywood. And for Hollywood, read: 'the world'.

The first thing that gets the chop in *Dogville* is the charm and comforts of make-believe. *Dogville,* despite the name, is not only not a Dogme film, it is reverse Dogme. The first rule of Dogme, 'Shooting must be done on location,' is here brazenly and wantonly defied by choosing to do away with location altogether. The movie is filmed entirely on a set and the set here is only partially constructed, so the film does not offer even the cozy confinement of filmed theater. It looks more like a backstage rehearsal in a giant warehouse. The film is narrated by John Hurt, thus violating Rule Two – 'sound must never be produced apart from images'. Rule Three, the one about hand-held cameras, is also discarded early on, as the first shot is an overhead establishing shot of the entire set. Although *Dogville* is in color, there is plenty of 'special lighting', most notably in the climax, that thumbs the nose at Rule Five. As for superficial action, forbidden by Rule Six, the film is rife with it, and positively wallows in rape and murder, ending with an orgiastic massacre to rival the most craven and superficial of Hollywood revenge fantasies. Regarding Rule Seven, *Dogville* is partially an exercise in 'temporal and geographical alienation,' offering no reassurance as to just when or where it is supposed to take place. In fact, the film deliberately confounds such questions, existing in a sort of 'neverywhere' limbo. As for Rule Eight: is it a genre movie? Here the rule seems inviolate, and it's inconceivable that any genre could exist into which *Dogville* might fit, unless it be the all-embracing 'genre' of melodrama. But the rest of the rules are joyously trashed, as if in a deliberate attempt to upset the director's Dogme devotees. *Dogville* is all about rule-breaking, so it's only fitting that it also defies the rules which von Trier and his Dogme brothers invented, back in 1995.

Dogville exists, like von Trier himself perhaps, expressly in order to confound. That is its *raison d'être*. To begin with, von Trier broke the ultimate (or original) unwritten rule, 'Thou shalt not sell out to Hollywood,' by casting Nicole Kidman in the central role, automatically turning his movie into a mainstream production (i.e. a Nicole Kidman movie; and since Lars also broke the final rule and took director credit, *Dogville* is also a Lars von Trier movie, though as products go, this one is considerably less in demand). It did not matter that in this case the mountain – Hollywood – had come to Mohammed; the fact remained that the 'twain-never-to-meet' had met, and agreed upon terms. The terms were those of Mohammed, however, and not the mountain. *Dogville* not only exemplifies von Trier's refusal to 'sell out' or compromise his vision for commercial gain, it even tells a story about it. That is to say, not only is the style of the film designed to alienate audiences and deny them any possibility of 'entertainment', the content itself, in metaphoric form, describes the necessity, and tragedy, of this defiance. *Dogville* is about the price of alienation.

To clarify: the heroine of *Dogville,* Grace, is on the run from her father, a gangster, and his hirelings; not because she's done anything wrong, but merely because she doesn't wish to be a part of the family business. The only way she can escape her background is by fleeing and hiding out in a small, backward, isolated town called Dogville. On arriving there, Grace first encounters Tom, a 'writer' who has written not a single line but takes pride in his craft. (Tom is von Trier's embodiment of 'evil', of the mincing ineffectiveness, the puny vanity and negligence, of the intellectual man.) The inhabitants of the town – once Grace has been introduced to them by Tom, and after putting it to the vote – agree to shelter her, on the condition that she perform services for each of them on a daily basis and thus justify her presence amongst them. At the end of the month, Grace is brought once more before the inhabitants, and they vote on whether or not she is to remain. One vote against and she must leave.

During the course of the month, Grace successfully ingratiates herself to the entire town and so is allowed to stay. Over time, however, the inhabitants of the town, though at first quite enamored of Grace, begin to mistreat her. They exploit her kindness, treating her with less and less consideration or respect, until finally she resolves to sneak away. She hides herself in the back of an apple truck, conspiring with the driver whom she believes is sympathetic, and he drives her outside the town. The apple man deceives Grace however: having revealed her plan to the townsfolk, he takes her a short distance then forces himself on her sexually. He then drives her back to the town and hands her over to the townsfolk.

Disgraced, Grace is chained up like a wild animal and used as a sex slave by the male inhabitants, while simultaneously reviled and spurned by the womenfolk. Tom, who has admitted he is in love with Grace, stands by and does nothing. He is in fact, through passivity, complicit in her torment, and is even tempted to take advantage of her incarceration for his own pleasure. There follows a long, drawn out period in which

Grace is dragged down to the status of the non-existent town mutt. (This mutt, also chained up, is the first person Grace meets, though we never see it, since von Trier uses a chalk drawing to designate the dog.) In the end, Grace's father, identified in the credits only as 'The Big Man', finally tracks her down, whereupon, in terror, the inhabitants release Grace. She goes to speak with her father, played by James Caan, in the back of his vehicle. He asks Grace to join him (the business), suggesting that now she has learnt more about the world, she is perhaps ready to assume her responsibility as his daughter. He promises her the highest position of power, a position second only to himself, if she will agree to return with him. 'Power is not so bad,' he tells her. 'I am sure that you can find a way to make use of it in your own fashion.' They discuss it, and Grace contemplates the town and its deeds. She asks herself, 'How could she ever hate them for what was at bottom their weakness?' The full moon breaks through the clouds and shines its light upon her, and she has a sudden realization. 'Light reveals the flaws. If she had acted like them she could not have defended a single one of her actions. The sorrow and the pain finally assumed their rightful place. What they had done was *not* good enough, and if one had the power to put it to rights, it was one's duty to do so.'

Realizing her true nature, Grace accepts her father's offer and uses her newly claimed power in order to 'solve the problem of *Dogville*' and 'make this world a little better'. She orders the destruction of the town and all its inhabitants and, after everyone else is dead, takes a pistol and shoots Tom in the head. After all we have witnessed, there is no question that, through such a brutal act of revenge, justice has indeed been served. The town of Dogville has got what it deserves, and we, in the audience, have been given what we needed. Retribution.

Now let us interpret *Dogville* in the following manner.

Lars von Trier breaks free of his 'Dogme mantle' and flees his past as ruthless avant-garde Danish filmmaker ascetic (his Mafia background), in order to take refuge in the small provincial town of Hollywood (represented by Nicole Kidman). Once there, it is uncertain if he will be accepted or not. He must ingratiate himself to everyone that he is obliged to work with (it is a community after all, and he is an outsider; it does not matter that von Trier never went to Hollywood, it is enough that he imagined doing so and made a movie about it). So he must set about pleasing, making himself useful or at last familiar to everyone he encounters within this community. This he succeeds in doing, but at a price. His short sojourn in 'Hollywood' begins to turn sour. He is accepted only to the point of being taken for granted. The exotic novelty of his presence wears off and all that remains is the knowledge that he is an outsider and not to be trusted. Hence subtle abuse follows, and Lars soon decides that Hollywood is not for him – too late, alas, for he has already entered the trap (he has taken on the responsibility of making a Nicole Kidman movie!). His attempt to escape serves only to confirm Hollywood's distrust of him, he is treated with open contempt and becomes a slave to Hollywood. Existing only to satisfy its base lusts, for money, fame and glory, he has become a whore.

All ends well, however, because von Trier's links to his Dogme past, his fellows warriors of the avant-garde, are strong. And soon those very same elements he had foolhardily but of necessity fled, in search of new experience, return to rescue him. He rejoins the Dogme Mafia, accepts his true calling, claims his natural birthright and power as artist–avenger, and – kills everyone in *Dogville*.

Or – makes the movie *Dogville*, in which he kills everyone in Dogville.

So you see how *Dogville* is a movie about how Lars von Trier has no choice but to make a movie like *Dogville*. No matter how hard he may try to sell out, he can't do it. He does not have it in him to be a whore. For Lars, it is freedom (revolt) or it is death (revulsion).

Dogville is a revolting picture in both senses. It is a picture in revolt, and a picture that revolts. It is designed to revolt and to incite revolt. It is a movie about the necessity – the rightness – of revenge, and it is an act of revenge in itself. Few people saw it as such, though they certainly felt it and responded to it that way (they hated it).

Dogville is far too long; it is repulsive and eventually becomes boring (once the repulsion becomes too great, and we get bored with being repulsed). And yet, it is exactly as long as it needs to be, as boring and as repulsive as necessary, to achieve its effects. Because, I think, von Trier not only wants us to feel revolted with the inhabitants of *Dogville*, he wants, and needs, us to feel revolted with his movie, and even, I suspect, with him for making it – for forcing it upon us and causing us to feel such revulsion, when we only want to be entertained! This is his methodology, and it is profound and inspired and all of a piece. It is a vision. A disgusting one, yes, but also a glorious and beautiful one (if we can only get past our disgust). Von Trier needs us to need his apocalyptic ending. After all, apocalypse, which is when an avenging God lays waste to a world devoid of redeeming qualities, is something we only get to enjoy at the movies. And usually only then because we are on God's side, delivering His vengeance; and not on the other side, receiving justice and being destroyed.

In *Dogville*, there is no familiar and comfortable frame of identification within which we can side with the avenging hero, and enjoy with impunity (zero guilt or misgiving) the wholesale destruction of evil – be it Arab terrorists, giant lizards, serial killers, Vietnamese soldiers or whoever, just so long as it is not us. The inhabitants of *Dogville* – repugnant as they may be – are ordinary people, everypeople, living in 'anywhere' USA. Their destruction is necessary to us, yes, but not simply because they are evil. It is because they are so goddamned ordinary. Their destruction isn't revenge, either for Grace or for the audience, those of us who have stuck it out. It is justice, the simple and necessary removal of what is devoid of value or decency: the eradication of corruption. Von Trier has worked hard to create in us a democratic contempt, not for any particular group or race, or even type, but for people in general, for human nature itself.

Grace's only virtue in the movie is having the strength (and grace) to wipe out the town of *Dogville*, and so relieve the awful burden of disgust and loathing with which the film would otherwise leave us. Von Trier's only virtue in making this movie is having the wit and cunning to know what the audience needs, and giving it to them. *Dogville*'s only virtue is to justify all its failings – its ugliness and ungainliness, over-length, awkward, unconvincing scenario and stilted performances – by cancelling them out with a timely, orgiastic, quite beautiful and immensely satisfying climax of divine destruction and wanton murder.

Von Trier is the town's creator, after all. He has the 'right' – the authority – to destroy it. Maybe even he has the obligation?

The Revenge of Art

'Style is what an artist uses to fascinate the beholder in order to convey to him his feelings and emotions and thoughts.'

Stanley Kubrick

Von Trier is a Catholic, but he was raised believing himself to be a Jew – his mother only broke the news to him on her deathbed, in what Lars called 'a very *Dallas* moment'. The message of *Dogville* is Christian, after a fashion (a Dostoyevskian fashion). It is apocalyptic. But it is von Trier's method of delivery that is remarkable here, more than the message per se, though they may be one and the same. The message is: 'Do unto others as you would have them do unto you'. Von Trier is not about turning the other cheek (Christianity is a bundle of contradictions, few of which are reconciled by the Book of Revelations). He is about meting out justice in the same measure that he would have it meted out to him. 'Do unto others' means here: make movies the way you would wish movies to be made. Give audiences the same kind of movie experience that you would wish for yourself. This is not quite the same as making movies for yourself, but it is close enough.

Von Trier is clearly aware of his audience, he just doesn't give a damn. And it goes further. He appears to be wilfully inflicting upon them – not merely the experience he wishes for himself (from movies) – but the very inverse of what audiences generally seek out, expect, demand, and pay to receive at the movies. At the same time, he gives them what they need: catharsis. He just exacts a much heavier toll than Hollywood movies generally dare to ask. This he does by forcing his viewers to be aware of the machinery of melodrama. He allows them to observe – to fully feel – how they are being manipulated into their responses.

Dogville is, in this regard – as a machine designed to create a cathartic reaction in its audience – little different from a Hollywood action-revenge melodrama starring Arnold Schwarzenegger or, to take it up a few notches, Clint Eastwood. An Eastwood flick, when effective, creates a state of tension in the audience that demands the release and relief of a violent and vengeful climax. The difference here lies only in the method used to create the tension. With Eastwood's action films, say *Dirty Harry*, *High Plains Drifter*,[1] *The Outlaw Josey Wales* or *Unforgiven*, a movie is a means of forgetting. It allows us to be absorbed into its melodramatic scenario ('entertained') and entails, even depends upon, creating a sense of righteous anger and loathing in us for the villain(s), and a full identification with the hero who will eventually destroy them. We are

1 There are some curious and amusing parallels to be made between *Dogville* and Eastwood's second film as director, the supernatural revenge Western *High Plains Drifter*. In the film, Eastwood plays the ghost of a murdered marshal who returns to his town to seek revenge. While he was the marshal there, the citizens arranged his death to protect business interests (or else simply stood by and allowed it to happen) by hiring three gunmen to kill him. The townspeople then double-crossed the killers and sent them to jail. The killers (who have sworn revenge) are due to be released from prison, and the town has hired three more gunmen to protect them from the original killers. When the drifter arrives, it is in a state of dreadful anticipation, and partially as a result of this, the hired gunmen pick a fight with the drifter while he is being shaved, and are instantly killed. The citizens, in desperation, and impressed by the stranger's shooting, seek to hire him to protect them instead. The drifter refuses, until the townspeople agree to give him a free hand in the town, 'anything he wants' (including, as it happens, the women, the first of whom he rapes, the second seduces). The stranger sets about training the inhabitants to defend themselves when the time comes. They are a useless bunch of weaklings, however, and moments before the killers are due to arrive (having had the townspeople paint the town red, and having renamed it 'Hell'), the drifter gets on his horse and leaves. Without his aid, the town is helpless to defend itself, and only when

treated more or less as children, duped (albeit willingly) into acquiescing to Eastwood's 'nihilistic dream world',[2] and succumbing to the logic therein. We are never asked, or even permitted, to question the hero's actions, any more than we are asked to question the actor/director's intentions (which are simply to entertain/dupe us). This is Clint, after all. We trust him. He is a superior moral (and creative) intelligence, a force both of nature and of 'art'. (I am of course referring primarily to Eastwood's 70s period, and not to more mature works such as *Mystic River* or *Million Dollar Baby*.) Von Trier does not ask – nor I suppose will he ever ask, not wishing to get it – the kind of blind trust and good will from his audiences that Clint does. He is rightly regarded with curiosity and suspicion, as someone whose movies and methods are obscure to us. *Dogville* creates its tension – the audience's need for the catharsis of violent climax – not by seducing us into its fantasy but by denying us the comforts and familiarity of melodrama. It is not a means of forgetting but a means for realizing – becoming more fully aware of – the subterfuges of movies, and of 'art' in general. Hence the anger and distaste we feel is only partially for the characters in the melodrama. More generally it is for the movie itself, and for von Trier for inflicting it on us, for his stubborn refusal to 'entertain'. Nor can we identify with the heroine, except so far as she is played by Nicole Kidman, and at least until she becomes an Eastwood-esque avenger, so displaying the force and righteousness that audiences are happy to identify with. They are less comfortable being inside the skin of a weak and indecisive victim.

Unlike the fantasy-heroic Eastwood, or Hollywood in general, of which Eastwood is perhaps the tallest still-standing icon and practitioner, von Trier does not treat us like children but as equals. (As mentioned, *Dogville* is primarily a film for other filmmakers.) He does not try to dupe us into emotional responses and so curry our favor, as Grace curries the town's favor. He asks us to question the logic and the credibility of his world, and once we have done so, if we are still with him, then, and only then, does he provide us with catharsis. It is a conscious catharsis, and so immeasurably more valid and satisfying,

---

the inhabitants have been rounded up by the killers does the drifter return to take his revenge. In a similar climax to that of *Dogville* the town is consumed by fire, revenge is served, and justice is done. The ghost disappears as he came, into the shimmering sunlight, there to find rest. Von Trier's fable might be seen as a sort of inversion of Eastwood's film (written by Ernest Tidyman), in which Grace is an angel sent to give the town one last chance to redeem itself. When it fails, she turns into the avenging angel of death, and burns it to the ground.

2 Pauline Kael, 'Killing Time,' from *Reeling*.

primarily because we did not have to be tricked into it, but also because von Trier is not interested in making us *like* him or his movie. The catharsis is not in service of the movie, the movie is a vehicle for creating catharsis. The joy of sitting through *Dogville* depends upon – is inseparable from – the misery and discomfort of sitting through *Dogville.*

Hollywood may entertain us and give us what we want, but we usually feel cheapened and sullied by the end of it and are unlikely to remember the movie for long. Von Trier – the high priest of 'indie' (independent) cinema as much as Eastwood is the sheriff of Hollywood – may not entertain us much, nor give us what we think we want from a movie; but we are likely to feel enriched, even purged, by the experience once it is over; and we will probably remember it, too.

The obvious question is: which do we prefer? Which way should movies be going? The less obvious and I think more useful question, the question this book wishes to ask, is: can the two 'schools' (movies as entertainment and movies as catharsis) be combined into a single discipline and a unified intent?

In *Dogville,* these two approaches are – aptly enough – described in the final, pre-holocaust scene as two specific kinds of arrogance: that of Grace's father and that of Grace herself. The arrogance of Grace's father is, as described by Grace, 'to plunder a God-given right'. Grace's father counters that it is also Grace's arrogance that he dislikes about her. Grace argues that she is not the one who is passing judgment, to which her father replies: 'You do not pass judgment because you sympathize with them. A deprived childhood and a homicide isn't really a homicide. The only thing you can blame is circumstances. Rapists and murderers may be the victims according to you but I, I call them dogs. And if they are lapping up their own vomit, the only way to stop is with a lash!'

'But dogs only obey their own nature,' Grace responds, 'so why shouldn't we forgive them?'

'Dogs can be taught very useful things,' her father replies, 'but not if we forgive them every time they "obey their own nature"!... You have this preconceived notion that nobody can possibly attain the same high ethical standards as you, so you exonerate them. I cannot think of anything more arrogant than that. You forgive others with excuses that you would never in the world permit for yourself!... The penalty you deserve for your transgression, they deserve for their transgressions! Does every human being need to be accountable for their own actions? Of course they do. You don't even give them that chance.'

The arrogance of Hollywood is that of Grace before her awakening to humanity's basic irredeemability (in Dogville). It is the arrogance that wishes to protect others from 'reality', from the truth, under the guise of compassion. It is arrogance that thereby denies us the possibility of growth, of facing the challenges of choice, of developing self-consciousness and conscience, that treats us as children and consumers to be amused and kept out of trouble, the matches always out of our reach.

The arrogance of the artist (which is what 'indie' represents, or must represent, if it is to mean anything at all juxtaposed with 'Hollywood') is that of Grace's father. It is the arrogance that already 'knows' – assumes – that humanity is unfit to govern itself, but states that it must be treated *as if* it had the potential to learn, i.e. treated *as if* it were responsible for its choices and actions, *as if* possessed of self-consciousness and conscience, in the hope that (there being no other hope besides this) it may develop this potential as a result. At which point, we are left with no choice but to grow, if we are to survive (or grok Lars' movie). It leaves the matches in easy reach, and encourages us – dares us – to play with them, in the belief that only direct experience of fire counts as true knowledge. If we must be burned to a cinder as a result, well, that is the price of free will, and of adulthood. Tribal coming-of-age initiations were traditionally difficult to survive. If it were otherwise, they would not constitute an initiation, nor precipitate the coming of age.

What *Dogville*, and this book, proposes is a reversal of the traditional concepts of virtue. In the hands of Hollywood, 'tolerance' or 'compassion' has become sentimentality and indulgence. Since the artist is ever drawn to restore equilibrium through extremes, he offers ruthlessness as the new measure of respect. Hollywood 'considers' its audience to the point of patronizing and indulging it, so revealing its secret contempt for it. The artist (the independent spirit of cinema) respects his audience enough to show his total and utter contempt for it. If you don't like it, he says, then do something about it. (We can start by proving ourselves undeserving of such contempt.)

Pauline Kael once said, 'If art isn't entertainment, what is it? Punishment?' *Dogville* is art as punishment, but by the end, we have been entertained, too. We are lighter, stronger for the experience – unlike after most Hollywood movies, which pummel us into submission and drain the life out of us while 'entertaining' us. But, like the Dogme exercise, we trust that von Trier only has to do this once to get it out of his system. Movies can be entertaining. They can be escapist fantasies and at the same time cathartic, enlightening experiences. They can be art, without the capital 'A' that accuses us of complacency and lack of depth.

To give four movies of recent years as examples: *Natural Born Killers, Fight Club, The Matrix* and *Phone Booth* are all, in their ways, as subversive as *Dogville*, or any other 'indie' film. Yet these movies are almost shamelessly entertaining. The function of these movies is primarily to entertain us, in fact, yet they do so not in spite of their subversive style and content, but *through* it. There is something that separates these movies from *Dogville*, however: they are products of the very same system which they are subverting. They are made by men and women (and groups of men and women) who – despite their creative sympathy for the apocalyptic – appear quite comfortable living within and benefiting from the system whose destruction so inspires them. Von Trier, I presume, also shops at supermarkets and uses gasoline, and the difference I am suggesting is one of temperament, of degree, and not absolute. What I am suggesting is that the people behind these movies – Oliver Stone, David Fincher, Brad Pitt, the Wachowskis, Keanu Reeves, Joel Schumacher et al., men also responsible for movies like *Alexander, Panic Room, Troy, Matrix Reloaded* and *Batman Forever* – are artists only when (and so far as) they are inspired by their material to be so, and only when obliged to be. The rest of the time, they seem to mix comfortably enough (if they will forgive me the phrase) with the other whores and pimps of Hollywood.

The movies I cite have a special dynamic, an intensity that comes from internal conflict that more 'pure' indie films rarely if ever exhibit. They are richly imbued with the doubt, despair and self-loathing that characterizes the momentarily repentant. Like whores who briefly become evangelists in order to escape the corrupting demands of their chosen lifestyle, they exhibit the joy and fervor of the recently converted. They suggest the conviction and intensity of doubt, of the dilettante-rebel who compensates for his lack of experience or commitment with excess enthusiasm.

It's doubtful, for example, that David Fincher would have taken such glee in trashing consumer culture and Western values as he did with *Fight Club* if he didn't also feel enslaved by them. Or that he could have adopted so anarchic a sensibility so whole-heartedly were it not for the awareness that, at the end of the day, he would be returning to the comforts of a bourgeois lifestyle. These movies, most nakedly and purely with *Phone Booth*, which even has a Dogme feel to it, are the impassioned fantasies of frustrated egos longing to unplug. Made by rich, decadent, probably unprincipled (since Hollywood actively discourages principles) movie fat cats, they are expressions of defiance, of the will and the right to have our cake and eat it – to get fat and complacent off the system while making movies that denounce it as corrupt. They are also, not despite but because of this, almost perfect works of art/entertainment.

They do not justify Hollywood, however. The exception proves the rule. They signify the completion of Hollywood's purpose, the end of its rule. For when the system delivers messages that betray its own corruption, then, clearly, the end of that system is at hand.

There is a saying in the (US) legal world – much used, little publicized (for obvious reasons) – that is as follows: 'Any prosecutor can convict a guilty man; it takes a great prosecutor to convict an innocent man.' Such 'game rules' have now replaced more traditional 'moral' principles in modern institutions such as Law, Politics and Hollywood, and the same basic principle might afford us a better understanding of the evidence, when it comes to the world of mass media. For the thrill of the challenge, and a perverse satisfaction at the rank stupidity of the public, publishers may, for all we know, take special pride in turning the most inexorable books into bestsellers. This is a rationale/motivation that can only come about when love of money has supplanted love of literature, naturally; the same applies in the legal world. In Hollywood in recent years, the game appears to have reached its apotheosis with works such as *Phantom Menace, Godchild* and the *Matrix* sequels, or indeed any number of summer blockbusters that – no matter how bad – are guaranteed to recoup their costs and garner a tidy, if not substantial, profit for the studios, for all concerned in fact. Everyone, that is, except the public.

In Robert Altman's *The Player*, the Faustian producer-executive played by Tim Robbins makes a quip to the effect of: 'Now if we can only do away with the writer, we'd really be cooking.' Hollywood has yet to succeed in this goal, but it has come close. Nowadays big Hollywood movies are worked on (not only before but even during shooting) by so many different writers-for-hire that the end result is that the movies seem to have been written by no one, or not to have been written at all. The situation is thus: a seemingly inexhaustible stream of worthless movies that make money for studios to make more worthless movies with, and so keep the public hungry for ever-more worthless movies. The medicine that forever promises but never delivers the cure. It is a blueprint for everlasting dominance over the masses, Hollywood supreme, worlds without end. Save for one single factor – time.

Time means change; time means impatience with and intolerance for no-change. One way or another, change must come to pass. When a system refuses to change, when it establishes itself – finds 'stability' from – a refusal to change, then the need for change builds and builds, until a point where it can only come about apocalyptically, i.e. suddenly and catastrophically. A long period of apparent no-change, then, is the ideal lead-in to a short period of transformation.

A system that is corrupt is by definition already dead. Corruption comes not before but after death has occurred.

This simple logic can – and must – be applied to the world today: the legal world, the political world, the world of media and entertainment, and the world of Hollywood. Concepts such as Art, Science and Religion, since they are eternal and abstract, cannot be corrupt, nor can they be corrupted. They stand outside any institution or discipline that claims to represent them. The institutions themselves, however those lifeless structures, ideologies, theories or styles – are like shells, crusts that form around the abstract, in order to make us conscious of it. As such, they are by their very nature corrupt; the only question is how corrupt they are. This usually relates to how long they have been around.

Like bodies, the moment such institutions or ideologies are created, they begin to rot. When systems designed to host and transmit abstract principles instead serve to imprison and distort them, it is safe to say that the corruption has reached a critical stage; that it has in fact nullified the original function of the system. It has high-jacked its meanings (those of Art, Science, Religion) to its own ends, ends which are the precise inverse of those it was created to serve. This is only natural, since in order to further itself, the corruption – the system – must overrule and oppose the will of its creator.

This is the point of total revolt, when the cells become the disease and the body becomes death. There is nothing left but for the shell to collapse, to fall away under the pressure of the original principles (those principles which the system – while still a host to them – has strived in vain to repress). This is the inevitable revenge of art, over any and all institutions that claim, but finally fail, to represent it. Like Hollywood.

Whoops, Apocalypse. What is wrong with this picture?

Hollywood! How far hast thou fallen, down to Dogville and beyond. The revolution has begun, O Hollywood, and the rule of the Mediocracy is over!

The revenge of art is the emergence of the original principle and intent of 'Art.' Being one with that of Science and Religion, the intent is simply to enlighten, through any and all means necessary, the heart and mind of mankind, in order that Truth and Beauty may come to dwell once more therein.

In the meantime, let's go to the movies.

Chapter One - Hollywood Genesis: A Brief History of the Movies

'Hollywood was invented by hoodlums from central Europe. And today a Hollywood lawyer is not a hoodlum. He's a bureaucrat.'

Jean-Luc Godard

It all began with a toy.

The first photographs (beginning in the 1840s) were produced on a piece of glass. In 1887, an alternate method was discovered by Hannibal Godwin, and used a transparent material (called celluloid) coated with a chemical film sensitive to light. When exposed to light, the celluloid retained the image. A manufacturer of photographic equipment, George Eastman, heard about the miraculous new development and started making celluloid. Soon after, Thomas Edison began experimenting with it, and eventually came up with the kinescope.[1] Patent applications were made in 1891 for a motion picture camera called a kinetograph, and a motion picture peephole viewer, called a kinetoscope.

The kinetoscope worked by winding the film inside a box, from one spool to another, whereupon the pictures on the film appeared to move. That tiny miracle of technology was the birth of motion pictures. Naturally the public was curious, and kinetoscope parlors first appeared in New York in 1893, soon spreading to the other major cities. A motion picture studio, the Black Maria, opened at the West Orange complex for the creation of short films, generally of current variety acts, to play inside the kinetoscopes.[2]

[1] Actually the first machine was designed by Edison's associate, William K.L. Dickson, who experimented with a cylinder-based device for recording images before turning to a celluloid strip. In October 1889, Edison returned from Paris to be presented by Dickson with a device that projected pictures and contained sound.

[2] 'In 1893, the world's first film production studio, the Black Maria, or the Kinetographic Theater, was built on the grounds of Edison's laboratories at West Orange, New Jersey, for the purpose of making film strips for the kinetoscope. In early May of 1893 at the Brooklyn Institute of Arts and Sciences, Edison conducted the world's first public demonstration of films shot using the kinetograph in the Black Maria, with a kinetoscope viewer. The exhibited film showed three people pretending to be blacksmiths. On Saturday, April 14th, 1894, Edison's kinetoscope began commercial operation. The Holland Brothers opened the first kinetoscope parlor at 1155 Broadway in New York City and for the first time, they commercially exhibited movies, as we know them today, in their amusement arcade. Patrons paid twenty-five cents as the

In those early days, the moving image was just another curiosity, alongside the human skeleton and the bearded lady, something to marvel at without any (apparent) purpose. There was plenty of profit in peephole viewers, however, and Edison was initially reluctant to develop a motion picture projector, thinking it would render the new toy obsolete. He eventually capitulated and invented the kinescope, a device for projecting images onto a screen that allowed larger audiences to share the experience. The invention (dubbed the vitascope) was unveiled to the public on April 23rd, 1896, at the Koster and Bial's Music Hall, New York. The film included images of a dancer, a prizefighter and waves lapping the shore. With these images, the American movie scene began.[3]

At first, it was a sort of circus act, a technological marvel, a toy for grown ups; presumed to have more 'important' uses soon to be discovered. Children eventually grow out of their toys, but since adults have nowhere to 'grow' to, they tend to hold on to their toys for life. So it was with the movies. One of the first, little-credited (perhaps because he was French) pioneers to exploit the potential of this new toy was Charles Pathé. While broke and jobless, Pathé was inspired by hearing one of Edison's phonographs at a fairground, borrowed enough cash to buy his own machine, took it to a fairground near Vincennes and set up a stall. That first day he made enough to live on for several months, and after a few weeks, he was a rich man. Pathé then branched out by buying some of Edison's old films, making copies and selling them to fairground showmen. Soon after, he teamed up with a wealthy entrepreneur, Claude Grivolas, and, with a loan from the Crédit Lyonnais bank, transformed his company Pathé Frères into a major film company.

At the turn of the century, Pathé took an unprecedented step and

admission charge to view films in five kinetoscope machines placed in two rows. Nearly five hundred people became cinema's first major audience during the showings of films with titles such as *Barber Shop, Blacksmiths, Cock Fight, Wrestling* and *Trapeze*. Edison's film studio was used to supply films for this sensational new form of entertainment. More kinetoscope parlors soon opened in other cities (San Francisco, Atlantic City and Chicago).' See *History of Film*, http://www.filmsite.org/filmh.html

3 Officially, it was the Lumière brothers in France, in 1895, who first showed a movie to a group audience. 'In 1897, the first real cinema building was built in Paris, solely for the purpose of showing films. The same did not occur until 1902 in downtown Los Angeles where Thomas L. Talley's storefront, two hundred seat Electric Theater became the first permanent US theater to exclusively exhibit movies – it charged patrons a dime. By 1898, the Lumiere's company had produced a short film catalog with over one thousand titles.' *History of Film*, website as previous, and all *History of Film* quotes hereafter. (In those early days, films were sold rather than rented to exhibitors.)

began film production, hiring Ferdinand Zecca to oversee this end of the business. In 1901, Zecca made *L'Histoire d'un Crime*, a six-part melodrama.[4] Pathé also hit upon the idea of using a regular troupe of actors, thereby prefiguring the contract system soon to be established in Hollywood. 'Without knowing, and ten years before the creation of the first major American studio, Charles Pathé had laid the foundations of the system that would enable the Hollywood moguls to reign over the movie industry for decades to come.' By 1907, Pathé's studios were making films at the rate of one per day; by 1908, 'Pathé's domination of world cinema was complete. He was selling twice as many films in the United States as all the American companies put together.' Pathé later admitted, 'I didn't invent cinema, but I did industrialize it.' [5]

Initially, as stated, the makeshift movies were shown in vaudeville shows and at fairgrounds and carnivals; then as they began to attract greater audiences, the back of supply stores or any other public venues were used, the profits shared between the property owner and whoever supplied the 'movies'. These were the 'nickelodeons'.[6] Naturally, as this practice gained momentum, the need for new movies to satisfy the ever-growing public interest likewise increased. The public's fascination (contrary to the expectations of many) did not diminish once the novelty wore off. As David Puttnam writes (in *Movies and Money*):

'The members of this audience were, almost without exception, the urban poor, the new immigrants who could not in their wildest dreams afford the admission prices of the more conventional forms of entertainment to be found in the theater or in vaudeville houses. And even if they could afford the prices, millions of these slum dwellers were excluded by the even more impenetrable barrier of language: most of them spoke little or no English... The nickelodeons changed all that forever. They gave the urban poor a cheap, affordable entertainment of their own, located – unlike the traditional downtown theaters – in converted stores just a few yards from their homes. Most important of all, no one

---

4 This wasn't only happening in France. 'British filmmakers had been among the first to respond to the demand for stories that thrilled the audience; James Williamson's *Fire!* appeared in 1902, and Frank Mottershaw's chase picture *A Daring Daylight Burglary* a year later.' David Puttnam (with Neil Watson), *Movies and Money*, pg. 28.
5 All quotes, Puttnam, pg 36-7.
6 Harry Davis invented the nickelodeon, using empty stores to house picture shows and charging a nickel for entrance. 'His simple idea spread like wildfire' (Puttnam, pg. 31). The earliest actual movie theaters were converted churches or halls.

was excluded on grounds of origin or education. Films created a common experience that drew together all the disparate communities then crowding into the New World.'[7]

These audiences returned to see the same 'movie' over and over, bringing family and friends to share in the experience. Even if the novelty was eventually to wear thin, the fascination did not, and shows no signs of dwindling over a hundred years later. Inevitably, there arose a demand for new moving images, and for a greater variety, and it soon began to dawn on the more attentive entrepreneurs at the time that here was a potential industry. In the early days, when films were sold to individuals or companies (who then took them around the country to fairgrounds or nickelodeons until the public's interest dwindled or the film wore out), there was a limited potential for profit. All that changed in 1903 when, as Puttnam explains:

'...a number of American film manufacturers simultaneously hit upon an entirely revolutionary idea. They began to buy films from other firms and rent them on to individual exhibitors. Among these pioneers were the Miles brothers who were based in New York. Hearing that the Biograph Company was about to sell off a pile of old films at bargain prices, they bought the entire stock and then traveled around the country renting the films out to individual theaters on a weekly basis. New companies began to emerge that specialized in the renting of films; in the process, they created outfits that came to be known as film exchanges. Thus was born the modern idea of the film distributor, the specialist middleman controlling the territory between producer and exhibitor.' [8]

The first motion pictures were as basic as the public appetite demanded, requiring merely a camera, a couple of 'actors' (attractive people capable of following simple directions), a set or stage (or an outdoor location) and a rudimentary crew. The idea of a director did not yet exist: all that was needed in the early days was someone to organize the shoot, make sure the camera was running and place the actors in the frame.

Since 'flickers' (as movies were originally known) came into being before the existence of studios, it might be fair to say, then, that

7 Puttnam, pg 32-33.
8 Puttnam, pg 29

independent cinema existed before Hollywood. These crude little enactments hardly merit the designation of movies, however, and it was not until certain individuals decided to invest large amounts of money in the burgeoning industry (when, as Steven Bach put it, 'mere flickers of light inspired flickers of greed'[9]), to build actual studios (factories for producing images), that 'cinema' (as we think of it today, as an 'art form') was born. Most of these individuals were Jewish immigrants with little or no capital but the vision to build an empire out of nothing.[10] As Puttnam observes, movies 'were a diversion for the poor and rootless. Hardly surprising, then, that it was from exactly this group in society that the next wave of successful film pioneers emerged.' [11]

The first official motion picture (retrospectively at least, and certainly the first movie 'hit') appeared in 1903, when Edwin S. Porter made an eleven-minute long film for the Edison Company called *The Great Train Robbery*. People all over the country flocked to the nickelodeons (named for the nickel entrance fee) to experience it. This was the beginning of narrative cinema in the US. In 1910, the population of Hollywood was 5,000; within ten years, it had grown to 35,000.[12] Realizing the need to counteract the increasing competition from Europe, in 1908 Thomas Edison had initiated a merger with the various US film companies – Armat, The American Mutoscope and Biograph Company, Vitagraph, and his own – to form a cartel, the Motion Picture Patents Company, soon to be known as 'The Trust'. The Trust began operating at the end of 1908, at a time when foreign imports made up around seventy percent of the short films seen in the US. Within less than a year, the European portion of imported films halved in number. Thus began a process that would inexorably turn

9 Steven Bach, *Final Cut: Art Money and Ego in the Making of Heaven's Gate, the Film That Sank United Artists*, pg. 30.

10 To name a few of the major players: Adolph Zukor, Marcus Loew, Jesse Lasky, Sam Goldwyn (Goldfish), the Warner brothers, Carl Laemmle (Universal Pictures), William Fox, Louis B. Mayer. The fact that most of these individuals were Jewish is documented by the book, *An Empire of Their Own*, by Neal Gaber.

11 Puttnam, pg 31.

12 'By 1911, New Jersey film producer David Horsley [no relation] established/opened Hollywood's first motion picture studio, the Nestor Film Company, in an old tavern at the corner of Sunset Boulevard and Gower Street (later dubbed "Poverty Row") and "Hollywood" was soon on its way to becoming the film capital of the world. (Many years later, the site of the Nestor Studio was occupied by the West Coast headquarters of CBS.) It was also developing a "movie colony" and distinctive carefree lifestyle for its filmmakers and actors. By 1912, fifteen film companies were operating in Hollywood, and large studios were becoming the norm. Nickelodeons were on the decline and were

movies into 'America's first truly indigenous form of mass culture.'[13]

Hollywood came into being as a result of the endeavors of individuals with the foresight and the means to take full advantage of the new technology (and of the public's obvious interest in it), and to use it for their own empowerment and enrichment. It is highly doubtful however – at this early stage – that there was much thought of inventing or exploring a new art form. It was simply a business prospect, risky, but of possibly limitless potential. That said, the moguls in question could hardly have failed to be aware that they were embarking on a form of marketing that was entirely new, and therefore unmapped, and that they were, in effect, endeavoring to profit from a product that they (like anyone) had only the vaguest idea of how to manufacture. As Steven Bach observed, 'The key to the box office was not production but distribution, and the great pioneers who were to become moguls and tycoons and czars were almost never producers (though they often called themselves that). Rather, they were exhibitors who had a clear, simple need that continues to the present day: product.'[14]

D.W. Griffith and George Méliès: the Two Movie 'Schools'

'Sometimes I think our aims are still old. All the discoveries seem to be discoveries of means. I think perhaps I'm conservative in that way. I wonder if there is anything to discover. I mean, things that are not superficial. We discover and invent new ways of finding out the same old things.'

Hal Hartley

being replaced by larger movie palaces, and audiences demanded longer films beyond one or two reels. Movie production was becoming divided between the East and West Coast studios.' *History of Film.*

13 Puttnam, pg. 52. 'Eventually, a successful anti-trust suit, instigated by William Fox (founder of the Fox Film Corporation), was first heard by the US government in 1913 (on behalf of independent film companies including Paramount, Fox and Universal) against the MPPC. In October, 1915, the MPPC and its General Film subsidiary were declared an illegal monopoly. The trust was ordered to pay over $20 million in damages. Following litigation for anti-trust activities and its 'restraint of trade', the MPPC was finally ordered to disband by the US Supreme Court in 1917 and officially dissolved by 1918. But the independents had already outmaneuvered the ineffectual trust. The dominance of East Coast studios was over, as Hollywood became the center of film production, and many of the independents on the West Coast combined into bigger companies.' *History of Film*

14 Bach, pg. 32

As everybody knows, the first movies were silent, short and clunky and characterized by exaggerated (not to say hammy) performances, meant (one supposes) to compensate for the absence of exposition that came later through dialogue. Mary Pickford was perhaps the first movie star, D.W Griffith the first (to many still the greatest) movie star director. Griffith is attributed with more or less single-handedly inventing what we think of today as basic film grammar: establishing shots, close-ups, flashbacks (which Griffith called 'switchbacks'), fade-ins and fade-outs, the use of the iris lens to zoom in on details of action, the use of titles, editing for parallel action and 'dramatic continuity', atmospheric lighting, and for encouraging 'restraint in expression' in screen acting. In fact, as is usually the case, history is not quite so cut and dried.[15]

When Griffith saw his first picture show, he is reported to have described it as 'silly, tiresome, inexcusable,' adding that 'any man who enjoys such a thing should be shot at sunrise.' Perhaps the first (though certainly not the last) filmmaker to be inspired by an 'I could do better' epiphany of disgust, Griffith set to work correcting the situation. Within a few years, he was describing movies as 'the greatest spiritual force the world has ever known.'

By 1920, Griffith had pioneered the concept of widescreen cinema, introduced the expressionist use of color tinting, and been the first to commission original music scores (he also sent a camera up in a balloon).

On the other hand, well before Griffith began his pioneering work, in 1903, Porter's *The Great Train Robbery* had made primitive use of parallel story-telling. Porter's other Edison productions make use also of dissolves, close-ups and camera movement. In Russia, meanwhile, Sergei Eisenstein was doing pioneer work of his own, most notably with *Battleship Potemkin*, with which he put into practice his theory

---

15 'The first feature-length film made in Europe was from France – Michel Carré's *L'Enfant Prodigue* (1907), an adaptation of a stage play. The first feature film produced in the US was Vitagraph's *Les Miserables* (1909) (each reel of the four-reel production was released separately). A second feature film, Charles Kent's Vitagraph five-reel production titled *The Life of Moses* (1909) was also released in separate installments. The first film to be released in its entirety in the US was *Dante's Inferno* (1911, It.). The first US feature film to be shown in its entirety was H. A. Spanuth's production of *Oliver Twist* (1912). *Queen Elizabeth* (1912, Fr.) was the third film to be shown whole. Although US production and exhibition of feature films started slowly in 1912, the next few years demonstrated tremendous growth when foreign competition encouraged development.' *History of Film*. According to David Puttnam, the first ever feature film (over an hour in length) was actually made in Australia, by J. & N. Tait in 1906, and called *The Story of the Kelly Gang*.

of montage.[16] Griffith's true innovation was that he made use of all these various techniques with an unprecedented skill, dramatic savvy and audacity. While working at the Biograph production company, he kept up an output of around nine films a month, finally totaling nearly five hundred productions in five-and-a-half years. Griffith had almost limitless opportunity to experiment with film at a time when the rules were still being invented, and while audiences were waiting for their expectations to be met and exceeded.[17]

In the end, Griffith had made one-reelers of almost every conceivable genre before 'genre' had even been invented.[18] He was the first to explore (and take full advantage of) the medium's potential to create a sustained experience of *otherness*, to tell a complex story over a long period. Inspired by the classic novels (particularly those of Dickens), he aspired to simulating an almost dreamlike state in audiences and thereby creating a surrogate reality for them. Through celluloid, most of the ingredients of everyday life could be re-created, using elaborate sets, special effects, ingenious camera work, and impassioned performances. None of this sounds the least bit unfamiliar to today's audiences, of course, since that's precisely what they expect movies to do. But before Griffith, they didn't.

16 To illustrate the theory, Eisenstein famously juxtaposed a shot of a man's face with images of food, a woman, a starving beggar, and so forth, to 'reveal' an expression of hunger, lust, pity, etc, on the man's face. He then showed the image in an isolated context, demonstrating that the man's face was in fact devoid of expression. This was the basic principal of montage: the conveying of emotion, effect and meaning through the juxtaposition of images (editing).

17 'A little credited player in the Hollywood Genesis was Thomas Ince. Ince decentralized and economized the process of movie production by enabling more than one film to be made at a time (on a standardized assembly-line) to meet the increased demand from theaters, but his approach led to the studio's decline due to his formulaic, stale, mechanized and systematized approach to production. Ince mysteriously died one night in November, 1924, aboard William Randolph Hearst's yacht in the harbor of San Pedro while celebrating his 42nd birthday. (The murder was recreated in Peter Bogdanovich's *The Cat's Meow* (2002), which speculated that he was shot when a drunken Hearst caught his mistress, Marion Davies, in amorous circumstances with Charlie Chaplin and shot at him, accidentally hitting and killing Ince instead.)' The *History of Film*. US cable network HBO's film of the making of *Citizen Kane* (*RKO-281*, which made Hearst its subject) speculated the same thing. Today, few of Ince's films from his days of film production are left, one exception being *The Italian* (1915), which was preserved by the National Film Registry

18 A one-reeler was ten to twelve minutes of film, the maximum capacity of projectors at the time. Film historians give Griffith credit for the invention of every genre save that of fantasy cinema (pioneered by George Méliès and Thomas Edison) and the epic, which he was forced to leave to Italian filmmakers until he had enough money to outdo them.

Griffith's real breakthrough came when he staked over $100,000 of his private funds (with a cast that followed him from Biograph) to make *The Birth of a Nation* in 1915. Originally titled 'The Clansman', and based on the novel by Rev. Thomas E. Dixon, it was the longest movie ever made in the US at the time. Widely regarded today as a politically naïve and slightly embarrassing masterpiece, the film advocated white supremacy and climaxed with members of the Ku Klux Klan 'riding to the rescue of besieged farmers threatened by Piedmont's black militia.'[19] With its brazenly racist message, its use of white actors in black-face, and its glorification of the Ku Klux Klan, the film stirred up a fierce controversy. Woodrow Wilson, the US president at the time, described *Birth of a Nation* as 'like writing history with lightning,' adding that, 'my only regret is that it is all terribly true.' The film was denounced by the NAACP, and incurred protests in Atlanta, Boston, and Chicago, while the Ku Klux Klan enjoyed a resurgence of popularity. The following year, a contrite Griffith responded with *Intolerance* (1916), his three-hour epic that interwove four stories about the evils of prejudice; at a cost of $400,000 and released in the midst of the First World War, the film was a commercial failure, in part because of the growing pro-war sentiment in the country. Despite the film's failure, it is now commonly considered to be Griffith's masterpiece, and the critic Pauline Kael (among others) regarded it as the finest movie ever made.

'We are playing to the world,' Griffith once said with characteristic grandiloquence. 'We've gone beyond Babel, beyond words. We've found a universal language – a power that can make men brothers and end war forever.'

But reaching higher than Babel only means having further to fall. By the time of his final film (1931), aptly titled *The Struggle*, Griffith was faced with commercial ruin. For the last seventeen years of his life, the greatest pioneer in the history of film was unable to work, shunned by the studios and forgotten by the public. When the D.W. Griffith Corporation went bankrupt and his films were auctioned, Griffith bought the rights to twenty-one of them for $500. It somehow perfectly encapsulates the nature of Hollywood – the Babylonian empire which more than any other filmmaker Griffith helped establish – that he was also its first victim.

19 *History of Film.* 'The film premiered in Los Angeles, with a ticket price of $2 (higher admission prices could be charged for feature-length movies), and on Broadway in New York, it played to packed houses for almost a year. Although its investment was $110,000, it became one of the highest-grossing films of all time ($10–14 million dollars, although some figures were probably exaggerated).' Ibid.

As stated, Griffith's method was one of realism, the staging of historical scenes to create the illusion of actual events. Some years before Griffith, however, the French filmmaker George Méliès was working towards very different ends, ends relating to the creation of worlds not of history (or even reality) but of the imagination. Méliès' approach to the new medium was expressionistic, even Surrealist. Illusionist, conjurer and theater owner/manager, Méliès wanted to use film as a means for making the fantastic happen; looking for a new medium in which to expand his repertoire of stage effects, he heard about the Lumière Brothers' projected film screenings (in late 1895) and from 1896 on, he began showing films regularly at his theater. That same year, while filming a street scene, his camera jammed for several seconds; when he processed the film, he was enchanted to see objects suddenly appear and disappear, 'transforming' into other objects (a carriage turning into a hearse, for example); it was via this serendipity that Méliès discovered a previously untapped potential in celluloid, and went on to develop a series of complex special effects for manipulating time and space. Setting up the very first European film studio in 1897, Méliès was the creator of the first double exposure (*La Caverne Maudite*, 1898), the first split-screen shot (with the actors appearing opposite themselves, in *Un Homme de Tête*, 1898), and the first dissolve (*Cendrillon*, 1899). He was also the pioneer of screen nudity, with *Après le Bal*, 1897. His most famous film is 1902's *Le Voyage dans la Lune*.

Like Griffith, however, Méliès' career ended ignominiously. Squeezed out by commercial rivals, and suffering diminishing returns as the novelty of his films wore off, he abandoned filmmaking in 1912. In 1915 he converted his studio back into a variety theater and resumed his career in stage magic. By 1923, he faced bankruptcy, and his theater was torn down. He was eventually acknowledged for his pioneering film work, however, awarded the Legion of Honor, and given a rent-free apartment, where he lived out the rest of his days (he died in 1938). Even while in his prime, Méliès' approach – directly opposed to that of Griffith, but seemingly even more suited to the medium – for some reason did not enjoy the same measure of success, nor have the same influence or endurance within the industry, as Griffith's. To this day, if we posit two opposing schools of cinema – that of Griffith and that of Méliès – it is clear that only one of them has held sway over the medium. Fantasy cinema exists, of course (Gilliam, Burton, Lynch et al), but it is an exception that proves the rule. Everything else belongs to the Griffith school. For whatever reason, the public opted for realism over fantasy. Perhaps, since they sought in movies an escape from reality, they didn't want to be reminded that their new refuge was only make-believe?

Sound, Color, World War II and Film Noir

'Before there were any stars and especially during the unlamented days of the Trust, most pictures were rented or sold at a flat rate regardless of content or cast. Suddenly the entire structure of pricing individual pictures changed, with higher prices demanded for bigger star names and, in some cases, director names in much the same manner that prevails today... The early moguls now found themselves being wagged by what had seemed the most negligible of tails: actors.'

Steven Bach, *Final Cut*

In 1919, in the first case of artists taking over the asylum, Charles Chaplin, D.W. Griffith, Mary Pickford (Chaplin's wife) and Douglas Fairbanks Sr. created United Artists, an independent studio that aimed to cater to the needs of the 'artists'. (The very word must have sent shivers down the spines of the reigning studio heads.) United Artists was created to provide actors and filmmakers with the freedom to devote themselves to personal projects without suffering interference from the studios, and to distribute only independently-produced films (including those of Buster Keaton, Rudolph Valentino and Gloria Swanson). The company was initially a success, and endured for several decades.[20] In 1922, following a series of Hollywood scandals that led to an increase both in government scrutiny and public distrust of the movie industry, the various studio heads collectively invited Will Hays, the head of US Post Office or 'postmaster general', to preside over a new organization, to be called the Motion Picture Producers and Distributors of America (MPPDA). As Puttnam describes, The MPPDA (or 'Hay's Office', as it soon became known):

'...would implement what amounted to a healthy degree of self-censorship by the studios. What was much more important from the industry's point of view, it would provide a single corporate voice and thus enable the industry to engage in active

20 By the end of the 1940s, however, the company was losing $100,000 a week and the various artists, no longer united, were not even talking to each other. The company was sold to Arthur Krim and Bob Benjamin, two lawyers who became legendary in the business (especially Krim), in 1951 and became solely a financing and distributing company. In 1967 it was bought up by Transamerica. It's ironic that United Artists was finally destroyed by the indulgences of a runaway 'artist', Michael Cimino, whose

lobbying at home and abroad. It also had the effect of reassuring nervous financiers on Wall Street... Hay's crusade against what he considered morally undesirable "alien customs" converged with the moguls' desire to ensure that American movies dominated markets the world over. Indeed, in his battle against the protective measures put in place by foreign governments, Hays would invoke ideals with which the moguls themselves could naturally identify.'[21]

By the mid-20s, the US movie business was worth over $2 billion; by the end of the decade, there were twenty studios in Hollywood, and the public demand was at an all-time high. In fact, the largest number of movies produced in the US to date was during the 20s and 30s, averaging roughly eight hundred releases a year (compared to today's average of perhaps a quarter of this). To meet the growing demand, the budding film industry needed to improve methods of production, and this led to the assembly line structure of studios designed to produce more films at a lower cost. Carl Laemmle had been the first, having merged his business with several others and formed Universal in 1912. After that, Adolph Zukor led the way with Paramount Pictures, the largest American movie company at that time, and it was Zukor who initiated the practice of 'block booking' by which theater owners were obliged to rent less desirable movies in order to get the films they wanted, ensuring that all the studio's films found distribution. The other studios soon followed Paramount's example, and by the end of the 20s, the moguls were single-handedly shaping the movie business. The various studios, each possessing their particular style and stock players, came into being over a period of a few years: in 1923, Walt Disney, whose speciality was animation, formed his company in Los Angeles with his brother Roy. Warner Bros. appeared the same year, and Columbia in 1924; also in 1924, Metro-Goldwyn was formed by a merger of Loews, Sam Goldwyn (formerly Goldfish) and Louis. B. Mayer's Metro (later renamed Metro-Goldwyn-Mayer or MGM; under Mayer's helmsmanship, MGM would become the most successful Hollywood studio during the 'Golden Age' of the 30s); and then there was RKO, in 1928. All this more or less coincided with what would become known as

Heaven's Gate went so far over budget, and was such a catastrophic failure on release, that it effectively finished off the studio (what was left was bought up by MGM).
21 Puttnam, pg. 102-3

the star-system, which would be further consolidated by the arrival of sound.[22]

If the silent era is remembered by the moviegoers of today, it is certainly not for the fantasies of Méliès, the epics of Griffith, or the romances of Valentino, but for the comedies of men like Charlie Chaplin and Buster Keaton, both of whom exercised almost complete control over their films. They wrote, directed, starred and brought the full expression of their personality to them (and thus to the audience), in stark contrast to the rest of the 'workers' in the dream factory. Contract players, in service to whichever studio 'owned' them, were obliged to make a set number of pictures each year and paid a weekly wage (whether or not they worked). Such contract players (this included directors) had little or no say in what movies they made: they were cast according to their 'type', and expected to show up and hit their marks in much the same way that factory workers are required to show up and punch their ticket.

This situation quickly changed, however (as happened with Chaplin and Keaton), the moment a performer became sufficiently well-known to the public to negotiate the terms of his or her contract.[23] It was quickly apparent, for example, that people were paying expressly to see Valentino, Chaplin, John Barrymore or Greta Garbo, leaving the studios little choice but to acknowledge the star's talent and individuality, and to afford them some measure of consideration, regarding money earned

22 'By 1929, the filmmaking firms that were to rule and monopolize Hollywood for the next half-century were the giants or the majors, sometimes dubbed 'The Big Five'. They produced more than ninety percent of the fiction films in America and distributed their films both nationally and internationally... The Big Five studios had vast studios with elaborate sets for film production. They owned their own film-exhibiting theatres...as well as production and distribution facilities. They distributed their films to this network of studio-owned, first-run theaters (or movie palaces), mostly in urban areas, which charged high ticket prices and drew huge audiences... Monopolistic studio control lasted twenty years until the late 1940s, when a federal decree (in U.S. vs. Paramount) ordered the studios to divest their theatres, similar to the rulings against the MPPC – the Edison Trust. Three smaller, minor studios were dubbed The Little Three, because each of them lacked one of the three elements required in vertical integration – owning their own theaters.' *History of Film.*

23 'Initially, actors and directors were not even credited. The first performer to receive credit was Florence Lawrence, the first "Biograph Girl," whom Carl Laemmle lured over to Universal and increased her salary to $1,000 a week. Mary Pickford, another Biograph Girl was the first major star and became known as "America's Sweetheart". In 1916 she became an independent producer and "the highest-paid star in the business after accepting a two-year, million-dollar contract (that included a percentage of the profits)". Then in 1918, Pickford joined First National with a production deal worth

and (even more importantly) the freedom to choose which movies they made. Since public opinion ruled the day, the studios were obliged to placate their stars with at least a semblance of autonomy.

This was less the case with writers, and even directors, since in those early days (besides Griffith), no one really knew or cared who the director was, or what he did (this is still largely true today of writers). The only directors from the silent era (besides those already mentioned) still widely known today are those who successfully made the transition to sound, and who thereby extended their careers into a new cycle, a cycle in which the director came to be recognized as a primary creative force behind movies. If the studios had had their way, however, such a change might never have come about at all. The director who most memorably made the shift from silents to talkies (which began in 1927 with *The Jazz Singer*) is undoubtedly Alfred Hitchcock. A young Englishman who began working in the 20s, Hitchcock had already captured the interest of audiences and critics by the time he made his first sound film, *The Lodger*, in 1927.[24] Unlike most filmmakers, Hitchcock seemed to have no trouble adapting to the new technology. The same skill and cunning he had developed with his few silent films, he now applied to sound.

It was due to the ingenuity and enthusiasm of men like Hitchcock – more than any actual initiative from the studios – that 'talkies' (initially considered a passing fad) quickly superceded the silents. Sound was the first (and to date last) 'revolution' to occur in Hollywood, and as with all good

millions of dollars. At the same time, actor Charlie Chaplin signed up with First National… The first truly great film star…began working as an apprentice for Sennett in 1913, playing small parts as a Keystone Kop. In 1914, he debuted his trademark mustached, baggy-pants "Tramp" character (in *Kid Auto Races At Venice*) and appeared in his first Mack Sennett short comedy *Making a Living*. In the same year, Chaplin appeared in the six-reel *Tillie's Punctured Romance*, Sennett's first feature-length picture (and the first US multi-reel comedy feature). Charlie Chaplin also added his famous walk to his familiar tramp character in *The Tramp* (1915), created under the Essanay Company. He soon began directing, writing, producing and starring in his own films. Having perfected his Little Tramp character by mid-decade, Chaplin left Sennett in 1916 and began working for the Mutual Film Corporation for $10,000/week, making short films such as *The Rink* (1916), *The Pawnshop* (1916), *The Immigrant* (1917) and *Easy Street* (1917). Soon afterwards, Chaplin signed the first million-dollar film contract in 1918 with First National and made *The Kid* (1921),' *History of Film*

24 The film is famous for the scene in which the lodger (wrongly suspected of several Ripper-esque murders – the first of Hitchcock's many innocents accused) overhears a conversation below, and is only able to make out a single word, repeated over and over. By this method, Hitchcock emphasized the lodger's growing paranoia, while simultaneously making innovative use of the soundtrack. The word in question was 'knife', a fitting enough introduction for a man who (three decades later) would terrorize the world with *Psycho*.

revolutions, heads were quick to roll. Those who could not adapt to the new dimension – those whose elocution did not complement their visual presence, who were possessed with sadly shrill voices or impenetrable accents – watched their careers go down the toilet with a single feature. Others, such as Garbo, Chaplin and Hitchcock, able to embrace the new dimension gracefully, only grew in stature and popularity.

The next technological development after sound to transform movies was the introduction of color. Besides a few early experiments, color came about in 1937 with *Snow White and the Seven Dwarves*, followed in 1938 by *The Adventures of Robin Hood* and in 1939 by *The Wizard of Oz* and David O. Selznick's grand folly, *Gone with the Wind*.[25] Unlike sound, there was never much doubt that color films would eventually replace black and white ones, yet it took considerably longer for this to happen (black and white was still the norm in the 60s, and it was only when color became cheaper to process that it supplanted black and white altogether). In the early days of color, the new potential was perhaps most fully exploited by the English filmmaking duo Michael Powell and Emeric Pressberger, who made their unforgettable excursions into color with expressionist zeal, in the mid-40s (*The Life and Death of Colonel Blimp, Matter of Life and Death*). Most directors, however (Hitchcock and Hawks, for example), preferred the simplicity and contrast of black and white, and did not deign to employ the new technology until the late 1940s or early 50s. (Hitchcock's first color movie was *Rope*, in 1948.)

While Technicolor slowly seeped onto the screens, the US was gearing up to enter the Second World War. Hollywood (the studios' combined wealth and talent) began to rally its workers to support for war. The Bureau of Motion Pictures was formed in 1942 by US Office of War Information, expressly to this end, to stir up patriotic fervor and turn popular opinion against Germany. It was for a time a patriotic duty to support the government, and movies were expected to serve the ends of propaganda rather than art. The war was a global concern; movies were a frivolous pastime at best, designed to make money for the studios and pass people's time. They could – and should – be proud to surrender to a greater agenda.

As a result, a vast number of patriotic but simple-minded (and

25 A movie that transfixed the public before it was even fully cast, thanks to Selznick's publicity skills (the famous hunt for Scarlet O'Hara that finally ended with Vivienne Leigh), and that had already staked its claim as 'the greatest motion picture of all time' before it was even completed.

largely worthless) movies were made. Whether they helped win the war (debatable), they did nothing to further the cause of filmmaking. Yet there was a curious side effect to this wholesale debasement of an art-form to political ends, a reaction *against* it, a stirring in the ranks that led to the emergence of a new strain: film noir. Film noir was the cinema of deceit, betrayal, mistrust and despair, and it did absolutely nothing to inspire patriotic feeling. What it did however was fulfil the function of 'art', by speaking for the collective mood of the times in a way that propaganda never could.

It was in more ways than one that the war gave rise to film noir as a genre. Because of the conflict, American movies were not distributed in Europe between 1939 and 1945 and as a result of this, there was a large backlog of movies that arrived on the continent, over a period of months, once the war ended. This served to emphasize certain developments of the art form that otherwise might not have been apparent, including a new trend in crime movies which the French (ever on the look out for such things) dubbed film noir. Noir was an expression of a subversive spirit in American film, and implied the same in the public (who, after all, 'dream' into being the movies they desire). Noir was the voice of doubt and dissent; it said, simply, something ain't right. Yet as studio genre movies, the movies arose through the very same channels as those absurd and puffed up propaganda pieces had; to all appearances, they were traditional crime melodramas, but with an unfamiliar sensibility, something darker, more despairing, and truer to the national mood. (It was a mood even more predominant in Europe, which had experienced the full effect of the war).

Film noir endures to this day – not only as a genre but as an independent 'movement' – due in part to this fact: it evidenced the possibility of a creative (unconscious) and subversive *will* expressing itself through mainstream channels, and so transforming them.

Orson Welles, King in Exile

'A good artist should be isolated. If he isn't isolated, something is wrong.'

Orson Welles

During this same period (in 1942), one of the most creative and subversive talents in America, Orson Welles, made *Citizen Kane*. Although not a film noir as such, *Kane* is possessed of a similar mood – a look, tone, and sensibility – to that of the noir films. It's subversive and playful, yet gloomy and despondent; cynical, yet also surreal and dreamlike. It's also, like noir, characterized by a desire to expose the corrupt underbelly of civilization, and of the human soul. Above all, *Citizen Kane* had a grown up quality. It had the skill and audacity to address its audiences as equals, on a level, to entertain them without patronizing them, and without succumbing to the unspoken will of the studios (and of audiences) to infantilize, dumb down, and blur the rougher edges of the current social conditions. These were conditions that everyone was aware of but (it was tacitly assumed) went to movies expressly in order to forget about, and not in order to think more deeply about them. *Kane* defied this assumption.

Citizen Kane was so unique, so personal and iconoclastic a vision, that it didn't seem to be the product of the Hollywood system at all. In a sense, it wasn't. In an article from the *Saturday Evening Post* published in 1940, long before *Kane* was completed much less released, Welles' impact on the industry was described as follows.

'No other newcomer's arrival in Hollywood ever caused so much indignation as Welles'. It is difficult to understand why. Somewhat more understandable is the bitter resentment at the fact that Welles has the nerve to be only twenty-four years old. Hollywood today (1940) is a sort of Old Infant Prodigies Home... It is the nature of things that the superannuated infant prodigies and their cohorts should disapprove of a fresh young infant prodigy. Welles' youth might have been condoned if it had not been for his extraordinary picture contract. Probably more screwball contracts have been written in Hollywood than in the rest of the world put together, and ordinarily, the most fantastic of them attracts no attention, but the Welles contract has caused a furious war of words. It provides that he should write, produce, direct and act in the pictures he makes; it pays him $150,000 a picture plus a percentage of the gross; it stipulates that neither the president nor board of directors nor anybody else can interfere with him in any way. No one in authority over Welles has the right to see the work until it is completed. This would seem to concern only Welles and the picture company, but that is not the way Hollywood sees it. There it is everybody's business. The idea that such a contract should have gone to a twenty-four-year-old carpetbagger with a beard is a menace to the public welfare.'[26]

26 'How to Raise a Child: the Education of Orson Welles, Who Didn't Need it,' by Alva Johnston and Fred Smith, from the *Saturday Evening Post*, Jan/Feb, 1940, reprinted in *Orson Welles: Interviews*; quote from pg 17-18.

When the movie was finally released – despite multifarious efforts to stop it – its irreverence and artistry put the studios to shame, challenging their line of homogenized product, by stating baldly and boldly that movies *were* an art form, if only audiences could realize it. (Welles' crew consisted of many European lights, and in Europe there was no question – with artists like Jean Renoir, Fritz Lang and Ingmar Bergman – that movies were art.) *Citizen Kane* (which was not a popular success on its release, or even fully embraced by the critics) brazenly demonstrated that 'art' and entertainment were neither incompatible nor, in fact, so different (they might even be synonymous). Welles suggested that it wasn't the medium – or even the public's perception of it – that needed to grow up, but the filmmakers themselves; and that it was up to the studios to give them room to do so.

That Welles was a true independent spirit, and a force of possible renaissance for American movies, is perhaps best evidenced by the fact that the system itself (with some encouragement from William Randolph Hearst, the newspaper tycoon whom Welles based his film on) did all it could to suppress him, and that it eventually succeeded. Initially, once Hearst discovered the movie was based on his own life and his affair with actress Marion Davies – including the use of his pet-name for her clitoris, 'rosebud' – he did everything in his power as press magnate to prevent the film ever reaching the eyes and ears of the public. What this entailed – besides a barrage of negative press in his various periodicals – was the covert blackmailing of the various studio-heads, using the threat of scandalous material (including photographs) relating to the more sordid aspects of some of their bigger stars' private lives (Errol Flynn was particularly embarrassing, with his penchant for underage girls).[27] Using the leverage of negative publicity, Hearst demanded that Selznick and the other studio heads band together and buy *Citizen Kane* back from RKO, expressly in order to burn all prints. This came close to happening, and one reason it didn't appears to be that Hearst was even then on the brink of bankruptcy, and hence his threats were largely empty.

Nevertheless, when the film was released it was not a major success for Welles – at least not compared with the amount of trouble it had caused

[27] According to the TV movie, *RKO-281* (the working title of *Kane*), Hearst's trump card and ultimate threat was to make open mention of the Jewishness of the studio heads, this in a time (before Hitler's policies were exposed to the world) when anti-Semitism was still common and fairly acceptable.

him – and his next film, *The Magnificent Ambersons*, though not actually destroyed, was mutilated almost beyond recognition by RKO pictures while Welles was in South America (shooting the documentary *It's All True*). As Welles described it (in 1982, three years before his death):

'The real point of *Ambersons*, everything that is any good in it, is that part of it which was really just a preparation for the decay of the *Ambersons*... It was thought by everybody in Hollywood while I was in South America that it was too downbeat, a famous Hollywood word at the time. Downbeat. So it was all taken out, but it was the purpose of the movie to see how they all slid downhill... While I was in South America, RKO was sold to Howard Hughes and another group of people. And a new studio head came in and they asked to see the movie and they previewed it and said it was downbeat and they started cutting it... There are three scenes at the end I didn't even write or shoot... So they destroyed *Ambersons* and the picture itself destroyed me. I didn't get a job as a director for years afterwards.'[28]

The treatment of *Ambersons* appeared to be an express act of vengeance by Hollywood for Welles' impertinence and for all the trouble he had caused. Perhaps more pragmatically, it served as a warning to anyone who might have dared to follow his example. Welles would never again make a movie with the same level of freedom and funding that he'd enjoyed on *Kane*, and he never made another movie that came close to realizing his genius. What he did (and it only needed to be done once) was show that it could be done. 'I had luck as no one had,' Welles said in 1964; 'afterwards, I had the worst bad luck in the history of the cinema, but that is the order of things: I had to pay for having had the best luck in the history of cinema. Never has a man been given so much power in the Hollywood system. An absolute power.'[29]

Orson Welles may have changed Hollywood, but if so he paid the price. It took thirty years for the changes to become observable, the time, roughly, that it took for the generation growing up with *Citizen*

---

28 *Interviews*, pg. 187–88
29 See *Orson Welles: Interviews*, pg. 119. In 1960, Welles commented to Huw Wheldon, 'There's a certain kind of filmmaker who really wants to make the film entirely on his own and that sort of fellow is the sworn enemy of the system... and the system is at great pains to denigrate such a person... They rightly regard the artist as the enemy of their profession.' Ibid, pg. 83.

Kane to come of age. Inspired by Welles' divine hubris, they would take on the system in imitation of their exiled king, and while many (like Francis Ford Coppola) would succeed where Welles had failed, an equal number would wind up paying the same exact price, that of exile.

*

'The 50s decade was known for many things: post-war affluence and increased choice of leisure time activities, conformity, the Korean War, middle-class values, the rise of modern jazz, the rise of "fast food" restaurants and drive-ins (Jack in the Box – founded in 1951; McDonalds – first franchised in 1955 in Des Plaines, IL; and A&W Root Beer Company – formed in 1950, although it had already established over 450 drive-ins throughout the country), a baby boom, the all-electric home as the ideal, white racist terrorism in the South, the advent of television and TV dinners, abstract art, the first credit card (Diners Club, in 1951), the rise of drive-in theaters to a peak number in the late 50s with over 4,000 outdoor screens (where young teenaged couples could find privacy in their hot-rods), and a youth reaction to middle-aged cinema. Older viewers were prone to stay at home and watch television (about 10.5 million US homes had a TV set in 1950).'

A History of Film

With World War Two now over, and film noir diagnosing something rotten in the heartland, Hollywood was embarking on a war of its own, in the person (and fanatical agenda) of Senator McCarthy. If there was ever a movement to crush the spirit of independent thought and action in Hollywood, it was McCarthyism. For a time (a time eerily echoed in the US today by the current post-9/11 climate), any tendencies towards freethinking, creativity, non-traditional beliefs or a questioning of the mores and conventions of society (which is, after all, what artists are temperamentally and vocationally obliged to do), was considered to be 'un-American.' As a result, many of the most talented writers and directors of the time – whether actual Communist sympathizers or merely insufficiently anti-Communist – were blacklisted. The investigations which the House of Representatives' Un-American Activities Committee (HUAC) carried out, starting in 1947, were supposedly directed at suspected Communists and political subversives within the Hollywood community, but an inevitable side effect was that any more liberal themes were slowly banished from movies as well. Just as today criticism of the US government is often interpreted as 'terrorist sympathies,' in 1947 anything less than a full-blown reactionary stance was suspected of being 'pinko'.

The famous 'Hollywood Ten' consisted of Hollywood filmmakers who refused to testify before the committee in 1948, and who, because of their refusal, were branded as criminals, facing jail time of up to one year and fines of $1,000 for 'contempt of Congress.'[30] They were also blacklisted by the US film industry, unable to work save under pseudonyms (or, as the Woody Allen/Martin Ritt film *The Front* depicted in 1976, by using 'fronts'). Most of those blacklisted actors, writers, and directors that were banned from working in the film studios never recovered, and many resorted to working in Europe. Walt Disney, Louis B. Mayer, Bud Schulberg, Elia Kazan, Gary Cooper and Ronald Reagan (President of the Screen Actors Guild at the time), co-operated completely with the Committee, but there were many others who did not. Between 1947 and 1954 (when the HUAC investigation finally ended), some three hundred plus Hollywood players had their careers destroyed. Movie giants such as Charlie Chaplin, Orson Welles, Myrna Loy, Sterling Hayden, Zero Mostel, Gregory Peck, Katharine Hepburn, Gene Kelly, Danny Kaye, Joseph Losey, Frank Sinatra, John Garfield, Paul Muni, Arthur Miller, Robert Rossen, Lionel Stander, Fredric March, Edward G. Robinson, Judy Holliday, Jose Ferrer, and Melvyn Douglas were among those who refused to co-operate. As a result, they were accused of being Communist sympathizers, investigated as suspected Communists, or of being part of a Hollywood 'Communist Fifth Column'.

Besides the individual persecutions, the covert objective appeared to be to make it more or less impossible to create thoughtful adult entertainment. Brainwashing was the agenda of the day, and it was an agenda that the Hollywood system was all-too temperamentally inclined to go along with.

For daring to defy McCarthy's relentless persecution drive, these stars and filmmakers risked the destruction of their careers (Chaplin for one was banned from the US for several decades). Anti-Communist paranoia was a force unto itself, and seemed intent on decimating Hollywood.

---

30 The Hollywood Ten were: screenwriters Lester Cole, Dalton Trumbo, Alvah Bessie, Ring Lardner Jr., John Howard Lawson, Albert Maltz, and Samuel Ornitz, directors Edward Dmytryk and Herbert Biberman and producer Robert Adrian Scott.

In passing, it's curious to note that, during the same period, one of the most popular new genres was that of paranoid sci-fi movies depicting invasion by flying saucers (objects which were actually being seen in the skies at the time, the sightings having led to the movies and not vice versa), attacks by giant insects, lizards, 'blobs', or other monsters, all of which suggested symbolic representations of *anti*-Communism, as much as Communism. Most of the monsters in these films resulted from the catch-all 'evil' of the genre: radiation. In the early 50s, after the atom bombs ended the war and before cancer scares had begun, radiation was considered a technological miracle and a boon to modern living. Apparently, these movies served as an outlet for the as-yet unconscious (or at least unspoken) awareness that such optimism was, shall we say, somewhat unfounded.

It was the arrival of the drive-ins (also in the 1950s) that allowed more trashy, inexpensive and 'low prestige' movies to reach audiences, but even before the drive-ins, B-movies existed. With hindsight, it might be said that a forerunner to the indie movement of the 60s was the B-movie of the 50s. B-movies were second-string productions made on the cheap with lesser known actors and unknown directors, and used as support features for more prestigious studio fare. The B-movie (which on occasion, though rarely, outshone the A picture and developed a following of its own) was ideal training ground for up-and-coming filmmakers. It was also a means for them to exercise (if inclined) more subversive and radical ideas, free of the disapproving gaze of the studios. Since B-movies were cheap and more or less disposable – and despite the heavy budget restrictions – they offered a kind of freedom for directors that made them eminently desirable. Here was a field in which filmmakers such as Don Siegel, Sam Fuller, and Robert Aldrich could learn their trade and come slowly to prominence. In the process, they produced not only some of the best B-movies of the time, but some of the best movies per se, and certainly some of the tougher, more uncompromising, cynical, and realistic ones.[31]

31 It's impossible to imagine, for example, a movie like *Pick-Up on South Street* (which Sam Fuller made in 1953 with Richard Widmark) being made as an A picture by any of the studios. It is simply too subversive. The sentiments of the pickpocket 'hero' – cynical, brutal, anti-patriotic, misogynist – seem more in line with the 70s, and the movie is so much fresher and more alive than most of the 'classics' from this period (the 50s marked a low point in Hollywood filmmaking) that the only wonder is why it took the French to recognize Fuller as a formidable film artist. (Unlike Aldrich or Siegel, Fuller never graduated to A pictures; he did not enjoy even retrospective success in the US.)

A forerunner to these men – and as much of a mentor to them as Welles was to other, more 'artistic' filmmakers – was John Huston.

John Huston's Dust and Dreams

'Hollywood has always been a cage... a cage to catch our dreams.'

John Huston

John Huston embodies what we mean when we talk of a maverick filmmaker. In the style of Hemingway (and as documented by Peter Viertel's *White Hunter, Black Heart*), he was a brawler, a boozer, a man not easily intimated by wild elephants, much less Hollywood moneymen. Consequently, he was one of the first directors to bring his personality whole to the movies, to imbue them with his own particular temperament and disposition, while staying true to the demands of the movie (the story and character) which he was making. Howard Hawks or John Ford generally gave a special 'spin' to their movies, a laconic spark or melancholy ache, but their movies were still more or less compatible with other factory-line products. What marked their movies (and Hawks' works were as varied and diverse as *Scarface, Only Angels Have Wings, Bringing Up Baby* and *Red River*) was not so much a consistent tone, or even style (much less a sensibility), but an overall quality, the economic plotting, lack of sentimentality and refreshing dialogue, for example. (Ditto Ford, and even Hitchcock, whose movies remained fairly traditional until the mid 50s). Huston's films were even more eclectic a bunch than Hawks', and there were at least as many misfires. But his career was as remarkable and exemplary as any director's in Hollywood. Spanning from his cracking debut *The Maltese Falcon* (1941), some four and a half decades to his elegiac swan song *The Dead* (which he directed from a wheelchair, with an oxygen tank), Huston covered a spectrum of subjects and styles as wide as their quality was varied (from rank mediocrity to excellence and back again). During this time he was never, for more than a movie or two at a time, assimilated by the system.

Huston's adaptability and durability – the persistence of his vision and artistry – turned him into something of a legend in Hollywood. What other director can be said to have peaked in four successive decades: in the 40s with *The Treasure of the Sierra Madre*; in the 50s with *The Asphalt Jungle* and *The African Queen*; in the 60s (just barely) with *Night of the Iguana*; in the 70s with *Fat City* (for which Huston toned down his grandiose style to suit the period) and (more characteristically) *The Man Who Would Be King*; and finally in the 80s with *The Dead*?

Huston grew up surrounded by the vaudeville (his father Walter was an actor, and the family traveled the vaudeville circuit). He enjoyed youthful pursuits as a boxer, competitive horseman, Cavalry officer and major in the US Army. He spent time in Mexico, riding horses, and later reporting for a magazine in New York, before finding work in Hollywood writing dialogue. He took up acting and wrote a play, *Frankie and Johnny*, traveled to London and then Paris, making a living as a street performer and artist. Back in Hollywood, he found work as an editor and writer, and worked for several years as a scriptwriter. Finally, through a combination of determination, charm and connections, Huston managed to persuade his employers at Warner Brothers to let him direct his script for *The Maltese Falcon*. The film was a success, and Huston was immediately established as a bright new light in Hollywood.

He followed *Falcon* with *Across the Pacific* (both films starred Humphrey Bogart), and then in 1948 with *The Treasure of the Sierra Madre*. Probably Huston's masterpiece (at least until *The Dead*), *Treasure* burnt up the screen with the intensity of its vision, razing the barren terrain of the Hollywood melodrama and making it fertile again. The film's psychological undercurrents of greed, paranoia and despair (familiar to the current film noir genre which Bogart had made his own) were all but non-existent in popular movies at the time, and Huston and Bogart took them to new extremes. Not even Hitchcock (and certainly not Hawks) dared (at that time) to go so deeply into the characters' psyches or strip them down to reveal such a fetid underlayer. Huston succeeded, while still being accessible (and entertaining) to mass audiences, in bringing psychological realism to the movies. Huston was a pioneer of film technique who brought more than just a new aesthetic, however, he brought a new modus operandi. For *Treasure*, he shot on location (just as Siegel and Fuller would), using natives for extras; he filmed scenes in Spanish and did away with subtitles. It was hardly a documentary approach, but compared to the house style of Hollywood, such injection of realism appeared radical. Huston liked to get his hands dirty when he shot his films.

Treasure (adapted from the novel by B. Traven) tells the tale of three impoverished workers making a pilgrimage south of the border to Mexico to pan for gold. The story would have had instant historical (and archetypal) appeal to Huston. Having spent seven years as a director in Hollywood, getting to know the system, he knew if there was one thing Hollywood held close, it was greed. In the middle of the 20th century, Hollywood was the land of dreams. The previous century it had been California, and hundreds of thousands had made the trek cross-country in search of employment, food, money, and, in those early days, gold. Huston had already developed a great affection for Mexico and shooting across the border would have had a strong appeal. It would have offered a way to escape the 'cage' of Hollywood (just as, a few years later, he would escape to Africa for *The African Queen*).

Treasure was an adventure story combined – cunningly and gracefully – with a psychodrama, a ruthless exposé of human weakness and obsession, specifically obsession for material gain. Without a shred of Hollywood moralizing or proselytizing, Huston offered it up as a cautionary fable – one perhaps geared specifically to the Hollywood set – in which the simple pursuit of a dream (making movies, for example) becomes instead a demented lust for wealth and power. Yet Huston made the film as a comedy, though certainly the blackest kind; it oozed a dark and cynical awareness of human corruptibility that was somehow inseparable from its humor. Humphrey Bogart (who played the sweating, whining, gibbering Fred C. Dobbs) was by then a hugely popular and romantic leading man, albeit of the anti-heroic mold, and Huston took obvious delight in stripping him of his movie star accruements – those of dependability, strength of character, decency, nobility, and even, finally, of sanity or humanity (to say nothing of his physical appearance: never Bogie's prime asset, he is here rendered grotesque). Along the way, the film did away with the usual devices of melodrama, having neither hero nor villain (the film's apparent hero has by the end become its villain), nor resolution, save in defeat. What defeated the characters (as it no doubt defeated many of Huston's Hollywood peers) was obsessive lust for gain and overwhelming ambition. With skin-crawling realism, Huston showed how such obsession leads to blindness, and finally madness. He took one of the oldest stories of all – the quest for an ever-elusive (and finally immaterial) gold – and treated it with unprecedented frankness. His film revealed how an illusory quest possesses men's souls and unhinges their minds, until they find themselves doing things they never imagined themselves capable of. Rather like in Hollywood, perhaps?

If there was redemption in the film, it was the redemption of self-mockery. When the ignorant Indians throw away the gold dust (mistaking it for dirt), the old man (played by Huston's father Walter), can only laugh. The laughter signified the old man's realization – the folly of chasing after such ephemeral things as dreams. With his laughter, Huston suggested that ironic detachment was the only thing that saves us. Perhaps Huston was fast realizing the same thing – that an ability to see through the folly of ambition was essential to his survival in Hollywood. If so, it came in the nick of time. *Treasure* won Oscars for both John and Walter and took Huston to the top of his game, a mere seven years after setting out. Four decades later, he was still on top. If anything made such improbable persistence possible, it was detachment and irony. Throughout his career, Huston showed a unique willingness to make light of his own dreams, and to laugh at the dust they left behind.

Stanley Kubrick, Independent Pioneer

'I don't think that any work of art has a responsibility to be anything but a work of art. There obviously is a considerable controversy, just as there always has been, about what is a work of art, and I should be the last to try to define that. I was amused by Cocteau's *Orpheé* when the poet is given the advice: "Astonish me". The Johnsonian definition of a work of art is also meaningful to me, and that is that a work of art must either make life more enjoyable or more endurable. Another quality, which I think forms part of the definition, is that a work of art is always exhilarating and never depressing, whatever its subject matter may be.'

Stanley Kubrick, 1972

During the period, pre-1960s, with blacklisting only having intensified the pressure to conform, it was a slow and laborious process to get a movie made (at least one that would receive any serious attention outside the drive-in). The contrast between then and now cannot be exaggerated: it was a different world and a different business. Nowadays, Quentin Tarantino, Robert Rodriguez or Kevin Smith can bring together a cast, crew and budget, and, through skill, persistence, and cunning, eventually make his movie and become a 'major league player', often in the space of two or three years. In the 50s, Sam Peckinpah spent over ten years working in theater and television before getting his feet wet in the world of directing. (His first break was as Don Siegel's assistant, and later script supervisor.[32])

---

32 Don Siegel was directing B-movies for just as long a period before his breakthrough came, with *Invasion of the Body Snatchers* (1957, a B-movie that broke through, and in which Peckinpah has a small role). *Body Snatchers* might have been forgotten too, along with dozens of other sci-fi cheapies of the same period, had it not stood out from the crowd by its tight direction and a sneakily topical, paranoid plot (the film was Siegel's covert jab at McCarthyism). Even so, Siegel wasn't helming any major studio productions for another ten years or so. *The Killers*, one of his best movies, was made for TV (in 1964, though it was eventually given a cinema release), and Siegel didn't really hit the big time until he hooked up with Clint Eastwood, in 1968, for *Coogan's Bluff*.

Unless they were Hitchcock, Hawks, or Ford, directors were dependent as much (or more so) on their wiles, cunning and discretion to succeed and survive in the studio system as they were on any ostensible talent, much less vision. One early exception to this almost inescapable process was Stanley Kubrick, a man who made a career out of being the exception.

It was during the early 50s that Kubrick came to prominence. The first 'independent' filmmaker since Welles to actually break through, Kubrick defied convention by ascending not through the ranks but through his own invention, talent and persistence. In fact, Kubrick's ascent would become more or less standard practice by the 70s, but he did it two decades ahead of the trend, and this may be one reason that he gained such an exaggerated, almost unassailable, reputation within the industry. (His reputation was mostly among filmmakers and critics, however, less so with the public). Sam Peckinpah was roughly the same age as Kubrick, and embarked on his career at roughly the same time (he and Kubrick briefly collaborated on what would become Marlon Brando's *One-Eyed Jacks*). Unlike Peckinpah, who trained in TV and as a director's assistant, Kubrick, in a practice now almost *de rigueur*, set about funding his own movies. He learnt his trade and eventually attracted the attention of the studios simply by *doing it*.

An avid photographer from an early age, Kubrick's career began more or less by chance when he caught an image of a newspaper salesman holding a paper with the news of the death of the President Roosevelt. The photograph, which amply communicated the nation's despair, was sold to *Look* magazine for $20. Kubrick went on to work at *Look* from the age of seventeen to twenty-one, and his experience with the camera held him in good stead when he finally embarked on his movie career. As he himself put it, 'To make a film entirely by yourself, which initially I did, you may not have to know very much about anything else, but you must know about photography.'[33]

In 1950, at the age of twenty-two, he made a short documentary film on the life of a boxer, also for *Look*.[34] Kubrick then made several short films in rapid succession, again seeking funding from family, friends, or wherever he could find it (he even played chess in the park for money). In 1954, at the

---

[33] See http://www.filmmakers.com/artists/kubrick

[34] Kubrick borrowed money from family and friends to cover the $3,900 budget, and later sold the film (named *Day of the Fight*) to RKO-Pathe for $4,000, so making a $100 profit. As a result of this, RKO gave Kubrick $1,500 for his next short. The movie ran in RKO's 'This is America' series and premiered at the Paramount Theatre in New York, on April 26th, 1951.

age of twenty-six, he graduated to feature filmmaking with *Fear and Desire*, for which he borrowed $10,000 from friends and relatives, persuading his millionaire uncle to invest (his uncle provided the funds in return for an assistant producer credit). *Fear and Desire*, Kubrick's first film, told the story of four soldiers trapped behind enemy lines during an unknown war. It was made with a thirteen-person crew. The following year, backed by a Bronx pharmacist named Morris Bouse and with a budget of $40,000, he made *Killer's Kiss*. Kubrick described his approach as 'guerilla-filmmaking', working on busy New York streets and bribing the New York Police Dept. to look the other way. Once it was completed, United Artists bought the film for worldwide distribution. Kubrick was officially a movie director, at the tender age of twenty-seven – in those days, almost unprecedented.

His early films displayed enough talent and technique to get Kubrick through the gates of Hollywood. Kubrick and his new partner, James B. Harris, worked out a script with novelist Jim Thompson and presented it to United Artists. Once they had secured a bankable star (Sterling Hayden), United Artists agreed to a budget of $200,000 and filming began. *The Killing* was a suspenseful thriller about a racetrack robbery that was presented (forty years before Quentin Tarantino) in a non-linear fashion; the film owed a substantial debt to Huston's *Asphalt Jungle*, also a taut, character-driven, noirish heist piece with existential undertones and Sterling Hayden. A poem of futility, it captured the changing zeitgeist and anticipated audiences' need for harder-edged dramas. Kubrick's sensibility was anything but populist. It was the antithesis of studio mentality, an uneasy mix of humanism and nihilism (in the end, nihilism won out), and for a while it gave Kubrick a leading place in the new, slowly emerging avant-garde of independent-minded Hollywood filmmakers. Kubrick had the razor-sharp technique, the coolness and detachment, and the hard edges of Huston, Fuller and Siegel; but he had something else too, something new to Hollywood (at least since Welles): his touch was impressionistic, European. It distinctly resembled 'art'.

Kubrick's next film, his first 'mature' work, was *Paths of Glory* (1957), a political film (at least by Hollywood standards) that was also an absorbing character piece and an unprecedentedly bracing war movie (one of those who praised the movie's authenticity was Winston Churchill). *Paths of Glory* was a cry of dissent and despair, a cinematic protest and an open mockery of the hypocrisy of government and war.[35] And yet, for all the

35 A far cry from the jingoistic posturing of the 1940s, if Kubrick had made the film a few years earlier he might have had McCarthy on his tail. So incendiary did the film prove to be, in fact, that French troops protested it, and the movie was banned in Europe until 1974.

uniqueness of its content and message, it was perhaps the film's *style* that had the more profound effect. Kubrick was a self-taught director, relatively free of the more insidious tendencies to conform that studio-line directors usually displayed (even the best of them). His realistic treatment had freshness and urgency – a lack of the familiar, hackneyed devices of melodrama – that must have seemed almost shocking to audiences at the time.

In 1960, with *Spartacus*, Kubrick got his fill of studio filmmaking. Reunited with Kirk Douglas (with whom he had not got along well on *Paths of Glory*), Kubrick had ample warning from the start of what to expect. Spartacus had been shooting in Death Valley (with Anthony Mann directing) for three weeks before Douglas had the director fired and called upon Kubrick; Kubrick had no choice but to agree, since he had signed a five-picture deal with Douglas' production company, Bryna. Two of the five movies he made after *Paths of Glory* were to star Douglas and Kubrick was now effectively on the payroll of his star.

Even then Kubrick was the most inflexible of directors, and he inevitably found his idiosyncratic vision hampered by such an arrangement. In the end, hog-tied by the demands of his star (Douglas was also executive producer), he wound up wholly dissatisfied with the film, and utterly disgusted with the process of studio production. Kubrick never made the same mistake again. He quickly extricated himself from his contract with Douglas (no doubt by mutual agreement), and Kubrick (who became his own producer with *Dr. Strangelove*) would exercise complete, even obsessive, control over all his subsequent pictures, down to the size of the small print on the posters and the choice of release date. By the time of *2001: A Space Odyssey* (1968), Kubrick had become a near mythical figure in Hollywood, in equal parts revered and indulged as a creative force unto himself, a unique visionary whose domain was sacrosanct and inviolate, and not to be trespassed upon by the coarse minds and commercial agendas of studio heads.

For the duration of his career, and despite the size of his productions and the fact that they were all (of necessity) studio-funded, Kubrick was very much an independent filmmaker. Such autonomy and complete fidelity to his vision, more than the quality of the films themselves (which steadily diminished over the decades, culminating with *Eyes Wide Shut*), perhaps accounted for the awe (and envy) with which he was regarded by the industry. Whatever you may think of his movies – which in the end sacrificed character and depth for the cold allure of technique – Kubrick was a giant. He was the embodiment and fulfillment of the hope and dream (so often vain in Hollywood) that talent can prevail over the dictates of commercialism.

★

'Maybe the reason why people seem to find it harder to take unhappy endings in movies than in plays or novels is that a good movie engages you so heavily that you find an unhappy ending almost unbearable. But it depends on the story, because there are ways for the director to trick the audience into expecting a happy ending and there are ways of very subtly letting the audience be aware of the fact that the character is hopelessly doomed and there is not going to be a happy ending.'

Stanley Kubrick

Like Huston only more so, Kubrick was a forerunner of things soon to come. By the 1950s and early 1960s, the days of contract players were over. Already, in the early to mid-50s, the star system (that of studio-contracted players) had begun to collapse, and by the 60s it was a thing of the past. The stars became independent agents, moving freely from studio to studio, ushering in the age of the superstar. The forerunner was James Stewart, who in the early 1950s decided to freelance and set the precedent of the percentage deal, in which he was guaranteed up to half the profits of his movies. Yet despite this, and even by the end of the 50s, studios (and even audiences) continued to regard directors (with a few exceptions) much as they always had, as hired hands, craftsmen little different from set designers, whose abilities were intrinsic but not essential to the shaping and completion of the product.

The battle between directors with a personal vision and studio heads with budgetary considerations has raged since the first days of film, but until the 60s, there was never the slightest question as to who had the upper hand. Until then, the war between auteur and industry was never seen as a match of equals, more like the relationship between a stern father and a not-yet adequately disciplined child. Sooner or later, the studio agenda prevailed and the vision (if it survived intact at all) was duly 'cropped', the director brought down to size. That was what made Welles so remarkable. Coming from a background in theater and radio, and bringing his own company of actors and collaborators, for a brief moment he held the studios captive to his vision. This was presumably also why he had to be swiftly made an example of: if Welles had received the honors – and enjoyed the success and freedom – that everyone knew he deserved after *Citizen Kane*, it could have opened the flood gates to a hundred other such renegade artists. Hollywood forbid. These flood gates were not destined to open (and even then only briefly) until the late 60s.

In the meantime, it fell to a small group of such renegades to chip slowly away at the dam.

Chapter Two - The Two Faces of Hollywood: The First Independent Wave, 1960-68

'The important thing in films is not so much to make successes as not to make failures, because each failure limits your future opportunities to make the films you want to make.'

Stanley Kubrick

There were originally eight major studios: Paramount, MGM, 20th Century Fox, Warner Bros., RKO, Universal, Columbia and United Artists (the latter three being considered 'minors', because they owned no actual theater-chains). According to John Belton:

'The dismantling of the studio system began just before World War II, when the US Dept. of Justice Antitrust Division filed suit against the eight majors, accusing them of monopolistic practices in their use of block booking, blind bidding, and runs, zones and clearances...The major studios delayed the process of divorcement and divestiture as long as possible, maintaining a certain degree of control over their theaters until the mid to late 1950s. As a result, the initial mechanism or structure that gave rise to the studio system remained more or less in place until roughly 1960.' [1]

1960, the year in which Alfred Hitchcock made *Psycho*.

Although the separation of social and cultural development into decades may seem arbitrary, it can be useful. For example, whatever sense of unease and dread was lurking beneath the shiny, optimistic surface of the 50s, it came to full expression in the 60s. There was a loss of innocence that followed World War Two, a new sense of instability, paranoia and apprehension that resulted from the detonation of the atom bomb and the inception of the Cold War, and from the rank intolerance and totalitarianism of the McCarthy era. There was also an increasing pressure, and a sense of doubt and cynicism, in the American people that inevitably had to surface. Film noir had been an early ripple of this unease. The social conscience films of the 50s could not whitewash the basic anxiety and suspicion that was increasingly predominant in the public psyche, and which manifested in sci-fi horror movies, low-budget nightmares rife with SFX symbolism (films

1. American Cinema/American Culture, pg. 78-9.

that Roger Corman would eventually make his métier). By the time the horror movie came of age with *Psycho,* these anxieties no longer seemed so childish.

Hitchcock's *Psycho*

'It is difficult to say what the director's responsibility is. It can be either commercial or artistic – only in rare cases can it be both. I think a director's responsibilities are to his employers to a great extent. After all, they have invested a large amount of money in the picture. But the director also has a responsibility to his conscience not to compromise too much. So, in the end, it is really a kind of constant tight-rope walking.'

Alfred Hitchcock

Inspired by the real-life serial killer (and mother-killer) Ed Gein, *Psycho* is an interesting hybrid. It can literally be cut in two halves, one an independent 'art' movie, dark, subversive, surreal, visionary and unique; the other (the second part) a standard studio genre flick, dull, predictable, slick and routine. The second half of the picture is perfectly effective, enough for the two halves (which may be seen to reflect a split in Hitchcock himself) to more or less seamlessly co-exist, to the point that few critics have commented on the film's schizoid qualities, or upon the fact that it is really only half a great movie, and half a cop-out.

One exception was Larry E. Grimes, who points out that:

'*Psycho* stands as a completed film, a unified narrative unit, the moment Marion Crane's car is swallowed by the swamp. Hitchcock knows this and marks the event with the only complete screen wipe in the film. This, I suggest, is the body of the film. Untouched by alternate endings, the body of the film speaks of corruption and death. Its biblical message is clear: The wage of sin is death… As far back as *The Lodger*, Hitchcock told Truffaut, he was aware that there was a difference between the film he wanted to make and the film the studio system would allow him to make. In *Psycho*, I suggest, he has it both ways. Through his clever use of multiple endings he makes a one-hour film to his own satisfaction while delivering a feature-length movie to the studio… His *Psycho* is the film that is completed when Marion's body sinks into the swamp, and it is (re)membered through the powerful, though ambiguous, shot of her car being resurrected from the depths.'[2]

By creating a world in which good and evil, right and wrong, have no real significance, *Psycho* may be seen as an unconscious expression of the growing dread, uncertainty and menace within the American psyche, as it readied to face its own inner demons, and found instead its own familiars. The apprehension which Hitchcock had for so long trafficked in no longer appeared a simple divertissement, but a warning of the times we were living in.

This is implicit in the first section of the film, an almost surrealist meditation on unconscious motives, of psychic undercurrents, guilt, anxiety, dread, and the hidden menace of everyday America (or everyday anywhere). Perhaps, when Hitchcock filmed the blood-tinged water circling down the drain, dissolving into the dead eye of Marion Crane, he was suggesting something about the unconscious, primal terror of our own demons, and that the nightmare which he had so ruthlessly thrust us into was not some awful aberration, but rather a universal horror lying just beneath the surface of our existence? The water spinning down into darkness (deservedly the film's most famous shot) becomes a whirlpool into the abyss, an abyss into which we are all inexorably drawn. The film seemed to provide audiences with two options: either of plunging into the abyss of their own free will, or being sucked in, like Marion, by random causes. This was the only freedom the film, with its macabre and irresistibly fatalistic pull towards death, offered, and with such a message, *Psycho* was the first truly nihilistic horror film ever made. It was also a harbinger of things to come.

Hitchcock was a man for whom work – movies – was everything, and whose films seemed to take place within a specifically cinematic realm: the Hitchcock Universe. Hence his films were, in some peculiar way (and for all their apparent adherence to conventional form and plot structure) the first surrealist body of work in American cinema. (Welles of course would have given us such a body, but he was cut down at the starting gate by the terrified studios.) Hitchcock's films are not realistic, but they're not fantastic either; they are a form of heightened realism, created by Hitchcock's subtle but precise control of the medium, and directed towards an intensification of our reactions – our emotions – in order to lead us into his dream world.

2 'Shall These Bones Live?' from *Screening the Sacred: Religion, Myth and Ideology in Popular American Film* edited by Joel W. Martin and Conrad E. Ostwalt Jr., p. 20.

This is roughly the definition of surreal (and of cinema also), as what is 'above reality', and Hitchcock's preoccupation with violence, with murder, crime, intrigue, madness, obsession, and, of course, suspense, was due to an interest not in the subjects themselves but in their *effects* upon the audience – namely, to heighten or intensify our awareness (unlike, say, a love story, which tends to blur audiences out). For all his 'conventionality,' Hitchcock never really worked within a standard genre – he never made a Western or an ordinary comedy, and his crime thrillers and horror movies were all somewhat eccentric, to say the least. They drew upon the conventions of the genre, but only in order to pervert – or reinvent – them. Hitchcock used genres as a vehicle for his own obsessions (the mark of a true auteur), but his films were characterized by these obsessions, rather than by their actual content, which was secondary.[3]

Hitchcock's compromising of his vision with *Psycho* may have related to the failure of his earlier film, *Vertigo*, in 1958. Now generally regarded as his masterpiece, *Vertigo* was a magnificent, wholly personal vision, dark and uncompromising, and a film that refused to make concessions (besides the hokey plot, which was really the Trojan horse for Hitchcock's subtext) to audience requirements of genre entertainment. Perhaps Hitchcock, burned by the film's failure, was leery of making the same mistake again? If so, he was probably right, because *Psycho* would never have had such an enormous influence on Hollywood filmmaking had he not compromised his vision and so ensured the film's (equally huge) financial success.

Hitchcock himself was unusually frank on the question of a director's responsibility, to the studios as well as the Muse:

'I have too much conscience to take a million dollars and make a film that would please only me and the critics. I don't think that's really what one should do. I might like to make a film that would satisfy only me completely but a lot of people probably wouldn't like it. One often hears of films that play art theaters and are seen by very few people. But our medium happens to have a universal appeal, and it would seem to me that making a film to show to one's friends and to critics who are rarely satisfied, is a different

3 *Vertigo*, for example, is not a 'thriller' but a dream-nightmare about sexual desire and terror; *Psycho* could be likewise defined, though in a very different way; *Rear Window* is about voyeurism, sensation-seeking and the morbid urge to imagine and see the worst in others; consequently it is really about cinema itself.

thing from making films to appeal to the vast public. I would say it is harder to make a film that has both integrity and wide audience appeal than it is to make one that merely satisfies one's own artistic conscience.'

Hitch had learnt his lesson well: render unto Hollywood. If you want to poison the masses with your vision, then you have to be sure the masses swallow your poison. You have to get by not only the studios, but the public's own instinctive defenses against 'art'. In a word, they have to be seduced. Hitchcock is best known as the master of suspense; really, he was a master of seduction.

Coincidentally or not, 1960 was the year not just of *Psycho* but also of *Peeping Tom* in England (from director Michael Powell, whose career the film ended), and the year Roger Corman hit his stride with both *Little Shop of Horrors* (shot in two days and one night) and *The House of Usher*, the first of his melancholy, macabre Poe adaptations (all starring Vincent Price). Stanley Kubrick, meanwhile, was wrestling with the big studios over *Spartacus* – aptly enough the tale of a slave's successful revolt against the Empire – while Francis Ford Coppola was signing up for a film course at UCLA. The 60s had begun. Almost simultaneously, as if summoned from the collective unconscious, the first truly independent movies – John Cassavetes' *Shadows* and Jean-Luc Godard's and Francois Truffaut's *A Bout de Souffle (Breathless)* – appeared within months of each other.

Cassavetes and Godard were innovators with a limited audience, however. Their influence was more on fledgling filmmakers than on the moviegoing public. This has always been the nature of personal filmmaking. It is its limited appeal, its exclusivity, that distinguishes it from mainstream moviemaking, the latter being geared towards commercial gain and of necessity impersonal, unshaped by individual vision. Naturally, the more personal a movie is, the more exclusive its appeal, and vice versa – the more a movie is calculated to reach a wider audience in style, subject, etc, the less of a personal vision there will be behind it. It was Hitchcock's ability to personalize commercial projects (and commercialize personal ones) that made him so uniquely regarded in the industry, both consciously by critics and filmmakers, and less consciously by audiences.

Hitchcock, Welles, Huston and Kubrick notwithstanding, the idea of personal filmmaking didn't really come about to any significant degree until the arrival of Godard and Truffaut and the New Wave, in Europe, and of Cassavetes and then Brian De Palma, Francis Ford

Coppola, Martin Scorsese, Jim McBride, et al. in the US during the 1960s. (Although Kubrick was an early practitioner of indie cinema, as we've seen, Kubrick's movies were never really *personal*.) In the US, it was down to John Cassavetes to more or less single-handedly pave the way for independent cinema.

John Cassavetes, Original Dogme

'As in classic Greek drama, each of Cassavetes' films ends with a moment of insight or self-recognition. Characters discover something about themselves – not by thinking but by listening to their feelings. One day they finally hear a little voice of discontent that may have been nagging away for years, and, if they are lucky, wake up. *Shadows* ends with four recognition scenes. Lelia, Ben, Hugh and Rupert each realize something about how they have been false to themselves. Cassavetes is a very spiritual artist. All of his work is about learning to hear that still, small voice. What is wonderful is that he never gives up on even his most doomed characters. He is an artist of hope – a poet of the miraculous, transforming power of love and grace... Cassavetes' understanding of expression was an actor's. That is to say, for him, there was no essential difference between the expressive situations of acting and of life: what happened in one had its equivalent in the other. The artistic impoverishments of timid or derivative forms of acting were inextricably linked in his imagination with the disappointments of timid or derivative ways of living; and, conversely, the aesthetic excitements and challenges of original and brave acting were indistinguishable from the stimulations of original and brave living.'

Ray Carney, *Shadows*

There was initially an apparent – even blatant – discrepancy between personal (independent) film and popular Hollywood product, not merely in the methods used and styles employed, but in the aims of the people who made the films. It's doubtful if there was ever a director less willing to sugar coat the bitter pill of 'art' than John Cassavetes. In films like *The Killers, The Dirty Dozen* and *Rosemary's Baby*, Cassavetes was an undeniably seductive actor, but when it came to filmmaking (perhaps out of distaste for 'whoring' his acting talents to raise the money he needed to make his own movies), he went out of his way to turn off the charm. Although Cassavetes is usually credited with initiating independent cinema in 1960, with *Shadows,* this is not strictly true. Cassavetes didn't actually give birth to or invent anything, though it would be fair to say that he helped deliver it. At precisely the time Kubrick was inching towards the mainstream with *Paths of Glory* (1957), and more or less in tandem with the New Wave of French critics turned filmmakers, Cassavetes was experimenting with a new kind of moviemaking on the streets of New York.

Cassavetes bought his own equipment and film stock, and, like Godard, took it out on the streets. He brought together a group of fellow actors and, with no script to speak of (just rudimentary plot and characters), he began to improvise.[4] The method was as far removed from Hollywood as the beat poets were from Shakespeare, and it expressed a similar spirit: that of invention and revolt. Classicism and formalism (and cliché) were out; spontaneity and irrationality (and novelty) were in, even if that meant being crude and amateurish. Cassavetes was not the first to realize it, but he was one of the first to act on it. He was the first beat filmmaker. (Fittingly, *Shadows* makes a mockery of the beat poseur with one of its main characters.)

What Cassavetes' method embodied was the validity of creative expression – just do it – as its own end. The means was the end (just as the medium was the message). Along with Godard, he was the first to attempt to use film as a means of exploration rather than simply a device for recording. Cassavetes perceived the camera as a tool for discovering the truth, rather than for capturing fiction. He used it to strip the artifact away, instead of building it up. In a sense, his approach to movies was the direct opposite to that of Hollywood, and the results, predictably enough, were equally alien: unfamiliar and ungainly, to most viewers they were largely inaccessible. If Hollywood was about manufacturing dreams, Cassavetes (and the spirit of independent cinema that emerged along with him) was all about getting back to reality. (Essentially, Cassavetes was doing Dogme 95 forty years before Dogme 95.)

While Cassavetes' intent remains what is most essential and valuable about his work, the actual results are another matter. If his first couple of movies (*Shadows* and *Faces*) are still his best, that is partially because his method never evolved beyond his initial vision, and his movies often

4 *Shadows* was not, in fact, a wholly improvised work, despite the claim to this effect at the film's start. In fact, Cassavetes spent three years on it, and after the initial shoot in 1957, he went back (in 1959) with a more or less complete script and shot new scenes in a more traditional (though still loose) fashion. He edited the two separate shoots together and came up with the film that audiences finally saw, and hailed, or dismissed, as a brave (or foolish) new step for American cinema.

mistook tedium and discomfort for realism. Godard – a great filmmaker as well as a creative visionary – had the instinct to blend and blur his raw methodology with heavy doses of fantasy, irony, surrealism and a blatant and unabashed love of movies. The result was that – though his films were always hit-and-miss affairs, and sometimes didn't come off at all – they continued to evolve and mutate, retaining a freshness and vitality throughout the 60s. Cassavetes' films, on the other hand, became increasingly wearing on the viewer, growing more self-conscious and indulgent over time. Professionalism did not become Cassavetes the way it did Godard; and as with many pioneers, Cassavetes' best work was done while he was still getting warmed up. Yet his inspiration and innovative courage – and above all his integrity – were never in doubt. Cassavetes' greatness was less in the films themselves and more in his overall career, above all in the fact that he never came anywhere near to selling out to Hollywood. He was a foreign element that could not be assimilated, and as such, Cassavetes' warming up was like a rallying cry to other filmmakers to find the courage to follow their own inner light. It was a cry that was to be swiftly answered. As Peter Bogdanovich once put it: 'Shadows was the beginning of the New Hollywood.'

Roger Corman's Trash Utopia

'God was a very important character. He was down to a bit part when the picture came out.'

Roger Corman, on Gas-s-s-s

If Cassavetes was the spiritual mentor of independent cinema (he directly tutored Scorsese and indirectly inspired dozens of others), then it's fair to say that Roger Corman was its godfather. After getting his degree (in engineering) and a brief stint in the Navy, Corman became a story analyst at 20th Century Fox at the age of twenty-three. The studio way of doing things did not mesh with Corman's personality, however, and he went back to college, this time in England. After returning to Hollywood, he worked briefly as a literary agent; at twenty-seven, he sold his first screenplay (Highway Dragnet) to Allied Artists and was associate producer on the film. (It was around this time that Sam Peckinpah was working at AA for Don Siegel.) Soon after, Corman went to work at American International Pictures (AIP), and there embarked on a career that spanned nearly forty years and included well over five hundred pictures as producer and/or director (and occasionally actor). As a director, Corman is best remembered for his series of luscious and sombre Edgar Allan Poe adaptations in the 60s; as a producer, his name is legendary among filmmakers, as much as is Cassavetes', and for almost diametrically opposed reasons.

If Cassavetes was the indie artist who never sold out and always remained an anomaly – a freak of cinema and an art house tough guy – then Corman became a studio system unto himself. Corman dedicated himself to 'exploitation' movies, catering to the lowest common denominator of audience taste – sex, violence, drugs, monsters and spaceships, prisons, bikers – the crudest, rawest (yet in a sense also the purest) genre films imaginable. If Cassavetes was all about using film as a means for personal exploration, Corman was about mass exploitation. Yet he did it in such an open, direct, and unabashed (even gleeful) fashion that his personal integrity (the autonomy and independence of his vision) remains as far beyond question as Cassavetes'.

Corman was a unique player in the history of Hollywood. Like Cassavetes, he seemed to emerge less of his own accord and more like an avatar bringing a new religion – in response to a need, a void within the medium itself. It's not that the films which came into the world through Corman were of any great value, either, or even all that entertaining. They were basically trash, but trash of the happiest kind, trash that seemed to improve the atmosphere rather than pollute it. It was trash-art, like Warholian artifact but freed of Warhol's need for self-justification as 'art'. Corman took the crude materials – the lowest ingredients of movie entertainment – and forged from them tidy, unselfconscious, wholly disposable products. Rather than making new trash, he recycled what was already out there, taking all the crap and draining it of pretensions, bloated budgets, lifeless production 'values' and easy morality, and stripping it down to base essence. By this method (and in the opposite sense to Cassavetes' work), he revealed the true core of movies.

Not that this was ever Corman's intent (I'm sure he would laugh at the suggestion), since Corman's goal was simply to make money. But that was precisely what made his movie so pure (hence the tag 'exploitation'). Just as Cassavetes' complete indifference to money made his movies pure, Corman's indifference to 'art' gave his work a different kind of purity – the hedonistic variety, compared to Cassavetes' asceticism. Corman fully believed in making movies as well as possible within the limitations he imposed on himself (for as little money as humanly possible, and with a minimum of original vision). As such, Corman's method was that of an artist, and in the process, he developed his truly phenomenal gift for spotting and recruiting new talents, talents which he then gave the opportunity to make cheap movies for AIP, some of which even transcended the trash pile.

During his time at AIP, Corman pretty much established his own film school/studio and recruited and nurtured a legion of up-and-coming players in what would soon become the New Hollywood; among them, Peter Fonda, Dennis Hopper, Bruce Dern, Francis Ford Coppola, Jack Nicholson, Monte Hellman, Woody Allen, Peter Bogdanovich, Charles Bronson, Robert De Niro, Brian De Palma, Martin Scorsese, Paul Bartel, John Sayles, Jonathan Demme, John Milius, Joe Dante, Jonathan Kaplan, Ron Howard and James Cameron. Corman created a unique arena for writers, directors, and actors to develop their gifts in and discover their strengths. Everybody was happy and everybody won. Ironic that this methodology was reviled (by both Hollywood and critics) as 'exploitation', since it was a far less exploitative environment than that of Hollywood. At AIP, the artists got to make movies, Corman got to make money and audiences got the movies they wanted (and no doubt deserved). It was a trash movie utopia.

Francis Ford Coppola: Hollywood Caesar

'Francis was the great white knight… He was the one who made us hope… He has charisma beyond logic. I can see now what kind of men the great Caesars of history were, their magnetism.'

George Lucas[5]

One of Corman's most celebrated protégés was Francis Ford Coppola. The first of the new generation who had grown up with *Citizen Kane*, Coppola was the leading light of a loose collection of filmmakers who followed in the footsteps of Welles, Kubrick, Cassavetes, and the French New Wave and set about making movies *their* way, without rejecting entirely the allure (or the funds) of Hollywood. This group became known as 'movie brats'; they were still in their twenties (unprecedented in the business at that time), went to film school and, like the French critics-turned-filmmakers (having grown up on a diet of movies), they were movie literate. Their approach was both a synthesis and an evolution of all previous styles and genres, fusing them into something

---

5 An opinion seconded by John Milius: 'Francis was going to become the new emperor of the new order, but it wasn't going to be like the old order. It was going to be the rule of the artist.' Quoted in 'Godfatherhood,' by Michael Sragow, *The New Yorker*, 24th March 1997

personal, visionary, and wholly new. For a time, their influence would be so prevalent as to give rise to the term, 'The New Hollywood'.

Coppola was the first of a generation of filmmakers trained in film school to hit the big time. Though they may now be seen as a mere transitional phase, film schools at that time served as a bridge between the age of studio filmmaking and the digital era yet to come. Before film schools, and besides Roger Corman's private recruiting ground, there was no alternative for aspiring filmmakers (save rare exceptions like Kubrick) besides working their way up through the ranks, in the hope that, if they persisted long enough and worked hard enough, they would eventually get to direct a movie. Film schools meant that instead of spending years doing menial work on B-movies – or simply twiddling thumbs and writing screenplays no one would read – it was now possible to spend time learning the trade, and even get one's hands on a camera, by going to film school. Not that there was any guarantee at the end of it that one would find work (there were no titles that could secure a directing job), but at least one would have gained experience should the opportunity ever arise.[6]

Initially, studios did not consider film school graduates to be potential directors, or even employable at all, but merely as inexperienced upstarts. But in the 60s, with the emergence of directors like Kubrick (self-made), Roman Polanski (who came out of Lodz film school in Poland) and Coppola, this began to change. Studios no longer felt so confident that their way of working – the old studio system – was necessarily the best, or that it could even keep abreast of the rapidly changing times, much less anticipate (or cater to) the mutating tastes of the public. Movie audiences appeared to be getting younger, and the youth, meanwhile, was definitely getting stranger.

Coppola signed on a UCLA for a two-year course in film in 1960.

Carroll Ballard, a co-student at the time, describes Coppola thus:

---

6 'Coppola's timing could not have been better. He was entering UCLA during a period when film schools were about to explode in a proliferation of talent that, within a decade, would change the face of the motion picture industry… In the past, an aspiring director wouldn't have dreamed of attending classes to learn the business. He would have worked his way up the industry ladder – the industry at the time was definitely an old boys' network – beginning with a menial job and advancing through the ranks over the years. Prior to the 1960s, film students were scorned by an industry that believed it was a waste of time to study how to make a movie when you could learn through experience… In theory, students entering a two-year program would be exposed to what usually took many years to learn through on the job experience.' Michael Schumacher, *Francis Ford Coppola: A Filmmaker's Life*, pg. 18-19.

'Francis showed up at UCLA and within a very short period of time he seemed to have the whole department wrapped around his little finger. Who was this guy? He got everything he wanted and had everybody working for him like a bunch of slaves. What qualified him for this? I have since come to realize that the qualities that he had – and chutzpah, to a large degree – were the most important qualities for making it in the business.'[7]

Coppola's first break in the movie business was in the world of porno, so we will need to take a brief digression into that world. In the early 60s, Russ Meyer – the undisputed don of indie cinema – came to prominence. Since Meyer made (ultra soft-core) porno, however, he has been mostly ignored by film historians. In his book *Danse Macabre*, Stephen King referred to the impossibility of true 'independent' filmmaking and pointed out that the closest to it must be Russ Meyer. Meyer not only wrote, produced and directed his films, he edited and shot them too.

His first noted work was called *The Immoral Mr. Teas* and came out in 1959. Meyer's genius – if genius it was – was in crafting a sexploitation film that slid under the radar of the censors and, by managing not to offend anyone, escaped obscenity charges. As a result, the film was successful enough to create an instant demand for soft-core nudies. Since the level of artistry required for such films was low, and the amount of funding equally limited, aspiring producers, eager to cash in on the new permissiveness, began to seek possible recruits among film school students, judging (rightly) that said recruits would be willing to work cheap – and have little concern about the dubious nature of the material – so long as they got a chance to make movies. One of these early recruits was Coppola.

Coppola was approached by a small group of investors and asked to write a script along the lines of *Mr. Teas*. Bored with the slow and methodical pace at UCLA and eager to get his feet wet (and hands dirty), he threw together a script that was immediately approved by his investors. They refused to consider him as the film's director, however, and since this was what had attracted Coppola in the first place, he took the script to another investor who offered $2,000 and agreed to let him shoot the film himself. The film – shot in an abandoned department store in Venice, California – was called *The Peeper*, about a Peeping Tom. Coppola's artistic aspirations somewhat interfered with the more simple ends of pornography, however, and the finished film proved insufficiently raunchy to attract a distributor. Coppola then hooked up with a group of filmmakers who had also recently completed a nudie (a comedy about a drunk cowboy who hallucinates naked women in place of cows), and they agreed to splice the two movies together. The result, called *Tonight for Sure*, had enough naked females to meet the demands of the market, and the film now appears on some of Coppola's filmographies as his debut feature. An auspicious start for the man who would soon become the godfather of the New Hollywood.[8] Soon after, Coppola hooked up with Roger Corman.

In common with the skin flick companies, Corman favored film students for his movies because they came cheap, and Corman was all about budget. Corman was looking for a cheap editor when a teacher at UCLA recommended Coppola to him, and since Corman's offer came at a time when Coppola was too broke to pay his phone bill, he accepted the job: six months editing work, for a total of $250. His first project was a B-movie called *Battle Beyond the Sun*, a Russian sci-fi flick for which Coppola was required to write dialogue in order for it to be dubbed into English. Coppola assured Corman that he spoke Russian (a lie), confident he could make up dialogue to fit the action based on the images alone. (That was exactly what he did, and even had the opportunity to shoot a few extra scenes for the film.) In an unrelated development, Coppola then won the highly prestigious Sam Goldwyn award for a script he'd submitted as a UCLA student. The script was called *Pilma, Pilma,* which Coppola had written during a single, sleepless night, ostensibly so he would be too exhausted to pass the physical the next day and so avoid being drafted. Coppola passed the physical but was not drafted, and went on to win $2000 for the script, later selling it for $5000, all for a single night's work. Corman, already impressed with Coppola's hard work ethic, took pride in his new found protégé and placed ads in the variety papers announcing the award.

For his next Corman project, titled *The Young Racers*, Coppola volunteered to work on the sound; despite the fact that he knew nothing about sound recording, he gave himself a crash course on the subject and pulled the job off to Corman's satisfaction. Then, as *Young*

---

8 Coppola followed this with a similar job, shooting additional scenes to (literally) flesh out a German soft-core film, eventually retitled *The Playmates and the Bellhop*. (The original was in black and white, and Coppola shot 3D color scenes and spliced them into the film.)

Racers was finishing up, and aware that the movie had come in under budget and that Corman liked to economize by shooting movies back to back, Coppola suggested they make another movie with the left-over funds, using the same cast and crew. 'I knew that whenever Roger takes a crew on location,' Coppola said later, 'he can't resist the temptation of doing a second picture, having already paid the crew's expenses there. I played on this, managing to convince him that I should direct it. At the time, Roger wanted to make a movie molded on the success of *Psycho,* so I told him a zesty horror scene which more or less turned him on.'[9] The scene involved a string of dolls and a body in a swimming pool, enough to inspire Corman apparently, because he gave Coppola the go-ahead, on the condition he change the man in the scene to a woman (Corman always required plenty of sex as well as violence in his films). Corman coughed up $20,000 for the budget and Coppola managed to secure another $20,000 from a British producer, Raymond Stross (who gave the money in exchange for UK rights). The film was shot in Ardmore studios in Dublin in two weeks, with some of the *Young Racers* cast and crew. It was while making *Dementia 13* (as the movie was called) that Coppola met his future and life-long companion, Eleanor Neil (now Eleanor Coppola). Coppola was enthusiastic about the project. At last he was underway.

In 1963, while Coppola was making his aptly-titled debut, a nation in a state of flux had become a country in the throes of transformation. It was the year Hitchcock made his second and only other horror film (and his last great work), the dream-nightmare *The Birds.* Kubrick was peaking with his own doomsday scenario, the blackly comic vision of Armageddon *Dr. Strangelove.* H.G. Lewis (an authentic independent filmmaker whose interests steered well clear of the province of 'art') was inventing the splatter film with *Blood Feast,* while a sixteen-year-old Steven Spielberg was enjoying his first hit with *Firelight*; Hollywood was making concessions to the new cynicism with a post-Jimmy Dean Paul Newman, as the surly and irresistible heel, *Hud*; Brian De Palma threw together his first movie, *The Wedding Party,* starring Robert De Niro and Jill Clayburgh; and Martin Scorsese made a short film called *The Big Shave,* in which a shirtless man shaves himself in the mirror, cutting his face repeatedly until covered with blood, then cutting his own throat. (The film was intended as a visual parable for America, specifically the Vietnam war.) To cap it all, the year ended with the assassination of John F. Kennedy, an act that devastated the public psyche and altered the social fabric of America forever, not least for being captured on film for all to see. As befits a true artist-spokesman, Jean-Luc Godard gave the last word for the year with his masterpiece, *Le Mepris (Contempt)*, perfectly summing up the mood of the time.

As a direct result of Kennedy's death, the conflict in Vietnam escalated and public awareness of it begun to increase. The unshakable impression which Kennedy's murder (and the pungent odor of conspiracy that surrounded it) gave to the American people (most especially the younger ones, all those budding filmmakers) was that something had gone horribly and irreparably wrong in the homeland. The side effect of this creeping suspicion was a corresponding desire to *communicate* – the despair, rage, paranoia, and dread – through whatever means available. For the first time ever, those means included movies. Cassavetes and Godard had shown it could be done. De Palma and Scorsese were just getting warmed up. Don Siegel was putting his ten cents worth in with the brutal and nihilistic *The Killers*.[10] Clint Eastwood was acting in a cheap little Italian Western called *A Fistful of Dollars*. And of course, The Beatles, Bob Dylan, The Rolling Stones, The Doors, and The Jimi Hendrix Experience were all doing their thing. A revolution was underway, and the lunatics – far outnumbering the guards – looked about ready to take over the asylum. And in Hollywood, though it would take almost a decade to become fully apparent, Coppola was getting ready to lead the way.

Dementia 13 hardly put Coppola on the map, but it did serve to discredit him with his fellow UCLA film students, many of whom scorned Coppola for selling out to trash merchant Corman. *The New York Times* dismissed the film wearily and referred to Coppola's direction as 'stolid'. (At first, Coppola was pleased, having misread the word as 'solid'; his brother soon set him straight.) This was the beginning of a life long contention between Coppola and his critics.

---

10 Siegel's *The Killers* not only made a first-rate thriller several years ahead of its time, but, like his earlier film *Invasion of the Body Snatchers*, it served as a kind of cloaked joke/ parable. In this case, the joke was on Hollywood – the land of dirty dealings, cutthroat businessmen, and heartless vamps and fall guys, a land where the maverick agent will whore himself to the corporation only so long before his better instincts compel him to bite the hand that feeds him, even if it means starvation or death. Lee Marvin's Charlie – the maverick, self-motivated, indifferent but dignified loner – was Siegel's stand-in, the rebel-outlaw who bucked the system, or at least tried to, and who inevitably died trying. (Seen through such a lens, *The Killers* may have been the greatest movie that Sam Peckinpah never made, but more on that later.)

But whatever anyone else thought (and Corman at least was proud of his new protégé), he had made a movie; he was a director. What Coppola really wanted to do, however, was write. If he had to go to Hollywood and have a big hit to fund his personal goals, so be it. To this day, Coppola considers writing the real creative act behind movies, and thinks of himself as a writer who also directs, rather than vice versa. His ambition even at this early stage (despite what his peers may have assumed) was to make small, personal movies based on his own ideas.

Coppola's Samuel Goldwyn award had caught the attention of the studios, including Universal, who made him an offer. Suspicious that it would involve TV work, he turned them down, accepting instead an offer of $375 a week from Seven Arts to write a script based on Carson McCuller's *Reflections in a Golden Eye*. (The film was eventually made in 1967 by John Huston, who did not use Coppola's script.) Shortly after, he was asked to adapt Tennessee Williams' *This Property is Condemned*; as with *Reflections*, his work was never used. Desperate to make another movie, this time a personal one, on impulse Coppola invested his savings (around $20,000) in stocks for a new invention, the Scopitone (a juke box that showed short films on a small screen). He lost everything, not the last time that Coppola's technological vision proved his (temporary) financial ruin. Coppola was then hired to work on the script for *Is Paris Burning?* for which he met and collaborated with Gore Vidal. This time, Coppola's name wound up on the finished film, and as a direct result- – despite the film's disastrous reception – Coppola was offered another war movie, *Patton*, for which he was paid a grand sum of $50,000 to write the script.

Patton took several years to make (it wasn't released until 1970), but meanwhile Coppola (having recuperated his losses) was more determined than ever to make his own movie. Coppola's second production was ostensibly an adaptation of a novel by David Benedictus, *You're a Big Boy Now*. Initially, the project had been an original script based on Coppola's own life; when later he read Benedictus' novel, he found some remarkable parallels. He purchased the film rights and adapted sections of it into his screenplay; the final result was a peculiar hybrid with only a distant family resemblance to the source novel.

Coppola secured funding via a method that is now a standard part of the Hollywood hustle: he approached the actors he wanted for the film and told them he had made a deal with a studio. He then went to the studio (Seven Arts, a subsidiary of Warner Brothers) and told them he had signed his actors; it was by this method (remarkably audacious for one as inexperienced as Coppola) that he got 'the green light', and Seven Arts eventually gave Coppola $800,000 for the movie, $8000 of which was for him to write and direct (he had also secured 10% of the profits). As Michael Schumacher writes (in *Francis Ford Coppola: A Filmmaker's Life*), it was a breakthrough offer. 'No one had ever offered someone as young and inexperienced as Coppola the opportunity to direct a mainstream feature-length picture.'[11]

Released on March 21st 1967, the film attracted little public interest and got a mixed, though generally encouraging, critical response. At the very least, it silenced the scoffers at UCLA, especially when Coppola submitted the film for his Master's, and passed. Coppola was the first film student ever to submit a movie for his thesis, just as he was the first film student to break into the movies directly from film school. Among the favorable notices, *Newsweek's* Joseph Morgenstern wrote: 'Not since Welles was a boy wonder or Kubrick a kid has any young American made a film as original, spunky, or just plain funny as this one.' After such unequivocal praise (and despite *Big Boy's* poor box office), the offers were rolling in. Heady with success, Coppola began conducting interviews with characteristic grandiloquence, and the soon-to-be notorious Coppola persona began to take form.

'I pattern my life on Hitler in this respect,' he said of his cinematic ambitions. 'He didn't take over the country. He worked his way into the existing fabric first.' Coppola later qualified the remark, without in any way leavening it:

> 'My allusion to Hitler was simply that, contrary to what a lot of people think, he wasn't a revolutionary who came down from the hills and took the government over. He worked his way into government, became a part of it, and then used that to take it over… The way to come to power is not always to merely challenge the Establishment, but first to make a place in it and then challenge, and double-cross, the Establishment. Which is essentially what I've done.'[12]

Despite, or perhaps because of, such lofty claims, Coppola made his first major misstep for his third movie by accepting the reigns of a big Hollywood musical called *Finian's Rainbow*. 'The only reason

11 Schumacher, pg. 45.
12 Schumacher, pg. 50-51.

I got the job,' he later remarked, 'was because I was young. Warner's had this creaky old property lying around, and they wanted a young director to modernize it. It was between me and Billy Friedkin.[13] The film was a disaster, matched only by Coppola's next excursion into the genre twelve years later, *One from the Heart*. After the failure of *Finian's Rainbow*, Coppola again resolved to devote himself to small, personal films, and to helping others do the same. He began to spend time with George Lucas (whom he'd met in '67), and expressed an interest in Lucas' sci-fi project, *THX1138*. Coppola planned to make *The Rain People* as his next picture, a road movie based on a short story he had written while at UCLA about three women (eventually just one) leaving their husbands and traveling cross country in a station wagon. Once again Coppola resorted to bluffing to secure his funding. He let slip that he was working on a new personal movie, and had already started shooting it in secret. To substantiate the rumors, Coppola took Lucas and actor James Caan (who eventually starred in the movie) and shot some raw footage of a football match. He then invested $80,000 of his *Rainbow* earnings into state-of-the-art equipment necessary for on the road filming, including a mobile editing suite. By now, he was considerably short of funds to make the movie, but Seven Arts had no way of knowing this. Nor did they know whether someone else would step up and offer Coppola funding if they failed to. In Hollywood, the fear of losing a golden goose is even greater than the fear of winding up with a turkey, and Coppola's bluff paid off. The studio promised him $750,000, more than enough to hit the road with. George Lucas later described the project as follows:

'The crew for *The Rain People* was very, very small, and it was very anti-establishment. I think there were only about thirteen or fourteen people in the whole crew... Francis just didn't want to be part of that Hollywood scene. He wanted to be more independent. We were more anti-establishment than ever because it was the 60s. We didn't want to be part of the establishment. Francis wanted to be doing more artistic films, and not be forced to make commercial films. I was still interested in doing avant-garde, non-story, non-character films.'[14]

13 Schumacher, pg. 54.
14 Schumacher, pg. 66,72. It was while traveling with Coppola and the crew of *Rain People* (and shooting a documentary on the process, *Filmmaker*) that George Lucas came up with the idea for *Star Wars*. He was watching 'Flash Gordon' on TV at the time.

Coppola eventually brought the movie in for $740,000. Galvanized by the experience, he decided to put his money where his mouth was and began laying the groundwork for his great, anti-Hollywood dream. Inspired by a visit to Lanterne film studios in Denmark (based in an idyllic mansion by the sea, fifty kilometers from Copenhagen), he ordered another $80,000 of equipment (including a sound-mixing system) and set about finding a location to build his own studio, to be called American Zoetrope.[15] Zoetrope was the name given to the original movie maker, a cylinder-shaped gadget that produced a moving image by the simple act of spinning it. The word is Greek for 'life movement', exactly what Coppola – with his Napoleonic creative vision – had in mind. What Hitler had tried and failed to accomplish in Europe at a political, economic, and social level, Coppola would now achieve in the arts: a renaissance of classical values and the realization of a global vision. Coppola didn't just aspire to being the new Welles, he dreamed of realizing Griffith's goal and creating a universal language. At the same time (a paradox at the heart of Coppola that eventually precipitated his plunge into darkness), he just wanted to make small, personal movies.

The Rain People premiered on August 27th, 1969. It was not a hit. Regardless of this fact, American Zoetrope was off and running, the dream fast becoming a reality. Reality would finally prove to be incompatible with the dream, however. 'As Coppola would regretfully admit, the young filmmakers pouring into American Zoetrope were, almost to the individual, rebelling against the old Hollywood system, but in their idealism, they neglected to appreciate fully the fact that even small studios and films require capital to survive.'[16] Coppola's vision had been naive: 'My enthusiasm and my imagination far outpaced any kind of financial logic. I wasn't associated with anyone who was the businessman of the group. It was all me, and I was forging ahead without looking back and seeing whether we could afford this or that.'[17]

By now, Coppola had already secured a multi-picture deal with Warners, including future projects *The Conversation,* Lucas' *THX1138*, and a war movie scripted by John Milius called *Apocalypse Now.* Warner's gave Coppola a rather meager loan of $30,000, and

---

15 827 Folson St, in San Francisco, a three-story loft, eventually became the home of American Zoetrope.
16 Schumacher, pg. 76.
17 Schumacher, pg. 77.

an additional $300,000 for script development, money that would have to be returned if the studios decided to back out of American Zoetrope at a later date. True to his wont, Coppola invested it in new equipment, building himself one of the most technologically advanced studios in Hollywood. The first movie American Zoetrope produced was *THX1138*, and the film was a complete disaster. Coppola practically forced Warners to put up the money (the film took ten weeks to film and cost $800,000) and even before its release, American Zoetrope was in trouble. Many of the filmmakers who had come aboard, it soon transpired, were pursuing their own agendas, and equipment began to vanish from the studio at an alarming rate: 'Coppola's paradise for young filmmakers had turned into a personal nightmare.'[18]

When Coppola saw an early cut of *THX1138,* his heart sank to his knees. 'This is either going to be a masterpiece or a masturbation,' he said to sound man Walter Murch. Despite being ever the optimist, Coppola must have known which it was going to be.[19] Warner's people loathed it, and in desperation they took the film from Lucas, hoping to 'save' it in the editing room. One look at the film had been enough to quash all interest in American Zoetrope; they were anxious to cut their losses and get clear of it before Coppola's 'genius' undid them all. With no future projects in sight, and no offers forthcoming Coppola was now half a million in debt. 'Zoetrope was picked clean,' he recalls. 'Everyone had used it, no one had contributed, and there was a time when I was literally staving off the sheriff from putting the chain across the door.'[20]

During the making of *Rain People*, Coppola was heard loudly prophesizing that, 'The system will fall by its own weight. It can't fail to!' A few months later, Hollywood was still standing, but the Zoetrope dream had ended before it had had a chance to even begin, and Coppola

---

18 Schumacher, pg 81. 'Coppola likened the experience to the Beatles' founding of Apple, which had faced similar problems in England, though on a much larger scale. Like the Beatles, Coppola had been too trusting of people who, quite often, were ripping him off.' (ibid)

19 Coppola quote from *Easy Riders, Raging Bulls*, pg. 98. *THX1138* is a difficult film even to sit through, much less to like, and if Lucas had not gone on to become the second most successful filmmaker in Hollywood history, it would probably have vanished without a trace.

20 Schumacher, pg 86. Visiting journalist Gerald Nachman observed at the time, 'Zoetrope was down to one mini-skirted secretary, and instant coffee instead of espresso.' (ibid)

looked to be going the way of Griffith. By its own excess weight, his half-constructed Tower of Babel had fallen. True to his word, he had followed in Hitler's footsteps and been toppled by his own excess zeal and ambition.

Romancing Hollywood: Roman Polanski's Deal with the Devil

'The greatest danger for any artist is to find himself in a comfortable position; it is his duty to look for and remain in the most uncomfortable position possible.'

Orson Welles, to André Bazin

A continent away in Poland, while Coppola was still apprenticing under Corman, Roman Polanski was breaking through with his debut movie, *Knife in the Water*. Even at this early stage, Polanski had already set his sights on Hollywood, which he described as, 'the place that belonged more to my dreams than to my reality, at the threshold of where everything would be handed to me.'[21] When *Knife in the Water* was nominated for an Oscar for best foreign film of 1963, those dreams looked set to become reality.

Roman Polanski's life reads like a movie. It is a saga both tragic and comic, absurd, appalling and perverse in equal proportions. Early in life, he was confined to a Polish concentration camp, where he was separated from his mother and later from his father (the former was killed in the camps). Later, he went to the Lodz film school in Warsaw and enjoyed great success, winning prizes for his short films *Two Men and a Wardrobe* (1958) and *The Fat and the Lean* (1961). After *A Knife in the Water* (shot in Polish) was nominated by the Academy in 1963, he moved to London for his next film, *Repulsion*, a breakthrough in the genre – that of psychological horror – that established its young director as the natural successor to Alfred Hitchcock; all, one suspects, more or less exactly as young Roman had intended. A master of anxiety and dread more than actual suspense, Polanski's character and films were far more suited to the 1960s climate than were Hitchcock's later works, and if Polanski finally disappointed in this early promise, he at least enjoyed several years of unsurpassed success, both critically and commercially, as supreme artist-entertainer in the Hitchcock tradition. In the space of four years, Polanski pulled off a crude but effective horror 'classic,'

21 See *Polanski: His Life and Films*, by Barbara Leaming a sharp, disturbing sex comedy (*Cul-de-Sac*), a visually haunting and inspired horror spoof (*Dance of the Vampires*), and a masterly and chilling ode to paranoia called *Rosemary's Baby*, which would prove not only to be one of the most influential and successful horror movies of all time, but also a central work of the period. *Dance of the Vampires* was Polanski's first Hollywood film and it was something of a disaster for all concerned. The film was severely edited and re-dubbed by the studios, who apparently didn't know what to do with it. Doubtless they were bewildered by a finished product which must have struck them as neither fish nor fowl. In a vain and self-defeating attempt to cater to the imaginary 'public', however, it was absurdly retitled *The Fearless Vampire Killers; or, Pardon Me, Your Teeth Are in My Neck* (yes, all one title), and not surprisingly, the film was a flop. (It seemed as if someone was deliberately determined to kill the horse before it even got out of the running gate.)[22]

Rosemary's Baby came out the same year as George A. Romero's *Night of the Living Dead*; considering that they share a common genre, two movies could hardly be more different, but both, in their way, changed the face of the horror movie. *Rosemary's Baby* proved that a well-made, thoughtful movie dealing with outrageously gothic subject matter could be a box office success, paving the way for such films as *The Exorcist, The Omen* and *Carrie. Night of the Living Dead*, on the other hand, proved that a small-budget, grainy, thoroughly amateurish but wildly imaginative 'splatter' movie could strike a chord with cinemagoers and establish its own 'cult' audience – thereby paving the way for such filmmakers as Larry Cohen, David Cronenberg, John Carpenter, and Tobe Hooper (whose *Texas Chainsaw Massacre*, ten years later, officially opened the gates of low-budget hell, and unleashed the video 'nasty' upon the world). Directly or indirectly, Polanski was an inspiration to them all.

For a Polish immigrant with only three features behind him, *Rosemary's Baby* was an astonishingly assured piece of Hollywood artistry. It was also a movie mogul's dream – a hit movie from a

---

22 These attempts at salvage/sabotage notwithstanding, the film remains a lyrical and poetic work, as true an ode to vampirism as ever reached the screen, despite, or perhaps due to, its tone of fondest parody. *Dance of the Vampires* is a lightweight masterpiece, one of the very few of its kind. As a script-conception it's a piece of fluff in the popular but disreputable tradition of *Airplane!, Young Frankenstein, Love at First Bite*, etc – in a word, a spoof. But Polanski's film is a spoof that surpasses – in artistic merit – most of the films that it is spoofing. This alone gives it a place in cinema history, and – I presume – in the hearts of horror fans everywhere (the film deserves to be a cult, even if it isn't).

bestselling novel that satisfied just about everyone: fans of the book, aficionados of the occult, the ordinary public of thrill-seekers, even, at a pinch, the art-house crowd. Yet it's also rather soulless – slick, glossy, seamless and wholly mainstream. The director's personal kinks are largely restrained. Polanski took the job in the spirit of professionalism, fully determined to cut himself a niche in Hollywood and prove to the studio heads that he was a dependable, efficient and bankable talent. As a result, he seemed to consciously curb his more visionary impulses.

Although Polish by birth (and although his first two English-language films were shot in the UK), Polanski embraced US culture (and cinema) at once, demonstrating an affinity for it (and an understanding of it) that few American filmmakers can lay claim to. His early films sizzled with mischievous delight in the medium and a fascination for the filmmaking process which effortlessly translated to the viewer. Such film sense seems to be a distinctly American 'passion,' one that Orson Welles first brought to audiences and which Hitchcock (an Englishman) developed early in his career. Arthur Penn displayed it in *Bonnie and Clyde*, and Peckinpah with his early films, but it would be several more years before Robert Altman and Francis Ford Coppola would break onto the scene and usher in the 'new wave' of American cinema, whereupon, with directors like Hal Ashby, Scorsese, De Palma, and Spielberg, passion would become – for an all-too brief spell – the norm. In the meantime, along with a mere handful of others, it fell, ironically enough, to a diminutive Polish Jew and survivor of the concentration camps, to put the kinetic spirit back into American movies.

Speak of the Devil: Robert Evans and the New Hollywood Shuffle

'You can't make a deal unless you're prepared to blow it.'

Robert Evans

If this book were as comprehensive as I'd like, it would have taken me twice as long to write and clocked in at one hundred pages longer, the additional space being mostly devoted to what are commonly referred to as 'the money men', the producers, studio executives and moguls who make movies possible, and who so often make life impossible for the people who make movies. The most prevalent and persistent myth about producers and studio heads – a gross simplification at best – is that they are a necessary evil that the artist has to overcome in order to realize his grand vision; in short, that producers are the bad guys, in the black hats, directors and writers the good guys, wearing white hats. The real truth is that egos are egos no matter where you go or what your occupation, motivation, or calling may be, and that 'artists' can be the worst egomaniacs of all. Just so (albeit less frequently), Hollywood businessmen and women can be as creative, in their way, as the people they hire, without necessarily having the inflated egos of 'artists'.

Robert Evans started out as an actor, a 'pretty boy' whose first screen role was opposite his idol, Jimmy Cagney (as Lon Chaney, Jr.), playing the boy wonder movie mogul, Irving Thalberg, who became head of MGM while still in his twenties. It was a fitting debut, because ten years later Evans was appointed the head of Paramount (much to the bewilderment and consternation of everyone in Hollywood) and became a boy wonder movie mogul himself, as well as the first actor ever to run a studio.

As a young movie actor, Evans got his break playing the matador who wins Brett Ashley (Ava Gardner) in the film adaptation of Hemingway's *The Sun Also Rises.* Just about everyone on the movie (including scriptwriter Peter Viertel and Hemingway himself) objected to Evans in the role; the cast even signed a petition to walk if Evans wasn't removed. In response, producer Darryl Zanuck (who had 'discovered' Evans for the role in a Los Angeles night club) showed up on the set with a bullhorn and announced, 'The kid stays in the picture!' (the title of Evans' bestselling, prizewinning autobiography). It was at that moment, Evans writes (the moment he was temporarily rescued from ignominy by Zanuck's divine intervention), that he decided what he really wanted to do: produce. Despite being for a time hugely popular as an actor (for a short period he was touted as 'the next big thing,' but it never happened), Evans was determined to be the next Thalberg, or at least the next Zanuck.

In 1963, he sold the fashion business (Evans–Picone[23]) and set up a 'non-existent Robert Evans Production Company.' Through a connection to *Publishers' Weekly* reviewer George Wieser, Evans was able to get first look at new publications and sniff out potential bestsellers to make into hit movies, and one of the first books he bought the rights for was *The Detective*, which became a bestseller soon after. Suddenly Evans was a Hollywood player. As he put it, 'For the first time, the guy holding the aces was me.'[24] Evans was offered a deal at 20th Century Fox as associate producer on the film, but turned them down. Fox offered Evans half a million for the rights;

23 Evans made his fortune as a New York fashion tycoon – most celebrated for popularizing 'women in pants' in the 50s. After he quit acting, he dabbled briefly in Broadway theater production, but that also fizzled.
24 See Robert Evans' autobiography, *The Kid Stays in the Picture* for full details (quote pg. 103).

determined to get his 'foot in the door', Evans demanded a three-picture development deal, a suite of offices, and a picture in the trades of him signing the deal with the new head of Fox, Richard Zanuck (Darryl's son), all in exchange for the rights to the novel. Fox turned him down.

Undaunted, Evans continued to play the role of producer. Using chutzpah in lieu of experience, he began setting up a deal with actor Alain Delon for a film based on the French entertainer Maurice Chevalier. Evans introduced Delon to Chevalier (who happened to be in LA at the time), and persuaded them both to accompany him to a press conference at the Bistro in Beverly Hills. There, Evans brazenly informed the press that he was negotiating a deal with a major studio and that his first picture would be *The Detective* (to which he still owned the rights). His second picture would be a film based on the life of Chevalier, starring Alain Delon. On impulse, Evans then announced that Brigitte Bardot would play Chevalier's lover, the cabaret singer Mistinguett. The press was so enthused by Evans' address that they forgot to ask him what the third picture would be (fortunately for Evans since there wasn't one). Evans may not have been holding all the aces, but he played like he was. The following day, Fox agreed to Evans' terms, photo and all.

Shortly after, an article appeared in the Sunday edition of *The New York Times* written by Peter Bart (whom Evans met through his *Detective* scriptwriter, Abby Mann), in which Bart referred to Evans as 'the next Thalberg.'[25] Manifest destiny. As a direct, almost immediate result of the piece, Evans was called to New York to meet the head of Gulf & Western, Charles Bluhdorn, who had just bought Paramount Studios for a bargain-basement price. (At the time, Paramount was the least successful of the major studios, coming in at a distant ninth place, after the eight majors.) Inspired by Bart's article, Bluhdorn invited Evans to take over Paramount's European production department, based in London.[26]

---

25 Interestingly, according to the director Henry Jaglom: 'Orson [Welles] always said that Hollywood had been ruined by Thalberg, who invented the idea of the creative producer, the producer who told the director what to do. That lasted from the 30s to the 60s. Bert [Schneider, head of BBS, see Chapter 3] reversed that.' (*Easy Riders, Raging Bulls*, pg. 77)
26 Evans on Bluhdorn: 'The real love of his life wasn't family, sex or even business. It was negotiating. Charlie would negotiate for anything from an airline to a potato. His edge was his energy. The one thing he never accepted was "no".' Evans also says of Bluhdorn, 'The electricity of his embrace was possibly his most extraordinary asset.' (Evans, pg. 131, 232.) A distinctly different perspective on Bluhdorn comes from Peter Bart: 'He was a thug, a terrible person, an absolutely unmitigated awful human being.' Don Simpson, who would become head of production for Paramount in the 80s, described Bluhdorn as 'a mean, despicable, unethical, evil man, who lived too long.' Both quotes, Biskind, *Easy Riders, Raging Bulls*, pg. 144.

Evans accepted Bluhdorn's offer. He managed to squeeze free of his newly acquired contract with Fox (by giving up his rights to *The Detective* and any other projects in development), and moved to London; during his five-month sojourn in Europe, he fired over half of the staff at Paramount. When he was questioned by Bluhdorn and Bluhdorn's right-hand man, Martin Davis, Evans said simply: 'You know the business better than me...but from all the bullshit I've been hearing it seems that distribution is running the business, not production. We're going the wrong way, fellas. If the product stinks, you can't sell it. Certainly not these dinosaurs.'[27] Bluhdorn was of half a mind by now to close down the whole studio and cut his losses, but finally decided against it. As Evans has it, 'They didn't close down Paramount. Worse. They launched a third world war. Heads rolled faster than marbles. Paranoia became the name of the game. Politics first, films last.' Impressed by Evans' chutzpah, Bluhdorn appointed him head of production in the US. Evans was to take care of the creative end of things while Bernie Donnenfeld took care of business. The then-current head, Howard Koch, was ousted without ceremony, and went on to become a leading Hollywood producer. Evans, meanwhile, became 'the biggest joke in town.'[28]

Evans' opening speech to his distribution staff was short and sweet: he wrote two lines on a blackboard in capital letters consisting of his sole decree: 'Don't tell me what to make. And I won't tell you how to sell.' Evans' first move as studio head was to hire Peter Bart as his right-hand man, an unprecedented act to grant a position of such power within a conglomerate to a journalist (a liberal one at that). Bluhdorn accepted Evans' choice, and Evans' stint as Paramount's youngest ever head of production lasted until 1974, when he was ousted with the standard deal, and became a freelance producer for the studio (his first film was *Chinatown*). During his time there, Evans was embroiled in a constant series of battles on an almost daily basis. Evans even went head to head with J. Edgar Hoover over production of *The President's Analyst*, which

---

27 This and following quote, Evans, pg. 116–118.

28 'I was called "Bluhdorn's Folly" by *The New York Times* and "Bluhdorn's Blow Job" by *Hollywood Close-Up*, a local scandal sheet read by all. Army Archerd, the encyclopedia of the industry, was once asked: "In forty years of writing for *Daily Variety*, which of your columns caused the most outrage?" Without a moment's hesitation, he answered, "The day I printed Bob Evans would become head of production at Paramount! This actor from Twentieth-Century-Fox! With no experience!" ' Evans, pg. 119.

Hoover perceived as a 'security breach.'[29] His first battle was with the legendary and notorious German director, Otto Preminger, over Preminger's film *Skidoo*, a battle Evans (by his own account at least) eventually won.

During this early period, Evans was busy negotiating a deal for a film version of Neil Simon's Broadway hit, *The Odd Couple*, to star Jack Lemmon and Walter Matthau. He fought to get Bluhdorn to pay the stars' salaries, and finally prevailed; the film went on to become Evans' first big hit for Paramount. Then in 1968, Evans put together a deal to make *Rosemary's Baby* with producer William Castle (who owned the rights to the Ira Levin book) and director Roman Polanski, a major success for all concerned.[30] Evans made Ali McGraw a star with *Goodbye Columbus,* then fell in love with her while putting together *Love Story,* the picture that saved Paramount from ruin. Evans cast Jack Nicholson in his first mainstream part, opposite Barbra Streisand in *On a Clear Day You Can See Forever,* cementing a lifelong friendship with 'the Irishman.' He played Ping-Pong with Henry Miller and made *Tropic of Cancer* on a lost bet. He greenlighted *Harold and Maude,* a film that no other studio would have gone within ten miles of that went on to become a cult classic. And then, of course, there was *The Godfather.*

According to Evans, he commissioned the author Mario Puzo to finish his book (then titled *Mafia*), and though Puzo denies this, Evans claims he was pushing *The Godfather* as a movie not only before the book was a bestseller but before it was even written. Evans also claims that it was he (at Peter Bart's suggestion) who fought to sign Coppola as the film's director, determined to give the film 'the smell of spaghetti' that only an Italian–American director could provide. According to Evans – firmly disputed by Coppola – he was also largely responsible for the epic scope of the finished

---

29 Evans finally relented just enough to change any references to 'FBI' to 'FBE', and the film went on to become a popular cult favorite with the counterculture. According to Evans, his phone lines have been tapped ever since.

30 When crisis hit, Evans persuaded Mia Farrow (playing Rosemary) to stick with the film even if her new husband (Frank Sinatra) made good on his threat to divorce her if she didn't quit. Farrow made the film and Sinatra divorced her. Evans also helped Polanski through his dark night of the soul when, in August 1969, the murder of Polanski's wife Sharon Tate and their unborn child in California brought his dazzling career to a premature and devastating (though temporary) end. (In 1979, Polanski had another 'setback' when he was accused of drugging and seducing a minor at Jack Nicholson's Beverly Hills home; Polanski jumped bail and fled to Europe, where he remains to this day.)

film.[31] Truth, half-truth, or bold-faced lie, Evans makes a strong case when he laments how a producer never gets the credit due him but always gets the blame:

'A high school dropout knows what an actor, a writer, or a director is, yet a Rhodes scholar has no idea what a producer is. Generalizing a producer as a fat, bald guy who sits in a back room, smokes a cigar, hustles, extorts – name it, he'll do it, anything, to get his flick made… It's the producer whose vision (which he then shares with others) eventually ends up on the screen. He's the one who hires the writer and director. When a director hires a producer, you're in deep shit. A director needs a boss, not a yes man… An actor gives twelve weeks to a flick; a director, at most a year; a producer, rarely less than three to five.'[32]

One final Evans anecdote. In 1970, just before the release of *Love Story*, the film that would return Paramount to glory (by 1972 it was the number one studio in Hollywood), Gulf & Western's board of directors decided

---

31 Evans' version of events is that Coppola delivered a two-hour version with all the good stuff taken out and that he 'forced' Coppola to put it back in, against the director's virulent objections, so restoring the film to the three-hour masterpiece finally released. Coppola's version is that he delivered a two-hour version merely to placate Paramount, and had always intended to reinstate the removed footage later on, but that Evans took credit for it in order to steal kudos for himself. Schumacher quotes Coppola on the subject: 'I had the right to edit in San Francisco, but Evans told me he would yank it down to LA if the cut ran longer than two hours and fifteen minutes. When the cut was done, it was over two hours and forty-five minutes, and we were so terrified that they were going to yank it, as warned, that we lifted as much as we could, getting it down to two hours and twenty minutes. We showed it to them, and Evans said that we had cut out all the texture, the good stuff. Therefore, he said, he was taking the film down to LA. In LA, we put back the stuff that we had taken out to conform to his dictum, and then he said – and has been saying ever since – how much better it is' (Schumacher, pg. 123). As Evans likes to say in his book, there are three versions to every story: yours, mine and the truth. The truth is probably somewhere between his and Coppola's story, but probably closer to Coppola's. The animosity between the artist and the businessman cannot have been eased, however, when Coppola 'forgot' to acknowledge Evans in his Oscar speech, not only once but twice (both when *The Godfather* won Best Picture and when *Part Two* did).

32 Evans, pg. 331-2. See also Julia Phillips' *You'll Never Eat Lunch in This Town Again*: 'The producer is the only guy on the set who doesn't have a specific job. How good he really gets to be is entirely dependent on almost everyone else's moods and inclinations. The creative people like to think of him as the money guy. The money guys like to think he's the guy who talks to the creative people. Almost no one else thinks he's talented. He never gets his *ya yas* off, unless all he cares about is money, which would explain why there are so many really rich scumbags in Hollywood now.'

to sell Paramount and get Charles Bluhdorn back where he belonged, making money for Gulf and Western. (Even the boss man has his bosses.)

When Evans was unable to persuade Bluhdorn to give the studio one more quarter (three months), he begged the board of directors for a half hour's audience instead. Perhaps largely out of curiosity, they agreed, and in a last ditch attempt to save Paramount, Evans recruited Mike Nichols to direct him in a short film made solely for the eyes of the board of directors. In the film (which included clips of recent, current and up-and-coming Paramount releases), Evans appealed to the company's pride (and greed) and beseeched them to support a cutting edge studio, and allow it to continue making waves in the movie world. 'We at Paramount look at ourselves,' he said, 'not as a passive backer of films, but as a creative force unto ourselves.'

According to Evans, he gave the performance of a lifetime, a shameless and brazen sell that somehow worked. Paramount prevailed, and if Evans' account is even half true (and though much of his autobiography is undoubtedly dramatized, this event at least is historically verifiable), it's probably fair to say that without Evans' determination – his ingenuity, vanity, ruthlessness, business savvy, commercial acumen, entrepreneur's charm and total lack of shame – there never would have been a *Godfather,* a *Harold and Maude,* a *Chinatown* or a *Godfather Part Two,* because there never would have been a Paramount to fund them. Of course, there never would have been a *Love Story,* either; but nobody's perfect.

If Evans – whom many consider to be the epitome of sleaze – is a legend in Hollywood, you can bet there's a reason for it. One primary reason may be that he was the last major studio head to really understand or care about the art of movies, and to aspire to give audiences what they wanted, as opposed to what they'd settle for. The thing that comes through most strongly in his autobiography (and that can't be faked) is Evans' passionate love for movies, and for the filmmaking process in general. There can be little doubt that – even if his particular creative talent was for the organizational and 'packaging' side of things (for post-production and marketing) – Evans was as passionate and committed to movies as most filmmakers.

Who's That Knocking at My Door? & Martin Scorsese's Catharsis Cinema

'In a sense, you're just absurd. What are we doing here? I mean here we are living, breathing; we seem to be conscious… [Anger] comes from being human, just from being alive. It's something that can be destructive; it can certainly kill, it can eat away at you. But it can be constructive. Sam Fuller said you should only make a film if you're really angry... Anger's important. It can destroy you but you can channel it into expression. That's the key. If you don't get angry, if you don't feel strongly, don't make the picture. You'll see, there'll be no heart in it.'

Martin Scorsese

Whatever John Cassavetes was trying to do with his movies, he was not overly concerned with entertainment, and in consequence his films never reached the consciousness of the general public. He remains a forerunner, a mentor to many, highly regarded in certain circles (those of independent filmmakers and art movie buffs, mostly), but otherwise unknown. Martin Scorsese, on the other hand, has come all the way from the Cassavetes-inspired, guerilla film days of *Who's That Knocking at My Door?* to mega-Hollywood productions such as *Gangs of New York* and *The Aviator*. Today, he even hosts his own cable TV show: he has crossed over and been institutionalized. Such potential to be embraced by the public – and by Hollywood – was evident from his very first movie; despite its crudeness and spontaneity, the lack of structure, plot or familiar hand-holds for audiences (the film is a rocky ride), *Knocking* is a lot more entertaining – more visceral and cinematic – than any of Cassavetes' films.

From the first, Scorsese displayed technique, intensity of vision, and raw energy unique among similarly fledgling filmmakers. *Who's That Knocking at My Door?* showed such a talent to burn – and such willingness to burn it – that (despite the incomplete narrative) the film was every bit as entertaining as most studio movies of the period. With his first picture (and even more completely five years later with *Mean Streets*, his third), Scorsese managed to fuse the freshness and anarchism of personal filmmaking with the pleasures and escapist highs of Hollywood movies. Unlike Cassavetes, Scorsese's profound love for Hollywood came through, not only in the style of the film but even in the content. (His altar ego JR – a John Wayne buff played by Harvey Keitel – is always talking about movies.)

The central character of *Who's That Knocking at My Door?* is a Catholic small-time punk (possibly a hood, we never really find out what he does), and an obvious precursor to Charlie in *Mean Streets* (also played by Keitel). JR is Scorsese's troubled version of himself, or a part of himself that he is wrestling to understand and (presumably by making this movie) to exorcise. JR is Italian macho, suspicious, arrogant, glib, insensitive, insecure and finally cruel and destructive (even if mostly to himself). The story, such as it is, concerns JR's meeting with a girl (never named, played by Zina Bethune) and their aborted attempt at sex (for reasons never made clear, JR stops it, apparently out of Catholic guilt, though possibly due to impotence). This is followed by the girl's revelation that she was date-raped some years before and therefore no longer a virgin. In JR's perverse, quasi-religions view, this makes her ineligible for marriage. He finally decides to 'forgive' her for her 'sin' (that of naiveté), whereupon she rejects him, and he returns to his seedy, solitary existence.

Like many of Scorsese's subsequent films, *Knocking* was preoccupied with male violence, and even though here (unlike the later works) it remained potential, dormant, it was no less disturbing for that. JR's sexual guilt and repression is redirected (deviated) into violent fantasies and a vicarious (rather than cathartic) identification with Hollywood Western heroes such as John Wayne. As a result of this, JR is basically insincere, unreconciled to his demons (his fears and desires), hence unable to make love to the girl. When he hears of the rape, he is haunted because some part of him would like to do the same. He is jealous of the rapist and sees the girl's submitting to him as a kind of infidelity. (He is also unable to believe that anyone could be so innocent as to allow it to happen, and assumes complicity on her part.) JR's separating women into girls and 'broads'– virgins and whores – is indicative of this schizophrenic inability to accept his own violent side. The male equivalent of a whore (a bad woman) is a killer, and when JR quips about Lee Marvin (another of his heroes) that he not only kills people but breaks furniture too, he is emphasizing the 'uncivilized,' brutish qualities of the tough guy, qualities that he admires but is unable to accept in himself.

Scorsese was struggling to communicate – and come to terms with in himself – these potentially crippling issues of manhood, issues of sexual guilt and desire, and of deeper, more violent impulses. He was wrestling with the shadow side of male sexuality. Yet he was also being swept away by the sheer joy – the rush of freedom and possibility – of filmmaking itself, and of finally getting his hands on a camera. The film communicated this joy, the joy of moving over to the other side of the screen, from witness to participant in, and creator of, the action. The amateurishness of *Who's That Knocking at My Door?* – its lack of cohesion, occasional indulgences (the sex scene was shot to meet a distributor's demands for nudity) and overall roughness – only enhanced the film's intensity. They gave it a purity that complemented its message, that of the virtue of sincerity and the pitfalls of hypocrisy. Such amateurish qualities of rawness and roughness were inseparable from the film's appeal; whatever flaws it had, they came from the heart.

George A. Romero's *Night of the Living Dead* and the New Darkness

'There's the belief that you must do what the audience wants, but there are feelings you must pursue as a filmmaker. Success has nothing to do with what the audience wants, because we don't know what the audience wants.'

Thomas Vinterberg

While Scorsese was raising funds for *Who's That Knocking At My Door?* (in 1967, the year of the summer of love, when the Beatles went psychedelic with *Sgt. Pepper's Lonely Hearts Club Band*), Mike Nichols released *The Graduate*, the first Hollywood movie that directly aspired to represent the counterculture. There were no hippies in the movie, but the message was geared towards them just the same. *The Graduate* was an ode to the disaffected. That same year, *Bonnie and Clyde* set a different kind of precedent by being the first movie to reflect the violence of the times (and so evoke Vietnam) without flinching. Not only did it not flinch, it actively wallowed in it, rubbing audiences' faces in it till they were appalled by their own responses. The effect was explosive, but as with all breakthroughs, it took a while to adjust to.[34] As ever, Godard got a word in with his grotesque damnation of Western civilization (and the promise of its impending descent into madness), *Weekend*.

Following the early blossoms of 1960, 1968 proved to be the watershed year for independent cinema. While Polanski was sidling up to Hollywood with *Rosemary's Baby* and Kubrick was ingratiating himself to the counterculture with ('the ultimate trip movie') *2001: A Space Odyssey*, Peter Bogdanovich made *Targets*

---

[34] The film was a failure on its initial release, and had to wait for a second wind, which came about due to the intervention of Pauline Kael. Kael hailed the film as an American classic and forced other critics to rethink their original judgment (which had been severe), after which the film was re-released, to great success.

for AIP[35]; Brian De Palma made his first semi-mature work, the anarchic anti-draft comedy *Greetings* (with Robert De Niro as a draft-dogging amateur pornographer), and so broke onto the movie scene (albeit its fringes); Coppola made his first fully-focused work, *The Rain People*, establishing himself as a major film artist; and George A. Romero made a little apocalyptic number called *Night of the Living Dead*.

George A. Romero was making 8mm films while still in his teens. He studied art and design and theater in Pittsburgh and went on to found his own company, Latent Image, to produce industrial films and TV commercials. In 1967, he teamed up with another advertising company, Hardman Associates, to produce a cheap horror movie, hoping to break into the film industry. (Horror films are eminently more marketable than any other kind of movie, save perhaps porno.) *Night of the Living Dead* had been intended more as a calling card than anything, but it became a huge hit. Made for $114,000, and originally distributed by a Manhattan theater chain, the film gradually developed a cult audience; by 1979 it had grossed $12 million.

The way in which Romero subverted the conventions and constantly departed from the formula of the horror picture was remarkable at the time, and it was this fact, as much as the depiction of violence and gore, that made the film such a breakthrough. Nothing turned out in the film the way audiences expected it to, and with one solid blow,

---

35 Another filmmaker who got his big break with Roger Corman, Bogdanovich studied acting with Stella Adler at the tender age of fifteen, worked in directing and acting off-Broadway, and in his twenties began writing film criticism for magazines. As for so many others, it was the French New Wave that gave him sufficient impetus to try his hand at filmmaking. He went to Hollywood in the early 60s and (according to Bogdanovich) learnt to direct by watching his heroes, Alfred Hitchcock and Howard Hawks work, hanging out on the sets of *The Birds* and *El Dorado*. Bogdanovich eventually found work with Corman, acting alongside Peter Fonda and Dennis Hooper in *The Trip* (Corman's LSD movie), and working on *The Wild Angels* doing rewrites, second unit direction, and dubbing. In 1967, on the condition that he write a part for Corman's in-house star Boris Karloff, Corman gave Bogdanovich the go-ahead to make his own movie. Inspired by Charles Whitman, the water tower sniper of Texas, Bogdanovich dreamed up *Targets*. The film concerned an aging horror star who laments the fact that the modern world, with all its all-too-real horrors, has made him obsolete. As a case in point, Bogdanovich gives us a young man with homicidal tendencies who takes to shooting people on the freeway with a telescopic lens. Prescient for its time, *Targets* was a choppy, uneven debut that didn't quite qualify as exploitation, yet fell somewhat short of the criteria for an 'art' film. Bogdanovich didn't have the intense vision or style of Scorsese to bind his ideas together, but the film was sufficiently intriguing and promising a work to bring him to the attention of Hollywood. His next film was *The Last Picture Show*.

Romero sent the horror movie out of its comic-book formula into a new realm, one of realism and nihilism. An awareness of true horrors (such as the Vietnam War and the assassinations) permeated the film. Romero was making a movie about the breakdown of order, and it must have seemed logical – essential – for him to fit the form to the content, to break down the conventions of the genre, even as the story broke down those of reality. It was the only way to represent the material, finally, and his approach was masterly. *Night of the Living Dead* was an art house splatter movie, closer to *Psycho* and *Repulsion* than to H. G. Lewis' 'blood fests' (or even to Romero's follow-up films); and for all its weaknesses (which were prodigious: a hammy overwrought score, some shoddy acting, a superfluous and atrocious 'love-scene' between the young couple, and some rather silly looking ghouls), the film was a truly original work. Even today it retains its power to disturb; at the time – with its vision of Hell at the heart of the family Man – it cut distressingly close to the bone.

What all these emergent filmmakers had in common was a powerful, irrepressibly creative desire to reflect the darkness and confusion of the times, and to express their own despair, frustration, and disgust with them. Combined with invention, determination, ingenuity and resources gave rise to a new strain of movies, made without either the support or the interference of the studios. Kubrick had done it in the 50s, but mainly just to get started and be noticed. (Kubrick's passion was always for images rather than ideas.) Cassavetes had broken out the mold and proved that there was life for movies outside Hollywood and a whole universe of untapped subject matter to work with. Coppola had shown that it took only a small step (or at most an audacious bound) to move from film student to filmmaker. Now this new stream of artists with 16mm cameras in their hands and a few thousand dollars in their pockets were promising something. Beyond the reach and influence of the odd exception, they were formulating (and shaping up to be) a new rule. And what strength they lacked in numbers (or dollars), they made up for with the force and intensity of their vision.

Finally, movies were being made by the people who went to see them. The gap between audiences and filmmakers was closing. Studios didn't know what audiences wanted anymore. The same old entertainments and reassurances just weren't washing, and the public wasn't buying. As if by design, the awareness of studios (that audiences were hungry for something new) and the emergence of a whole slew of untrained but inspired filmmakers (offering exactly that) had coincided. The result was that, for a brief moment during which the system (like Dylan's Mr. Jones) didn't have a clue what was happening, the floodgates burst open.

For that moment, as if predestined from birth, an art form came of age.

Chapter Three – Hollywood At War: Avant-Garde Vs. Old Guard, Early 70s

> 'In the early 70s, when I heard Scorsese talk for hours with my brother, with De Palma, with Spielberg, about how to play the power game, the assumption, never questioned, was that power was a means, not an end. We wanted to make great films, we wanted to be artists, we were going to discover the limits of our talent. Now what was left was power for its own sake, not as a means, but as an end. The generation started out as believers. They behaved as if filmmaking were a religion. But they lost their faith.'
>
> Paul Schrader

Between the years 1967 and 1971, a mere handful of movies changed the face of the film industry forever. Films like *Easy Rider, The Wild Bunch* and *Midnight Cowboy* spelt not only the end of a decade but also the end of an era. In a sense, they spelt the end of a dream, the moment when the dream broke through into nightmare. Bent on communicating this new awareness, a handful of auteurs – artists with a personal vision to share – forged a new path, a new sensibility, one that audiences were hungry to partake of. These films questioned everything and answered nothing. They were products of a new age, an age of uncertainty when all that *was* clear was that the old values, the old beliefs, were no longer valid; and that even if new values could not be found, the old ones would have to be destroyed.

There was a growing sense of anarchy in America, and artistic imagination thrives upon nothing so well as anarchy. The violence in American movies was partly a result of this new freedom, but it was also an expression of authentic rage and despair. The blood signified life, a new awareness, a new understanding, dark but essential, vital, coming to light. Many of the films were raw, clumsy, contrived; yet they were fresh, honest attempts to do away with familiar forms and come up with something new. After *Bonnie and Clyde*, *Easy Rider* was the work that kick-started it all. The film began an all too brief period of renaissance which would later become known as 'the New Hollywood', a period that ended a scant eight years later, with *Star Wars* and a new era of techno-pop junk movies. During those eight years, American cinema enjoyed its golden age.

Easy Rider, Jack Nicholson, BBS & *The Last Picture Show*

'I want to make movies about us. We're a new kind of human being. In a spiritual way, we may be the most creative generation in the last nineteen centuries... We want to make little, personal, honest movies... The studio is a thing of the past, and they are very smart if they just concentrate on becoming distributing companies for independent producers.'

Dennis Hopper, 1969

Easy Rider was a counterculture dream (as well as nightmare) in which two of its own managed to infiltrate the system and pull off a miracle.[1] Ironically, though the film signified the brief victory of auteur over industry, *Easy Rider* tells the exact opposite tale: the inevitable triumph of the establishment over the individual. Captain America and Billy the Kid (Peter Fonda and Dennis Hopper, the film's producer and director, respectively) are like blood sacrifices on the altar of 'art'. Like Abraham, Hopper was prepared to sacrifice his own creations in order to establish his integrity with his audience – the filmmaker's only visible 'god'. By this time, any other ending would have been seen as a cop-out: despair was the only honest reaction to a world in which violence and conspiracy ruled. (In a sense, despair was also the only solution.) America was now synonymous with the abyss: where its untarnished heart had been was now nothing but rot. Certainly, the heroes of *The Graduate, Midnight Cowboy, The Wild Bunch* and other films were seen to be lost causes, adrift on a sea of hypocrisy and intolerance, too lost to even know it. *Easy Rider* confirmed the counterculture's worst fears, that its lurking sense of dread – its distrust of everyone, even itself, and its feeling of approaching disaster – was not merely runaway paranoia but a fully-founded intuition, a new, emerging state of awareness.

The success of *Easy Rider* also confirmed what Hollywood brass had already suspected: they didn't have a clue. It was the kind of movie they would never have deigned to release (much less fund), barely distinguishable to them from a legion of other cheapo biker/drug movies that Roger Corman and his ilk were unleashing on the world.

---

1 The fact that director Dennis Hopper and co-star Jack Nicholson, and possibly the film's producer-star Peter Fonda also, were high on drugs for most of the production and still brought in a respectably coherent and good-looking movie, is something of a miracle in itself.

Yet somehow, it had broken through.[2] It had escaped the drive-ins and infiltrated the art houses, finally reaching mainstream audiences to become one of the year's biggest hits. *Easy Rider* was quickly followed by a sleazy, grungy little movie called *Midnight Cowboy,* which would go on to become the first X-rated film to win the Academy Award. The film's willingness to portray the seamier, seedier side of American street life struck a chord with audiences and critics alike, making the film an equally unlikely success.[3] Also that same year, Sam Peckinpah's *The Wild Bunch*, with its raw depiction of violence, went even further than *Bonnie and Clyde* had, affecting viewers in a powerfully visceral manner new to American movies (at early screenings of the film, people ran out vomiting). *Midnight Cowboy* was released in May, *The Wild Bunch* in June and *Easy Rider* in July of 1969. And then of course, the following month, there were the Manson murders (which included the killing of Roman Polanski's wife, Sharon Tate).

Hollywood (and the studio people who liked to think they ran it) was reeling, shaken to the core. It had been hit at such a deep level that the entire community was in a state of shock. Zen masters whack their students on the head with a stick to stun them and open them up to a new program, and perhaps something similar was happening in Hollywood. Over the next six years or so there was a temporary suspension of 'business-as-usual' – a loss of certainty among studios as to what audiences wanted or how to give it to them – accompanied by a realization that artists knew the answer better than they did. As a result, Hollywood began to produce movies characterized by personal vision – by a desire to take chances – instead of films shaped by commercial requirements that insisted on playing it safe.

Although the countercultural audience was far from being a majority, it was perhaps the most vocal and demanding section of moviegoers at the time. The last thing a disenfranchised youth wants is more franchise products, clearly, and for a time, Hollywood began to specialize in making one-off films that were the products of

2 Peter Biskind quotes Buck Henry (writer of *The Graduate*) on the film: 'Nobody knew who wrote it, nobody knew who directed it, nobody knew who edited it… it looks like a couple of hundred out takes from several other films all strung together with the soundtrack of the best of the 60s. But it opened up a path. Now the children of Dylan were in control.' (*Easy Riders, Raging Bulls*, pg. 75.)

3 *Midnight Cowboy* was directed by an Englishman (John Schlesinger) and starred two barely known actors at the time, Jon Voight and Dustin Hoffman. Hoffman, still fresh from his success with *The Graduate*, was fast becoming the poster-boy for a generation, at least until the counterculture opted for a rough n' readier anti-hero in Jack Nicholson.

individual visions rather than corporate agendas. The simple fact was that they sold, and so, all of a sudden, there was a corporate agenda to make 'individual vision' movies.

Perhaps the Hollywood personality who best embodied this new trend of individualism and revolt was Jack Nicholson. Nicholson had worked for many years with Corman at AIP, appearing in some of his best known movies, such as *The Little Shop of Horrors* and *The Raven*; he had finally broken through into public consciousness with his small but poignant role in *Easy Rider*, in which Nicholson played the sacrificial lamb, George Hanson, the 'straight' who hitches his wagon to the Easy Riders of the title and is murdered for his troubles (forewarning the fate of the film's heroes). Nicholson's was the most likeable character in the movie, and he was by far the most entertaining and memorable thing about it.[4] He milked the part for all it was worth without unbalancing the rest of the movie, and gave the picture its heart; without Nicholson's Hanson to care about (and for straight people to identify with), it's highly unlikely the film would have resonated with audiences as it did.

Nicholson played his hand deftly and gave the right answer, one sufficiently dramatic to satisfy, but mysterious enough to leave the question open. The answer he gave (in 1970) was *Five Easy Pieces*. Directed by Bob Rafelson, with whom Nicholson had co-directed *Head* in 1968, the film was as much the carrier of the zeitgeist as *Easy Rider*, and was also a far superior film. It's impossible to imagine *Five Easy Pieces* being made at any other period in history, even as little as five years earlier or later: it has the slow, brooding quality, the understated menace and smoldering rage and yet the irony and disenchantment (all qualities embodied by Nicholson), that characterized the best of American (semi-independent) cinema in the early 70s. As such, it reflected the general mood of the public to a 'T' (the youth, that is). Nicholson became the unofficial Hollywood spokesman of the disenfranchised youth and the personification of the rebel spirit, a James Dean for the 70s.

As it happened, both *Easy Rider* and *Five Easy Pieces* were funded by a small, independent company called BBS (after the first names of its three founding members, Bob Rafelson, Bert Schneider and Steve Blauner)[5], and BBS pretty much adopted Nicholson as their own. Like

4 The part had been intended for Rip Torn (a genuine Texan actor), but when Torn backed out, Nicholson was called in, being a long-time associate of Hopper and Fonda at AIP.

5 According to Biskind, 'BBS realized it had a good thing in Nicholson, who was the de facto fourth partner, and he was automatically considered for every project.' (*Easy Riders, Raging Bulls*, pg. 76.)

Corman at AIP, only with an eye to 'art' rather than 'trash', BBS took a personal interest in selecting and backing films that would be consistent with the company's unifying vision and direction. When its position in Hollywood was consolidated (and its vision confirmed) by the success of *Easy Rider*, BBS negotiated a deal with Columbia studios to produce six films with Columbia funds, on a budget of up to $1 million per film, free from studio interference. BBS had final cut provided they covered extra costs out of their own pockets, if and when any of the films went over budget; they would share the profits fifty-fifty with Columbia. With a big studio backing behind them, BBS went on to produce several films that embodied the new aesthetic of the 70s, capturing the mood of alienation and malaise of the times, and so appealing directly to audiences (as had *Easy Rider* and *Easy Pieces*).[6]

BBS followed *Five Easy Pieces* with *The Last Picture Show*, the film that made Peter Bogdanovich a star.[7] Based on the novel by Larry McMurtry about a small Texas town in the 1950s, *The Last Picture Show* was an astutely observed dust opera, an aria of ennui. The characters in the film were like goldfish in a bowl, lost souls floating through desert limbo, living lives of aimless melancholy and quiet desperation. The grown ups (Ben Johnson, Ellen Burstyn, Cloris Leachman) existed in a nostalgic twilight zone between resignation and regret, while the kids (Timothy Bottoms, Jeff Bridges, Cybil Shepherd) languished and groped through the moral wasteland they had inherited.

Everyone in the movie[8] was looking for sexual gratification of one sort or another, and the film's frank depiction of sexuality was a cause for some controversy. For these characters, sex was a means to relieve the tedium and emptiness of their existence, and the film's treatment of coming of age and the accompanying disillusionment was (consciously or not) almost perfectly shaped to appeal to the disenfranchised counterculture audience. Like *Easy Rider, The Wild Bunch, Five Easy Pieces* and *Midnight*

---

6 The agreement didn't last long. 'In December [1973], BBS got a letter cancelling the sixth picture. Columbia was playing hardball, withholding money due Schneider from his previous films.' (*Easy Riders, Raging Bulls*, pg. 185.)

7 Bogdanovich directed the film for a fee of $75,000 with a deal for twenty-one percent of net profits; Bert Schneider stipulated some nudity in the movie, a budget of $1 million, and an eight-week shoot, all of which Bogdanovich agreed to.

8 Besides Sam the Lion (Ben Johnson), the movie house and pool hall owner and the only man in town who seems content with his lot. Sam is the heart of the town, but it's a sickly heart. He is the unlikely bearer of the fast-fading values of the Old West, and his wistful presence provides what little grounding the community has. The last picture show of the title is *Red River*, Howard Hawks' psycho-Western, a film that also dealt with the erosion of communal values, and the inevitable conflict that results.

Cowboy, Picture Show was a bleak and troubling picture of a country reaching the end of its innocence, a timely diagnosis of the terminally sick soul of America. Consequently, it was a big hit.[9]

While both BBS and Columbia were having their cake and eating it, something similar was occurring to the other major studios. In 1969, Warner Bros. had been bought up by Kinney National Service, a company best known for funeral homes and parking lots. The head of Kinney was Steve Ross, and Ross – much like Bluhdorn at Paramount – had no desire to be directly involved with running a movie studio. Instead, he hired Ted Ashley, a forty-seven-year-old agent at the William Morris agency. Ashley went straight to work, firing eighteen out of twenty-one Warners executives and assembling his own team, starting with John Calley, who at the time was Mike Nichols' producer.[10] In tune with the New Hollywood, Calley's vision was strictly about the empowerment of the auteur. Calley's argument was that, 'If this is the guy who is looking through the camera, and evaluating the lines, he better be in charge. We started doing pictures without producers almost immediately. Directors had to run the fucker.'[11] Calley enthusiastically made up a list of twenty-odd directors with whom he wanted to work; in less than three years, Warners had greenlighted such diverse, director-driven projects as Don Siegel's *Dirty Harry,* Kubrick's *A Clockwork Orange*, Sydney Pollock's *Jeremiah Johnson*, Alan J. Pakula's *Klute*, Truffaut's *Day for Night*, Visconti's *The Damned* and *Death in Venice*, and John Boorman's *Deliverance*. In 1973, they bought up Martin Scorsese's *Mean Streets*. Most of these pictures were not only prestigious but also, amazingly, commercial hits for the studio.

Less fortuitous in its bid to keep abreast of the times was Universal, the most conservative of all the studios. The head of Universal was Lew Wasserman, one of the uncontested kings of old Hollywood

9 *Picture Show* put its director on the map, whereupon he vanished again a few years later. Apparently Bogdanovich only had one or two classics in him, and within five years of *Picture Show*, the now unemployed director was introducing himself as, 'I used to be Peter Bogdanovich.'

10 Calley had also produced *The Loved One*, *The Cincinnati Kid* and *The Americanization of Emily*; besides Calley, Ashley also hired Frank Wells, Clint Eastwood's lawyer at the time; Wells later died in a skiing accident.

11 'Calley created an atmosphere congenial to 60s-going-on-70s filmmakers. The production executives put in long hours, but they dressed in work shirts and jeans instead of suits.' (See *Easy Riders, Raging Bulls*, pg. 84.) Biskind also notes, 'Throughout the decade, producing credit would become *de rigueur* for successful directors. It was at once an expression and a guarantor of their power.' (pg. 86.)

and by then an old man. Wasserman (and his equally aged executive staff) couldn't even sit through *Easy Rider,* much less appreciate its groundbreaking effects on the business. A younger production executive who would soon be in charge of the new unit ('the youth division') was Ned Tanen, who described the situation thus: 'These were aging gentlemen who did not remotely understand where their audience had gone.'[12]

According to Peter Biskind, Universal's attempt to get with the New Hollywood proceeded as follows:

'Borrowing a leaf from Schneider's book, the idea was to produce films for under $1 million, preferably $750,000. [As Danny Selznick, David O. Selznick's son and assistant to Tanen, said:] "For $5 million they could have five pictures, five chances at a breakthrough." The talent would be paid scale, but they would be given a hefty chunk of the back end, as much as fifty percent. Universal offered final cut, an extremity from which even BBS shrank. [Biskind quotes Ned Tanen:] "When the companies started making these movies, they didn't go gently into them. They said to kids who could not have gotten an appointment on the lot two weeks earlier, 'It's your movie, don't come back to us with your problems, we don't want to know about them.' These were not movies where the studios were dealing with someone they trusted. They were dealing with kids whom they didn't trust… They viewed them with absolute dread. Beyond dread.' "'[13]

The first movie that Tanen's new unit agreed to was Dennis Hopper's follow-up to *Easy Rider,* prophetically titled *The Last Movie.* It was a complete disaster and all but destroyed Hopper's career for the next two decades. The new unit was off to a shaky start, and indeed, the movies that Universal's 'youth division' funded, though definitely auteur works, were considerably less successful than those backed by BBS or Warners. In fact, they were disastrous. *Diary of a Mad Housewife, Taking Off* (from director Milos Forman), Peter Fonda's *The Hired Hand*, Monte Hellman's *Two-Lane Blacktop*, Cassavetes' *Minnie and Moskowitz*, Doug Trumbull's *Silent Running*, all failed at the box office despite favorable

12 *Easy Riders, Raging Bulls,* pg. 125. Biskind also quotes Paul Williams on the confusion of Hollywood executives at the time: '*Blow-Up* had confused the hell out of them. People really started feeling they didn't know what was going on. It was much easier to get stuff going.' (Ibid, pg. 22.)
13 *Easy Riders, Raging Bulls,* pg. 125.

notices; the sole hit among the bunch was George Lucas' *American Graffiti,* in 1973; but by that time Universal had already had it with youth divisions and auteur works (two years later, Spielberg would save Universal's bacon with *Jaws*). As Biskind observes:

> 'In fact, none of Tanen's pictures did any business. There was a fatal flaw in the whole idea. The pictures may in fact have had audiences, but they never had a chance to find them. They were released through the studio's marketing and distribution divisions, which, like the departments of physical production, were still in the dark ages, geared to big-budget mainstream movies. The fifty-something executives didn't have the foggiest idea how to market pictures like Hopper's, and worse, didn't care.'[14]

The Young Lions: Altman Does *M*A*S*H* & Coppola Gets *The Godfather*

> 'There's always been a kind of collective madness that takes place in Hollywood and it's very attractive and seductive, but you could lose yourself in it… The success of *The Godfather* went to my head like a rush of perfume. I thought I couldn't do anything wrong.'
>
> Francis Ford Coppola

Robert Altman joined the air force at age nineteen, and was a co-pilot fighting the Japanese towards the end of World War II. As a young man, it was seeing *The Bicycle Thief* that first stirred an interest for making movies, and Altman began writing short stories and scripts soon after. In 1955, he made a low-budget feature, *The Delinquents,* funded by a small Midwestern exhibitor. The year after, he got a job on the 'Alfred Hitchcock Presents' TV show and spent several years working in television. In 1963, Altman set up his own company, Lion's Gate, in L.A., and in 1968, he finally got a job directing on *That Cold Day in the Park.* Two years later he broke through with *M*A*S*H*, the film that made his name, and Altman's only real success of the 70s (or, for that matter, the 80s). *M*A*S*H* took the fading pulse of America and concluded that suicide may be the most painless option. It was a glib film about taking nothing seriously, not even death. Genuinely anarchic, it attempted to answer to (and for) the spirit of the times; by sending up everyone and

14 *Easy Riders, Raging Bulls,* pg. 137

everything, it seemed to have no position to fall back on save total cynicism. Yet the mood of the film was not outrage or disgust, rather bewilderment. The insanity and the anarchy of the players (juxtaposed with the Korean war, which was really Vietnam, disguised so as not to jeopardize the film's success) was a liberating madness, allowing the film (along with its characters) to perform a sort of mental back-flip. For all its cynicism, it gave audiences something suspiciously like a redemptive message: with supreme irony, it gave them the healing power of war.

M*A*S*H struck a chord with the counterculture and was a huge hit. The heroes of the film (Donald Sutherland and Eliott Gould) were cynical, devil-may-care heroes who had apparently found freedom in despair, liberation through alienation. They may have believed in nothing, but they were saving lives (they weren't soldiers but surgeons), and not giving a damn about anything besides having a good time was their way of dealing with the despair. These heroes rejected the stale values of dignity, nobility, integrity – they rejected heroism – having seen where such ideals led (to the war in Vietnam, for starters); whatever good they did, they did in the same spirit as they played their infantile pranks – for the hell of it. These were heroes the counterculture could identify with.

The film that had the profoundest effect on audiences, studios and filmmakers alike at the time, however, was Francis Ford Coppola's *The Godfather* (1972). After being almost ruined by the collapse of American Zoetrope, Coppola was sorely in need of a hit. Even so, he had taken on the project only with the greatest reluctance. Coppola wasn't interested in gangsters, thought the pulp novel by Mario Puzo (now a bestseller) was trash, and only wanted to make small, personal movies like *The Conversation*. He knew the only reason Robert Evans and Paramount had offered him the film was because he was Italian and there were no other Italian-American filmmakers in Hollywood. Coppola finally agreed to do the film, however, mostly for the money. Though initially nowhere near as well thought of as it has now become, *The Godfather* was a huge commercial success, so much so that it introduced the studios to the possibility of the 'blockbuster' movie (a film that, through blanket advertising and word of mouth, opens 'big' across the country and keeps on growing). It also turned Coppola into the most successful young director in Hollywood, though in some ways he would come to regret it.[15]

15 'The great frustration of my career is that nobody really wants me to do my own work. Basically, *The Godfather* made me violate a lot of the hopes I had for myself at that age.' Coppola, quoted in 'Godfatherhood,' by Michael Sragow, the *New Yorker*, 24th March 1997.

It was the beginning of the age of the superstar director. Bogdanovich had just made *The Last Picture Show* and was due to be nominated as best director by the Academy (the film was also nominated as best picture, though in the end it won awards only for supporting actors Ben Johnson and Cloris Leachman). William Friedkin had a runaway hit with *The French Connection* and was about to win the Academy Award for best director (the film also won best picture, and its star Gene Hackman best actor). Sam Peckinpah (one of several directors initially considered for *The Godfather*), having just made *Straw Dogs*, had been described by Pauline Kael as 'the youngest legendary American director'. It was an epithet which Coppola and the others were no doubt rabidly competing for.

In Hollywood, youth is even more coveted than status. In fact, being young *bestows* status, status of a particular kind. Ever since Welles wowed the industry with *Citizen Kane* at a mere twenty-four years of age, there had been an unspoken challenge to filmmakers everywhere to match or beat his record. And whatever traditional values had once been embodied by John Ford and Howard Hawks (and even John Huston) were now passing away (a fact lamented by *Last Picture Show's* Sam the Lion, and by the films of Sam Peckinpah). It was no longer character, age or even mileage that conferred legendary status upon a man or filmmaker; it was simply success. *Shane* and *High Noon* were out, *The Wild Bunch* was in. It didn't matter how honest or upstanding or hardworking you were, either; what counted was how many bodies you left lying in your trail.

Sam Peckinpah's Studio Wars

'Directors, in order to stay in the game, are among the worst people we've got. You have to be absolutely ruthless. Many of them are sociopaths.'

Don Devlin, producer

Sam Peckinpah is a man who to this day invokes strong reactions in people. In many ways he is the epitome of the film auteur, and if there is irony in his story (as there is irony in that of Welles), it is, like that of his films, a melancholic irony. For one of the greatest American directors in cinema history, Peckinpah, like Welles, was almost criminally frustrated in his attempts at personal filmmaking. Of his thirteen movies, perhaps only three or four of them can be considered representative of his talents. The rest were either projects that he was compromised into making in order to work at all (such as *The Getaway, The Killer Elite* and all his films thereafter), or else they were personal projects that were disfigured by the studios (most notably Peckinpah's third film, *Major Dundee*, set a pattern of studio interference repeated throughout his career). Like Welles, Peckinpah only managed to release a single film wholly representative of his talents and intentions.

Unlike Welles, Peckinpah had a perverse desire to squander his own talents, as if at heart ambivalent about their true worth. Peckinpah was at constant odds with studio heads, producers and anyone else he considered part of 'the system' as opposed to the artistic process. Yet in a weird way, Peckinpah's battles with the studios – and the businessmen he so openly despised – was his way of retaining his integrity. One of the reasons Peckinpah became legendary was that he was the quintessential maverick, and he had all the traits required of a movie director. He was an absurdly unlikely mix of poet, general, sports coach, drill sergeant, psychologist, preacher, choreographer and samurai warrior, all competing for prominence in his psyche. His methods, though controversial and definitely not appreciated by the countless causalities they incurred, were regarded with respect and awe within the Hollywood community, at least so long as the fruits they produced were of the caliber of *The Wild Bunch*.

Peckinpah was indeed a visionary (and legendary) film director who found via his art the diabolic justification to fuel his obsessions and neuroses, until the day they consumed him. In Hollywood he was granted complete license to raise hell and take no prisoners, to turn the world into his own personal battleground and loose his demons upon it, without ever having to take responsibility for the consequences. Such madness was to Peckinpah part of the necessary and holy function of 'Art'. Put more plainly, Peckinpah fell into the trap reserved specifically for those creative individuals who enjoy some measure of worldly success, become 'artists,' and behave like egomaniacal monsters with complete impunity. This is a disease particularly prevalent in Hollywood, but even in Tinsel Town there is no such thing as complete impunity, and Peckinpah's kicking up of the dust would eventually reap him a whirlwind. In the end, Peckinpah was destroyed by his own rage, frustration and bitterness at being unable to work within the industry or to follow the dictates of his genius. Yet tragically, he was equally unable to break away and seek an alternative arena to work in and sought refuge in drinking instead, living out the last of his days like a trapped genie, released only for moments at a time (even his last film, *The Osterman Weekend*, had momentary highs).

Peckinpah's peer, Roman Polanski, undoubtedly took the harder blows, yet ironically, survived better. Weird perversions aside, Polanski was for a time the most adaptable and amenable of 'geniuses' that Hollywood – bent upon the destruction of all genius – could ever hope to find. Whenever possible, Hollywood has always preferred to drain a genius of his talent and originality rather than actually destroy him; that way, it can secure the genius – whatever's left of him – for its own prestige. The *name* of the genius is more important to Hollywood than the actual work, after all, and studios are happy to tout Welles, Peckinpah or Polanski as part of their roster, conveniently forgetting that they once did everything they could to crush these geniuses.

Welles was ostracized but found his own means of creativity outside the industry and continued to do unique, if flawed work such as *Touch of Evil, Macbeth, Othello, Chimes at Midnight, The Trial* and *F for Fake*. The fact that, after *Citizen Kane*, he never got to make a film the way he wanted to (with American funding, crew and locations, free from studio interference) is a loss which Hollywood has to answer for; yet it was perhaps less Welles' loss than audiences'. Welles remained a legend to the end of his days, his legend only increased by the battles he fought and lost. Polanski had to literally flee the country (rejected not by Hollywood but by the US legal system) where he continued to make American-style films and preserve his status, finally attaining the ultimate pedigree when he won an Academy Award for *The Pianist*. Peckinpah, on the other hand, was unable to live without his work, and he was unable to separate himself from the glamour and the excitement of Hollywood. He had the option to go off and make small, personal films outside the industry, as Welles did, and retain his integrity that way (he might have worked in Mexico, for example). But like the heroes of *The Wild Bunch*, his pride and his passion compelled him to stay and fight to the bitter end. And bitter it was.

Of course, filmmaking, unlike any other art form, *is* a business, first and foremost, a business in which the artist is forced into an alliance (at best uneasy, at worst diabolic) with essentially uncreative entrepreneurs who are indifferent, even antagonistic, to the plight of the artist. The result is that a work by definition individual, uncompromising, becomes compromised in the worst possible way, subjugated to the will and the authority of others (and filmmaking depends on a veritable council of others). In the process, the artist becomes a hired hand, a whore. Peckinpah repeatedly referred to himself as such, with comments like, 'I'm a good whore – I go where I'm kicked.' The melancholic irony of 'Bloody Sam' was that, the more aware he was of it, the angrier and the more embittered he became, the truer it was. His resentment fed the resentment of the studios, and he was treated increasingly like an unruly child (a prodigy, but still a child), to be disciplined and restrained if he was to produce any goods at all. His drunkenness, though it was presumably in part a reaction to (or a retreat from) this intolerable situation, once again only served to consolidate it: in later years, Peckinpah *was* like a child, unable to see his own movies through, unable to meet the responsibilities he had taken on for himself. As Pauline Kael (who knew Peckinpah personally) wrote, 'His whole way of making movies has become a revenge fantasy: he screws the bosses, he screws the picture, he screws himself.'[16]

A major – perhaps principle – part of Sam Peckinpah's legend came from these battles with the studios. Not since Welles was a filmmaker so temperamentally at odds with the Hollywood way of doing things as Sam Peckinpah, whose whole method and personality seemed not merely incompatible with the men that hired him, but actively opposed to them. Peckinpah worked his way into movies the slow, hard way, doing menial jobs on film sets (most auspiciously as an assistant to Don Siegel, whom Peckinpah considered his mentor), then later in TV (during the early days of the 1950s). Peckinpah's first real experience of filmmaking was *The Deadly Companions*, on which he was given almost no creative control and barely managed to come through with dignity intact. Filming a mediocre script with a producer in equal parts meddlesome and inept, breathing down his neck every step of the way, the result has accordingly disappeared from film history; Peckinpah's directorial debut is generally considered to be *Ride the High Country* (1962), a film which Peckinpah had to fight to film his way (on location), but which he managed to imbue with personal style and vision and which is now considered a classic of the genre.[17]

It was on his next film, *Major Dundee*, that Peckinpah's troubles really began. There were several elements at play that brought about the disaster of *Dundee*. First of all, there was the studio (Columbia) and the producer Jerry Bresler, both of whom had high hopes for a prestige hit from their

---

16 'Notes on the Nihilist Poetry of Sam Peckinpah,' from *When the Lights Go Down*, pg.116. Kael goes on to say that, 'a lot of the time he wasn't fighting to protect his vision, he was fighting for torturous reasons. He doesn't start a picture with a vision; he starts a picture as a job and then perversely – in spite of his deal to sell out – he turns into an artist' (pg. 118).

17 *Ride the High Country* is an example of a B-picture that, through its own superior quality and audience-critical response, ousted the movie it was supposed to be supporting and became an A-picture.

star (Charlton Heston) and their bright young director Peckinpah. But Columbia and Bresler refused to take any chances, so far as budget and schedule went, and once they had Peckinpah on board they did everything they could to reign him in and prevent him from being carried away by his visionary tendencies. Another factor at play was the star, Heston. As strong-willed and bull-headed as Peckinpah, they inevitably (if not literally) came to blows. (On one occasion, Heston reputedly charged at Peckinpah on horseback, his saber drawn for the kill.) Then there was the script (by Harry Julian Fink, Oscar Saul and Peckinpah, which was still not completed to anyone's satisfaction even when shooting began, resulting in a production that seemed to get lost half way in, perhaps the primary reason *Dundee* finally came off the rails.

The film was shot on location in Mexico and took several long hard months in some of the worst conditions and climate imaginable. Inevitably, it went over budget and schedule. At one point, the studio was preparing to oust Peckinpah and have him replaced, and they probably would have had it not been for Heston's intervention.[18] When Peckinpah handed in a rough cut of almost four hours, his input was no longer required. Whatever Peckinpah's vision of the film, it wasn't theirs. Peckinpah was out of the picture, and *Major Dundee* was released as a 134 minute film, momentarily possessed of brilliance, visually beautiful with some powerful performances (or half-performances), but overall a muddy, shapeless, incoherent mess.[19] The effect on Peckinpah was devastating. Having worked months of his life and sweated blood to make what he was convinced would be his masterpiece, to have it taken from him and butchered by a money-hungry studio can only have compounded his bitterness and contempt for Hollywood.

Soon after, Peckinpah suffered a second ignominy when he was fired from *The Cincinnati Kid* (starring Steve McQueen, and produced by the

---

18 Heston threatened to walk if Peckinpah was fired, and offered up his own salary as a sop to placate the studio. Columbia accepted Heston's offer, much to his and his agent's chagrin, and Peckinpah stayed on as director.

19 To be fair to Columbia, it's likely that, since the script was never properly completed, even Peckinpah's cut would have been full of inconsistencies, and lacking a third act. It is also worth noting that, after the success of *The Wild Bunch* in 1969, Columbia offered to hand the original footage back to Peckinpah and allow him to make his own cut of the film. Peckinpah declined. Apparently, he had bigger fish to fry. Or perhaps, as David Weddle noted (in *If They Move, Kill 'Em*), he preferred to lay the blame for the film's failure at the door of the studios, rather than take responsibility for it himself. A mutilated masterpiece was more in keeping with the legend he was creating than a well-intended failure.

afore-mentioned John Calley), ostensibly for shooting 'unauthorized nude scenes.' After the *Dundee* debacle (the film's financial failure and the rumors that Peckinpah had gotten out of control), being removed from *Cincinnati Kid* rendered Peckinpah effectively unemployable, and it would be four more years before he made *The Wild Bunch* (due largely to the intervention of an old Marine buddy, and producer Phil Feldman). The film's runaway success re-instated Peckinpah at the front ranks of American directors, but even then (after being nominated for an Academy Award as the film's co-scriptwriter), he had trouble making the movies he wanted to make. He promptly followed *The Wild Bunch* with *The Ballad of Cable Hogue,* but when the film was a flop with the public, it cemented the studios' prejudice that Peckinpah could only attract audiences with bloodbaths. Peckinpah capitulated and made *Straw Dogs*, a crude, simple-minded film well below his talents, after which came *The Getaway,* a blatant and undisguised concession to the marketplace that was Peckinpah's most successful film to date, despite being a two-dimensional trifle more suited to a Roger Corman apprentice than one of the most talented filmmakers in the country. But that was Hollywood, and Peckinpah knew the rules of the game better than anyone. Having been on the losing end of them for half of his career, he wasn't about to risk winding up unemployed again. He was a good whore, and he would go where he was kicked.

*

'The woods are full of killers, all sizes, all colors… A director has to deal with a whole world absolutely teaming with mediocrities, jackals, hangers-on and just plain killers.'

Sam Peckinpah

In 1972 Peckinpah made the character-driven piece, *Junior Bonner*, another futile attempt to escape being typed as an action director; the film bombed as badly as *Cable Hogue* and so Peckinpah returned to safe ground to make *Pat Garrett and Billy the Kid* for MGM, the film that proved to be his undoing. This was the beginning of the end for Peckinpah. From the outset, Peckinpah and James Aubrey, the head of MGM, were destined to become mortal foes. Aubrey (known in the community as 'the smiling cobra') was notorious among Hollywood filmmakers for his penchant for sabotaging director's movies on a whim, apparently for his own personal satisfaction.[20] Peckinpah entered into his collaboration with Aubrey knowing full well that the studio head would do everything in his power to obstruct his (Peckinpah's) vision of the movie, yet irrationally confident he would come through the experience unscathed, if not victorious. [21]

MGM agreed to let Peckinpah shoot in Mexico (the Durango desert) – foolishly thinking it could cut down on costs – but despite Peckinpah's warning that the silicon sand would play havoc with the equipment, Aubrey refused to let Peckinpah have a camera repairman on set. Within a week of shooting, and by the time the first dailies came in, they had a serious problem: half of the image was out of focus. Though Aubrey finally agreed to a camera mechanic, he refused to authorize any re-shoots, forcing Peckinpah and his crew to shoot the

[20] While Blake Edwards was filming *The Carey Treatment* for MGM, without warning Aubrey cut two weeks off the shooting schedule, leaving Edwards with no recourse but to abandon his vision of the picture. Edwards lamented, 'Aubrey, who'd just become head of MGM, personally destroyed *Wild Rovers,* cutting out forty minutes and changing the ending and a lot of the relationships. Then he suckered me into directing another film for him, *The Carey Treatment,* by Michael Crichton. I said I'd do it only if I could make certain changes, and Aubrey agreed. Then he simply reneged. I found out Aubrey was cutting the movie even before I finished shooting it.' See http://www.films42.com/tribute/blake_edwards.asp

[21] Regarding Jim Aubrey, the *Smiling Cobra,* it is amusing to note Robert Evans' account (in *The Kid Stays in the Picture*) of how Al Pacino was finally cast in *The Godfather.* Evans didn't favor Pacino for the part (no one at Paramount did), but he finally had little choice but to concede to Coppola's insistence; by the time he did, it was too late – Pacino, convinced he would never get the part of Michael Corleone, had signed on with MGM to do *The Gang That Couldn't Shoot Straight.* According to Evans, Pacino's agent at the time (unnamed) refused to attempt negotiations with Aubrey, the head of the studio, knowing that, 'Getting a pardon from a prison warden's easier than getting a favor from Aubrey.' (pg. 228.) Evans called Aubrey himself – he claims they were friends – and was turned down flat. Evans then called Sydney Korshak, whom Evans refers to as 'The Myth,' 'a lawyer living in California, without an office,' and whom Peter Biskind describes as 'the real godfather of Hollywood.' (*Easy Riders, Raging Bulls*, pg. 144.) According to Evans, 'a nod from Korshak and the Teamsters change management… A nod from Korshak and Vegas shuts down.' At twenty-one, Korshak had been 'one of Al Capone's top consiglieres' (a consigliere is what Robert Duvall's Tom Hagen was to Brando's Don Corleone in *The Godfather*). Evans and Korshak were close friends, and according to Evans' account (which may be part-myth too), after speaking with Evans' Korshak called Kirk Kerkovian, the owner of MGM, who at that time was interested solely in 'building his Las Vegas empire.' Kerkovian had given Aubrey 'total control' in running MGM, but he had no intention of getting on the wrong side of Korshak, and had no choice but to break his word and intervene on Evans behalf. Evans got his way, and Coppola got Pacino. The Smiling Cobra, meanwhile, was no longer smiling; he swore revenge on Evans but, so far as Evans' account has it, never did.

lost scenes between set-ups or at the end of the day, snatching a half hour whenever they could. Filming was completed twenty-one days behind schedule and half a million dollars over budget. As soon as Peckinpah was back in Hollywood, Aubrey reneged on their agreement and gave Peckinpah a mere three months to get the film ready for release. It was stipulated in the contract that Peckinpah's first cut would be given two public showings, but Aubrey informed Peckinpah that the two screenings would be on the MGM lot (a public place), whereupon MGM would take over and re-edit the film to suit their own requirements. Peckinpah had no recourse. Though he was careful to invite a number of influential Hollywood people to the screenings so they would back him up in his fight with Aubrey, Aubrey countermanded him, and struck the names off the list. Understandably discouraged, Peckinpah was too drunk to show up for the screenings. He showed his cut-in-progress to a few friends and associates, including critic Pauline Kael and Martin Scorsese. Scorsese for one thought Peckinpah's cut of the film was a masterpiece; Kael insisted it needed shaping. Peckinpah, losing confidence rapidly, his energy flagging, took a break just when he most needed to stand his ground.

When he returned, Peckinpah discovered that his editors (Roger Spottiswoode and Bob Wolfe) had cut a deal with Aubrey behind his back, agreeing to cut the film down to under two hours in length (the alternative being to let Aubrey and his studio hacks do the cutting). Peckinpah was appalled by the betrayal; to add insult to injury, when he arrived at the MGM lot he found his parking space painted over, and was refused entry to the building. The film was property of MGM. He may have helped deliver it, but his input was no longer required.

Pat Garrett and Billy the Kid was eventually released in a mangled, 106 minute version – by all accounts a far cry from what Peckinpah had intended – and fared poorly with audiences and critics alike. Aubrey was later fired as MGM head, though not (we may assume) in the interests of justice. Peckinpah never again made a film that did anything like justice to his talent or exhibited the intensity, passion or craftsmanship of his earlier works, making *Pat Garrett* his last half-great picture. Although it would be wrong to call Sam Peckinpah a victim of Hollywood – he was a victim of his own alcoholism and of the demons of self-destruction – it would be fair to say that Hollywood helped him along. His experiences showed how insidiously damaging the studio system can be to an individual artist (sensitive, as an artist must be, to his environment) who allows that system to get under his skin.

There is a basic antipathy between studio heads and filmmakers which is more or less parallel to the antipathy between outlaw and government (partly what *Pat Garrett and Billy the Kid* was about, ironically enough). Essentially, though the State depends on individuals to exist (as much as Hollywood depends on artists), still it can only perceive them as a threat to its existence. In this it is not wrong. The individual rebel-outlaw-artist exists primarily to oppose and – if successful, which he never is – overthrow the system. At best, the outlaw exists despite the system, while the system serves to spite the outlaw. And yet both depend on each other for their identity – the Law needs outlaws to justify itself, and the outlaw needs the law to rebel against. The relationship is a symbiotic one, but it's also a diabolic one. It is part creative, part destructive, and the only question is which part is emphasized, which prevails and is victorious, and which defeated. But if the artist is to prevail over the system – the filmmaker to beat Hollywood at its game – the first thing he has to realize is that you don't beat it by fighting it. It is too big for that, as Peckinpah found out to his everlasting regret.

The tale of auteur vs. industry is like that of David and Goliath, with a touch of the hare and the tortoise thrown in. The system indeed has to fall by its own weight, not by being charged head-on as Peckinpah attempted. It's a matter of cunning, ingenuity, humility, precision, heroic levels of patience and persistence, and a healthy dash of indifference (like that tortoise). Most of all, what gives the artist the advantage is the continuing awareness that such opposition is just what his creativity thrives on, and that the more the system resists the artist's vision, the stronger that vision becomes.

For all his bravado, his machismo, brilliance and dedication, Peckinpah was unable to hold his own against a machine that chewed him up and spat him out, incapable of actually devouring him. His story, more than any of his movies, is a modern tragedy of everyday proportions – the lone fighter unable to resist the encroaching influence of 'progress', who can only stand his ground and endeavor to hold on to his beliefs and die, as he lived, fighting for them. And while he was busy parrying blows with his external foes, the enemy within devoured Peckinpah whole. [22]

---

[22] Peckinpah died in 1984 of heart failure.

Breaking in the Broncos: Hollywood's Many Mutilated Movies

'If a person can tell me the idea in twenty-five words or less, it's going to make a pretty good movie. I like ideas, especially movie ideas, that you can hold in your hand.'

Steven Spielberg, 1994

Major Dundee and *Pat Garrett and Billy the Kid* are just two of the more notorious cases of a studio destroying an existing work and scuppering a director's vision through a mixture of timidity and avarice, with some spite and envy thrown in for good measure. In fact, the cases are legion. Perhaps the most memorable early example is, aptly enough, the film that Orson Welles' made immediately after *Citizen Kane: The Magnificent Ambersons. Ambersons* was a film into which Welles invested all his talents while they were at their very peak, making what we can now only assume was a fitting follow-up to *Kane*, and possibly even his masterpiece (Welles, at least, insisted it was a better film than *Kane*). The original cut of the film ran over two hours. Welles was such a prodigious worker that, unfortunately, before the film was fully edited, he had left for Brazil to work on his next project (the documentary *It's All True*). Partially as a result of his absence, the studios were able to intervene (in their own interests) and cut the film down to a meager eighty minutes. Welles' original cut was lost in the confusion, and to this day has not surfaced. It is now the holy grail of film enthusiasts, a great lost treasure that aficionados still dream will some day show up.

As we've seen, it's likely that the treatment of *Magnificent Ambersons* was more than just cynicism, avarice and heathenism at work, but part of a deliberate, anti-Welles agenda following the release of *Kane*, intended to chastise and 'discipline' the young wunderkind, letting him know who was boss, and exactly who was working for whom. Perhaps it was also meant to ensure that Welles' fame and influence – his power within the industry – was not further augmented by a second masterpiece. The butchering of *Ambersons* may not have done much to kill Welles' spirit (by definition unkillable), but it must have dampened his enthusiasm for Hollywood considerably; it also somewhat tarnished his reputation with audiences.[23]

---

23 In fact, it's doubtful if *Ambersons* would have been any more successful with mass audiences in a longer form; its dark and turbulent family saga, with its gloomy psychological undercurrents, was never intended to be a crowd pleaser.

The same tactic was undoubtedly applied with Peckinpah, who, like Welles, never seemed to learn. There is something about the temperament of the visionary, rebel-artist – perhaps his mere existence? – that causes studio heads (those men in suits whom Peckinpah so despised) to see red, awakening an almost predatory (or territorial) need to make a show of power and superiority. Studios are like ranch-owners who invest in the most powerful, dynamic bucks and then endeavor to break them in, put reigns on them and ride them. Some bucks just won't be broken, however, and have to be kept from the other horses, or else destroyed completely.

There have been many more recent examples of films that were taken away from their directors and recut, ostensibly in order to increase the films' commercial potential but also as a means to discourage and demean the filmmakers who put their life-blood into them; Sergio Leone's *Once Upon a Time in America* and Terry Gilliam's *Brazil*, for example (though both films were eventually restored to their proper length). In the more extreme cases of studio meddling the director may wind up so disgusted and dispirited that he takes the only option left open to him, that of having his name removed from the picture. This is an occurrence mercifully rare in Hollywood, but it is still common enough for the existence of a catch-all pseudonym used in such cases, namely, Alan Smithee, which is an anagram of 'the Alias men'. The first respectable director to resort to the Smithee option was Don Siegel, whose name is nowhere to be found on a film he made in 1967 called *Death of a Gunfighter*. Instead, a new auteur was born, the estimable Alan Smithee. Following in Siegel's footsteps and taking the Smithee route were Stuart Rosenberg, for *Let's Get Harry* in 1986; Dennis Hopper, with *Backtrack* in 1989; and Arthur Hiller for (aptly enough, in what may have been partly a publicity stunt) *An Alan Smithee Film: Burn Hollywood Burn*, in 1994.[24] Of course, the Smithee option is mostly used by directors whom audiences have never heard of anyway, since when a well-known (hence bankable) director threatens to remove his name from a picture, it is usually enough of a bargaining chip for him not to have to.

The fact remains, however, that the most effective way to get at an unruly artist director is by attacking what he most cares about: his work. As is so often the case, however, such desperate tactics did not manage to save the film from commercial oblivion, and in fact they probably

24 A far more respectable rotor of names can be found on films recut for American television, where Smithee's oeuvre now includes Michael Mann's *Heat*, Martin Brest's *Scent of a Woman*, William Friedkin's *The Guardian*, Sidney Lumet's *Q & A* and David Lynch's *Dune*.

only guaranteed it. But they did succeed in somewhat diminishing Polanski's until-then impeccable reputation, and thereby (one supposes) undermining some of his confidence as a film auteur, thus making him that much more amenable to studio 'guidance'. In a word, he was broken in, and his next film (for Paramount) was *Rosemary's Baby*. The eccentric and unmanageable European auteur had become an efficient (and bankable) Hollywood worker.

Another director who endured studio 'harnessing' at the start of his Hollywood career was Brian De Palma.

Blood Work: Brian De Palma & the Poetry of Pain

'You've got to know what you do well and not be embarrassed by it – even if it brings you great wealth and success... Nothing wrong with Hollywood. If you're in a position to control your destiny, it's the greatest place in the world.'

Brian De Palma

Born September 11th, 1940 in New Jersey, Brian De Palma moved to Philadelphia while still a child. His father was an orthopedic surgeon, and at an early age De Palma became fascinated by surgical procedures. When he was still a teenager, he was allowed to sit in on some of his father's operations, including amputations. Doubtless a formative experience for young Brian, he went on to work part-time as a lab assistant at the hospital and sat in on many more surgical operations, including brain and eye work, thereby further increasing his familiarity with human anatomy and viscera.

While he was in high school, Brian won first prize in a regional science fair for designing an analog computer. He won second prize in a national science fair for a critical study of 'hydrogen quantum mechanics' (including reference to cybernetics). The young prodigy then went to Columbia University to study physics; he soon joined a student theater group, acquired a 16mm camera, and began making short films. In 1962, his short *Wotan's Wake* won an award from the Rosenthal Foundation for 'best film by an American under twenty-five.' It also won him a graduate fellowship for Sarah Lawrence College, where he went after graduating from Columbia in 1962. *Wotan's Wake* was also nominated most popular short at Midwest Film Festival in 1963. De Palma graduated for Sarah Lawrence in 1964 with an MA, and made a living briefly making documentaries and business promo films. In 1966, he raised $43,000 and shot his first feature, *The Wedding*

Party, with a young Robert De Niro and Jill Clayburgh. He made *Murder à la Mod* the following year, and then *Greetings* in 1968, the first non-pornographic film ever to receive an 'X' certificate.

De Palma quickly forged for himself a niche and a small following as an underground filmmaker with an uncharacteristic gift for satire.[25] *Greetings* gave Robert De Niro his first starring role and was a minor cult hit with young audiences, mostly due to its subject matter – draft dodging and voyeurism – and for the playful, anarchic technique which De Palma employed, his refreshing amateurishness and idiosyncratic vision. De Palma made a sequel in 1970, also with De Niro, *Hi Mom!* The two films showed certain promise, but in between them, in 1969, he made a fumbling excursion into the mainstream with *Get to Know Your Rabbit.* The film starred Tom Smothers and Katharine Ross, with a supporting role for Orson Welles (then at the nadir of his career, reduced to doing commercial voiceovers and cameo roles). As with the films mentioned above, De Palma found the studios uninterested in supporting his vision, or even helping him make a decent movie, and concerned only with using him as a hired hand to herd the cattle (i.e., the public). De Palma wanted an extra week's shooting on *Rabbit*, to improvize; Warners told him to forget it and John Calley threw him off the picture (the supposed 'directors' friend,' Calley had also allowed Peckinpah to be removed from *The Cincinnati Kid*). The final result was a peculiar blend of De Palma's quirky, fast-developing talent with a thoroughly contrived and clumsy appeal to 'hip' audiences; neither fish nor fowl, the film promptly disappeared, of interest today only to De Palma completionists (of which there are few) and film historians. Following *Hi Mom!*, De Palma's talents appeared to be in abeyance with *Sisters* (1973), which he made for AIP for $500,000 and with which he began developing the themes and the style that would characterize the majority of his later films, albeit gauchely. (*Sisters* has little to recommend it besides a witty opening sequence and a sassy performance from Margot Kidder.) The following year, De Palma's talents exploded on the screen in an appropriately pyrotechnical fashion with *Phantom of the Paradise*, a send-

---

25 De Palma began his career making comedies and it may be that his most natural inclination is towards the comic side of life. He is more irreverent than Hitchcock and less morbid than Polanski, and of the three directors, only De Palma has ever made an out-and-out comedy (not only his early works but also *Home Movies* in 1980 and the rather witless *Wise Guys*, in 1986). De Palma was actually the first American auteur of the New Hollywood ('the movie brats') to emerge, but the last to come to prominence (not counting George Lucas, who is hardly an auteur in the true sense). He is also the most gleefully, perversely derivative of them all, and perhaps for this reason the most in tune with the times.

up of horror movies (specifically *The Phantom of the Opera*) and the rock industry. De Palma had originally written the film in 1969, when Marty Ransohoff was intending to produce it. There had been production difficulties, however, so De Palma bought his script back and resold it to Ed Pressman, who agreed to make the film after the success of *Sisters*. The four-year interim gave De Palma time to develop his talents and perfect his technique sufficiently to do justice to the material, and if we delegate the half dozen or so films he made previously to the realm of juvenilia – accomplished home movies on which he cut his creative teeth – *Phantom of the Paradise* might be seen as De Palma's debut film, his graduation to real moviemaking. As such, it was one of the most auspicious debuts in motion picture history.

The film was a kinetic feast, a wild, whacked out orgy of imagery, pop references, old movie plots, quotes, homages, in-jokes and otherwise idiosyncratic touches, an unruly hodgepodge of sensibilities that miraculously coheres into a whole. A film with its very own spin to it, *Phantom* was unlike anything else in American movies and had a demented integrity. Watching the film was like gazing into a kaleidoscope. The images shifted, transmuted, morphed into each other, all moving with such a frenetic buzz, waltzing over the rough spots, that the glaring ineptitude of some of the scenes seemed part of the movie's charm. De Palma had a natural gift for comedy, and his twisted sense of humor was the most redeeming, and defining, thing about him. Like Buñuel, he saw everything through the lens of absurdity.

Phantom of the Paradise was De Palma presenting himself to the industry and screaming, 'Here I am!' (or better yet, 'I *am* here!'). After ten years of working in relative obscurity on small-scale movies and being summarily ignored, he had finally found a project scaled to his talent. With an inhuman cry of berserk and agonized laughter, he came crashing into the big time. De Palma's audacity was matched by his assurance as a filmmaker: with 'inspired amateurishness',[26] he pulled off his movie despite the glaring inconsistencies and plot blunders. What held it all together was more than just technical skill or creative ingenuity, however; it was something more unusual, something that marked De Palma as a genuine artist: absolute commitment to his material.

Phantom had an ache – an under layer of sadness and of pain – that ran through it like a pigment. With its effortlessly screwy updating of

---

26 Pauline Kael, 'Spieling,' her review of the film, from *Reeling*, pg. 367.

the Faust legend, the film deftly portrayed the pain of the artist. The story concerned a gifted young composer, Winslow (William Finley), who has his masterwork – a rock opera based on Faust – stolen from him by the music producer giant Swan (played by midget songwriter Paul Williams). When he tries to see Swan, Winslow is beaten, framed and carted off to Sing Sing, where he has all his teeth removed. He manages to get shot while escaping, stumbles into a record press and has his face hideously disfigured. Presumed dead, he pursues his revenge under a new identity, that of the Phantom. Despite his disfigurement, Swan recognizes Winslow and talks him into making a deal, promising to produce his music the way Winslow wants it to be produced, as a part of the grand opening of Swan's latest project – The Paradise. The childlike Winslow, deceived and betrayed a second time, now loses not only his music but his soul into the bargain.

Swan is Faust and Mephistopheles, wrapped up in one dwarfish package. He's De Palma's maliciously cheeky depiction of the soulless producer who controls, and thereby ruins, everything the artist tries to achieve. So far as Winslow is concerned, Swan is the devil. Though Swan sold his soul out of vanity – if he couldn't stay young and beautiful forever, he preferred to die – Winslow sells his soul unwittingly. He's in such a wretched and desperate state, he doesn't think twice about trusting the man who turned him into a monster a second time. All Winslow has left is his art, his creativity. If he has to make a deal with the devil to fulfil his artistic goals, so be it. As Swan says to Winslow: 'What choice do you have?'

The contracts are signed in blood, 'an old tradition.' Winslow's art – his passion – has brought him nothing but trouble from the start. His talent, his obsession, utterly overwhelms his personality (which is the reason Swan is compelled to take the music and dump the artist). Winslow, one of the purest losers in movies, represents De Palma's most morbid, masochistic vision of the artist, and of himself. This artist not only suffers for his vision, he actively tortures himself for it. In the end, he kills and dies for it, too. When you have talent to burn, De Palma seems to be saying, you are likely to be its first victim. It was a remarkably astute (and as it happened, prescient) statement on the director's part. A true independent artist with a rare gift for drawing music from pain and poetry from blood, De Palma would never find much peace (or respect) within the film industry.

73-74: Hollywood Peaks, Creative Compromise and the Directors Company

'I need things to fight against. You need walls. You need parameters to bang your head against. You have to have people say, "You can't go that way!" Then you say, "I can't go down that way? Fuck it! I'll go down this way." Sometimes it becomes a better way out... I don't want to have a situation with no parameters. I don't know how to work like that. Films are products of specific times and places and combinations of people.'

Terry Gilliam

If there is one thing we can say with impunity that artists have in common (besides suffering), it is a desire to communicate their vision to the world and subvert the current view of things – to (super) impose their vision onto that of the mass, and so provide it with a new perspective. (Not, of course, for any philanthropic reasons, but merely as a means to alleviate their own sense of alienation.)

If there is one thing we can be sure that unites Hollywood studios, it is the very opposite concern: a desire to cater to (and thereby enforce) the mass perception of the world, and so ensure the public's attention, approval and attendance (in a word, their money). Yet, as already described, any artist wishing to communicate his or her personal vision has to ensure that someone *see* it. A tree falling in an empty forest may as well be silent, and a movie that no one sees is a movie that might never have been made at all. The artist has to 'compromise' (adjust) his vision to ensure the public's interest in and openness to it, just as Hitchcock had done with *Psycho* after the disappointment of *Vertigo*. At the same time, studios that desire the public's continued attendance have to compromise their agenda (that of business), in order to allow for a certain degree of novelty (creative vision) to inform the product, making it sufficiently fresh and attractive to audiences. There is a double program at work, then – a commercial agenda and an artistic vision – and ideally the two halves should complement each other; just as a movie's commercial success is increased by the influx of 'art' (witness *The Godfather*), so a film's artistry may be enhanced by a necessary concession to commercial demands and popular tastes (witness *The Godfather).*

The Godfather is a movie that was sourced in a popular pulp novel that nonetheless attained the depth and poignancy (and durability) of high art, and became the Hamlet of our times. If we look at many of the most interesting works of American cinema, we will find the same dynamic at play. From *Citizen Kane, Treasure of the Sierra Madre, A Streetcar Named Desire, Rear Window, Vertigo, The Manchurian Candidate, The Birds, Dr. Strangelove, Dance of the Vampires, Bonnie and Clyde, The Wild Bunch, Cabaret, Deliverance, Badlands, The Last Detail, Chinatown, Phantom of the Paradise, Alice Doesn't Live Here Anymore, The Godfather Part Two, Dog Day Afternoon, All the President's Men, One Flew Over the Cuckoo's Nest* and *Taxi Driver*, all the way to recent works such as *Fight Club, Three Kings, The Matrix* and *Eternal Sunshine of the Spotless Mind*, we can find the same 'compromise' in evidence. Yet these are also the very best that American cinema (independent or otherwise) has to offer.

When a movie leans slightly more towards creative vision, away from commercialism, we get films like *Paths of Glory, Shadows, Night of the Iguana, Cul-de-Sac, Who's That Knocking At My Door?, The Rain People, Five Easy Pieces, The Last Picture Show, McCabe* and *Mrs. Miller* (and most of Altman's films), *Harold and Maude, The Last Tango in Paris, Mean Streets, Fat City, The Conversation* or *The Tenant*, less dynamic works (and perhaps less exhilarating ones), but no less impressive for that.

When films lean too far towards satisfying the director's personal desire to 'communicate,' on the other hand, we often find they don't communicate at all, and wind up with Arthur Penn's *Mickey One*, Cassavetes' *Husbands*, Dennis Hopper's *The Last Movie*, Altman on a bad day (*Brewster McCloud, Images*), Lucas' *THX1138*, Antonioni's *The Passenger*, Rafelson's *The King of Marvin Gardens*, John Boorman's *Zardoz*, Peckinpah's *Bring Me the Head of Alfredo Garcia*, and some truly intolerable fare such as Norman Mailer or Andy Warhol (or Peter Greenaway) films.

On the other side of the scale, when the commercial agenda supercedes artistic vision, the results can still be art, albeit of the more populist variety, for example: *Night of the Living Dead, Rosemary's Baby, North by Northwest, Spartacus, M*A*S*H, Straw Dogs, Dirty Harry, The French Connection, Serpico, Carrie* and *Jaws*. Stray too far in this direction, making too many concessions to popular tastes, and we end up with lamed beasts like *Finian's Rainbow, The Chase, Major Dundee, Get to Know Your Rabbit, Boxcar Bertha, Sisters*, or else with soulless potboilers like *The Getaway*, enjoyable trash like *The Omen*, or grotesque freaks of art-pulp like *The Exorcist*, from trash artist *par excellence*, William Friedkin.

*

'We all remember the Directors Company. We all do remember
First Artists. Do you really want to discuss American Zoetrope?...
If you put four directors in charge of choosing what films are to be
made in the course of a year, they'll end up shooting each other.'
                        Ned Tanen, former production chief
                        of the 'youth division' at Universal

William Friedkin's star first ascended in 1971 with *The French Connection*,
the same year Peter Bogdanovich scored with *The Last Picture Show*, and
shortly before Coppola conquered with *The Godfather*. In 1972 the
three directors – the front line talent of the New Hollywood – banded
together to form The Directors Company, a business proposition that
required all three filmmakers to produce and direct one new project
each (and executive produce at least one other film) over a period of six
years. On its end, Paramount would fund and distribute at least twelve
films at a total cost of $31.5 million. Profits would be split fifty-fifty, half
for Paramount and the other half to be shared by the three directors.
Coppola described his reason for joining the project thus:

'Part of my desire to get involved with them is revenge. Part of
me really wanted to take control and own a piece of that film
business, for lots of vindictive, Mafia-like reasons – because I'm so
mad at Warner Brothers. And I know that I can't do it alone. Billy
Friedkin, Peter Bogdanovich and I are old friends, and we've all
had a super-success this year. What if we get together? We could
really take over the business. In a company like that, for six years'
work, you could make $20 million, and then spend the rest of
your life making little movies that don't have to make money.'[27]

Such naiveté was understandable at the time, and indeed for a brief
moment it looked as though a genuine coup was in the air, and that
an assumption of power by the artists was not only being allowed,
but actively endorsed by the studios. It was a changing of the old

---

27 Schumacher, pg. 134. 'On paper, the Directors Company had looked fail-safe to
all parties involved. The risks seemed minimal and the potential rewards boundless.
The directors involved…had been given a wide berth to create the kind of films
they wanted, in exchange for their allegiance to Paramount. All three had displayed a
knowledge of the business aspects of filmmaking uncommon to directors their age; all
three had directed huge critical and financial success. Paramount's hopes were high at
the time.' (pg. 180)

order. The promise was short-lived, however, as the three directors proved incompatible at a basic level, and the Company (as Michael Schumacher put it) became another 'victim of the never-ending battle between commerce and art':

'Artistic vision...became a major obstacle. At the time of the formation of the Directors Company, Gulf & Western CEO Charles Bluhdorn was confident that Coppola, Friedkin and Bogdanovich had graduated from making arty, film-school movies to the more grown-up world of big commercial pictures, and he encouraged the formation of the company. Paramount president Frank Yablans was not so certain, and he expressed his reservations... he was certain that the Directors Company was headed towards failure, to be sunk by the egos of its participants. Despite these feelings, Yablans went along with the idea – at least in public. "They've gone through their growth period, indulging their esoteric tastes," he said of the three directors during an August 20th, 1972, luncheon announcing the formation of the Directors Company. "Coppola isn't interested in filming a pomegranate growing in the desert. They're all very commercial now." '[28] Such brazen optimism would prove unfounded. Though Bogdanovich (who made the first movie for the Company) maintained his winning streak with Paper Moon[29], Coppola wanted to film pomegranates in the desert.

'When Yablans tried to shuffle Godfather II to the DC, he was blocked from doing so by other Paramount officials. Then to Yablans's horror, Coppola delivered The Conversation, a movie that [he] correctly predicted would not stand a chance at the box office.'[30] When Paper Moon was a hit, 'Yablans, sensing a ripe opportunity to create discord among the three directors and possibly break apart a company that he despised more and more with each passing day, filled Bogdanovich's ears with talk of how he was being taken advantage of. "When are these guys going to make a movie?" he asked Bogdanovich. "They have your money, what's going on here." Bogdanovich listened.'[31]

But then Bogdanovich made Daisy Miller, and all of a sudden he was in no position to complain. The movie met with a high consensus of critical derision, landing with a deafening crash. Friedkin, having no desire to be

---

28 Schumacher, pg. 180–81
29 He also scored with What's Up Doc? but spiralled into artistic folly and professional oblivion with his next three movies, Daisy Miller, At Long Last Love and Nickelodeon. His career never fully recovered.
30 Schumacher, pg. 181
31 Schumacher, pg. 181

connected with such critical and financial turkeys as *Daisy Miller* or *The Conversation* (a film Friedkin actively hated), bailed out of the company. [32]

★

'When someone achieves a degree of success you tend to alter your lifestyle in a way that is not conducive to staying in touch with the zeitgeist.'

William Friedkin

The following year, Friedkin went on to have the biggest hit of his career with *The Exorcist*. A film that scared and repulsed audiences in equal parts, it became the first blockbuster since *The Godfather* (rather more unaccountably, it was also a critical success). *The Exorcist* was a thumbscrew of a movie, a ruthless and unflinching treatment of a genuinely nasty subject that somehow managed to pass for entertainment. The story concerned a sweet, virginal girl who, for no good reason (the film gave a few hokey pointers) is possessed by 'the ancient force of evil' (guess who?) and takes to vomiting green bile, spinning her head around like a pepper grinder, speaking in a hoary male voice, and (the showstopper) masturbating with a crucifix. All of this was presented with a kind of brutal realism that was quite revolutionary at the time, and even today, few horror films have topped *The Exorcist* for sheer bad taste (though many have tried).

Friedkin's 'touch' displayed all the subtlety of a sledgehammer, yet apparently this was the film's main appeal. Audiences seemed to enjoy being sledgehammered, and *The Exorcist* was roundly embraced as one of the first ever 'roller coaster' movies (though it's hard to imagine a horror movie less enjoyable than Friedkin's). [33]

---

32 Friedkin on *The Conversation*: 'I thought it was like watching paint dry or listening to hair grow' (Schumacher, pg. 181). Coppola remarked: 'There was a disagreement between us and Paramount, the nutshell being that we wanted a truly independent company. The three of us got along well, and even to this day we never had an argument, although Bogdanovich and Friedkin were always feuding to some extent. But I think the reason we ultimately liquidated it was because Paramount never really wanted there to be a company with the autonomy that we wanted' (Ibid pg. 182).

33 What was particularly disturbing and even repulsive about the film was how (unlike later gross-outs such as George A. Romero's films and Raimi's *Evil Dead* series) it maintained an earnest, devout tone throughout. Did Friedkin (the director, working from the book by William Peter Blatty) believe he was giving audiences a cautionary tale of demonic possession for their edification? Anything was possible. It seemed more likely, however, that he was cynically exploiting audiences' more morbid fears and worst tendencies towards voyeurism and masochism.

Friedkin had been the studios' darling ever since *The French Connection* brought credibility and realism (and incoherence and cynicism) to the police thriller and walked away with a stack of Oscars. The film was hailed as a masterpiece and a classic of the genre, and Friedkin was hailed as the latest film auteur. He was Hollywood's idea of an auteur, anyway: a talented hack with commercial acumen and a minimum of the troublesome 'visionary' tendencies which drive businessmen to despair. As Pauline Kael wrote, 'Friedkin [was] beloved of studio heads for such statements as "I'm not a thinker… If it's a film by somebody instead of for somebody, I smell art."… [He's] a true commercial director – he confuses blatancy with power.'[34] A filmmaker who briefly enjoyed both critical and commercial success, Friedkin initially appeared as a genuine (albeit lowbrow) artist driven by personal creative goals. With *The Exorcist*, however, he revealed himself as little more than a gifted craftsman with a wholly commercial agenda.

Apparently Friedkin only had two 'classics' in him, in any case, and his next movies (*Sorcerer, The Brink's Job, Cruising*) were hung out to dry. By the 80s, he had become as negligible a creative force in American cinema as Bogdanovich, though (like Bogdanovich) he continues to make movies to this day. If anything, it was Friedkin's cynicism briefly coinciding with the spirit of the times – the crudeness and opportunism of his approach to filmmaking – that allowed him his period of glory, and that has afforded him a place (however minor) in film history. Yet that same coarseness and obvious (self-professed) lack of artistic vision or sensibility also brought his career as an auteur to a rapid and ignominious end.

Friedkin lacked the integrity and the inspiration of Coppola or Scorsese (filmmakers who also floundered commercially in the late 70s, but who continued to do artistically challenging work). More fatally, he also lacked the lightness of touch and the commercial savvy of the next cycle of filmmakers – those who would inherit Hollywood in the 80s and hand it back to the studios – Spielberg and Lucas being at the head. These new auteurs were every bit as commercially-minded as Friedkin, but they were more in tune with what audiences wanted: not gritty realism or crude sensationalism (though that would play its part), but escapist fantasy.

In 1973 (the precise mid-point between *Bonnie and Clyde* and *Taxi Driver*), while *The Exorcist* was becoming the hit of the year, New Hollywood was enjoying full expression and nearing the peak of its

---

34 'Back to the Ouija Board,' *Reeling*, p. 250. Friedkin also claimed, 'I have no image of myself as an artist. I'm making commercial films, I'm making a product designed to have people buy it.' (Quoted by Peter Biskind, *Easy Riders, Raging Bulls*, pg. 206.)

reign. Robert Altman hit his stride with *The Long Goodbye* (swiftly followed by *Thieves Like Us* and *California Split*). Terence Malick appeared out of nowhere with the sleepy, creepy classic *Badlands*. Hal Ashby let Jack Nicholson loose in the edgy, melancholy *The Last Detail*. George Lucas broke through with *American Graffiti*. Steven Spielberg made his dazzling debut, *The Sugarland Express*. Clint Eastwood painted the town red in *High Plains Drifter*. While old Hollywood battled on with *Papillon, The Sting* and *The Way We Were,* Woody Allen made his first 'mature' comedy with *Sleeper*. Peter Bogdanovich lived up to expectations with the sentimental favorite *Paper Moon*. Sydney Lumet gave Al Pacino his best role since *The Godfather* with *Serpico*. In England two outstanding horror movies came out, *The Wicker Man* and *Don't Look Now*. And while Sam Peckinpah was crashing and burning with *Pat Garrett and Billy the Kid*, Martin Scorsese was burning a trail straight to Hollywood with *Mean Streets* and (the following year) *Alice Doesn't Live Here Anymore*. *Mean Streets* was the film that more or less brought indie cinema into the mainstream, and incidentally revolutionized acting styles in American movies as much as Brando's *Kowalski* had twenty years previous, back in 1954.

1974 was the year that Coppola was nominated for an Academy Award twice as best director, for *The Conversation* and *The Godfather Part Two* (a stunt not to be repeated until Steve Soderbergh in 2001) and that Polanski (also a nominee) was reintegrated (briefly) into the mainstream with *Chinatown*. It was also the year that *The Texas Chainsaw Massacre* did what *The Exorcist* aspired to do and dragged the horror film screaming into reality. In October of 1974, Barry Diller was appointed head of production at Paramount by Bluhdorn, ousting Robert Evans and Frank Yablans. It was the beginning of the end of Evans' brief reign, and he left Paramount soon after Yablans. According to Yablans, 'When I left, Bob lost his bulletproof vest, and there was no way he could survive under Diller.'[35]

The independent movie was finally creeping into the mainstream (two years later, David Lynch released *Eraserhead*), fortunately enough because the New Hollywood already appeared to be on its last legs. By 1975, when *One Flew Over Cuckoo's Nest* swept the Oscars, and as

---

[35] Peter Biskind, *Easy Riders, Raging Bulls*, pg. 270. Biskind continues, 'But Evans made the best of it, took a production deal, and replaced himself with Dick Sylbert... Sylbert hired an impoverished Don Simpson as his assistant.' (Ibid.) Simpson, of course – who became head of production in the 80s – was one of the pioneers of the 'high concept' executive-driven action movie that became prominent in the 90s and that continues to reign over Hollywood to this day.

Scorsese was nearing his apotheosis with *Taxi Driver*, something had begun to shift in Hollywood, both in audiences and the studios. There was a drawing back, a retreat, a moving away from the strange (if fertile) ground of experimental filmmaking that had started in '67 with *Bonnie and Clyde* and *The Graduate*, and an edging back towards safer, more familiar ground. The huge success of *Jaws* (1975), a work that made the horror film into family fare, clearly marked the moment at which this shift began to occur.

Steven Spielberg's Commercial Throne and the Age of the Blockbuster

'My influences, in a very perverse way, were executives like Sid Sheinberg, and producers like Zanuck and Brown, rather than my contemporaries in my circle in the 70s. I was truly more a child of the establishment.'

Steven Spielberg

Steven Spielberg began making movies (and making money making movies) while still a pre-teen. His first home movies centered around wrecks staged with his Lionel train set, but he soon made an eight minute Western called *The Last Gun*, for which young Steve charged admission to his family and friends, while his sister sold popcorn. At the age of fourteen, Spielberg won a prize for a forty minute 8mm war movie *Escape to Nowhere;* he made another short, *Battle Squad*, using existing WW2 footage mixed with all-new sequences which he shot at an airport. In 1963, at the age of sixteen, he exhibited a one hundred and forty minute film called *Firelight* (about UFOs, later remade as *Close Encounters of the Third Kind*) at a local movie theater, and made a tidy profit of $100. It was the first of a long series of commercially successful Steven Spielberg enterprises, and the beginning of a career that would eventually take the director to the very pinnacle of success, as the undisputed (if unofficial) King of Hollywood.

Legend has it that Spielberg got his start in movies through an ingenious subterfuge and a healthy supply of chutzpah. According to this legend, he was touring Universal Studios when he slipped away and found an abandoned janitor's room which – either on a whim, a burst of temporary insanity, or a piece of low cunning born of true ambition – he turned into an office. He then procured himself a black suit and a brief case and installed himself as a Universal employee. In time, the legend has it, he became such a familiar sight that the security guards waved him through the gates without question, while other employees simply assumed he worked there.[36] A charming tale, and further testament to the filmmaker's prodigious talents for storytelling, since almost none of it is true. As the 'Urban Legends Reference Page' has it:

> 'So much for the legend. In fact, Steven Spielberg's entree to the Universal lot was gained while he was a sixteen year old on break from his junior year of high school in Arizona (in late 1963 or early 1964), and it had nothing to do with his sneaking onto the premises – his visit was arranged in advance by his father (through an intermediary) with Chuck Silvers, assistant to the editorial supervisor for Universal TV… [The] tale about Spielberg's finding and occupying an empty office at Universal was nothing more than a bit of creative fiction on the fledgling director's part to romanticize his rather menial official duties… In his accounts of his early days at Universal, Spielberg has never mentioned his office work with Julie Raymond. Instead he has gone to considerable lengths to turn mundane reality into romantic myth.'[37]

Spielberg came to the attention of Universal as a result of *Amblin'*, a twenty-four minute film he made for $15,000 that won several film festival awards and was shown at the Atlanta Film Festival in 1969. When Sid Sheinberg saw *Amblin'*, he reputedly told the young

---

36 'In a 1969 interview with the *Hollywood Reporter*, Spielberg claimed… "Every day, for three months in a row, I walked through the gates dressed in a sincere black suit and carrying a briefcase. I visited every set I could, got to know people, observed techniques, and just generally absorbed the atmosphere." Two years later, an account in the same publication revealed Spielberg had embellished this story, claiming that he had set up shop in a vacant office at Universal which he occupied for a full two years before being found out: "One day in 1969, when I was twenty-one [sic], I put on a suit and tie and sneaked past the guard at Universal, found an empty bungalow, and set up an office. I then went to the main switchboard and introduced myself and gave them my extension so I could get calls. It took Universal two years to discover I was on the lot." By 1985, Spielberg had pushed the timing of his story back four years and added the detail that he first made his way onto the Universal lot by sneaking away from a studio tour: "The fateful day when this movie-mad child got close to his Hollywood dream came in the summer of 1965, when seventeen-year-old Steven, visiting his cousins in Canoga Park, took the studio tour of Universal Pictures. 'The tram wasn't stopping at the sound stages,' Steven says. 'So during a bathroom break I snuck away and wandered over there, just watching. I met a man who asked what I was doing, and I told him my story. Instead of calling the guards to throw me off the lot, he talked with me for about

Spielberg, 'You should be a director.' Spielberg agreed and Sheinberg offered him a seven-year contract at the Universal Television division (the same work Coppola had turned down a couple of years earlier). Spielberg accepted, making him the youngest director in history to be signed by a major Hollywood studio. After working on a diversity of TV shows (at twenty-two he directed Joan Crawford in the pilot episode of Rod Serling's 'Night Gallery'), he made a TV movie called *Duel*, which was so well-received that it was had a theatrical release in several European countries. The wunderkind had arrived, ostensibly out of 'nowhere.'

If Spielberg was not one of the film school auteurs, it was partly because he had been refused by the University of Southern California film school (instead, he went to California State University to study English); but there was something else different about him. Other filmmakers – Spielberg's peers such as Coppola, De Palma, and Scorsese – had been drawn to their medium by a desire, a need, to express their personal passion and pain, to release the images and emotions that possessed them, so as not be consumed by them. They simply *had* to master their chosen medium, to give form to their inspiration. Spielberg, on the other hand, seemed to be motivated by a simpler desire, the desire to make images. With Spielberg, technique came before art: form sought substance, not substance form. A true child of the TV age (he once commented that he was raised by a third parent: TV), in Spielberg's work the medium *was* the message. His films existed purely in order to exist, they were spectacles, and their function was to excite the senses and expand the limits of the medium, not to stimulate thought, and certainly not to express the filmmaker's unconscious.

In his feature debut movie, *Duel* (1971), a giant truck stood in for the

an hour. His name was Chuck Silvers, head of the editorial department. He said he'd like to see some of my little films, and so he gave me a pass to get on the lot the next day. I showed him about four of my 8 mm films. He was very impressed. Then he said, "I don't have the authority to write you any more passes, but good luck to you."' The next day a young man wearing a business suit and carrying a briefcase strode past the gate guard, waved and heaved it a silent sigh. He had made it! "It was my father's briefcase," Spielberg says. "There was nothing in it but a sandwich and two candy bars. So every day that summer I went in my suit and hung out with directors and writers and editors and dubbers. I found an office that wasn't being used, and became a squatter. I went to a camera store, bought some plastic name titles and put my name in the building directory: Steven Spielberg, Room 23C."' 'Urban Legends Reference Page,' by Barbara and David P. Mikkelson, also quoting John Baxter's *Steven Spielberg: The Unauthorised Biography*. http://www.snopes.com/movies/other/spielberg.asp

37 Mikkelson, http://www.snopes.com/movies/other/spielberg.asp

forces of irrational, unstoppable evil. Spielberg's 'genius' (it was a hokey kind of genius – wizardry would be a better word) was in making the truck (which seemed to move of its own will) seem like an actual, living creature, a beast like no jungle ever spawned. Spielberg followed *Duel* with *The Sugarland Express,* today something of an anomaly in his oeuvre. In fact, after *Jaws, Sugarland* may be seen as Spielberg's most flawless film, but it is also his least characteristic. Oddly enough, despite this, it is also one of his most personal[38].

And then came *Jaws. Jaws* was your basic monster movie, overhauled and tuned to perfection by a twenty-five-year-old boy wonder. The film stands alone in the subgenre – yet in its own way it was as guilty as *Star Wars* for ushering in the age of the blockbuster and bringing a premature end to 'the New Hollywood'. Spielberg and George Lucas were the answer to the studio heads' prayers. They were commercial wizards, and with them the studios could have their dream and eat it. Like Scorsese and Coppola, Spielberg and Lucas were 'movie brats' – auteurs with their own vision – but they were naturally disposed to the popcorn market. Their visions were popular visions, and their 'genius' – their instincts – were geared towards trash and not art. *Jaws* accomplished what *The Exorcist* and *The Omen* had only attempted – it turned the horror movie into family fare. Both *The Exorcist* and *The Omen* made money, but they were restricted movies; *Jaws* was something even children could enjoy, and it moved with all the punchy drive and the visceral kicks of a live-action cartoon (just as the later Lucas-Spielberg *Indiana Jones* films would).

With *Jaws*, Spielberg, who may be the real inheritor of Hitchcock's

---

38 *Sugarland* was a chase comedy with at least one spectacular set piece (an almost endless procession of police cars trailing after the hero and heroine on a sun-drenched highway), but it was also an intimate family drama, a graceful character study more akin to the early works of Jonathan Demme than to anything else in the Spielberg canon. Based on this evidence, it might be fair to suggest that, had Spielberg not gone on to helm the biggest box office hit in history (*Jaws*, in 1975) and so fallen into the role of master of escapism, his career might have taken a very different direction, a direction indicated by *Sugarland Express* but otherwise only suggested by specific scenes and moments in his other films. Spielberg's true strength, his most unique and valuable gift, may not be in the assembling of mega-budget spectacles or 'event' movies, but in his absorbing, wholly heartfelt depictions of domestic life and family relations. This is evident all through *Sugarland*, and in the few scenes sprinkled through his best movies: the dinner scene in *Jaws*, for example, when Chief Brody plays with his son and Hooper barges in and talks about sharks (attacking the family's leftovers). In *Close Encounters of the Third Kind* – again with Richard Dreyfuss – Roy's prickly intimacy with his kids has an immediacy and veracity remarkable in American movies, and even in *Poltergeist*, this

'commercial throne,' made the horror-comedy that the Master never had. Spielberg lacked the perverse, slightly sadistic streak of humor that characterized Hitchcock's work and made his 'comedies' mostly private ones.[39.]Unlike Hitchcock, he was interested in fantasy, dreams and in human beings – not as flawed or troubled obsessives but as ordinary dreamers. His sensibilities were closer to those of Jonathan Demme or Frank Capra than to Hitchcock's, and he was the perfect director for a horror-comedy/family picture, because never for a moment did his film betray the disturbing undercurrents that suggest something amiss in the American home (or soul). His shark was just a great big fish that ate people, and if it represented the wild and terrible forces of Nature (like *Moby Dick*, or Hitchcock's *Birds*), then that was all it represented. Nature was still out there, after all. Like the ocean, it was something to go to; it didn't come to us. Like the majority of Spielberg's films (and in accord with Friedkin's motto), *Jaws* was not a film *by* someone but a film *for* someone. It was expressly for 'us', and that was the principle pleasure of it.

Despite being a movie for the masses, *Jaws* was informed with wit and cunning, and with the freshness and vitality of the best of the 1970s movies. As such, it was exactly what the studios had been waiting for: a way to harness the chaotic, creative (subversive) energy of the counterculture and render it both harmless (less volatile or unpredictable) and profitable. Spielberg was the answer to the studios' prayers. Here was a wunderkind with talent, energy and originality, but none of the darker, more disturbing, rebellious qualities that made artists like Peckinpah, Coppola or Scorsese all but impossible to control or predict. *Jaws* was a movie both mass audiences (with their profane demand for simple thrills without complexity or depth) and critics (film lovers and filmmakers) could appreciate. It was a movie for everyone, even kids.

gift is in evidence. If *E.T.* remains Spielberg's most beloved work, it's probably because it's the only one of his blockbusters that stays rooted in a domestic milieu: even the relationship between Eliot and E.T. is one of siblings and not of different species. But, besides *E.T.*, Spielberg has used this remarkable gift – his power of observation and his affinity with the ordinary American heartland – merely as a convincing backdrop for his magic shows. He has not, since *Sugarland* (with the partial exception of *Catch Me If You Can*), had the courage (or the desire) to go back to these roots and make a simple domestic comedy-drama, despite proving himself amazingly adept at exactly that. Instead, he has moved from kiddy spectacles to weighty moral dramas and back again. In the process, he may have overlooked his greatest talent.

39 To date, Spielberg has refrained from working in the horror genre at all, not counting *Poltergeist*, ostensibly directed by Tobe Hooper, though by most accounts Spielberg took over direction himself.

★

'*Star Wars* was in. Spielberg was in. We were finished.'

Martin Scorsese

Hollywood is notorious for its lack of imagination when it comes to trying out new things. If the men who run the studios – making decisions on what gets made and so having a hand in setting 'trends' and determining what's 'in' – find what works, their tendency is to stick with it as long as possible and so avoid the unpleasantness of taking risks. In the eight years between *Bonnie and Clyde* and *Jaws*, Hollywood studio people had been in a state of uncertainty about what audiences actually wanted. As a result, they had allowed the filmmakers to do what *they* wanted, in the hope that audiences would want it too. To some extent, they had, but it was not until *Jaws* (*The Godfather* and *The Exorcist* being forerunners) that studios finally let out a collective sigh of relief. Here it was! This was what audiences wanted: giant sharks. Blockbusters.

The following year, De Palma made *Carrie* (his biggest success of the decade) and momentarily ingratiated himself with the studios. For the schlock-horror merry-go-round movie that it was, *Carrie* had a remarkable depth of feeling and of meaning, and may have been one of the most emotionally disturbing horror films ever made. Although it was a minor work of art, all told, it was a major cinematic feast for the popcorn crowd and a genuine, bloody carnival for the senses. As audiences wandered out the theaters, wondering exactly what hit them, De Palma's devilish laughter was the music in their ears. Horror, of the schlocky, giggly kind, was definitely in. On the other hand, *Taxi Driver* (which offered horror of an altogether different kind, the troubling, haunting variety) lost out as best picture to Sylvester Stallone's *Rocky*, an old-time movie about the triumph of the underdog and the American Dream. Such a preference would have been unthinkable five (or even two) years earlier. It was a sign of the times. It was also a statement on the part of the Academy – enough is enough.

Taxi Driver unfolded with the force and inescapable logic of an authentic nightmare. It put audiences squarely and wholly inside the point of view of its steadily deteriorating protagonist (Robert De Niro's Travis Bickle), and dragged them ever deeper into his fevered dementia. The film had the breadth and scope of vision to create an all-inclusive world for us to inhabit – the world of a tormented soul. Few, if any, films had gone this far before. It was Scorsese's vision, but it was Travis Bickle's point of view, and Scorsese never rubbed audiences noses in the squalor, or asked them to judge it or condemn it; on the contrary, he drew them into this world, seductively, like a master, and bathed them in its colors. *Taxi Driver* was a hellish baptism, and the swan song of the New Hollywood: its peak and pinnacle, and its culmination.

Scorsese was an artist of expressionism, with a visionary gift close to madness, which is exactly what qualified him for the subject. His art with *Taxi Driver* (and *Mean Streets*) was to take audiences where they would normally never dare to go – into the darkness of their psyches. *Rocky*, on the other hand, was a movie that precluded deeper thought and existed for audiences to cheer and weep to, to bask in the glow of simple values. It allowed them reprieve from the relentless despair, confusion and paranoia of the decade, with all its assassinations and conspiracies, its Manson murders, Vietnam, Jonestown, Watergate. For a brief period, movies had reflected the uncertainty and horror of the times, offering zero relief from it unless it was the relief of a better understanding (which mass audiences weren't that interested in anyway). With *Jaws*, and *Rocky*, and finally *Star Wars*, the movies reclaimed their traditional function – that of escape, refuge, reassurance. The forgetting chamber was again open for business.

Audiences flocked in droves, in numb relief, grateful to be put back to sleep again. It was the beginning of a new era in American movies, and the end of a renaissance. Despite all the blood and thunder, the 'revolution' had been still-born.

Chapter Four - Hollywood Prodigals: Four Auteurs and an Apocalypse

> 'The auteur theory killed all these people. One or two films, the magazines told them they were geniuses, that they could do anything, they went completely bananas. They thought they were God.'
>
> Mardik Martin[1]

By now a trend may be observable in the trajectory of most independent filmmakers and their prevailing relationship with Hollywood. With very few exceptions (Cassavetes for one, but also John Sayles, John Waters and Jim Jarmusch), filmmakers who come to notice through their own efforts – who, like Kubrick, Coppola and Scorsese, rely on their wiles and resources to make their first movies – generally wind up making films for the studios in the end. Usually they jump aboard the Hollywood bandwagon as soon as a suitably attractive offer comes along, one that is both lucrative and sufficiently non-restrictive. What is notable about filmmakers of this period (the late 60s and early 70s) is that they often did their very best work for the studios. During the transitional period, while they still held on to their anarchic, independent sensibilities and accepted the financial benefits and production perks of the industry, many filmmakers seemed to enjoy the best of both worlds. Both Coppola and Scorsese, for example (and also Kubrick), actually made their 'sell-out' movies before they hit the mainstream, as a means of getting the necessary experience and commercial qualifications. A very different order to that which prevails today, when independent filmmakers squander their gifts before they really understand them, and go from promising debuts to tawdry and faceless Hollywood products in no time at all.

Whatever the individual cases, the fact remains that the dividing line between 'independent' and 'mainstream' is both blurred and constantly fluctuating. It is not like the border between states but more like a twilight zone separating day from night, so-called 'independent artist'

---

1 Peter Bart: 'At the beginning of the decade, you have a group of people who really wanted to be on budget and on schedule. They were earnest young people who couldn't believe that they were being allowed to work within the system, and that the studios would be able to accommodate them. By the end of the decade, they became the big exploiters of the system.' John Milius: 'These guys got too good for everyone. Everybody got very, very distant. George had his entourage around him. Could do no wrong. Everything was for George. And Steven you can't talk to. He's not a human being anymore.' *Easy Riders, Raging Bulls*, pg 340, 406.

from 'sell-out'. As Alexander Payne put it, 'I don't think independent implies necessarily the source of the funding, but rather the authorial and personal spirit in which the film is made.'[2] There are plenty of 'independent' filmmakers whose work is every bit as soulless, derivative and crassly commercial as the worst Hollywood drek, who clearly made their 'independent' movies solely as a means to hock their wares within the industry and go for the big payola. Likewise, successful and world famous moviemakers continue to work 'for' Hollywood – within the industry and with studio backing, making $50 or $100 million movies – while retaining their creative integrity, subversive vision, and stubborn individuality. Perhaps it even nourishes their rebellious spirit and keeps it alive, to work within an environment so manifestly antithetical to them? (Terry Gilliam comes most readily to mind.)

The 'war' between art and commerce, already a lazy division to begin with, becomes even more facile when extended to an imaginary 'war' between 'independent' cinema and Hollywood. Of course there is a war, and that no one can deny. As we have attempted to demonstrate (with our case histories of Welles, Coppola, Peckinpah et al.), it is a real war with real casualties, complete with assault strategies, intelligence operations and weapons of destruction (albeit psychological and financial rather than physical destruction). Yet there are no precisely definable sides in this war, unless they are the sides of the collective (represented by Hollywood) and that of the individual, represented by the 'auteur' filmmaker. This is also a shifting line of demarcation, however. A collective is made up of individuals, and Hollywood is made up (partially) of auteur filmmakers; in which case, it is an interior battle that is raging. It is the system (Hollywood) against itself, on the one hand (Hollywood's schizoid desire for commercial hits and popular appeal, opposed by its need for artistic credibility and prestige); and on the other hand, it is a conflict within the artists themselves, an inconsistency of the fluctuating goals of 'art' and 'trash' (commerce). Naturally, Hollywood (and the public) reflects and complements this split within the filmmakers and vice versa: Hollywood's ambivalence – and the public's fickle and unpredictable taste – is an unconscious response to (and a reminder of) *the lack of the filmmaker's commitment to his vision*.

The mass will always be just a mass (a temporary and arbitrary arrangement of units), and the system will never amount to more than a system (ditto). Likewise, artists are only human beings. However much the system may demonize them and the public deify them, they are subject to inherent whims and weaknesses – doubts, fears, the desire to be admired – every bit as much as they are to the external pressure of circumstances (sickness, adversity, failing marriages, financial ruin, etc, etc). To expect (or even desire) an unbroken chain of masterworks from any filmmaker, as continuing 'proof' of his integrity of vision and the independence of his goals, would be unrealistic. A filmmaker is going to have ups and downs just as much (or more so) as an ordinary person does, from day to day. The trouble is that with a filmmaker, an 'off-day' may last the duration of a picture, and sometimes more; unlike a painter or novelist, moviemakers can't set fire to their inferior works or stick them in a drawer and work on them later. Even when they know they have messed up – either in their original intent or in its realization, or both – they have no choice but to stand behind the work and send it into the world with a smile.

In this regard, the 'system' *always* 'wins', because, at the end of the day, no matter what has gone into it, the artist's work winds up as just another product. The means by which it enters into the world (public consciousness) is (save in rare, obsessive cases like Kubrick) out of its creator's hands. An artist – and this includes painters and novelists – has no choice but at some level to 'sell out' in order to reach his audience. Audiences are only interested in buying what is for sale, and this includes an artist's 'vision'; it is only a question of degree. The 'pure' artist who creates 'only for himself' would destroy his works, or keep them hidden, or at best allow them to be seen without charge and without taking credit for them. Only so could he be sure that his motives were pure, unleavened by personal desire for profit or gain – including the gain of being admired. And in the life of the artist, the desire for admiration is the most insidious and prevalent motivating force there is, and the system plays on this weakness for all it's worth. What else is celebrity but the poisoned prize by which artists' psyches are seized by the same system they once lived to defy?

Woody Allen: A Niche of His Own

> '[The] directors, the ones with the personal voices, had lost. The studios took the power back. Today you look at an ad and you don't even know who directed the picture.'
>
> Martin Scorsese

There is one 'mainstream' filmmaker who retains independence and autonomy within the system, however, and who exhibits apparent indifference, both to commercial success and audience favor. For the duration of his career, he has made movies exactly the way he wanted to make them. He has had 'final cut' (a relative, quasi-mythical term in Hollywood) on all of his movies, and has not only avoided but apparently been impervious to the kind of tooth-and-nail battles that all but destroyed Peckinpah and Welles. He is as close to a true auteur filmmaker as it is possible to imagine, yet he has made all his movies for studios and never once (so far as I know) suffered the ignominy of having a picture interfered with or a vision compromised. Not only that, but he refuses to promote any of his films with interviews or tours, or to perform any of the usual (now practically de rigeur) PR duties. How did he manage it? By being Woody Allen.

By his own account (and as his *Purple Rose of Cairo* testified), Allen grew up on movies. If there was ever a filmmaker who displays an unabashed affection for Hollywood, it is Allen. Time and again he betrays a wistful (if world weary) romanticism and a faith in the healing power of fantasy and escapism, the overt message of *Play it Again Sam, Zelig, Purple Rose, Hannah and Her Sisters* and *Alice*, and a recurring theme in many of his other films. No doubt such faith in – and predilection for – fantasy comes from his early years as a storyteller (apparently Allen was only seven years old when he first began to think about making movies), and then later, from his time as a stand-up comedian. Allen's roots in comedy would seem to belie his apparent indifference to his audience as a filmmaker, however. A nightclub comic lives or dies on the whim of his public, without the luxury of creating purely for his artistic satisfaction. A routine that gets no laughs is a routine that is promptly abandoned, and no amount of integrity or belief in oneself can outweigh the paralyzing silence of an indifferent audience. Perhaps Allen's professed disinterest in his audience is a rebellion against those early years of being so utterly dependent upon them?

Although Allen didn't start working the cabaret circuit until he was twenty-five, he first began developing his comedy gifts as a teenager writing skits. At sixteen, he was hired to write jokes for radio and TV performers, and when he was twenty-two he joined the cast of Sid Caesar's TV show. In 1965, he was hired by producer Charles Feldman and actor Warren Beatty to write a comedy script as a vehicle for the up-and-coming star. Feldman and Beatty scouted out Allen's act at the Bitter End, a comedy club in New York, and after the show, Feldman offered Allen $30,000 to write a script for them. Allen wanted $40,000, Feldman refused, Allen agreed to the original offer on the condition he had a role in the movie. Feldman agreed, and Allen went off and wrote the script for *What's New Pussycat?*[3] The part tailored for Beatty wound up being played by Peter O'Toole, but Allen got his role in the film. He was less than impressed with Clive Donner's direction, however, or with the finished film (reputedly he threatened to sue the producers to keep it from being released), and the experience left an indelible impression on him. He resolved never to let anyone direct one of his scripts again. (Despite this, in 1972, Herbert Ross made a film of Allen's play, *Play it Again Sam*, with Allen in the lead.)

Allen went on to play a small role in the feeble spoof *Casino Royale* and used the money earned (plus his writing fee for *Pussycat*) to purchase a negligible Japanese action movie, *Kagi-no-Kagi*, dubbing all-new dialogue over the action, now revolving around a quest to locate a secret recipe for egg salad. *What's Up Tiger Lily?* was released by AIP (home of Roger Corman) and became Allen's debut picture. Ironically, despite having had 'complete creative control' over how his script was 'shot' (since there was no shooting involved at all), Allen was less than happy with the results, and once again considered blocking the film's release. When the movie opened and received favorable reviews, Allen changed his tune and the film became a minor hit.

For his next script, Allen teamed up with comedian Mickey Rose (an old friend, and probably an inspiration for Allen's character in *Broadway Danny Rose*) to write *Take the Money and Run*, in which Allen would play an inept bank robber. Allen began to shop around for a studio to back the movie which would also allow him to direct, ending up at the recently founded company Palomar Pictures. There Jack Rollins and Charles H. Joffe agreed to Allen's terms on the condition he make the movie for under a million dollars. Allen took the money and ran, and to this day he continues to work with Rollins and Joffe. By all accounts, Allen's first cut of the film was a mess, and the producers persuaded Allen to work with the editor, Ralph Rosenblum to restructure the film. Rosenblum suggested Allen add a narration track, remove some of the dialogue and dub music over it, replace the existing music, and tighten up what he perceived as an excessively loose narrative structure. Allen capitulated to all these suggestions and salvaged his movie, thereby ensuring its success with critics and public alike. It may be that this early experience of studio 'meddling'– by which Rollins, Joffe and Rosenblum guided the inexperienced director (the very inverse of the kind of interference Welles and Peckinpah suffered) – softened Allen up to the idea of collaboration

---

3 Allen took the title from Beatty's well-known greeting to his lady friends; later, Allen confessed his greatest desire was to be reincarnated as Warren Beatty's fingertips.

from the start, because in future, Allen would be generally amenable to outside suggestions, and rarely if ever possessive of his movies.

Take the Money and Run (released in 1969) was crude and amateurish but sufficiently inspired and amusing to become a minor hit. It was successful enough, in fact, for United Artists' Arthur Krim to offer Allen a contract to make any film he wanted. From the outset, Allen's appeal – his talent – was so clearly unique and idiosyncratic that Krim intuited (or reasoned) that there was no sense in trying to restrict or shape it. Better simply to let it loose and hope to profit from it. As Steven Bach writes:

> 'Woody's UA deal was unique in the business. Contractually his pictures could be made virtually without approvals if they could be made below a specified budget figure... In practice, Woody submitted a script to Arthur Krim...and if Krim liked the script...that was it. There were no readers' reports, no committees, no creative meetings, no casting approvals (unless informal, from Krim), no dailies, nothing but Woody and his script and his budget and Arthur Krim's blessing. One reason this worked as well as it did was that Woody's pictures always came in on budget, on schedule and were what he had said they would be. For all the originality and iconoclasm and well-aimed satiric thrusts at the sacred cattle he saw munching away at the cultural landscape, Woody had an old-fashioned, deeply ingrained sense of honor about his commitments... Approval of the script was not contractual but by gentleman's agreement, inspired by Woody's punctiliousness. As he explained to me... "I wouldn't want the company to spend money on something it didn't believe in," and he meant it in both commercial and thematic senses.'[4]

Like Welles, Allen was a well-known actor-performer turned writer-director and film auteur. Unlike Welles, Allen was interested primarily (at this early stage) in making people laugh. He was not aiming to revolutionize cinema or propagate his own genius (and certainly not to subvert the status quo by going after a powerful public figure). Welles'

---

4 Bach, pg. 109–110. Bach quotes Allen on his unprecedented UA set-up: 'They never ever bother me... They would never come to a set without calling, and they never ask, "Could you show us somethin?" They see the picture when I'm ready to give it to them.' Ibid, pg. 108. In 1979 when Krim left UA with several of his closest associates to form Orion pictures (a studio that was remarkable for upholding the same artist-friendly atmosphere that Krim had created at UA), Allen soon followed him there and cut an identical deal to before. Orion went bankrupt in 1991.

aura – his large frame, chubby-handsome face and baritone voice, his irresistible charm and daunting self-regard – all combined to create a persona that was every bit as threatening (and galling) to people as it was charming. The net result was that Welles was someone that a lot of people needed to see fail. He seemed to be unwittingly goading fate to confound him, and of course, fate obliged. Allen had the profound (and rarely acknowledged) advantage of being short and homely, a nebbish that, no matter how talented he might be, did not inspire envy or resentment. He was also, for a struggling artist and forming genius, remarkably unambitious (at least compared to Welles, who wanted it all). From the outset, Allen seemed to be concerned solely with making movies his way, and in having the satisfaction of making people laugh (and getting women to fall in love – or at least bed – with him). Sights set suitably low, Allen proceeded to do just that, and United Artists knew that, as long as people laughed and paid to come back and laugh again, then they would make their money.

After toying with a more serious project (*The Jazz Baby*, which Krim rejected), Allen gave them what they wanted with *Bananas* (1971). The film (a screwball comedy about a nebbish who becomes a Latin-American revolutionary to impress his girlfriend) was an even bigger hit than *Money*. Allen's abilities were developing in leaps and bounds. He went on to write and star in *Play it Again Sam* (the play, which he filmed with Herbert Ross in 1972), and directed his third feature in 1972, *Everything You Always Wanted to Know About Sex (But Were Afraid to Ask)*, a series of sketches lacking in subtlety or finesse, and the weakest of his early pictures. Then in 1973, he graduated to the ranks of accomplished filmmakers with the sci-fi comedy, *Sleeper* (filmed for a cost of $3 million), and *Love and Death* (1975), a classic comedy inspired by Russian literature (probably a first). And then, in 1977, there came a breakthrough. However great the development between *Sex* and *Death*, it was nothing compared to the evolutionary leap Allen made with *Annie Hall*; with a single bound, he moved from the ranks of inspired amateurs to one of the most assured dramatic filmmakers in America.

In the period between *Money* and *Annie Hall* (roughly seven years), Allen had written and directed five films (the last four for United Artists), all precisely as he wanted them to be (with a little help and guidance from his collaborators).[5] A unique voice in American movies,

5 *Annie Hall* was originally a four-hour murder mystery called *Anhedonia*, a fact almost impossible to believe for anyone who has seen the 93-minute finished film, a sweet and touching romantic comedy with zero bodies in sight. Allen eventually returned to his original idea in 1993 with *Manhattan Murder Mystery*, also with Diane Keaton.

Allen already had a loyal fan base when he made *Annie Hall*; by the time it had swept the Oscars (winning Best Picture, Best Director and Screenplay for Allen, and Best Actress for its star, Diane Keaton), he had become one of the most adored and respected filmmakers in Hollywood. The film was a breakthrough not only for Allen (and Keaton), but also for the comedy genre and to some extent for movies in general. Its rough, loose, improvisatory style and its free-associative autobiographic humor – its blend of pratfalls with sophisticated wit and dramatic depth – suggested that audiences (and Academy members) were open to more refined kinds of entertainment than *Rocky*. Briefly (though it didn't last) the romantic comedy had come of age.

Annie Hall was by far the most personal movie at that time ever to win Best Picture (and still is, in fact). Allen had effectively put his life up on the screen and got audiences to laugh, smile and sigh with him, and to hail it as art. Of course, 1977 was the same year that *Annie Hall* and *Close Encounters of the Third Kind* flooded the collective consciousness of moviegoers and changed Hollywood forever; but significantly, they weren't winning too many awards for it.[6] The success of *Annie Hall* – especially after *Rocky* had won the previous year – was a belated nod to the New Hollywood, an endorsement of the delights of personal, experimental filmmaking. It was a tribute to the independent artist, and it suggested that, if a vision or a sensibility was fresh, vital and unique enough, it would be honored. At least for a time.

John Waters' Cinema of Sleaze

'I don't think that writers or painters or filmmakers function because they have something they particularly want to say. They have something that they feel. And they like the art form: they like words, or the smell of paint, or celluloid and photographic images and working with actors. I don't think that any genuine artist has ever been orientated by some didactic point of view, even if he thought he was.'

Stanley Kubrick

It's hard to imagine a sensibility more unique than that of John Waters, who, in the iconoclastic spirit of Russ Meyer and H.G. Lewis, invented his very own subgenre to live in. Like Roger Corman, Waters (the

---

6 This was before the days when the Academy, afraid to see seem out of touch with popular tastes, began giving awards to films like *Silence of the Lambs* merely for being successful.

anti-Stanley Kramer of movies) emerged as a reminder to Hollywood not to disparage or reject its trash roots. After all, before Griffith and Eisenstein had aspired to enlighten the world through movies, grubby little men were making nudie flicks for audiences who didn't give a plug nickel for 'art' but were happy to give a real one for some cheap thrills. Waters' movies existed as a raspberry at the high art of Hamlet, a burst of flatulence at High Mass. They were the full-bodied and mischievous rejection of art, edification, social responsibility, or moral instruction as being in any way relevant to the business (and pleasure) of movies. To Waters, movies were about self-expression in the same way that indecent exposure or acts of terrorism were about self-expression: a means to release the tension and pressure of correct social comportment and moral behaviour. Before PC-ism existed, Waters was bent upon trashing the sacred tenets of art, religion, politics and good, harmless 'entertainment'. Since Waters wasn't concerned with making art any more than he was with making moral statements, his films were freed from any obligation to be 'good', or even watchable. The fact that they existed was enough.

By his own (doubtless embellished and definitely relished) accounts, Waters grew up watching X-rated movies at a local drive-in through binoculars. One of the high-points of his childhood was discovering dried blood on the twisted wreckage of an automobile accident. (His early movies seemed designed to inspire a similar kind of morbid-squeamish fascination for the grotesque.) Waters got a 16mm camera for his 17th birthday and went straight to work, assembling a group of similarly-disposed buddies into a repertory group, The Dreamland Players. One of the group was the overweight Harris Milstead (Waters' classmate) who went on to adopt the screen name of Divine and, of course, was everything but. Waters and Milstead were in complete accord as to their mission: to assault and if possible destroy the middle-class system of values which they so despised, and to inspire an equal measure of horror, disgust and loathing in their complacent Baltimore audiences. Waters' first shorts had names like *Hag in a Black Leather Jacket* and *Eat Your Makeup!* and were screened (appropriately enough) in church basements hired for the occasion. (Invitations were distributed liberally about the town.)

Waters made his first feature for $2000 (borrowed from his father) in 1969; called *Mondo Trash*, it realized (and even surpassed) Waters' goals when he was arrested the night before the screening for 'conspiracy to commit indecent exposure' – a nigh-perfect description of Waters' subsequent career. Endorsed by the power of Fate itself (or at least Baltimore Law), Waters set about producing what would become his breakthrough opus (in 1972), *Pink Flamingoes*. Made for around

$10,000, the film quickly became (in)famous for a scene in which Divine – competing with other Dreamland Players for the title of 'World's Filthiest Person'– scoops up a piece of dog shit and eats it. Via the basest (and cheapest) of methods imaginable, Waters and Divine had succeeded in making an indelible impression. The film became a cult classic and Waters' name was established. He made two more films in the 70s (*Female Trouble* in 1975 and *Desperate Living* in 1977) but remained stubbornly outside the mainstream. (The most resolutely underground filmmaker ever to be embraced by Hollywood, the inevitable finally happened in 1988, when Waters made *Hairspray*.)

Waters stripped artistic expression down to its basic core, relieving it of all artistry until it was exposed as what it really was: simple (and pure) self-indulgence. Naturally, he gained a devoted following of moviegoers, equally sick and tired of Hollywood movies that represented a tiny portion of the populace (mainly white, middle-class Christians, or else tough police officers, rebellious students, hopeless drug addicts and so forth), neatly locked into boxes by which audiences could easily identify them. Even the movies that claimed to represent the counterculture (those hippies) did so in a facile, condescending manner, currying favor and approval from their target audience for deigning to represent them.

Waters' films were about real freaks, not generic stereotypical Hollywood 'freaks' (even *Easy Rider* was made by fringe-Hollywood freaks). They were filmed in the gutter, where the filmmakers themselves seemed most at home. The films were nightmarish to some – and equally hilarious to others – for portraying a world that couldn't be simulated on a Hollywood sound stage. This wasn't just a temporary illusion designed to tell a hackneyed story, but rather a glimpse into genuine depravity at the center of a twisted psyche. When Divine ate dog shit, he really *ate* dog shit. The motives of the character and that of the actor playing the character (to be the filthiest person alive) were indistinguishable, just as were the filming of the act and the act itself. This wasn't sleight of hand. This was John Cassavetes in Hell.

David Lynch: Into the Labyrinth

'The question becomes, are you giving them something to make them a little happier, or are you putting in something that is inherently true to the material? Are people behaving the way we all really behave, or are they behaving the way we would like them to behave? I mean, the world is not as it's presented in Frank

Capra films. People love those films – which are beautifully made – but I wouldn't describe them as a true picture of life.'

Stanley Kubrick

John Waters was not alone in his fascination for blood and car wrecks. Things had come a long way since the early days of movies when audiences fled from an approaching train, thinking it would flatten them. By 1974, audiences had wised-up immeasurably, and even the horror film – perhaps especially the horror film – required a new degree of subtlety and cunning to pull new wool over the old, jaded eyes of the public. It also required a new level of realism; or, in the case of David Lynch, of surrealism. Lynch was a genuine phenomenon, and his vision transformed the horror genre (and audiences' expectations of it) while remaining too unique, too weird, ever to be confined to it. Was ever so strange an animal as Lynch embraced by Hollywood? The bastard child of the Surrealists by way of the European expressionists and neorealists (Bergman, Fellini, Rossellini et al.), Lynch was the freakish yet inevitable fusion of a New Hollywood auteur with an indie schlock-horror filmmaker. The result was something wholly unique to movies.

Lynch began his creative career at art school rather than film school, and from his very first films his approach was as abstract and avant-garde as any to infiltrate the mainstream. Had he set out ten years earlier, he probably never would have, more than likely remaining with underground filmmakers such as Kenneth Anger or Andy Warhol. Yet despite his penchant for the avant-garde, and unlike Waters, Lynch was the all-American boy, an Eagle Scout who as a teenager had been an usher at John F. Kennedy's Presidential inauguration. Attracted by the graphic arts, Lynch signed up in 1963 at the Corcoran School of Art in Washington, D.C.; later he relocated to Boston and studied at Boston Museum School, then moved briefly in Europe. In 1966, he went to Philadelphia and attended the Pennsylvania Academy of Fine Arts. It was there he began to experiment with filmmaking, making what he called a 'moving painting', *Six Men Getting Sick*, in 1967. He then made *The Alphabet*, a semi-animated 16mm short, on the strength of which he was awarded an American Film Institute grant of $7,200. After this he temporarily abandoned filmmaking to concentrate on his marriage and his new daughter, Jennifer, and didn't make another short until *The Grandmother* in 1970 – a 34-minute film funded with the AFI grant. He then moved to LA and attended the AFI Center for Advanced Film Studies.

Lynch had fathered his first child in 1968 and by his own admission, the terrors and anxieties of fatherhood haunted him. In 1972, he set about making a feature-length movie to exorcise some of these fears, and this was the genesis of *Eraserhead*. Working together with actor Jack Nance, cinematographer Frederick Elmes and sound designer Alan Splet, initially funded by the AFI, the shoot took many years. Filming whenever they could, stopping periodically to raise money for film stock (when AFI funds ran out), the process continued for almost five years; for much of this time, Lynch had nowhere to stay (any money he could get his hands on went into filming) and he wound up sleeping on the film set, living and breathing the movie until, by the end, it seemed to be oozing out through his skin.

When he started *Eraserhead*, Lynch was twenty-six; by the time the film was finally released, in March of 1977 (for a total cost of around $20,000), he was thirty-one; shortly after, the film became a cult phenomenon, due largely to the timely intervention of sleaze-guru John Waters, who adored the film, and whose word was gospel in American cult circles. A genuine oddity, *Eraserhead* was Lynch's 'dream of dark and troubling things'; the most aggressively strange movie since *Un Chien Andalou*, it marked the arrival of perhaps the rawest, most threatening new talent in movies since Luis Buñuel. Like *Un Chien Andalou*, however, *Eraserhead* was as much a cultural phenomenon as an actual work of art, and much of its power and effectiveness derived from its novelty, audacity and capacity to shock and disturb audiences.

Eraserhead seemed to have been shot in another dimension, a film so lived in, so intensely alive with mood, atmosphere, detail and nuance, that it was as if Lynch had attained the age-long goal of art, projected his unconscious directly onto celluloid and captured his dreams in plastic. Clearly, Lynch wasn't just another independent filmmaker; he was a weaver of dreams, and *Eraserhead* was the most intensely personal movie ever to reach a mass audience. Beyond the wilful perversity of Waters or the raw honesty of Cassavetes – and beyond the self-conscious masturbation of Warhol – Lynch had made a movie that was an X-ray of his own head, that bared his psyche to audiences and dared them not to flinch from it. As with his early shorts, the film did not avail itself easily to the rational mind. Like a dream, it was necessary for audiences to let the images flow over them without trying to understand or interpret them, and to watch Lynch's film was to wander through the labyrinth without thought of where it was leading, or what to expect at the end.

Eraserhead was a bleak film, almost depressing, and it cut close to people's private terrors, those of madness, unreason, incoherence. The lack of familiar, reassuring sights and sounds (or even recognizable human beings) was all but suffocating; the film didn't merely disconcert, it practically deranged. Visionary as it undoubtedly was – one of the few sustained dream-nightmares ever put on film – *Eraserhead* was an insular, slightly self-indulgent fantasy, one which adequately displayed the director's gifts (and his primary preoccupations), but that didn't offer much for viewers to respond to.[7] There was humor in *Eraserhead*, but (like *Un Chien Andalou)* it was humor so wilfully personal as to be all but private, and certainly too perverse and disturbing to provide much relief (unless they were John Waters or Mel Brooks).[8]

There could be no doubt that Lynch was a genuine prodigy and that rarest of things: a born moviemaker with a natural gift for conveying the bizarre (and wholly irrational) world of dreams. *Eraserhead* started as a dream and moved progressively into nightmare, as if by its own internal volition. It depicted a world unknown but familiar, a world of irrational fears and inexplicable emotions. It was a world where machinery appeared alive, where blood and viscera and physical deformity seemed beautiful when looked at closely enough, and where the ordinary comforts of life became terrifying, when looked at too closely. Lynch was a pure 'right-brain' filmmaker, unshackled by plot or logic, and consequently there was simply no way of knowing what anything in his films *meant*. The image (and the sound) was all there was. Since there was little or no discernable 'filter' (of interpretation) between the audience and the filmmaker's psyche, the movie could 'mean' anything at all.

Nothing is more disturbing and potentially alienating to mass audiences than abstraction, however, since abstraction entails total freedom of interpretation. Whatever audiences 'saw' in a Lynch movie, they had to take responsibility for it, and that was the true horror. Lynch's lack of structure, logic, or fixed meanings wasn't the result of sloppiness or a lack of clarity.

7 The film perhaps played better in memory than on the screen, and images such as the Man in the Planet (sat by the window), the Lady in the Radiator, or the mutant offspring at the film's centre, were images with an almost terrifying resonance that seemed to have sprung whole from the collective unconscious. But the film as a whole was so alienating that – for those who didn't 'get' the humor of it – it was almost impossible to enjoy.

8 *Eraserhead* attracted the attention of the comedian and filmmaker Mel Brooks (who also had his own production company). Brooks adored the movie and felt drawn to meet the man who made it. The two men hit it off and Brooks – inspired by a filmmaker as unique as Lynch – hired the young director to make his next movie. *The Elephant Man* – though not initiated by Lynch – was a poetic development of the themes central to Lynch's art, and demonstrated the possibility of symbiosis (or at least collaboration) between auteur and industry. An honest weepy and a superb period drama, the film was another 'dream of dark and troubling things' by its director: brooding, trancelike and visually and emotionally devastating.

It was clearly intended, and his film sense – his ability to take viewers out of their own heads and into the labyrinth – was never in doubt. What was troubling (because new) was the way he used his gift. As Lynch himself put it, 'In Hollywood, if you can't write your ideas down, or if you can't pitch them, or if they're so abstract they can't be pitched properly, then they don't have a chance of surviving. Abstract things are important to a film, but very few people get the chance to really go all out with cinema. Creations are an extension of yourself, and you go out on a limb whenever you create anything. It's a risk.'[9] With *Eraserhead*, Lynch took the ultimate risk and went all the way out on that limb.

Lynch's movies required audiences not only to suspend their disbelief but to suspend thinking entirely. They weren't just fantasy worlds, they were altered states of awareness. Watching his movies was like getting caught in someone else's dream, and at times, Lynch's films seemed to simulate a state indistinguishable from madness. A far cry from the soothing lullabies of Hollywood, Lynch was there to remind audiences that art (unlike movies) wasn't necessarily a way to forget our troubles; it was also a means to remember them.

Making Tables: John Sayles and the Mysterious Film Sense

'There's a lot to be said for independent filmmaking. It's where a single mind determines what the story should be. The story itself is the thing, not the commercial aspects of it. Sure, movie making is a business. It must eventually appear on the screen so that people can pay to see it. It's a product made for money. But for me, it starts with the story I want to tell.'

John Sayles[10]

9 *Lynch on Lynch*, by Chris Rodley, pg. 64.
10 Sayles continues: 'It must be commercially viable, yes, but if I have to use the wrong actor because he's a star, then it's no longer that story. If I have to shoot it on a studio location that compromises the look I want, it's no longer that story. If I have to change a line here, another line there, it's no longer that story. This is what defines the eternal clash of interests. The studio contract reads: "Paramount Pictures, hereinafter known as The Author..." So you're doomed by contract. It's a question of who has the power over what finally appears on the screen. The answer to that is in the hands of who controls the money. If I were to make an independent film that grossed $100,000,000 say, a studio might give me financing for my own story, casting, final cut. But that's not about to happen, so I have to rely on small budgets banked mostly by my screenwriting jobs and various independent investors. I don't want to be a director for hire. I don't want to make someone else's story. I enjoy making my own movies. I want to keep telling those stories until I run out of them.' Interview from *DGA Magazine*, Vol. 22-5, Dec/Jan 1998.

Yet another alumnus of the Roger Corman school of film, John Sayles began his career working in the schlock horror genre (a perfectly respectable place to get started, as Coppola demonstrated). In the late 70s, Sayles wrote the scripts for *Piranha* and *Alligator* (and later *The Howling*), superior horror fare marked by sardonic humor and an ironic wink at audiences that is sometimes labeled 'postmodernism'. Since the arrival of Tarantino, such irony has become more or less standard for genre movies, but at the time it was relatively fresh, and with his early forays into the genre, Sayles distinguished himself with his sophisticated (by Hollywood standards) wit and intellect. His artistic temperament was a lot closer to John Cassavetes than to Roger Corman, however, and in 1980 he made his first feature, *The Return of the Secaucus Seven*, shot on a single location for $60,000 with a small cast of unknown actors (including Sayles in a supporting role). The film found itself a distributor and also an audience, albeit mostly in art houses and independent cinemas (still in existence in those days).

As Sayles himself describes it:

'I'd saved about $40,000. What could I do with that kind of money? I knew a lot of talented stage actors, all around thirty years old. I couldn't afford expensive camera-moving equipment for action shots, but I could substitute cutting for action. Robert Altman had done that in *Nashville*. So I wrote a story about young people, an ensemble film about a reunion of old friends who'd been arrested in New Jersey during the protest movements of the 60s. Plot and subplot. I got hold of a camera crew from Boston whose experience was limited to making commercials. No one had been in a movie before. We set up at a ski lodge that summer, $1 a day for a bed, all locations within a few miles – a neighbourhood bar, exterior locations like an old basketball court. Somehow, everything seemed to go smoothly during the five weeks of shooting. It wasn't until we got to Los Angeles for post-production work that all our mistakes became evident. Years would pass, 1978, 79, 80, and the $40,000 became $60,000. But when *The Return of the Secaucus Seven* was finally released, it grossed a couple of million.'

A lot had changed in Hollywood (and audiences) since John Cassavetes first cranked up his 16mm camera on the streets of New York in 1960. In a sense, movies had caught up with whatever Cassavetes had been trying to do, and such raw style no longer seemed a revolutionary new methodology so much as an alternate aesthetic, one that the films of the early 70s – films like *Easy Rider, Midnight Cowboy, The Last Picture Show, Alice's Restaurant, Last Tango in Paris, Mean Streets, The Conversation, Alice Doesn't Live Here Anymore, The Long Goodbye, California Split and Night Moves* – had made familiar to audiences. It was fly-on-the-wall filmmaking, often plotless, characterized by understated, improvised performances, location shooting and a lack of reassuring messages or tidy resolutions. These films appealed to audiences tired of being pummeled and patronized, duped and condescended into acquiescing to Hollywood's (plainly bogus) vision of the world, a vision that was all-too-obviously contrived to keep them happy consumers.

Film's natural aptitude for fantasy and escapism didn't necessarily have to be at odds with its (largely unexplored) capacity for capturing everyday reality, and nor were the two 'functions' of the art form mutually exclusive. Godard had more than adequately laid the groundwork for the fusing of realism with surrealism, whereby the fantastic, escapist qualities of movies could be allowed to complement and enhance the documentary ones. Godard had provided the example, and filmmakers like Scorsese and Altman were ready to follow it. A film like *Mean Streets* used its documentary realism to intensify its narrative, and vice versa – its use of rock and roll, hyper-charged performances, and expressionistic visuals gave an added degree of immediacy and urgency to the realism. The film was an almost perfect blend of the two styles, and no less of a 'movie' for being so raw and improvisatory. (Scorsese brought the same street sensibility to his big Hollywood production, *Alice Doesn't Live Here Anymore*, and successfully transformed it into the first grown-up movie of its kind.)

Sayles worked within a similar template to Scorsese, albeit with considerably less by way of visionary gifts or creative passion. Sayles' style was sparse and workmanlike, with little apparent interest in cinematic flourishes or the ordinary (or even extraordinary) devices of melodrama. *Secaucus Seven* was not really any closer to being a documentary than *Mean Streets*, but it was considerably closer to being a home movie. It was melodrama stripped almost naked of its usual adornments, and the impression it gave – for perhaps the first time since Cassavetes, only with none of the attention-grabbing 'innovations' – was of real people doing ordinary things while the camera just happened to film them. It provided a sense of the moment being captured without embellishments, of lives glimpsed in the raw. Sayles was almost anthropological in his approach to film, and he gave the impression that his primary concern was not to interfere with the purity and spontaneity of his subject.

As a director (despite his quirky appearances in many of his films), his presence seemed intentionally unassuming, discreet, all-but undetectable; in an odd way (self-effacingly, in service of the film as a whole), his touch as a director was negligible. As such, he distinguished himself from other auteur filmmakers of the period, all of whom without exception strove to leave a personal mark on their movies by suffusing them with their obsessions. Sayles didn't seem to care about being an auteur. He made movies less like a Van Gogh or Picasso – possessed by their searing visions and filled with flourishes – and more like a carpenter building a table, checking to make sure the legs were the right length and all the parts held together. Sayles cared less about any aesthetic qualities his movies might have than how well people could eat off them.

Despite his prosaic approach to filmmaking, Sayles displayed from the start a natural gift for the medium, albeit a gift that – being perhaps less than abundant – he has continued to use sparingly throughout his career. There is a mysterious factor when it comes to making movies, a quality that can't really be measured or defined, nor apparently can it be learned (though it can be lost). It is a quality that is as essential to the film director as his own eyes, and like vision, either he has it or he doesn't. Pauline Kael called it 'film sense'.[11] A filmmaker can be bereft of all other skills – of any aptitude for writing, plotting, honing performance – and still get away with making movies, just so long as he retain his mysterious film sense (witness Stanley Kubrick). On the other hand, if a director is lacking it – as in the case of Paul Schrader – it matters little how accomplished his cast may be, how brilliant the screenplay, or how lavish the production values, his film will sink like a stone in the minds of audiences and leave no traces.[12]

Audiences don't necessarily need to be seduced or tricked into

---

[11] Peckinpah had it in spades, to the point that even when his technique, his basic abilities, his sobriety and even his sanity had deserted him, his movies were still possessed of moments of brilliance. Lynch has it and it shows in his very first films, even the shorts. De Palma likewise, and Spielberg (who may not have much else besides), Altman, Scorsese and Coppola for the first part of his career, after which (somewhere during the making of *Apocalypse Now*) it seemed to abandon him, never to return. In a rare exception, Woody Allen seemed to pick it up as he went along.

[12] Witness also the works of Harold Becker, Bruce Beresford, Jonathan Kaplan, or Michael Apted, accomplished directors with no distinguishing features whose styles all seem interchangeable in their facelessness. No amount of technical ability can cover up a lack of basic vision.

entering the illusion of movies, but they definitely need to be wooed (and lulled) into it. Above all, what audiences need – and what the mysterious film sense enables a director to give them – is a feeling of complete confidence and trust that the movie they are seeing (and the people who made it) will take them on a journey and get them safely to their destination. Without this trust, audiences cannot suspend their disbelief or ignore the artifice of the medium; they cannot succumb to the experience of watching and partaking in the movie. This is probably why Hitchcock is so revered to this day, because – more than any other filmmaker who ever lived – he gave audiences what they wanted and needed: a sense of complete and total confidence in his ability to deliver. Hitchcock finally lost the gift of spell-casting; his film sense deserted him and audiences were lumped with *Torn Curtain* and *Topaz*, so consequently he lost his audience. This was presumably due to old age as much as anything, but what are we to make of filmmakers who are blessed with this (apparently unearned) gift of a prodigious film sense, only for it to desert them completely and leave them floundering in a sea of lackluster images and lifeless performances? The history of Hollywood is rife with just such cases. In fact, they are more the rule than the exception. And the reasons, though many and varied, all come down to the same thing: creative burn-out.

Raging Abysses: Scorsese's Quagmire and the Strange Case of Michael Cimino

'We poured all of ourselves into one movie, and if it didn't hit, our whole career went down with it. There are directors who, after certain titles, didn't have anything more left, any more fight.'

Martin Scorsese

Following *Who's That Knocking at My Door?*, Scorsese served his apprenticeship under Roger Corman at American International Pictures, and made the workmanlike but forgettable *Boxcar Bertha* (1972, with Barbara Hershey and David Carradine). Scorsese cites John Cassavetes as a greater influence on him than Corman, however. After a screening of *Boxcar Bertha*, Cassavetes told Scorsese, with characteristic candor: 'You've just spent a year of your life making a piece of shit.' Cassavetes urged Scorsese to stick to his personal vision and not to whore his talents to mainstream studios (or audiences). Scorsese followed the advice and made *Mean Streets*, a film which – as much as *Easy Rider* and *The Godfather* – helped change the face (and pace) of an art form. It's fair to wonder, however, what Cassavetes would have said about later Scorsese films such as *Cape Fear* and *Gangs of New York*. It's astonishing – and sobering – to compare *Knocking* with these later films, and see that, for all the slickness and professionalism now in evidence, the scenes in *Gangs* are far less convincing, less alive and vital, than those in *Knocking*, shot when he was a green, New York street kid still finding his feet. For all its clumsiness and indulgence, there is nothing in *Knocking* to compare with the rank insincerity of *Cape Fear*, or with the embarrassing shallowness of *Gangs* (or the dullness of *Age of Innocence* or *Kundun*).

The later films have straightforward stories and glossy production values; studios back them, and so audiences accept them, both as entertainment and 'art' from the legendary Martin Scorsese (in fact, they are neither). The same audiences would never accept *Who's That Knocking at My Door?* however. Scorsese has often remarked that, as a boy, the cinema was like church for him: a place to go and sit in the dark and be inspired. If so, he takes it one step further and turns filmmaking into a religion, a means of confessing his sins, on the one hand, and of atoning for them, on the other. If Scorsese – who has never sunk to sermonizing with his films – remains the undisputed high priest of American cinema, it is primarily because he never lost touch with the sinner inside. The movies he made in his first decade, following the advice of Cassavetes, were consistently informed by the same intensity and urgency, and evidently they acted as a form of personal catharsis.

Scorsese made a choice somewhere along the way, however, and decided that reaching wider audiences (and working with big Hollywood budgets) mattered more to him than personal catharsis. Or perhaps, after his first, failed attempt to 'sell out' with *Boxcar Bertha* – and following the string of masterpieces or semi-masterpieces that came after (*Mean Streets, Taxi Driver, The Last Waltz, Raging Bull, King of Comedy*) – he was all out of personal demons? Scorsese's 'choice' only became evident in the quality of his work after the failure of *King of Comedy* (his last truly personal work, and to date his last great movie), but probably it was made sometime during the shooting of *New York, New York* (1977); that was the film that got Scorsese beat, in the same way that *Apocalypse Now* was beating Coppola – at roughly the same time and for roughly the same reasons – from excess ambition.

Almost three decades later, Scorsese spoke about this period as follows:

'I think it [winning an Oscar] matters in terms of my ego, there's no doubt about that. But winning the Palme d'Or in Cannes mattered a great deal, too, and when I won it for *Taxi Driver*,

I went the wrong way, and I became overly confident. I was testing myself in the wrong direction, but I had to go there to find out it was wrong. I came back out the other side alive. But the recognition was part of that arrogance. Well, I'd always been arrogant, but the attention turned it into obsession.'[13]

New York, New York was Scorsese's valiant but misguided attempt to fuse his intense, street sensibility with a grand, old-style Hollywood movie musical production, and when the film failed – both commercially and critically (and probably even before that, while he was stuck in the quagmire of making it and knew intuitively that he had lost his direction) – Scorsese began to have doubts about what he was doing. For Scorsese, 'It was just the beginning of going into an abyss for about two years and coming out of it just barely alive… It hit me finally… that I didn't enjoy it anymore. There was nothing left…it was like rock bottom. I thought, I've lost my voice.'[14.] Was it worth putting so much heart and soul, so much blood, sweat and tears into movies? Racked by such doubts, and after narrowly escaping a bloody, drug-induced death, Scorsese finally agreed to make *Raging Bull*, convinced it would be his last Hollywood film.[15] It wasn't, but to many it was his last truly personal one. With his next film, *The King of Comedy*, Scorsese seemed to have deliberately stripped his filmmaking down to a TV-style simplicity: all the rougher edges and raw intensity were gone. It was as if (thinking it would be his last film) Scorsese had put everything he had into *Raging Bull*, figuring he'd never get another chance to show his stuff, so may as well give his all. Though *King of Comedy* was a great film (superior to *Raging Bull* in all but superficials), it was also a strangely impersonal one.

Though the falling off of Scorsese's talent in the 80s was by no means as marked as with Coppola, all of his subsequent films conspicuously lacked the searing brilliance that characterized his 70s work. Perhaps, having plumbed the depths of his own psyche, Scorsese hadn't liked

---

13 *Backstage West,* 29th January 2003, 'Director's Cuts: Interview with Martin Scorsese.'

14. *Easy Riders, Raging Bulls,* pg 315, 379.

15. According to Scorsese, a combination of bad coke and various prescription drugs (Scorsese is an asthmatic) landed him in the hospital, bleeding from every orifice. Scorsese acquiesced to making *Raging Bull* when he saw clearly his own self-destructive tendencies, and decided he was Jake LaMotta. Though it wasn't a commercial success, the film was nominated for several Oscars, and is now considered by many critics – however erroneously – to be his masterpiece.

what he found there? In which case, he would only ever skirt the edges of those abysses, and never again gaze unflinchingly inward.

*

'*Heaven's Gate* undercut all of us. I knew at the time it was the end of something, that something had died.'

Martin Scorsese[16]

Perhaps the most irrefutable and outstanding case of total director burnout is that of Michael Cimino. Ironically, Cimino began (and ended) his career as 'film genius' by emulating Francis Coppola, himself a bewildering and nigh-tragic case of a once-great director whose film sense fatally abandoned him. Cimino made three films and then effectively vanished, buried under the rubble of his own insane ambitions. He began, modestly and auspiciously enough in 1974, working with Clint Eastwood on the superior comedy crime thriller *Thunderbolt and Lightfoot*, and the film, like most of Eastwood's films of the period, was a success, and remains one of the actor's best films of the period. Cimino didn't direct another movie until 1977, when he began work on what would become *The Deer Hunter*, the first serious treatment of the Vietnam War and one of the most critically lauded films of the decade.

The film infuriated as many people as it seduced, however. Pauline Kael called *The Deer Hunter* 'a small-minded film with greatness in it.'[17] The film began magnificently; its first hour (the wedding sequence) was masterly, as Cimino, carried away by his love for the medium, successfully 'aped' his mentor, Coppola. Possibly the majestic grace of this sequence pulled the wool over everyone's eyes, to the point that most critics didn't notice that the film steadily declined afterwards, degenerating into preposterous masochistic fantasy by the end. For the first hour of *The Deer Hunter*, Cimino successfully simulated Coppola's style, and all the pre-war scenes were possessed of depth and quiet intensity. With their measured, almost hypnotic pacing and attention to detail, the impassioned yet understated performances, the film directly

---

16 Coppola concurs: 'There was a kind of coupe d'etat that happened after *Heaven's Gate*, started by Paramount. It was a time when the studios were outraged that the cost of movies were going up so rapidly, that directors were making such incredible amounts of money, and had all the control. So they took the control back.' *Easy Riders, Raging Bulls*, pg. 401
17 *When the Lights Go Down*, pg. 512.

evokes Coppola's *Godfather* masterpieces. It was only once Cimino got to Vietnam (actually Thailand) that his heroic restraint and subtle intelligence seemed to desert him, and the film turned into a different work entirely, closer in spirit to John Milius than Coppola.

Despite this, Cimino won a Best Director Oscar for the film and was immediately thrown into the front ranks of genius auteur filmmakers. Some are born to greatness, some achieve it through hard slog and some have it thrust upon them. And there then are those who don't seem to have a clue what to do with it. Cimino used his new-found, largely unearned status to make *Heaven's Gate*, the film that effectively ended his career and, in the process, brought a whole studio (United Artists) to its knees. Today *Heaven's Gate* has the rare honor of shouldering a sizeable portion of the blame, or credit, for ending the short-lived 'reign of the auteur' in Hollywood. And the reason was simple. As Michael Schumacher writes, 'There was great discussion about the death of the auteur in Hollywood. Bright, talented, yet largely self-absorbed directors, the rising stars in the industry less than a decade ago, needed to be reeled in and controlled by the studios backing the pictures. After all, when all was calculated, there was a price tag on ego and artistic vision.[18.]

Michael Cimino was an example of a runaway genius whose despotic egomania not only derailed his movie but bankrupt a studio in the process. Cimino's success with *The Deer Hunter* had been so prodigious, so unexpected and so impactful that for a brief spell, Cimino had Hollywood in his thrall and was able to do anything he pleased with it. What he did was shoot hundreds of hours of location footage with a cast of thousands and deliver a 'final cut' five-and-a-half-hour Western in which everyone dies. *Heaven's Gate* was considered unreleasable, but United Artists finally cut it down to two and a half hours and released it anyway; it became one of the most expensive flops in film history. The film was a sprawling mess; almost no one who saw it liked it, and just about no one bothered to go and see it. What appeared to have happened (as with *The Deer Hunter* only on a much larger scale, and far more critically) was that Cimino's ambition – his drive for glory, will to power, and the lure of 'genius' – capsized the simple desire to make a movie: he lost all interest in communicating with his audience, and so lost the ability to tell an entertaining story with interesting characters.

It's ironic that, though a mere 'auteur' very nearly undid 'Hollywood', it was only by allowing megalomaniacal drives to override creative

18. Schumacher, pg. 279.

common sense that Cimino lost control of his vision. In other words, it was not Cimino's visionary tendencies that undid him (and the studio that backed him), but his despotic ones. His was a cautionary tale indeed, and to this day filmmakers and studio heads alike shudder, covertly, at the mention of his name.[19] Cimino's story so fully encapsulates the great dread of both studios and filmmakers that his name has become a kind of malediction; it set a precedent that artists are loathe to be reminded of, and ill-advised to ever forget.

Francis Coppola's One-Way Trip to the Abyss

'Violating the boundaries between life and art to make their material their own was a dangerous way for these filmmakers to work. It was successful for a while, enriching both the life and the art, but as the two became more extravagant and interchangeable, New Hollywood directors lost the detachment of artists, and their lives and art sank into quicksand, joined in a fatal embrace.'

Peter Biskind, *Easy Riders, Raging Bulls*

At almost exactly the same time Cimino's career was spiraling into the abyss, something similar seemed to be happening to Cimino's unconfessed mentor Francis Coppola.[20] If Cimino had already begun losing his way before *The Deer Hunter* was ever completed, then the film's huge success – and Cimino's almost instantaneous elevation to Oscar-winning film genius – can only have intensified his estrangement from his talent. Cimino's hubris in defying not only Coppola but Hollywood with his storming of *Heaven's Gate* was inevitably going to be his downfall. What was remarkable was how quickly it came about.[21]

In his turn, Coppola was to descend from considerably greater heights than any attained by Cimino; and they were heights that Coppola had

---

19 The end result, as Peter Biskind put it, was that, 'The system of social Darwinism that is Hollywood took care of the problem in short order. UA, stripped of credibility, was devoured. Transamerica sold it to MGM's Kirk Kerkorian for $350 million.' *Easy Riders, Raging Bulls*, pg. 400. For the full story, see Steven Bach's *Final Cut*.

20 According to Schumacher, Cimino '…took cheap shots at Coppola, implying that he, Cimino, was more qualified to make an authoritative film on the war than Coppola. "Vietnam," he scoffed, "is not the only war in the history of the world where there have been terrible atrocities. There have been and there probably will be far worse. Vietnam was not the apocalypse."' Schumacher, pg. 247.

21 To date, Cimino has not made a single film of note since *Heaven's Gate*. His subsequent work, *Year of the Dragon*, was a tawdry affair, but was surpassed in shoddiness

inhabited that much longer, and consequently had made his own. There is perhaps no filmmaker in American movies – unless it be Griffith, and certainly including Welles – who displayed such monumental talent and so remarkable an ability to apply it on a grand scale as Coppola did in the 70s with the two *Godfather* movies, *The Conversation*, and the greater portion of *Apocalypse Now*. If anyone had earned the appellation of genius, it was Coppola in the 70s. So then what happened?

Of all the great American movie directors to emerge in the late 60s and early 70s, Coppola may be the hardest to pin down. His was the most baffling, the most evasive and finally the most fleeting and frustrating of talents. It was a talent that seemed to defy all attempts at analysis, while at its strongest, and then to disappear entirely, as if never having existed at all. Coppola has referred to himself as 'a genius with no talent', and though glib, the remark is telling. Coppola seemed to bypass the usual transitional phases between filmmaker apprentice and master director, and then later, between master director and empty craftsman. He went from the slightly dull but promising *Rain People* straight to *The Godfather* films, then from *Apocalypse Now* to *One from the Heart*, which was not the beginning of the end (it really began somewhere in the midst of *Apocalypse*) but the end itself, in all its tacky glory. Since then, he has made about a dozen movies, ranging from ungainly but intriguing (*Rumble Fish, Bram Stoker's Dracula*), to whimsical (*The Outsiders*) to grotesque (*Peggy Sue Got Married, Jack*), to well-made but less than memorable dramas (*Gardens of Stone, The Rainmaker*), to shapeless messes (*One from the Heart, The Cotton Club, Tucker*, and Coppola's segment in *New York Stories*, which was not only Coppola's but everyone else's personal low point).[22] Then, in 1997, he seemed to stop making movies altogether.

by *The Sicilian*, with which he demonstrated once and for all (by adapting the Mario Puzo novel) that he was not, nor ever would be, the next Coppola. If this wasn't enough to end anyone's career, Cimino came back a couple of years later with the excruciating *The Desperate Hours*, a film that exposed its director as not only devoid of artistic vision but bereft of even the most basic technical skills. He then made a film called *Sunchaser*, which few critics took the time to review (perhaps out of good manners?), and audiences failed to notice entirely.

22 His third *Godfather* film was an improvement over much of this, but an embarrassment nonetheless. Making the film was a move that he should never have attempted, because the talent that he had invested into the first two films had so obviously deserted him by then that attempting a third installment was only broadcasting the fact. The contrast between the early films and the later one is distressing, to say the least, and one would think they were made by different people. Only with *Bram Stoker's Dracula* did Coppola begin to hint at a possible, untapped reserve of talent still lurking somewhere within him. It seems a foregone conclusion, however, that he will never return to his former heights.

When *The Godfather* was released in 1972, its enormous critical and commercial success assured that Coppola would be 'typecast' forever after as the man who made it happen. If Coppola had retired after the second film (or after *Apocalypse Now*) and never made another picture, he would have remained in most people's minds the most intriguing and dazzling American film genius since Orson Welles. And as with Welles, we would forever have wondered about the films we never got to see. As it is, we may forever wonder about the genius whose talents evaporated into nothingness.

Coppola's *Godfather* films (the first two) were an almost magical blend of artistic and historic vision, possessing the depth and scope of authentic mythmaking. With the slow, sure rise to power of Vito Corleone, the second film showed the poetic motions of the artist, as he worked and struggled to render his dream a reality. From the first moment when he sees the Statue of Liberty from the ferry, Vito dreams himself into being, and through the subtlety of his direction and the grace of De Niro's performance, Coppola shows how Vito attains power not through force but through will. Vito's unbending will is a force unto itself, before which all other men's wills bend in order to accommodate themselves to it. Vito creates the path of least resistance for himself wherever he goes; slow and stately, like a king without a kingdom, he walks down his path towards his destiny. With Don Corleone, Coppola gave us far more than the customary 'rise to power' of the hood to gangster to crime lord. He gave us the birth of greatness, the realization of the artist's vision of himself in glory. On the other hand, because of the subject matter, Coppola showed us the darker side of this romantic dream – the side we always dreaded and secretly knew was there.

As magnificently as Coppola depicted Vito's rise to power, his real genius was in portraying the fall of Vito's son Michael, and the almost irresistible pull of the abyss which his once-honorable intentions and overweening ambition had opened up before him. The rise and fall of the Corleones – enacted by father and son over the course of the two films – was a grand tragedy that, in his own way and in the course of a single lifetime, Coppola's own career would appear to curiously and darkly mirror.

★

'The bigger the budget, the less freedom you have and the less money you have actually available... I think I'm better suited to a medium where the budgets are smaller and yet the imagination is bigger.'

Francis Ford Coppola

After the disbanding of the Directors Company in 1974, Coppola wasted no time forming a new company of his own, called Cinema 7, having bought 72,000 shares in New York-based distribution company Cinema 5 for $180,000, amounting to ten percent of the total company stock. 'When discussing Cinema 5 with the press, Coppola assumed his now familiar position of the embattled filmmaker searching for a way to circumvent an oppressive system.'[23] Coppola's vision was to distribute films (his own and those he produced for others) through Cinema 5, and so avoid the compromises that filmmakers invariably made when they sacrificed creative control and final ownership in exchange for money needed to make their films. Coppola intended his first project to be a war movie about Vietnam called *Apocalypse Now*. At first, he wanted George Lucas to direct the film; Lucas was ensconced in his fast-developing space opera, *Star Wars,* so Coppola went to John Milius (who had written the script), who also refused. Coppola finally assented to the inevitable and agreed to direct the film himself. It was a decision that would cost him dearly.

The first obstacle to making the movie was finding someone to star in it. Coppola approached just about everyone for the lead: Steve McQueen, Marlon Brando, Clint Eastwood, Jack Nicholson, Robert Redford; despite the allure of working with the man behind the two *Godfathers*, no one wanted to commit to what looked certain to be a long and arduous shoot in the Philippines jungle. There must have been certain prescience on these actors' parts, considering the fact that *Apocalypse* took about eight months (not counting four months' downtime) to shoot, and almost killed its leading man, Martin Sheen, who suffered a major heart attack midway into the shoot.

Coppola's original budget was between $12 million and $14 million, and at this early stage (before the film was cast) he had raised $7 million from foreign distributors. $1 million of his own money had gone into preproduction costs, and it was quickly becoming apparent that, much as he might want to, he would not be able to finance the film independently. His goal was to find funding without handing over ownership of the film, and finally United Artists offered an advance of $7.5 million in exchange for US distribution rights. Coppola flew to the Philippines on March 1st

1976, having managed to secure Marlon Brando for the role of Kurtz. (Kurtz is the renegade American colonel who has gone insane, and set himself up in the jungle as a demigod to the natives, and whom the main character, Willard, is assigned to kill.) Coppola had finally settled on Harvey Keitel for the role of Willard, though only once everyone else had turned him down. One reason for this was doubtless due to the unusual degree of commitment Coppola was now asking of his actors.

With *Apocalypse Now*, Coppola was striving for a greater degree of autonomy as a filmmaker, and in an unprecedented move (unprecedented since the days of contract players, at least), he placed a full page ad in *Variety*, in which he declared his wish to bind his actors to a seven year contract to Cinema 7. As Schumacher writes:

'Unlike the old studio agreements, in which actors were essentially treated as slaves, forced to work on pictures they would have preferred to avoid, and loaned to other studios in arrangements profitable to the studios but not to the actors themselves, the Coppola contract would encourage actors to work on outside projects, and they would be given a generous percentage of the profits for such work. The contracted actors would be paid for fifty weeks of work (as opposed to the forty weeks' pay in the old Hollywood system), and they would be encouraged to develop their careers further by writing and directing their own projects.'[24]

The announcement, which came immediately prior to the commencement of the *Apocalypse* shoot, reaffirmed Coppola's reputation as American cinema's foremost visionary – or megalomaniac, depending on your point of view. (Martin Scorsese, for one, approved the idea, tentatively stating: 'I think it's the right concept to break down the $3,000,000 syndrome.'[25]) As it happened, Harvey Keitel (who agreed to these conditions) didn't last more than a couple of weeks into the shoot, and was promptly replaced by Sheen.

The troubles, setbacks, and outright catastrophes that besieged the filming of *Apocalypse Now* came hard and fast, culminating in May with Hurricane Olga, which destroyed several sets and flooded countless habitations (including the Coppolas'), forcing the director to shut

24 Schumacher, pg. 201
25 Schumacher, pg. 201. The '$3 million syndrome' referred to the then-astronomical fees that actors were beginning to ask for at the time, mere peanuts compared to today's salaries, of course, which are now approaching ten times that figure.

down the film less than two months into shooting. By this time, he had already spent $7 million (half of his budget) shooting roughly fifteen minutes of the script (one-tenth of the final running time). Faced with his own apocalypse Coppola has no choice but to return to LA and meet with United Artists lawyers.

After negotiations, United Artists agreed to give Coppola $3 million in current overruns, '...but only on the condition that *Apocalypse Now* earn $40 million in rentals. If it didn't, Coppola would be personally responsible for paying back the loan. It was a gamble, but a calculated one. All Coppola had to do was complete the movie on his original budget and hope that his reputation carried it at the box office.'[26] The film wrapped in May 1977, over a year after commencing (shooting had been suspended for four months due to various natural disasters), at a total cost of $27 million, a nigh-historical figure at the time. Having shot over a million feet of footage, funds almost depleted, Coppola was forced to sell his shares in Cinema 5 back to the company (for precisely what he had paid for them), and to reach another agreement with United Artists. This time, he put his house and real estate up as collateral, in return for another $10 million to complete the film. 'As it now stood, *Apocalypse Now* would have to be a huge box-office success for Coppola to realize any profit for all his work. If the movie bombed, he would go down in flames with it. To protect its investment further, United Artists took out a $15 million life-insurance policy on Coppola, leading the director to remark that he was now worth more dead than alive.'[27]

By April 1978, Coppola had a rough cut of the film which he showed as a 'work-in-progress' for United Artists executives, and then, shortly after, for a select audience in San Francisco. Coppola made it clear that the film was unfinished and implored critics not to write about it. They did anyway, and the overall response to the film was tepid. At the end of the year, with *Apocalypse Now* still uncompleted, Michael Cimino released *The Deer Hunter* to an all-but unanimously ecstatic critical response. By now, *Apocalypse Now* was being churlishly referred to in the press as 'Apocalypse When?', and finally, 'Apocalypse Never'. In May of 1979, however, Coppola screened a near-finished cut at the White House, and then, in direct defiance of United Artists' wishes, took it to Cannes film festival and entered it into competition as a work-in-progress. The film won the Palme d'Or and was finally released to the general public in August 1979, four long years after Coppola had first started the film.

26 Schumacher, pg. 210
27 Schumacher, pg. 236.

Though critics were less than united in their praise, almost all of them agreed that Coppola had made a powerful movie that fell apart in the final section. Audiences were slightly bewildered by the film. Fortunately for Coppola, their curiosity had been stirred to such a pitch by the film's tumultuous shoot that they showed up in hordes to see for themselves whether the film was 'a masterpiece or a masturbation'. The film was a box office success, and Coppola avoided going down in flames. After so long teetering on the brink of financial and professional ruin, he had come through the ordeal; his vision had prevailed. Yet despite this, the overall impression was that *Apocalypse Now* had been a catastrophe and a folly; an inspired one, perhaps, but a folly nonetheless. Nothing short of an unequivocal masterwork or a blockbuster success could ever justify the turgid and grisly tales of hardship, excess, and indulgence – the hurricanes and the heart attacks – in the public mind. And *Apocalypse Now* was neither blockbuster nor masterpiece.

The film left audiences with a sense of uncertainty and confusion as to what Coppola had been trying to do, and if the end justifies the means, *Apocalypse Now* (whose means were so extreme they demanded justification) did not give audiences the conclusion they needed. The greatness of the movie, its being accomplished against all the odds, was outweighed, finally, by the greatness of the let-down. Coppola may have snatched financial victory from the jaws of bankruptcy, but artistically, he had barely saved face. *Apocalypse Now* was a searing *tour-de-force* that sustained its power and intensity for two hours and then, just when it all needed to come together, fell to pieces. Up to that point, it was an unparalleled work in the genre, but the messy, formless ending which Coppola gave audiences – in which both his talent and his confidence seemed to desert him – detracted fatally from everything that had gone before, all but erasing it from memory. As a result, the film seemed most memorable for being the greatest anti-climax in the history of Hollywood. Not only was it its own anti-climax, it was the anti-climax of Coppola's career and, ultimately, the anti-climax of the New Hollywood.[28] The movie was really finished as soon as Willard arrived at

---

28 Pauline Kael seemed to agree when she wrote: 'Part of the widespread anticipation of *Apocalypse Now* was, I think, our readiness for a visionary, climactic, summing-up movie… [Coppola's] film was posited on great thoughts coming out at the end – a confrontation and a revelation. And when they weren't there, people slunk out of the theatres, or tried to comfort themselves with chatter about psychedelic imagery. Trying to say something big, Coppola got tied up in a big knot of American self-hatred and guilt, and what the picture boiled down to was – white man-he devil. Since then, I think, people have expected less of movies.' 'Numbers, or Why Are Movies So Bad?,' *Taking it All In*, pg. 18

his destination, and Coppola must have known it, and been paralyzed by the burden of his own intentions. *Apocalypse Now*, like a blooming flower of napalm, consumed itself by burning too brightly.

As Peter Biskind observed, 'It was no wonder Coppola could not figure what to do with Kurtz. He existed at the intersection of too many issues that were deeply personal. To kill him would be to indict himself, commit suicide, metaphorically speaking. To let him live would be to capitulate to the dark side. Coppola's inability to resolve this dilemma prevented *Apocalypse* from becoming the masterpiece it might have been.'[29] Coppola had faced the abyss to bring his dream into reality, and then flinched. It was not only the realization of a vision but its complete and final termination. Coppola put more into his film than probably any filmmaker ever put into any film, before or since; he spent four years of his life, half his personal wealth, sacrificed his health, peace of mind, artistic reputation, and – most finally and crucially – all that remained of his inspiration. *Apocalypse Now* was a labor of love, and it drained Coppola dry. It was a work of rare and unparalleled intensity and feeling; but it was also a crazy, undisciplined – and at times rather silly – mess. It was the filmmaker's quest that led to his own apocalypse, and along the way, the artist got lost in the jungle.[30] Even at the time Coppola acknowledged his folly.

'We had access to too much money, too much equipment. We built villages in the jungle and the weather destroyed them, and we went insane. Eventually I realized I was not making the movie. The movie was making itself – or the jungle was making it for me... I think you can see it in the film. As it goes up the river, you can see the photography going a little crazy. After a while, I realized I was a little frightened, because I was getting deeper in debt and no longer recognized the kind of movie I was making.'

After simultaneously abandoning and completing his film (he completed it by abandoning it), Coppola may have emerged from the Philippines older and wiser, but his experience cost him dearly. He had gone from America's greatest filmmaker to an empty, talentless showman. Perhaps Coppola left his muse in the jungle, and swore never to go back for her? If so, the man who emerged may have been unburdened, and more at peace for it (let us hope so); but he was no

---

29 *Easy Riders, Raging Bulls*, pg. 375.
30 Quotes from Peter Cowie's *Coppola*, pg. 127, and Schumacher, pg. 214.

longer an artist. What else can account for the absence of Coppola's talent in all but a very few of his subsequent, post-*Apocalypse* film projects? This is only one possible explanation, but it is one which Coppola himself might have agreed with; he once said, '...the man who made *The Godfathers* died in the Jungle.'[31]

Apocalypse Now was preposterous, foolhardy, deluded – gloriously so. The overweening ambition of the film's director and the simple-minded grandiosity of its original writer (John Milius), combined, diabolically, to give rise to a beast stillborn in Hell. A classic case of artistic ambitions drowning themselves in excess of zeal, it was full of sound and fury but signified little (this was Vietnam, after all, where the sound and the fury were the only meaning). Coppola was so intensely involved in the process of revelation, and of suffering, that he got caught in his own devices and became a character in his own fiction: a cross between Willard and Kurtz, the passive, indifferent onlooker and the corrupt, insane perpetrator.[32] This madness was his own creation, and it had snow-balled to such an extent, grown so out of hand, that he could only have felt, like Frankenstein, in danger of being overcome by the monster of his own ambitions.

Orson Welles failed to realize his *Heart of Darkness* project; Coppola, on the other hand, went as far as he could with his. But, finally succumbing to the futility of his mission, he fell flat on his face and dropped the ball, sending it spinning into the abyss. Brando and Coppola weren't really to blame, and neither were Conrad or Milius. They had made the most of what they had, trying in vain to create substance from shadows and impose meaning onto a void. What artist hasn't tried this? Isn't it the one, impossible goal that every artist strives towards, knowing from the start that he is destined to fail but condemned to strive anyway, like Sisyphus?

But if the darkness has a voice (or a mouth, or a heart, or even an asshole), then *Apocalypse Now* wasn't it, and the truest words in the film may not have been those spoken by Kurtz but, fittingly enough, by his clown-jester (played with exasperating authenticity by Dennis Hopper), quoting Eliot: 'This is how the world ends – not with a bang but a whimper!' That was how *Apocalypse Now* ended, anyway.

---

31 *Easy Riders, Raging Bulls*, pg. 420.

32 Coppola admitted as much. He claimed, like Kurtz, to be 'taking his orders from the jungle'. Eleanor Coppola wrote in her *Notes*. 'More and more it seems like there are parallels between the character of Kurtz and Francis. There is the exhilaration of power in the face of losing everything, like the excitement of war when one kills and takes the chance of being killed.' (Quoted in *Coppola*, pg. 121)

★

'It's so silly in life not to pursue the highest possible thing you can imagine, even if you run the risk of losing it all, because if you don't pursue it you've lost it anyway. You can't be an artist and be safe.'

Francis Coppola

If *Apocalypse Now* was the end of Coppola's career, then *One from the Heart* was the means by which he confirmed it. Yet whatever had become of Coppola's creative abilities, his vision was still going strong. As Schumacher writes:

'The core of the dream had changed very little over the years. He still wanted to lead a company of writers, actor and production specialists, all working in a contemporary vision of the studio system, where he could take the best of tradition and infuse it with bright new business and creative practices. An electronics revolution was at hand, and Coppola wanted to integrate it into a new, more efficient way of filmmaking. In April, during the Academy Awards ceremony, he had spoken confidently of his vision. "I can see a communications revolution," he said, "that's about movies and art and music and digital electronics and satellites but above all, human talent – and it's going to make the masters of the cinema, from whom we've inherited the business, believe things that they would have thought impossible." '[33]

Overflowing with characteristic optimism and zeal, Coppola was confident that his revamped Zoetrope Studios would finally give him complete artistic control of his films, from the initial stages of preproduction to editing and distribution. His movies would evolve from original ideas hatched by the creative minds he nurtured, realized by the labor and dedication of a tight-knit group of actors and technicians loyal to Coppola's unifying vision. If they had their own sound stages, then the hardships and catastrophes of *Apocalypse* need

---

[33] Schumacher, pg. 268. 'Coppola also described his vision thus: "I believe the most natural forum for films to be made in is the repertory system, in which the talent is held together as a team, where actors, producers, directors and writers are encouraged to work and socialize together, and out of all the fraternization can achieve the same sort of craft that you find in a theater company or a ballet company." ' Ibid, pg. 272.

never happen again. By keeping his films within reasonable costs, he could make them according to his own vision and desire, and never again be hampered by the commercial demands of studios.

Predictably enough Hollywood, the collective, offered at best a dubious raise of the eyebrow, at worst a mocking scowl to Coppola's grand vision.[34] In April 1980, an undaunted Coppola bought the old Hollywood General Studios for $6.7 million.[35] In order to cover the costs, however, Coppola would have to make another movie as soon as possible, and it would need to be a hit. To this end, he began to develop *One from the Heart*, securing a $1 million loan from Security Pacific Bank, once again using his real estate as collateral. He repeated his request once a week, over eight weeks, until he had the $8 million he needed to finance his film. MGM agreed, meanwhile, to release the completed film.

Coppola's inspired (or deranged) vision drew the attention of the press and of the general public. Time and again Coppola had displayed his absolute commitment to his vision, his willingness to put everything – even his own livelihood – on the line to make it reality. He received loans from sympathetic sources, a half million here, a half million there. Applying his new 'electronic cinema' methodology, he made his movie according to his vision. First glimpses of the film were not encouraging, however. Citing large budget overruns and claiming that Coppola had broken his contract, MGM backed out of their agreement to release the film; Jack Singer, a wealthy Canadian investor, stepped in and offered to cover the costs to complete the film, whereupon Paramount agreed to distribute it. The budget, meanwhile, soared to $25 million, giving the lie to Coppola's promise of cheaper, faster, more efficient 'electronic' movies. Paramount screened the film in the hope of attracting investors, but the response was universally negative. It was generally conceded that the only thing Coppola's advanced electronic technology had done for his film was strip it of any substance. *Heart* had no soul.

---

34 'Here was Coppola, always the showman, popping off again about how he was going to reinvent the wheel – and this coming from a man who could barely scrape together the money needed to purchase a run-down, outdated studio lot. As far as Hollywood was concerned, Coppola could go off on his little adventure and experiment to his heart's content. Hollywood, like the American government, had gone along basically unchanged, governed by the same rules, because the old way worked.' Schumacher, pg. 273.

35 Hollywood General Studios 'housed nine soundstages, thirty-four editing suites, projection rooms, a special-effects lab, offices and bungalows, plus a history that could be traced back to the era of silent films… [It was also where] Michael Powell had made *The Thief of Baghdad* (Coppola's 'all-time favorite movie').' Schumacher, pg. 268.

The picture still unfinished, Coppola was once again facing the abyss of failure, and had no choice but to secure his own funds. He approached Chase Manhattan Bank, seeking one last loan, and put everything he owned (everything that wasn't already being used as collateral) on the line, including his Napa Valley estate, where he kept his vineyard, his primary source of income besides directing. With the money from the loan, *Heart* was completed, but now no one wanted to release it. In an unprecedented move, Coppola decided to go directly to the public and let them decide, screening the film without Paramount's approval. 'If this picture isn't strong,' he stated eight days prior to the screening, 'this will totally annihilate it.'[36]

Unable to resist an opportunity to wield their power over one who had frequently disparaged them, the press came down on Coppola like a ton of bricks. 'How do you feel,' they asked after the screening, 'now that everyone dislikes the picture?'[37] Coppola did his best to ignore the jibes. He still believed in his picture, even if no one else did. 'They call me reckless on a business level,' he defended, 'but I've had Zoetrope for twelve years. We've never made a flop. We've never lost large amounts of money. Exhibitors and theater owners have made money on pictures I either directed or produced, or on talent that I discovered or gave their first start to, and yet they resent even putting me in a position where I don't have to go to one of them with my hat in my hand and have them tell me what movies I can or cannot make.'[38]

Coppola shopped the film around but there was little interest. Having no recourse, Zoetrope announced that it would release the film in twenty-five theaters, in eight different cities (New York, Chicago, Los Angeles, Las Vegas, Denver, San Francisco, Seattle, and Toronto). As Schumacher put it:

> 'Realistically speaking, Coppola was reaching the endgame portion of his chess match with the major studios, and, like a chess player unwilling to concede defeat, he was praying for what amounted to a draw. He didn't have the money to make release prints for extensive national release, nor did he have time

36 Schumacher, pg. 305.
37 Schumacher, pg. 306. 'Coppola had taken some beatings from the critics in the past, but nothing could have prepared him for the salvos fired on *One from the Heart* in reviews that were smug, sarcastic, mean-spirited and downright sadistic, as if critics were using the occasion to puncture the bombast and arrogance of Coppola's past by hurling darts at his precarious future.' Ibid, pg. 307.
38 Schumacher, pg. 308–9.

to assemble trailers to advertise the film. He was dodging bad press from every direction; both Chase Manhattan Bank and Jack Singer were demanding repayment of their loans. Limited release could at least generate revenue and further interest in the film.'[39]

Coppola finally settled with Columbia to distribute the film, since this was the only way he could retain ownership of it. The picture was a resounding flop; earning a trifling $800,000 in the first twenty days, it was summarily removed from all but eight cinemas (one in each of the cities). Zoetrope was given ninety days' foreclosure notice, and Columbia withdrew the movie, preferring to write if off as a tax-loss. (A few weeks later, the company was bought up by Coca Cola.) On April 15th, 1982, Coppola put Zoetrope up for auction and bid farewell to a dream.[40]

*

'The new technology is as important to modern man as the discovery of fire was to early man. We are going to turn in the distant future into a race of people who possess extraordinary communication with one another – and the language of communication will be art.'

Francis Coppola

What oppressed and finally defeated Coppola wasn't the system – as in the case of Welles – or even his own demons (as in the case of Peckinpah). It was something else, something even more formidable and insidious: his ambition. Coppola wasn't satisfied unless he was reinventing the wheel. It wasn't enough for him to have helped to create two of the greatest Hollywood movies in history; or even to have played a key role in resuscitating an art form. No, Coppola was still just getting warmed up. It wasn't enough to make the great Vietnam War movie, either; he had to stage his own Vietnam and fight the war all over again. Coppola wasn't one to take snapshots of the abyss from a safe distance; he had to film it from the inside.

According to Biskind, by the time he was halfway through his personal Apocalypse, 'Coppola was in the grip of a full-blown, clinical case of manic depression.'[41] One of Coppola's supporting actors, Sam

---

39 Schumacher, pg. 310.
40 Zoetrope was sold on February 19th, 1984, for $12.3 million to Jack Singer. Coppola kept the name but nothing else.
41 *Easy Riders, Raging Bulls*, pg. 373.

Bottoms, started the project full of naïve optimism and wound up deeply disillusioned by what he saw:

> 'One of his big dreams was that we'd all work together in harmony for the good of the project, like communists. That's why I was attracted to him in the first place. But like any utopia, the truth is there is one person who gained, and everyone else suffered. He was living like a king – the cigars, the limos, the mansions – and complaining he didn't have any money. When someone's abusing their power to the point where they become inhuman, lashing out at people, criticizing people who were working for nothing, where's the humility there?'[42]

Coppola's ambition was Promethean in grandeur, and equally destined for failure. You can't steal fire from the gods without reprisals. The fire is forbidden for a reason, not merely on the whim of the gods. Such fire also proves a man's mettle, destroying anyone who is unready to wield it. Whom God wishes to destroy, Coppola once joked, He first makes famous (and gives them a taste of the fire). In Hollywood the forbidden (but also promised) fire is the fire of glory, limitless riches, endless adulation – and the most elusive and destructive fire of all – the fire of 'genius.' The irony of Coppola is that he did reinvent the wheel, briefly, and wield the Promethean fire, for a time. But he developed a head for heights, and a taste for glory, and it was not enough to pass the flame, he wanted to hold onto it for his own. It was never enough, and so Coppola was driven to ever greater heights, impossible heights, until the fall became inevitable, preordained.

Not content to serve in Hollywood, Coppola wanted to reign over his own domain. And in response, Hollywood cast him out and left him to his own devices, knowing full well what would happen. Both sides felt betrayed, though both had been true to their given natures. Coppola's nature was to rebel against the order that had formed him; Hollywood's nature was to reject its prodigal son, to damn him for the one, unpardonable sin of pride. That's just the natural order of things; it's always the brightest angel who falls.

42 Ibid, pg. 367.

Chapter Five - The Dark, Satanic Mill: Independent Cinema in the 80s

'It's called the age of marketing. In reality, it is the age of despair.'

Robert Evans

When it comes to film, a generation passes considerably faster than it does with ordinary human beings. Rather than taking twenty years for a new cycle to come about, one 'wave' of filmmakers can generate another wave – bearing similar characteristics to the first – within ten to twelve years, sometimes less.[1] Not only this but, as with human procreation, the process seems to be accelerating rapidly. Where once a generation took twenty-five years, teenage mothers have made it more like sixteen; similarly, where once Coppola and Scorsese's 'offspring' took some fifteen years to emerge (and where Welles' had taken twice that), Tarantino had already fathered a new wave of imitators within four or five years of *Pulp Fiction*.

It's ironic that, among so-called 'indie' filmmakers, the passing on of traits through celluloid DNA – imitation as the sincerest form of flattery – is even more in evidence than it is in mainstream movies. Studios are monolithic entities, and as such they have little time for questions of aesthetics or artistic innovations, much less revolutions. The only kinds of 'trend' these entities observe is one that relates to audience tastes. This is why studio movies have remained basically the same, stylistically, since the inception of sound and color. Studios (and their movies) imitate each other, and were it not for the subtle but insidious influence of individual artists working within the system, the medium would barely have evolved at all since *Gone with the Wind*. It's only when the studio aesthetic merges (and fuses) with a unique creative vision and a work of art becomes a phenomenon unto itself – as in film noir, *The Godfather*, or recently *The Matrix* – that 'trends' change at any profound level in Hollywood. The rest of the time, it's more like the slow, steady chipping away of a mountain, happening so gradually that the mountain (monolithic Hollywood) regenerates itself before its basic structure can be altered. However radical, subversive or innovative an artist may be, he is almost invariably assimilated by the system he is subverting. The system, like a parasite that constantly adapts itself to its environment in order not to be expelled from it, alters its

---

[1] As independent producer John Pierson put it, 'My theory is we're living in a world of ten-year cycles.' *Spike, Mike, Slackers and Dykes*, pg. 5.

form repeatedly, according to the new influence.

In the above metaphor, Hollywood is the virus in the 'body' of 'art'. We might better reverse the metaphor, bring it down to a more local scale, and instead posit Hollywood as the body or organism, and individual artists as the viruses that attempt to infiltrate and transform it by forcing it to mutate[2]. The host, Hollywood, adapts and mutates so rapidly, however, that it is immune to any single virus (artist, or new aesthetic); as a result, the virus is assimilated into the organism, and the filmmaker is swallowed up by Hollywood. This can happen only as a result of the system altering *itself* in response to the virus, however; so even though the artist has been absorbed into the commercial agenda, he has also triumphed over it, because that agenda has been obliged to mutate in order to assimilate the artist and his vision. The artist then becomes a 'sacrifice' to the greater cause, as it were, the higher entity of 'art'. What is normally sacrificed is the artist's uniqueness, artistry and vision. Having forced the system to accommodate that vision, he can no longer define himself or his vision as in any way different or new to the system.

This is why 'imitation' (and flattery) is the rule in Hollywood, the surest way to strip any new influence of its originality and therefore its power. This is also why, as a general rule, the more radical or subversive an artist is in the beginning, the more he will eventually be assimilated by the medium he once subverted. This is a necessary self-preservation on the part of Hollywood. The medium – Hollywood movies – has no choice but to recognize the influence of a new visionary element in its midst, and the safest means of defusing this potentially disruptive influence is to acknowledge it and, if possible, recruit it and adopt it as its own. Since such visionary sensibilities depend on their outsider status to thrive (and to define themselves by), when they are accepted and adopted by Hollywood, they are quickly drained of the very qualities that inspired them to make movies in the first place. Hollywood gets its 'auteur', and the auteur 'gets' Hollywood – wealth, fame, and the apparent freedom to make movies, albeit strictly in the house style. Everybody appears to be winning in this deal; but in fact,

2 Organisms procreate, generate and evolve, creating new organisms towards some unknown end, presumably that of perfection. Viruses, on the other hand, replicate themselves endlessly with ever-increasing speed towards a single basic end: that of turning everything into themselves. Yet viruses are organisms too, and so far as it requires a host of some sort to live off (an environment to sustain it), every organism is also a kind of virus. So whether virus or organism, and whether the end be of evolution or decay, finally depends on point of view.

everybody loses, and none more so than audiences. Generations – or imitations – are occurring with ever-greater speed and frequency in Hollywood, because there is less and less substance (original ideas) for the viruses to feed off, and they end up devouring themselves. And while generations evolve and improve over time, copies only degenerate. If a virus imitates its host in order to infiltrate it, then, by the same token, the host has also 'taken over' the virus. It's only a question of which comes out on top. Despite the gloomy evidence of countless individual cases (Scorsese, Lynch, Spielberg, et al.) – and despite the even more discouraging evidence of current Hollywood products – there can be no doubt that the medium *is* evolving, albeit in strange, non-linear directions.

Gilliam's Travels

'Something happens to people when they become movie-studio executives. I'm not sure exactly what it is. They're businessmen who have risen to the top because they are very good businessmen, but when they find themselves running a movie studio, they suddenly want to be filmmakers. They think they *are* filmmakers. But you know what? They're not.'

Terry Gilliam

There is perhaps no filmmaker, alive or dead, who more amply illustrates the war between individual creative vision and the Hollywood system that serves to obstruct it (in the process of profiting from it) than Terry Gilliam. For much of his career, Gilliam was the confirmation of Hollywood's worst prejudices against the runaway auteur. Unlike Michael Cimino, however (whose vision was paltry at heart, and reduced itself to dust), Gilliam does not seem likely to fade away with the passing of time. Like Coppola or Cimino, Gilliam is a big filmmaker in need of big funding to bring his unique vision to the screen. But unlike those filmmakers (and unlike James Cameron or Oliver Stone, equally large-scale moviemakers, though less for visionary than megalomaniacal reasons), Gilliam's grandeur is not a sign of self-importance but (for better or for worse) intrinsic to that vision. Gilliam's films thrive on mammoth sets, elaborate productions and hallucinatory special effects, and if anything, Gilliam's weakness is his lack of weight as a filmmaker, his tendency to hitch multimillion dollar budgets to what amount to little more than adolescent pranks (mostly infamously in *The Adventures of Baron Munchausen*).

Gilliam started his career as the animator for 'Monty Python', and his movies (with the exceptions of *The Fisher King* and *Twelve Monkeys*) retain a freakish, cartoon-like quality that as often undermines the stories as it liberates them.[3] In *Brazil*, for example, the hero's comic book dreams provide a much-needed burst of fantasy and are among the high points of the film. The grotesque caricatures of the hero's mother and others, on the other hand – apparently meant as comic relief – are nothing of the kind, and far too horrific to be funny. Gilliam's inspired visual sense characterized his work from the outset – his bizarre mix of the surreal and otherworldly with the mundane and antiquated, his futuristic medievalism, made for as unique and idiosyncratic a cinematic vision as any since George Méliès. Gilliam was a genre unto himself. His sensibility was complete and all-consuming. He was a giant with an infant's giggle.

As Gilliam liked to describe it, his battle to do things his way was eternal and never-ending. 'I go galloping out to Hollywood every few years with a big bag. I want to get it filled with money, without any strings attached and have control of what I'm doing. For better or for worse I pulled it off time and time again. That's all I really fight for.

---

3 Gilliam was born in Medicine Lake, Minnesota (on 22nd November 1940) and moved to California as a boy, where he enrolled at Birmingham High School. He achieved straight As in all subjects and became president of the student body, senior prom king, being voted 'Student Most Likely To Succeed.' It was around this time that he discovered Harvey Kurtzman's *Mad* magazine. In 1958, Gilliam graduated from High School and went to Occidental College to major in political science (after first dabbling in physics and fine art). Gilliam contributed to the college magazine, *Fang*, and later became the editor. After graduating, Gilliam spent a short time working for an advertising agency, before Kurtzman (Gilliam having sent him copies of *Fang*) offered Gilliam a job as the associate editor for his magazine, *Help!* It was during this time that Gilliam first met John Cleese. In 1965, *Help!* folded and Gilliam was in danger of being drafted into the Vietnam War. To avoid this fate, Gilliam joined the National Guard; on his release, he traveled through Europe, returning to New York broke and homeless, and ended up sleeping in Harvey Kurtzman's attic. In 1967, he moved to London and secured a job at the *Sunday Times Magazine*, also doing freelance art for American comics. Gilliam met and befriended Eric Idle, who helped him get a job on the show 'We Have Ways of Making You Laugh,' which led to Gilliam's hooking up with several more (equally desperate) artists (Idle, Cleese, Graham Chapman, Terry Jones and Michael Palin), a group that would eventually become known as 'Monty Python's Flying Circus'. For the show, Gilliam would provide the animation; he chose his now famous and highly idiosyncratic animation style largely because it was cheap and easy to learn. His use of cut-outs and bizarre sound effects (often made by Gilliam himself, working under a blanket with a cheap tape recorder) gave the animations a surreal, home-made feel that only enhanced their absurdity.

Let me fuck it up, not you guys.'[4] Gilliam in Hollywood was a bit like Gulliver on his travels: surrounded by tiny creations (those Hollywood execs) determined to pin him down and keep him under close scrutiny, to minimize the damage he could do simply by flexing those gargantuan creative muscles. As the undisputed creator and destroyer of worlds, Gilliam was regarded with a mix of awe, envy and dread by the citizens of Hollywood. And with his fiasco-turned-triumph *Brazil*, he may have been the filmmaker who came closest to following in Welles' monstrous steps – a subversive genius and master entertainer who defied the system and (at least in Gilliam's case) came through victorious. Despite this (and after *Brazil* was followed by *Munchausen*), Gilliam has ironically only been wholly successful (not just commercially but as an artist) when he swallowed his vision and became a 'director-for-hire.'[5]

Gilliam's comic temperament – playful, irreverent and unruly – naturally tended towards self-indulgence and excess.[6] His sense of humor is too compulsive for Gilliam to make anything but comedies (or partial comedies; his default setting is that infant's giggle). And yet his vision is that of a fantasist, and what seems to interest him more than jokes (which appear to pop up of their own accord, even when inappropriate) is the creation of worlds of the imagination on a grand scale. Gilliam is like a fusion of Méliès with Griffith, the epic with the fantastic: a true child of the movies.

Gilliam's unruly sense of humor has so far combined with his runaway visual imagination to create some of the most sheerly original and entrancing messes in the history of movies. The trouble has been that he didn't seem able to apply discipline when it came time to shape his ideas towards a finished product. Like many genius-auteurs besieged by financial restrictions and studio interference, what Gilliam needed, above all, was a good producer to rein him in. Gilliam's irreverence and irrepressible enthusiasm may have brought

---

4 *Terry Gilliam: Interviews*, pg 109.
5 His most fully-shaped and effective films are still *The Fisher King* and *Twelve Monkeys*, both studio-initiated films. Gilliam himself provides a clue as to what happens (or doesn't happen) when he takes on a project that is not his own. (Speaking of *The Fisher King*): '[T]his was the writer Richard LaGravenese's film, which I was merely working on as a hired director, bringing his vision to the screen. I actually worked hard on that film trying to get the Gilliam out of it – and this is where the film and its making began to merge, because the film is about becoming selfless and breaking down the ego.' *Gilliam on Gilliam*, pg. 196.
6 Perhaps this is one reason Woody Allen has been so amenable to input from his collaborators?

him through nigh-interminable struggles to get his films made and allowed him to deal with the small-mindedness and anti-visionary meddling of his backers; but these very same qualities may be what got him into these jams in the first place.

Gilliam became a director by a natural development of events, when his Python team decided to branch into feature films and make *The Holy Grail*.[7] The film was shot on a low budget that famously obliged such improvisatory tricks of business as coconut shells in place of horses; yet despite these restrictions (and largely due to Gilliam's rapidly-developing penchant for piss-and-grime realism), and despite being a comedy, the film was perhaps the most authentically medieval film ever made (it put John Boorman's *Excalibur* to shame). After the film was a success, Gilliam made his solo directorial debut with *Jabberwocky*, the first case of Gilliam's absurdist (or just plain silly) humor being in obvious conflict with the 'fantastic realism' of his story. *Time Bandits* was a more successful blend; Gilliam's first excursion into medieval sci-fi, the film's success fully established him as a serious filmmaker outside the antics of Python.[8] He made one last contribution to the team with *The Crimson Permanent Assurance* short (for *The Meaning of Life*) before embarking on his hugely ambitious personal opus, *Brazil*, a project that seemed destined to meet nigh-insurmountable difficulties from the outset, and did.

Brazil is the tale of Sam Lowry (Jonathan Pryce), a dreamer who denies his own dreams in exchange for a safe place inside the system, but whose dreams become too vivid and demanding to ignore them, even as the system grows too oppressive for him to hide in. In Gilliam's fable, the dreamer awakens to his reality and tries, vainly, to overcome and replace it with his dreams. And, like Lowry joining the Ministry of Information in order to get what he needs from it (information about the girl of his dreams), Gilliam was forced to go to Hollywood in order to get what he needed, and realize his dream. (The film was funded in the UK but needed a US distributor.) In the process, just like Lowry, Gilliam was very nearly swallowed up by the Machine.

When finally completed, Gilliam's baroque, surreal, macabre and

---

[7] When the TV series ended, Gilliam spent some time directing TV commercials and title sequences for films before reuniting with the team for 'Monty Python' and the *Holy Grail*. It was democratically agreed that anyone named Terry could direct the movie, and the task fell to Terry Jones and Gilliam, the sole American of the team.

[8] *Time Bandits* was both a critical and a financial success and enabled Gilliam to pay back Handmade Films, George Harrison's production company, which had also funded *Jabberwocky* (not a success).

melancholy vision was deemed by its American distributors, Universal, to be unreleasable. The head of the company, Sid Sheinberg, obliged Gilliam to cut the film down to 94 minutes, from an original cut of 142 minutes. Via the kind of brazen act of subterfuge that Hollywood is famous for, Universal required a happily-ever-after ending for its doomed lovers, nurturing the vain and delusional hope that they could somehow turn the film into a 'feel-good' audience-pleaser. Once they had obliged Gilliam to mutilate his own movie, Universal decided not to release it anyway, and the film was shelved. Resorting to drastic measures to meet the circumstances, Gilliam broke one of the great unwritten rules of Hollywood (no telling tales out of class) and placed a full-page ad in *Variety*: 'Dear Sid Sheinberg: when are you going to release my movie *Brazil*?'[9]

This audacious move made it extremely awkward for Sheinberg (and Universal) to sit on the film, and public and industry curiosity grew to almost unmanageable proportions. (Sheinberg's responded at the time: 'I'm not a cold piece of meat. I know he's devoted to this, that the minutes are as important as the money is to us. I am of this business. I am of this process. And I'm arrogant enough to think I'm as creative as the next guy').[10] The film was screened in Canada to an ecstatic response, and went on to win the US National Society of Critics award for best film – a first for a film as yet unreleased in the US. As Mathews writes in *The Battle of Brazil*, 'Universal, unless it wanted to send out a very strange signal indeed, would be required by its own marketing tradition to take out ads congratulating the winners of a movie that the studio's highest executives had called "unreleasable" and "interminable to sit through." The Los Angeles critics had provided a very strong second opinion.'[11]

9 Gilliam did TV interviews to plead his cause. As he later described it: 'I don't have a problem with the studio, I have a problem with one man, his name is Sid Sheinberg and he looks like this! And I'd pull out an eight-by-ten photograph and say, there, millions of Americans, that's the man! And he had never been treated like this. This is a man who was very powerful, who sat in his office and the world kowtowed to him, and it drove him crazy. And it was fun.' *Interviews*, 157. The struggle that Gilliam had with Universal studios is now legendary, and is covered in full by *The Battle of Brazil* by Jack Mathews.

10 Quoted in *The Battle of Brazil*, pg. 57. Sheinberg later admitted, 'One of my personal sadnesses is that I am not more involved in the making of films' (pg. 90).

11 *The Battle of Brazil*, pg. 67. 'Could they vote for a movie that had not been released, and was not scheduled for release before the end of the year? Logically, it didn't make sense. The best picture of 1985 won't be released until 1986? If it had been any movie other than *Brazil*, that argument likely would have carried the day. But the critics who

Universal had no choice but to finally release the film and unceremoniously dumped it on the public; critics' raves notwithstanding, the film was not a commercial success with American audiences. Like *The Matrix* fourteen years later, *Brazil* was an unequivocal indictment of bureaucratic western society and offered no hope save in 'unplugging' completely (or in Lowry's case, losing his mind). Unlike *The Matrix*, however, and despite the film's misguided attempts at humor, *Brazil* failed to sugarcoat its bitter pill with sufficient amounts of fantasy or wish-fulfillment action. The highs it offered (beside those of Robert De Niro's Tuttle) were those of a radical new movie talent unleashing his scabrous vision onto the world. And Gilliam's vision, mischievous as it was, was anything but reassuring. Unable to offset the darkness and horror with humor (*Brazil* was too intense for that), Gilliam employed unabashed romanticism instead, using his mythic imagination to imbue the standard romance of misfit lovers with a poignancy that few contemporary fantasy filmmakers were capable of, or even aspired to.

Gilliam was an anarchist auteur, and *Brazil* was an undisciplined, inspired mess of a film. In this case, the artist might have benefited from the restraining influence of the studio, if only the studio hadn't been so unsympathetic to the artist's vision. In her review of the film, Pauline Kael wrote how, 'Gilliam distrusts the conscious mind as if it would destroy his creativity – though it's probably the only means of bringing his creativity to fulfillment.'[12] Gilliam indulged his visionary gifts to the limit, and as a result, the film was overlong and poorly shaped, with at least half a dozen scenes that didn't play at all. *Brazil* had breadth and scope and intensity, but it lacked depth; by failing to do justice to the characters in his drama, Gilliam sold his vision short. The film was a pastiche; it wasn't about people so much as about Gilliam's ideas, not all of which were cinematic. Gilliam was a fantasist with a social conscience lurking underneath, and at times his hard-earned schizophrenia got the best of him.

liked *Brazil* had connected with its antiestablishment, antiauthoritarian point of view. What could be more appropriate, more Gilliam-like, than chucking the rules and voting for it? It would be the critics' version of blowing up the Ministry of Information Retrieval in *Brazil*.' Ibid.

12 Kael, *Hooked*, pg. 109. Actually, the director's 142 minute cut *is* too long, and could arguably benefit from some editing, albeit not of the kind that Sheinberg had in mind. According to his original contract, Gilliam might have avoided the entire fiasco if he had delivered a cut under 125 minutes in length, and *Brazil* could easily have stood losing fifteen to twenty minutes of superfluous material. Sometimes the artist fights the right battle for the wrong reasons; likewise, the studio can be right for all the wrong reasons.

Although Gilliam had Tom Stoppard and Charles McKeowan help with the screenplay, *Brazil* was Gilliam's baby all the way, one of the very few Hollywood movies of the 80s possessed by an authentic personal vision. It was also one of the most subversive movies ever given the green light in Tinsel Town, and of course Hollywood was to repent of its rashness in supporting the movie – and then later repent of its repentance for abandoning it. Perhaps the most surprising thing of all about the *Brazil* debacle, however, was that the battle was still raging at all. In the climate of those times, a climate of join-the-dot movie-making, the remarkable thing was not that Gilliam had to fight tooth and nail against the tyranny of corporate mentality (ironically, what his movie was all about), but that he managed to overcome it in the end. *Brazil* illustrated the possibility of individual vision winning out over consensus reality (the establishment), even as the movie gave audiences the precise opposite, the dreamer crushed by the state.[13]

Brazil was a tale of defeat and despair and of artistic glory, an ambiguity or schizophrenia that was at the heart of the film. Sam Lowry's tendency to daydream his life away spoke of a far higher function than mere idleness. It spoke of the most valuable gift an artist can have – and Gilliam's own special gift – the power to dream worlds into being. *Brazil* gave audiences the artist's dream, and placed it at the heart of the bureaucrat's nightmare. Most bizarrely of all, the two seemed made for each other.

Jonathan Demme, Hollywood Casualty

'If actors and directors have a corporate mentality, then who in the world doesn't have a corporate mentality?'

Ethan Hawke

A less felicitous case would be Jonathan Demme, an artist drained of individual qualities who became a proficient but wholly uninteresting Hollywood agent. Demme's original ambition was to become a veterinarian, and he studied at various animal clinics as a teenager. He went to the University of Florida in Gainesville but, stumped by chemistry, abandoned animal medicine and began writing film criticism for the university newspaper. After college, Demme wrote reviews for a small paper in Coral Gables, including a favorable review of the film *Zulu*,

13 'With every movie I've made, there's a connection between the making of it and what it's about.' *Interviews*, pg. 139.

which Demme's father passed on to producer Joseph E. Levine. Impressed by Demme's writing, Levine gave Demme a job as a publicist at Avco Embassy, and Demme went on to work for several film companies. In 1970, Demme was working in London when he met Roger Corman (then shooting Von Richtofen and Brown in Ireland); Corman offered Demme a job as unit publicist. According to Demme:

'Corman said, "Why don't you write a biker movie for my new company?" (He was just starting up New World Pictures.). Joe Viola and I worked on it and arranged to drop off the script at the London Hilton. As we were walking away, Roger called us back; he said, "Joe, you've directed commercials; why don't you direct the movie for me? And Jonathan, you've produced commercials; why don't you produce the movie?" That became Angels Hard As They Come.' [14]

Soon after that, Demme was producer and second unit director on another Corman production, The Hot Box, after which he graduated to directing with Caged Heat. [15]

After two more films for Corman – Crazy Mama and Fighting Mad, with Peter Fonda – Demme made his real debut with Citizen's Band (Handle with Care), a lightweight comedy about CB radio users made when CB was still a national fad (Demme was hired by Freddie Fields to direct the script by Paul Brickman – later of Risky Business fame). The film was not a hit but the reviews were good, and on the strength of the film Demme was hired by United Artists to direct Last Embrace, a lifeless, uninvolving Hitchcock imitation starring Roy Scheider. Demme quickly found his feet again for his next film, Melvin and Howard. Based upon the true story of Melvin Dummar, it was his breakthrough movie, and though the film was only mildly successful, it garnered several awards, including an Oscar for best screenplay and

---

14 From 'Jonathan Demme on the Line' by Michael Sragow, American Film, January/ February 1984. Demme and Viola adapted the premise of the Kurosawa classic Rashomon into a biker film and made Angels Hard as They Come.

15 One of Corman's penchants at the time was for steamy women-in-prison pictures, a sub-subgenre that offered ample opportunity for sex and violence, the sine qua non of Corman's output. Caged Heat was Demme's directorial debut, and indisputably the masterpiece of the genre. Although a far cry from the subtlety and dramatic finesse that Demme would later develop (and then abandon), it was evidence of a bright new talent in movies, albeit B-movies. Caged Heat may actually be preferable – more entertaining, at least – to subsequent high-prestige, overly worthy Demme pictures like Philadelphia or Beloved.

a best director award for Demme from the New York Film Critics Circle.[16] With his assured and understated technique and humane sensibility, Demme established himself as a unique movie presence with a bright future – the Frank Capra of the New Hollywood. Like Altman, Demme brought human beings to the fore. He was the most democratic of directors (a profession not known for its egalitarianism), and his vision embraced the common American experience without straining or condescending to it (or sentimentalizing it, as Capra did). Like Sayles, only with added lightness, Demme made movies that were proud of their ordinariness without being dull or worthy.

Early on in his career, however, Demme got caught up in a Hollywood power play (mostly with his star Goldie Hawn) for *Swing Shift*, a film that soured him to Hollywood dealings for some time after.[17] Demme followed the experience with a considerably more joyful one, collaborating with the band Talking Heads on the concert film *Stop Making Sense*, a critical triumph and a surprise commercial success. Demme then reached the peak of his career (so far) with *Something Wild*, an almost perfect blend of the idiosyncratic with the formulaic, and the quintessential Demme film. Demme had a naturally populist touch – what Kael called 'a true gift for informality'[18] – and a fondness for the ordinary quirks of life; he sought out and celebrated the eccentric, taking delight in everyday oddities.

After peaking with *Something Wild* (not a great commercial success, it still managed to bring Demme to public awareness), Demme immediately began to flounder with the insubstantial comedy *Married to the Mob*, before descending into gloomy sincerity for *Philadelphia* (a film about AIDS that pandered to Demme's worst humanistic impulses). As if to do penance for his PC-ism, he came entirely unhinged with the grisly and misanthropic *Silence of the Lambs*, a pulp-trash movie

16 *Melvin and Howard* (based on a script by Bo Goldman inspired by a real incident) was the tale of losers big and small. Melvin was a young blue-collar worker whose fate changes in a single night when he gives a ride to a shoeless bum on the highway, a bum he later discovers was Howard Hughes. Hughes remembers Melvin's random act of kindness in his will, and leaves Melvin $150 million; the will is contested on the basis of Hughes' unsoundness of mind, however, and Melvin never gets his fortune.

17 The film told the story of women working in defense plants during World War II, and Demme was most interested in the freedom working women experienced during wartime, while Hawn wanted the film to focus on her relationship with Kurt Russell. Demme and Hawn failed to reach an agreement during the production, and Demme and his editor left the project before the final cut was completed.

18 'I can't think of any other director who is so instinctively and democratically interested in everybody he shows you.' *Hooked*, pg. 232.

with aspirations of greatness. Not since *The Exorcist* had a film offered up sleazy gore and cheap thrills with such a hallowed, humorless aura of self-importance as *Silence*. No doubt Demme believed in the worthiness of his material, but in his attempt to enshrine schlock as art, he embalmed it instead. Demme was the worst director imaginable for the material; taken from the Thomas Harris bestseller concerning super-intelligent, predatory cannibal-psychiatrist Hannibal Lecter, the plot was more or less interchangeable with a thousand psycho-thrillers-cum-police-dramas-cum-slasher flicks. Basically a non-too-subtle combination of all three, it was a stalk 'n' slash chiller with added quasi-Freudian overtones, and at its most primitive level – muddle-headed metaphysical psycho babble aside – it was an old-fashioned monster movie. The difference was that it was a monster movie made by Jonathan Demme, erstwhile auteur of endearing, spirited human comedies.

By the time of *Silence*, there was no joy left in Demme's work. Demme seemed to believe he was taking audiences into a metaphysical realm and showing them the horror at the heart of existence, and *Silence of the Lambs* wanted to be the *Apocalypse Now* of horror movies. But all he really succeeded in was being as crude and ruthless at exploiting his audience as the next hack. With *Silence*, Demme seemed determined to dispel any rumors that he was a lightweight director, and the film (hailed as masterpiece and showered with Oscars) landed on Demme like a millstone around his neck, leaving nowhere for him to go but down.

Silence was as total and irrevocable a departure from the sensitivity and warmth of Demme's earlier films as is possible to imagine. If the film had been received less euphorically – i.e., if the response had been more in proportion to the film's (dubious) merits – perhaps Demme might have come to his senses. Instead, he seems to have abandoned his former strengths to pursue a singularly unrewarding career (artistically if not financially). If there was ever a filmmaker who needed simple, human stories – small, intimate shoots, loose scripts, moderate budgets, minimal production values and relatively star-free casts – for his imagination to thrive in (and his gifts to grow), it was Demme. Instead, he seemed to aspire to having Spielberg's career (or maybe William Friedkin's). By the end of his *Manchurian Candidate* remake, though the film starts strong and was far better reviewed than his previous remake, *The Trouble with Charlie*, it was apparent that Demme no longer knew, or cared, why he was making movies anymore. The thrill was gone.

★

'It's a natural evolution from avant-garde to mainstream. There's a reaction, [the reaction] becomes convention, and everyone falls asleep.'

Lars von Trier

Jonathan Demme's touching predilection for losers – his slightly naïve optimism and kitsch-tinted view of the American heartland – was the exception among independent filmmakers in the early 80s. The 70s had been a period of collective disillusionment, and movies of the period had helped the process along. They accelerated it but also made it less painful, tapping into the anger and despair and channeling it into something creative. The net result, the silver lining to the gathering thunder cloud (besides some of the finest movies Hollywood ever produced), was in the solidarity of uncertainty, a deepening understanding of the crisis. Then, in the late 70s, as if by a collective agreement to venture no further into the American heart of darkness, movies began to move back towards 'healing', reassurance and denial. It was an odd and unexpected throwback to the optimism and naiveté of the 50s (the very thing the 60s had been reacting against), and was fully manifest in the archaic heroics of *Star Wars* – with its *Triumph of the Will* finale – and the starry-eyed, slightly air-headed futurism of *Close Encounters of the Third Kind*.

The Deer Hunter evidenced this retreat from genuine soul-searching by taking refuge in self-serving macho fantasy instead. To some extent *Apocalypse Now* also evidenced a retreat, though for different reasons. Both films wore their existential nausea and self-loathing on their sleeves, and unlike more refined, subtler explorations of the American underbelly – *The Godfather* or *Taxi Driver* – these films carried an overt message, one of hopelessness, corruption, insanity and despair. As a result, they allowed audiences to maintain a safe distance from them, secure in the knowledge that the crisis they depicted was being diagnosed (by self-lacerating movies), and as such, under control.

Movies that attempted to say something big – whether the big cuddly reassurance of 'We are not alone' or the big, gloomy admonishment of 'the horror, the horror' – invariably sacrificed something in the process. By delivering an overt message, they lost the power to take audiences off-guard, to creep into their consciousness undetected and affect them at a more intimate level, as individual stories rather than polemics. Travis Bickle was far more disturbing a creation than Kurtz; he could be lurking on street corners or in convenience stores, waiting to strike when we least expected it, and we didn't have to go to the jungle to encounter his kind of madness. Kurtz, on the other hand, was as far removed from the average person's experience as the shark in *Jaws* or the UFOs in *Close Encounters*; Spielberg's movies were bigger than life and made for bigger entertainments, just as *Apocalypse Now* aimed for a bigger 'message'. But these films didn't reach audiences at deeper levels – where they lived and breathed – and they didn't get under their skins.

The big affirmation or big negation messages of the late 70s and early 80s gradually gave way to exclusively positive message movies, for the very good reason that the negations (*Heaven's Gate*) didn't sell, and the affirmations (*E.T.*) did. Ten years after *The Godfather*, Hollywood had changed its tune and found one that studios and audiences could dance to, but that more experimental filmmakers were seriously out of step with. When John Carpenter hit his creative peak with the dark, moody sci-fi remake *The Thing*, the film was swallowed up by Spielberg's cute and cuddly *E.T.* Brian De Palma likewise reached the culmination of his form with *Blow Out* but the film died a death, both with audiences and critics (Pauline Kael excepted). Having partially triumphed with *Raging Bull* in 1980, Scorsese made *The King of Comedy,* his most disturbing and scathing social commentary since *Taxi Driver;* the movie sank without a trace. Hollywood (and the public) was not interested in thought-provoking works anymore. They didn't want movies to lift the veil off the human psyche or reveal the corruption and dementia underneath. They wanted to be cocooned by the white light of New Age healing, and sung lullabies about benevolent star beings and eternal life.

Hollywood was once again becoming the kind of monolithic cookie-cutter industry it had been in the 50s. It was perhaps inevitable that – in response to this oppressive new 'zeitgeist' – there arose a corresponding need for an alternate, non-commercial agenda, an outlet for sensibilities unable to find a foothold in the old-new Hollywood climate, resulting in a new wave of independent lights. Many of the films that came out of the Hollywood suburbs were characterized by a new degree of cynicism, and by a stubborn refusal to address 'serious' social issues. These were not message movies, unless the message was 'To hell with messages.'

Ironically – perhaps inevitably – there was also a new degree of vacuity to many of these films, which often seemed to be actively proud of their lack of social value or depth. As with Cassavetes, minimalism was suddenly 'in'; only now, the minimalism extended not just to the style, but to the content as well.

1984: *Repo Man*, the Coen Brothers and the New Superficiality

'It's entirely personal, because the audience of a film doesn't exist…the audience of a film is inconceivable… We don't know who the film audience is, thus we can only make something we believe in.'

Orson Welles, 1974

One of the first – and still best – of these self-consciously affected 'up yours' movies was Alex Cox's *Repo Man*. *Repo Man* was a punk movie and one of a small group of films that spoke with the voice of that most dispossessed of generations; as such, it took disillusionment for granted. Its 'message' was that there *was* no message, and it took delight in trashing movies along with everything else. Its director, Alex Cox (an Englishman who seemed to have a stronger sense of American trash culture than most natives), appeared not to have to affect this nihilistic world-weariness but to be genuinely afflicted with it. The film began wonderfully and ended terrifically; in between was a sloppy, intermittently funny, generally inept but genuinely original mess of a movie. It was a film student kind of movie – hip and sleazy and superficially dark – and it was a hit with the midnight movie crowds by playing on their lack of regard for everything, even for the basic indispensables of plot construction or craftsmanship: in the last half hour or so, the plot of the film collapses entirely.

The first film by director Alex Cox (who wrote the script), *Repo Man* had 'cult' written all over it. From the Iggy Pop opening score to the flying saucer folklore and Harry Dean Stanton as Bud, it was self-consciously wacky throughout. In 1984, when the film came out, it was a breath of fresh air, one of the seminal independent movies of the period – violent, irreverent, stylish and, above all, anarchic. The film wasn't only anti-Hollywood, it was anti-everything (it was even anti-rebellion: Otto's outlaw pals are just dumb wasters). One of the problems with nihilistic movies, however, is that they tend to lack energy: there's nothing that they consider worth working up enthusiasm for, so there's nothing behind them. Being devoid of purpose, they tend to be devoid of momentum also, lacking in drive. *Repo Man* was all about cars, so it made sense that the only real momentum the film had it got from chase scenes and a frenetic soundtrack. But the film wasn't going anywhere, and its plot seemed like pure send-up, an irrelevant joke with no punch line.

Repo Man was a nasty, refreshingly cynical movie with occasional comic highs, yet finally, it lacked the necessary ingenuity to compensate for its heartlessness. All the characters in the film were eccentric individuals with no apparent interest in anything but themselves (a notable exceptions being Otto's zonked out parents, who spend their lives smoking grass and watching a TV-evangelist). The characters never really connected or interrelated, and even when they did it was at the crudest level. But *Repo Man* wasn't about its characters; it wasn't really about anything, save perhaps an attitude, a style which, in lieu of plot or subtext or meaning, carried the film along. Cox was no more interested in what was going on in his film than his characters were. Life in the movie was so corrupt and senseless that the only possible kind of experience worth having was one of danger – kicks and death. That was all that audiences seemed to want, too.

★

'There's a difference between being the marionette and being the puppet master. One is a director because one wants to be the master.'

Brian De Palma

The same year as *Repo Man*, the Coen brothers, Joel and Ethan, came out of New York University film school with their debut movie, a little gothic thriller (or possibly a comedy, the new nihilism made it difficult to tell) called *Blood Simple*. The film was greeted with such extravagant praise and adulation that the brothers must have wondered what had hit them. Apparently, audiences and critics were ready for something, anything, to alleviate the depression induced by too much Hollywood product. At first look, it was easy to see why critics were bending over backwards to find new superlatives for *Blood Simple*: the film was assured to the point of arrogance. It was a smart, slick, funny, obscenely involving noir-esque crime/adultery/murder escapade, filled to the brim with as many twists and turns as a bag of pretzels. It was also about as nourishing. Highly-stylized (as all their subsequent films would be), *Blood Simple* didn't lose a single opportunity to demonstrate the Coens' prodigious talents in their chosen medium. Characters, story, dialogue, cinematography – to say nothing of the film's non-existent subtext – all were placed in service of the filmmakers' single-minded desire to 'wow' the audience with their improbably sophisticated technique.

Joel Coen started in the business editing – most famously for Sam Raimi on his breakthrough *Evil Dead*, in 1981 – and for *Blood Simple*, the Coens borrowed Raimi's frenetic camerawork and displayed a similar penchant for gratuitous but impressive tracking shots. Compared to *Evil Dead, Blood Simple* was an ambitious work, at least in terms of storytelling; but in the end it didn't have much more depth or substance than Raimi's schlock horror movie, and was possessed by the same cheeky, trashy nihilism and visceral, anything-for-a-reaction 'aesthetic'. It was an impressive little machine however, and a suitable harbinger for the style-over-substance that would characterize the new wave of independent film, and which independent filmmakers (for obvious if dubious reasons) would soon embrace *en masse*, finding their Messiah in Quentin Tarantino.

The Coens layered their films with irony, pre-empting at every turn any option of taking them too seriously. After *Blood Simple*, audiences might reasonably have expected the Coens to become the progenitors of a new film noir nihilism updated for the 80s; instead, as if in response to the critical accolades, they made *Raising Arizona*, a movie about a baby co-starring Nicholas Cage's hair. *Raising Arizona* was anything but nihilistic and anything but noir. It was a rosy-colored, rambunctiously romantic comedy farce that pulled out all the stops and turned itself into an extended comic strip. The Coens seemed determined to prove themselves unafraid of looking silly, indifferent to serious criticism. Paradoxically, for all its goofiness, the film (their most touching work to date) was a much warmer and more heartfelt film than *Blood Simple*, which had never asked audiences to care about anything besides the moviemaking.

The one thing the Coens took seriously was their craftsmanship. They seemed obsessed with it, in fact, and their films were swamped in it. Bizarrely, they made 'auteur' works that were wholly impersonal, that gave nothing away about the men who made them besides the fact that they loved to make movies. The films suggested a case of auteur's retarded growth (or perhaps artistic autism). Few movies bore their makers' mark so baldly and brazenly, and few movies so well-made had so little depth to them. What the Coens' films had in common from the start was a lack of sincerity. Their films were self-referential, caught up in self-conscious irreverence, and the Coens were perhaps closer to cinematic hucksters than artists; their films were mostly about technique, the joy of the prank when applied to the medium of film. One thing you could say for them, however: they made audiences aware of the plasticity of the medium. In the 70s, the movie brats had brought their love of the medium and their extensive knowledge of film to their work (not just Hollywood but also European films). They blended their stylistic virtuosity and playfulness with meaty stories, fully-developed characters and weighty (though not bloated) themes. Then, with *New York, New York, The Deer Hunter, Apocalypse Now, Raging Bull*, the themes – the artists' aspirations, as they all-too obviously strained for greatness – began to capsize the stories. At which point, the until-then dazzling styles of these 'auteur' filmmakers began to seem a tad…excessive.

The new generation of (mostly indie) filmmakers were ones who had grown up on *The Godfather* and *Mean Streets* just as the previous generation had been weaned on Welles, Huston and Kubrick. But unlike their forefathers, they seemed to care only about style; it was as if all the good stories had been taken, and the only thing left to improve on was stylistics for their own sake. The Coens fully embraced this trend (and helped set it), and in the space of two or three movies they became the undisputed masters of the new superficiality. After the top-heavy moral-amoral melodramas of Scorsese, Coppola and Cimino – and especially after the candyfloss escapism of Lucas, Spielberg, and Ron Howard – the cool, nihilistic vapidity of the Coens, Jarmusch and others came like a breath of fresh oxygen inside a stalled elevator.

Jim Jarmusch and the Rule of Cool

'When you go out to shoot a film with all these people it's physically very demanding. It's almost like you're going through a marble quarry and you're carving a big chunk off the side of the hill, hoisting it down and taking it back. Then you are in the editing room, you start sculpting it and you might have thought it was a horse, but it turns out to be a moose. The editing becomes a way of letting the materials speak to you, telling you "this is what I want to be". When you impose your preconceived ideas rigorously on the material, then it tends to object.'

Jim Jarmusch, *Digital Babylon*

Despite the irreverence, eccentricity, and subtle mockery of the genre, *Blood Simple* had the surface appearance of a 'real' movie: name actors (sort of, M. Emmett Walsh for example), elaborate plotting, slick lighting, cinematography, even special effects. Though it was obviously the work of a unique creative sensibility (or two), it was as professional-looking as most Hollywood movies, and not necessarily the work of inspired amateurs breaking into the medium. Jim Jarmusch's *Stranger Than Paradise*, on the other hand, was the rawest, purest, most unabashed piece of 'I could do that' independent filmmaking since

John Cassavetes, and as a result, it had almost as profound effect on up-and-coming filmmakers. While the Coens played with the plasticity of the medium to their heart's content – stretching the genre conventions into new shapes until audiences no longer knew what kind of movie they were seeing – Jarmusch stripped it down to nothing. He achieved the unthinkable: he took minimalism (and even 'existentialism') and made it fun (or at least droll). Jarmusch made fly-on-the-wall movies in which the camera never moved and nothing much happened in front of it (his scenes didn't even cut). Yet somehow (mostly through Jarmusch's assured composition and his astute choice of performers), it was captivating.

Jarmusch exploited audiences' weariness with Hollywood excess and their satiety with the self-indulgent stylistics of auteur filmmaking, and offered them the relief of a movie unencumbered by either. *Stranger Than Paradise* (1984) had no plot, no stars, few locations and zero production values; it barely even had a script distinguishable from improvisation; it had no subtext and certainly no 'message.' What it had was three characters in a room (or car) in search of a story (and a life). The film seemed to aspire to being boring and yet – despite or because of this – it offered a strange and unfamiliar fascination. The relief that *Paradise* offered was a much profounder relief than the cynical ingenuity and gamesmanship of *Blood Simple*; it was the relief of solitude after too much time surrounded by crowds: the relief of silence.

Jarmusch allowed the spaces between scenes, between lines, to have their own voice. He created a cinema of loneliness without ever drawing attention to the characters' isolation or to his own intentions. He made film itself seem like a lonely medium, but also a clean one. Reminding audiences of the origins of the medium – when all that was needed to make a film was a room, a camera and a couple of human beings – Jarmusch brought it back to just that. This wasn't a statement (as it was with Cassavetes), or even an act of innovation; it was a response to the demands of the medium and to his own limitations as a filmmaker. Basically, Jarmusch shot what he could afford to shoot and, like Dogme 95 ten years later, he turned those restrictions into a kind of freedom. He freed the actors to act and himself to direct, to create out of next to nothing. And audiences felt freed up, too. By making a movie that seemed so basic, simple and attainable, Jarmusch sent a message (almost despite the movie itself) to the film industry: Film belongs to anyone who can get their hands on a camera. And in its own humble way, *Paradise* inspired filmmakers to pick up a camera and do it as much as *Citizen Kane* once had, in its less than humble way. Only now, the aspiring followers were legion.

Jarmusch graduated from high school in 1971; he spent time in New York then traveled to Paris on an exchange program, and stayed there for a year, infatuated by French culture, literature and movies. Once he got back to New York, Jarmusch transferred to Columbia University and got his degree in English literature. Despite a complete lack of film experience, he was accepted into New York University Tisch School of the Arts, and became teaching assistant for Nicholas Ray (the nigh-legendary filmmaker). With Ray's help, Jarmusch got his thesis project, *Permanent Vacation*, funded and made his feature debut in 1980. The film (though eventually released) failed to earn him his degree, however. Originally a thirty minute short called *New World*, *Stranger Than Paradise*, Jarmusch's follow-up effort, was made possible by the German filmmaker Wim Wenders, who gave Jarmusch a cache of unexposed film with which to finish his movie. When it was released, *Paradise* won a Golden Leopard at the San Locarno Film Festival, a Best Film of the Year award from the National Society of Film Critics and the Camera d'Or at the Cannes Film Festival for best first picture.

Jarmusch's filmmaking style was as alienating to some as it was refreshing to others. If it was a cinema of solitude, it was also (to many) cinema in which the director's 'vision' was everything, and rendered irrelevant plot, characters, even the actors. Such vision bordered on autism. The sparseness of *Paradise*, and of Jarmusch's follow-up film *Down by Law* (also with John Lurie[19] and two other actors, this time Tom Waits and Roberto Benigni), might be – to unsympathetic viewers – indistinguishable from vapidity. When Jarmusch graduated to color filmmaking (for *Mystery Train*), it seemed like a giant step: color appeared almost decadent after the one-toned monotony of his early films. Though he took to color like a fish to water, Jarmusch seemed all at sea when he tried for a conventional dramatic effect. The first segment (the film was a triptych of half-hour films), in which a young Japanese couple wander aimlessly about Memphis and languish even more aimlessly in their hotel room, was pure Jarmusch, further enhanced by the richness and sensuality of color. For a while, it looked like Jarmusch had found his strength, blending the monotony with wit and vibrancy to create something genuinely new to movies. Then the film fell apart; striving for substance and a

---

19 John Lurie remains the quintessential Jarmusch leading man, just as James Woods was the quintessential Cronenberg actor. Both of them resemble their directors in more than superficial ways.

narrative, it turned instead into awkward melodrama and bad acting, courtesy of Joe Strummer. It betrayed all the worst characteristics of Jarmusch's cinema, characteristics that might be summed up by the phrase, 'the self-indulgence of cool'.

Night on Earth was worse still: more films, even shorter and even more irrelevant. Jarmusch seemed to have lost his way entirely. His idea was to shoot five different films, in five different languages in five cities across the world, all taking place on the same night in the back of a taxi cab. No doubt Jarmusch considered the idea to be 'cool' enough for him not to have to bother creating interesting characters or intelligent dialogue (this was even more evident with his more recent compendium, *Coffee and Cigarettes*). Jarmusch's hipness was all-too often inseparable from, perhaps even an excuse for, his laziness as a filmmaker. Yet it was also intrinsic to his charm, and to whatever pleasures his films offered – their deadpan apathy often doubled for grace. When the balance was off – as in *Dead Man* – there was no center to Jarmusch's vision, it was all peripheral, oblique, finally obtuse. It seemed to be willfully, petulantly eccentric, and Jarmusch's indifference to the basic requirements of drama – his meandering plots, irrelevant interludes, half-written characters and half-baked situations, along with the overall lack of narrative drive – placed too much weight on the quirkiness and originality of his style; the whole thing unraveled into a bunch of shapeless scenes in search of a story.

When the balance was just right – as in *Ghost Dog*, Jarmusch's most conventional but also best film – the director's weaknesses became his strengths, and what had often seemed like apathy or indifference became Zen. Jarmusch made movies without half trying, and a lot of the time (as with *Coffee and Cigarettes*), he might not have bothered to show up on the set for all we can tell. But every now and then, his coolness paid off, and he became a master.

Jarmusch might have had his ups and downs as an artist, but as an independent filmmaker he is almost without par, as consistent and dedicated to independence as anyone working in the medium.[20] As he himself put it, 'I'm not even considered a real director in America. I'm a cult, marginal, fake director; which I don't mind

20 Jarmusch has received most of his funding from European backers, sometimes company dollars, sometimes that of individuals (or a combination of both). He has made films at a regular rate (since *Paradise* in 1984, he has made seven features), and has frequently supported up-and-coming independent filmmakers in their own efforts to break into the medium. His cameraman, for example (Tom DiCillo), went on to become a notable director. To this day, Jarmusch retains copyright of his films.

or resent. In fact I probably agree with it. I wouldn't be good at making a film that someone told me to make.'[21] Unlike so many of his immediate peers (the Coens, Sam Raimi), Jarmusch never went 'Hollywood', has never made a mainstream movie for a major studio and, consequently, never had a big, career-changing hit to put him on 'the A-list' of American filmmakers. Like Cassavetes and Sayles, Jarmusch appears largely indifferent to the allure of big-budget, star-studded moviemaking. Fame and fortune may not be entirely incompatible with the self-sufficiency of 'cool', but they certainly aren't essential, and so long as he can write and shoot his own scripts, work with the actors he wants to work with, and make movies the way he wants to make them (and get them seen, if not by large audiences then at least by his followers), Jarmusch could probably care less about achieving wider recognition or accolades. With his devotion to the sacred principles of cool, Jarmusch is a refreshing exception to the almost all-encompassing rule that all filmmakers, no matter how independent their beginnings or how 'grass' their roots, eventually fall under the spell of Hollywood.

Jarmusch remains one of an endangered minority who resisted the devil's promise of 'all this can be yours', and refused to bow down to Mammon. Of course, the first rule of cool (as any of Son of Lee Marvin knows[22]) is bow down to nobody.

---

21 'White Night: An Interview with Jim Jarmusch' by David E. Williams, *Film Threat* 25th April 2005. 'I wouldn't turn down money from anywhere, even Hollywood. My films haven't been commercially successful in America, but they have been in Europe and Japan, so that's where my money comes from now. My offers from Hollywood so far have been to direct *Porky's V*. They haven't seen my films, just my name in *Variety*, so it's kind of perplexing.'

22 At the curious web site 'The Sons of Lee Marvin' (a little known secret society of which Jim Jarmusch, Tom Waits, John Lurie and Nick Cave are reputed members), Phil Snyder writes of what he calls 'The Way of Lee Marvin' and how he 'became entranced by his mysterious American archetype and evolutionary throwback qualities, I began noticing other actors that transmitted similar signals, as if they shared a common bond, perhaps membership in a secret brotherhood or some common ancestor. Whatever the connection, it was a deep almost mystical kinship that transcended whatever physical resemblance they may have displayed. No longer just a great actor, Lee Marvin became the ultimate expression of a certain Eternal Spirit, if you will, the leader of a strangely familiar outfit of tough guys and character actors who seemed to possess secret knowledge and power. It started with Warren Oates and James Coburn, who both bore a physical resemblance to Lee Marvin, but later extended to include many other unique individuals, such as Robert Mitchum and Jason Robards.' url: http://home.earthlink. net/~cyclonepub/sonsmarv.html

Spike Lee and the Politics of Being Black in Hollywood

'If you want to be a writer, you got to write, if you want to be a filmmaker, you have to make films.'

Spike Lee

Another filmmaker who has defied assimilation (if not funding) by Hollywood, Spike Lee came to prominence – with characteristic audacity – in 1986 with the rough-and-ready black and white amateur flick, *She's Gotta Have It*. Like Jarmusch, Lee's independence and individualism as a filmmaker related directly to his personality and temperament. In Lee's case, however, it was anything but coolness that kept him uncorrupted. Lee was as hotheaded, prickly-tempered and combative a filmmaker as Hollywood had ever embraced, and no doubt he would be the first to admit that a great deal of this had to do with the color of his skin. No one would ever think to call Jarmusch (or Steve Soderbergh) a white filmmaker, any more than Scorsese or Coppola are referred to as 'Italian American filmmakers'. Admittedly, Spielberg (and Woody Allen) may occasionally suffer the ignominy of being labeled 'Jewish,' but Hollywood is predominantly white (though to this day, still largely run by Jews), and it's understandable, perhaps inevitable, when a black filmmaker becomes a formidable presence within the film community, if he is identified for the one thing that makes him 'special': his skin. Jane Campion, Katherine Bigelow and Sofia Coppola, are all known as 'woman directors,' and if a paraplegic was successful as a director in Hollywood, he would doubtless become known as 'the paraplegic filmmaker'. There is nothing necessarily offensive about any of this, but it is easy to see how it would quickly become annoying to be judged within the framework of a specific sub-category, rather than on the merits of the work itself.

If Spike Lee has by now transcended the category of 'black filmmaker', it is only partially by putting white people in his films, and mostly due to his having evolved and extended his gifts as an artist. At this point, no one can deny Lee his place alongside the leading directors of the day, and not merely at the head of black filmmakers. But it did not come easily, as Lee would be the first to tell you.

Born 1957, the son of jazz musician Bill Lee, Spike (whose first love was sports) made his first movie in 1977, *Last Hustle in Brooklyn*, with a Super-8 camera. On graduating from Morehouse College, Atlanta, Lee (like Jarmusch) signed up at New York University Tisch School of the

Arts and earned his Master of Fine Arts Degree in film production. His senior feature was in 1982 and called *Joe's Bed-Stuy Barbershop: We Cut Heads*. It was the first student film to be screened for Lincoln Center's 'New Directors, New Films' series, and won the Student Award from the Academy of Motion Picture Arts and Sciences. The film's success secured Lee representation at the William Morris Agency but didn't lead to any studio offers, so Lee looked into alternate means for financing his next film, eventually securing $125,000 dollars to make *She's Gotta Have It* in 1986. The film won the Prix de Jeunesse award at Cannes and earned around $9 million at the US box office. The offers came rolling in after that, and Lee made his first studio film, *School Daze*, in 1988. It was a flop, but he followed it with *Do the Right Thing* the following year, fully establishing himself in Hollywood as a force to be reckoned with (especially when the film was nominated for best screenplay by the Motion Picture Academy).

Lee's blackness may have been an obstacle to his working and advancing in white-dominated Hollywood, but (as Lee himself might admit) it may also have been a considerable advantage. Any filmmaker with a degree of autonomy, self-confidence, and attitude – such as Lee possessed from the outset – is in for a difficult time in Hollywood. Studios and the (white, male) people who run them, like all humans in (usually unearned) positions of power, tend to make a point of asserting their authority gratuitously. This entails challenging, obstructing, and generally making life hell for anyone and everyone who depends on them to get their films made, and who consequently comes under their power. In Hollywood, as elsewhere, it is the simple (never pure) play of egos that prevails, and egos can only aggrandize themselves by pitting themselves against (and if possible crushing) other egos. When a small-minded and spiteful studio executive is given the opportunity to deny and obstruct an ostensible 'genius', how much greater must the temptation be to abuse his power? Said genius, for all his or her talent and popularity, *needs* the studio's assistance simply in order to work; said studio likewise needs (for purely emotional reasons) to abuse its power over the genius, for the rush of dark satisfaction that ensues.

Sam Peckinpah was only the most extreme and famous of examples of this sticky syndrome, and any filmmaker at all will have stories to tell and scars to show. For Spike Lee, being black no doubt intensified the degree of adversity he encountered in Hollywood and the extent to which his advancement as a filmmaker was resisted. But it also may have given him a special kind of leverage that Peckinpah never had, and a not-inconsiderable boost of righteous wrath and indignation. Every time a studio executive blocked Lee's idea or attempted to interfere with his work, he could (quite legitimately, but also conveniently) cry racial discrimination. If a white filmmaker tried telling a meddlesome studio exec, 'You hate me because I'm more talented than you are,' he would quickly see how far it would get him. If, on the other hand, Spike Lee challenged the same exec with, 'You're only saying that because I'm black,' he would almost certainly have hit a nerve and scored a point, maybe even a winning one. Studio execs are a lot more aware of their incipient racism than they are of their latent envy and hatred of artists.

None of this is intended to diminish Lee's achievements within the industry, of course, merely to place them in a slightly fresh (hopefully more revealing) perspective. Lee established himself first of all as a black filmmaker for black (and a few white) audiences. He was the first, and for a while the only, black director and became the reluctant spokesperson for the African American movie-going population. When Lee made *Do the Right Thing* (still his most highly-regarded film, though far from his best), he both shocked and impressed white audiences, and some black ones, with the audacious and provocative message. ('Doing the right thing' seemed to entail starting a riot, an idea considerably more digestible to black audiences than to white.) By simple virtue of the color of his skin, Lee was suddenly a political – even a 'revolutionary' – filmmaker. It was as if he had no choice: for a black man in America, watching his people (as Lee sometimes claimed) being systematically destroyed by governmental policies, everything was political (except maybe Nike commercials).[23]

From the start, Lee made movies in genuine guerilla fashion, partly as an act of war but also as a simple means of survival. But it was only when, after *Do the Right Thing* and *Malcolm X*, Lee ceased to make overt 'statement' movies that he really began to develop as a filmmaker. This he has done in leaps and bounds, and his films have become increasingly effective, not as statements but as films. Ironically – and it may be the author's own bias at work here – Lee's best movies have often been the ones that gave leading roles to whites as well as (or even instead of) blacks (namely, *Clockers*, *Son of Sam*, *25th Hour*).

Like Jarmusch, Lee has never made a film that didn't seem to come out exactly as he intended it at the time. Though his artistry, and at

[23] Lee's willingness to earn extra dollars promoting Nike sneakers, and later Orange cell phones (in a parody of the studio-beleaguered filmmaker), throw into question somewhat his political savvy and commitment. Certainly, we can expect that Michael Moore (who went after the head of Nike in *The Big One*) would have something to say to Spike on the matter.

times his vision, may have been open to question, his integrity mostly wasn't. As such, and at the risk of patronizing the most volatile, user-unfriendly filmmaker in America today, Lee has probably inspired more young black men – not only filmmakers, either – to seek out empowerment through self-expression than anyone since Muhammad Ali (and that includes Sidney Poitier).[24] In many ways, he is the exemplary independent filmmaker – never satisfied unless he can do it his way, in his own good time and on his own sweet terms. As much as filmmaking has empowered Lee and given him his voice (and it's some voice, Lee will never need a bullhorn to get across), Lee has returned the favor by showing that independent film – for those who know how to use it – is indeed a force to be reckoned with.

A (Very) Brief History of Indie Cinema

'The original sin of the American independent cinema, when it shifted away from the avant-garde, was the introduction of narrative. Once you do that, you're inserting yourself into the commodity system. At that point, whether or not you have seized the means of production, à la Karl Marx, doesn't matter, because what you haven't done is seize the means of exhibition, marketing, and distribution, and so you end up having to play by the rules of the big boys.'

James Schamus (Focus Pictures)

The history of American independent cinema is a history of stops and starts – repeated 'breakthroughs' – followed by brief resurgences of original, 'groundbreaking' work from first-time filmmakers. With only a handful of exceptions, these filmmakers have swiftly graduated to mainstream, studio-backed movies. (John Cassavetes was one of the only maverick filmmakers who stayed faithful to his roots to the bitter end and continued to make small, personal movies seen by a relatively small audience of aficionados. John Sayles and Hal Hartley also remain tried-and-true outsiders.) Though Louis Malle made *My Dinner With André* – perhaps the first 'I could do that!' indie art movie to reach the mainstream – in 1982, and Paul Bartel inflicted his *Eating Raoul* on the world (and John Sayles made *Lliana*) in 1983, 1984 was, by all accounts, the breakthrough year. In the year 1984/85 alone, Jim

---

24 Lee consistently gave employment to struggling black technicians on his films (his crews were generally ninety percent black), and also cleared a path for up-and-coming 'black filmmakers' such as John Singleton, Matty Rich, Darnell Martin, Ernest Dickerson (Lee's one-time cinematographer) and Albert and Allen Hughes.

Jarmusch, the Coen brothers, Alan Rudolph and Alex Cox arrived on the scene, with *Stranger Than Paradise*, *Blood Simple*, *Choose Me* and *Repo Man*, respectively. 1984 also saw the release of John Sayles' *Brother from Another Planet*, Jonathan Demme's *Stop Making Sense*, Wim Wenders' *Paris Texas* and Robert Altman's *Secret Honor*.[25] In the following years, independent cinema has enjoyed a predominant position in movie history, and a substantial percentage (perhaps as much as one third) of the best American movies released in the last twenty years have been independent or semi-independent features.

A mixed bag includes Henry Jaglom's *Always, Static*, Spike Lee's *She's Gotta Have It*, Jarmusch's *Down By Law*, David Byrne's *True Stories* (all 1986); Robert Townsend's *Hollywood Shuffle*, Tim Hunter's *River's Edge*, Sayles' *Matewan*, John Huston's *The Dead* (all '87); Jaglom's *Somebody to Love*, Rudolph's *The Moderns,* John Waters' *Hairspray*, Errol Morris's *The Thin Blue Line*, Penelope Spheeris' *The Decline of Western Civilization II*, Keith Gordon's *The Chocolate War*, Paul Schrader's *Patty Hearst* (all '88); Bob Babalon's *Parents*, Michael Lehman's *Heathers*, *Tapeheads*, *Vampire's Kiss*, Steven Soderbergh's *sex, lies and videotape*, Gus Van Sant's *Drugstore Cowboy*, Jarmusch's *Mystery Train* (all '89); John McNaughton's *Henry – Portrait of a Serial Killer*, Michael Moore's *Roger and Me*, Hal Hartley's *The Unbelievable Truth*, Whit Stillman's *Metropolitan*, Alan Moyle's *Pump Up the Volume*, Altman's *Vincent and Theo*, Abel Ferrara's *King of New York* (all '90); Stephen Frears' *The Grifters*, Alexandre Rockwell's *Sons*, Todd Haynes' *Poison, Truth or Dare*, Richard Linklater's *Slacker, Hearts of Darkness* (all '91); Altman's *The Player*, Tim Robbins's *Bob Roberts*, Tom DiCillo's *Johnny Suede*, Allison Anders's *Gas, Food and Lodging*, Hartley's *Simple Men*, Rockwell's *In the Soup*, Tarantino's *Reservoir Dogs* (all '92); Robert Rodriguez's *El Mariachi*, Philip Haas's *The Music of Chance*, *American Heart*, *Menace II Society*, Gordon's *A Midnight Clear* (all '93); Rose Troche's *Go Fish*, Stillman's *Barcelona*, Roger Avary's *Killing Zoe*, *Pulp Fiction*, *Hoop Dreams*, Kevin Smith's *Clerks*, John Dahl's *The Last Seduction*, David O. Russell's *Spanking The Monkey*, Louis Malle's *Vanya on 42nd Street*, Rudolph's *Mrs Parker and the Vicious Circle*, Boaz Yakin's *Fresh* (all '94); Ed Burns' *The Brothers McMullen*, Haynes' *Safe* ('95); *Bodies, Rest and Motion, Welcome to the Dollhouse, Trees Lounge, Unhook the Stars*, Gordon's *Mother Night*, Wayne Wang's *Smoke* and *Blue in the Face*, Larry Clark's *Kids*, and *Shine* ('96). DiCillo's *Living in Oblivion, Palookaville*, Paul Thomas Anderson's *Hard Eight, I Shot Andy Warhol, Dream with the Fishes, Kissed* ('97); Smith's *Chasing Amy, Fine Art*, Anderson's *Boogie Nights*,

---

25 Altman went independent after a decade of studio 'flops' – as well as some of the best films in the 70s – in 1982, with *Come Back to the Five and Dime, Jimmy Dean, Jimmy Dean.*

DiCillo's *The Real Blonde*, Greg Araki's *Nowhere*, Haynes' *Velvet Goldmine*, Hartley's *Henry Fool*, John Turturro's *Illuminata*, Darren Aronofsky's *Pi*, Solondz's *Happiness* ('98). More recently there's been *The Blair Witch Project*, *Things to Do in Denver When You're Dead*, *The Suicide Kings*, *The Alarmist*, *Montana*, *The Boiler Room*, *The Opposite of Sex*, *Rushmore*, *Run Lola Run*, *Citizen Ruth*, *The Apostle*, *Little Odessa*, *Looking for Richard*, *Dogma*, *Being John Malkovich*, *Boys Don't Cry*, *Magnolia*, *Girlfight*, *Priest*, *Happy, Texas*, *Election*, *Storytelling*, *Safe*, *Jesus' Son*, *Requiem for a Dream*, *The Believer*, *In the Bedroom*, *Waking the Dead*, *About Schmidt*, *Ghost World*, *Ghost Dog*, *She's So Lovely*, *Crazy/Beautiful*, *The Virgin Suicides*, *Crouching Tiger, Hidden Dragon*, *Waking Life*, *Tape*, *Human Nature*, *julian donkeyboy*, *The Yards*, *Monster's Ball*, *Iris*, *Ken Park*, *Igby Goes Down*, *City of God*, *The Good Girl*, *Donnie Darko*, *Punch-Drunk Love*, *Sexy Beast*, *Full Frontal*, *Memento*, *Bend It Like Beckham*, *One Hour Photo*, *Kissing Jessica Stein*, *Personal Velocity*, *The Royal Tennebaums*, *Far from Heaven*, *24-Hour Party People*, *Mulholland Drive*, *Adaptation*, *United States of Leland*, *Laurel Canyon*, *The Rules of Attraction*, *The Quiet American*, *Wonderland*, *Lost in Translation*, *Jersey Girl*, *The Singing Detective*, *Eternal Sunshine of the Spotless Mind*, *Hero*, *Capturing the Friedmans*, *Supersize Me*, *American Splendor*, *Sideways*, *Bad Santa*, *Before Sunset*, *I Heart Huckabees*, *Steve Zissou and the Life Aquatic*, *A Love Song for Bobby Long*, *Around the Bend*, *Napolean Dynamite*, *Mean Creek*, *The Machinist* and *The Woodsman*.

Since 1984, there has been the emergence of Jim Jarmusch, Spike Lee, the Coens, Alex Cox, Mike Leigh, Hal Hartley, Gus Van Sant, Neil Jordan, Abel Ferrara, Penelope Spheeris, Lizzie Borden, Errol Morris, Julian Temple, Keith Gordon, Steve Soderbergh, Wayne Wang, Todd Haynes, Atom Egoyan, Joyce Chopra, Whit Stillman, Richard Linklater, Allison Anders, Tom DiCillo, Robert Rodriguez, Alexandre Rockwell, the Hughes brothers, Mario Van Peebles, John Singleton, Jane Campion, Ang Lee, Boaz Yakin, John Dahl, Kevin Smith, Greg Araki, Tim Robbins, Danny Cannon, Danny Boyle, Quentin Tarantino, Nick Cassavetes, Billy Bob Thorton, Neil LaBute, James Mangold, Alexander Payne, Peter Jackson, Paul Thomas Anderson, Larry Clark, Terry Zwick, David O. Russell, Harmony Korine, Kimberley Pierce, Lynne Stopkewich, Henry Bean, Rebecca Miller, Lisa Cholodenko, Wes Anderson, Darren Aronofsky, James Gray, Chris Nolan, Charlie Kaufman, Spike Jonze, Michel Gondry, Sofia Coppola, Richard Kelly, Jordan Roberts, Jared Hess and Matthew Ryan Hoge.

These artists came to light through their own will and ingenuity, and a determination to make films on whatever budgets they could, independent of – and largely indifferent to – 'Hollywood'. Such an upsurge of new talent was partly a result of the increasing accessibility of technology to young, insolvent, would-be filmmakers, and the growing realization that anyone could make a movie if his heart and mind were in it. Above all, it was the response of a diverse group of like-minded artists to a demand for some alternative to Hollywood product. If not an actual 'revolution', the independent revival was at least a sign of revolt; in that it was a reaction against an intolerable situation, however, it was a largely 'negative' phenomena. After staring incredulously at one piece of Hollywood crap too many, many young filmmakers seemed to have reached the same realization (just as Kubrick had in the 50s): even they could do better. A great many of these films – *Repo Man, Blood Simple, Stranger Than Paradise, Down By Law, River's Edge, Heathers, sex, lies and videotape*, and many others – were willfully nihilistic expressions of despair, and served as an outlet for a growing exasperation, disgust, boredom, and scorn for the old Hollywood system. Yet they were also offering a genuine alternative, even if only a superficial one.

Pauline Kael's *Cri du Coeur* to Filmmakers

'The big change in the system is that everybody got really rich in the 80s... It used to be, executives worked for the company. Now, you're dealing with executives who are worth $20 million. That changes how they deal with you. The big hurdle now is getting them interested in what you're doing. They're not very interested in movies out here anymore.'

Brian De Palma, 1992

In 1981, Warren Beatty, the star and producer of *Bonnie and Clyde* and *Shampoo* and the director-to-be of *Reds*, whose fingertips Woody Allen dreamed of being, successfully seduced arch-critic Pauline Kael to leave her hunting ground of New York for a sojourn in Hollywood. Beatty's idea was that Kael apply her remarkable acumen for film, her special gift for spying the weakness in script construction, casting, etc, to the process of preproduction, and act as an executive consultant at Paramount.[26] Kael

26 Paul Schrader has a different theory regarding Beatty's motives: 'Because of her power, executives used to be terrified of her. There was a feeling in the industry that Warren was the only one who could bring Pauline down. The ultimate smooth move was to flatter her to death, give her a little power, and put her in an office until she was gradually exposed as being one of us and therefore not dangerous. I really believe he brought her out there to humiliate her, maybe not consciously, but some part of him did. He gathered a lot of respect from the industry for that.' Schrader quoted in *Easy Riders, Raging Bulls*, pg. 366.

did not greatly enjoy her time in Hollywood, nor did she feel that there was much she could do to check the rapidly increasing momentum of corporate Hollywood, as it moved towards the complete debasement of an art form. (One film she helped to greenlight was David Lynch's *The Elephant Man*.) But she did get to see just how far her reputation extended. By her own accounts, and much to her surprise and dismay, she was regarded with awe bordering on terror by the Hollywood community. As Derek Malcolm wrote of her after her death, in *The Guardian*:

'Pauline Kael could make or break reputations at will. And she was not averse to doing just that. A brilliant writer, she slammed and praised with equal ability, coining memorable phrases to castigate those she thought fundamentally untalented and to boost the reputations of her favorites… One of her chief sources of power was a network of lesser critics who she caused to be hired, and sometimes fired, across the United States. The Kaelites were a group who thought like her, even if they couldn't write like her, and she often kept tabs on them, like a slightly malicious mother hen. Hollywood took note of what she wrote, even if it did not prevent them pursuing their own course of commercial mediocrity. If a director was praised by Kael, he or she was generally allowed to work, since the money-men knew there would be similar approbation across a wide field of publications. Even after she retired, editors would seek her advice on whom to appoint – even if they didn't always take it. Kael, who was wrong almost as often as she was right, was not a balanced writer. She got stuck in as if the cinema were politics. She had a profound effect, most of all on the acolytes she supported. The rest of us tagged along behind. At the height of her career, it was difficult to raise one's voice sufficiently to mask hers. But, particularly on non-American films, it was sometimes worth trying. When she was off beam, she was very off beam indeed. When she was right, you felt you had, in some way, been blessed.'

While in Hollywood, Kael was afforded a rare, inside view of the process of filmmaking that greatly enhanced her understanding of movies, and forever changed her view of Hollywood. She wrote about it extensively for the *New Yorker* on her return, in a piece called, 'Why Are Movies So Bad? or, The Numbers.' Yet whatever she had seen can hardly have come as any great surprise, considering that, ten years previously, Kael had written extensively on the corruption of the movie business, and the all-but hopeless plight of the artist within it, in a historical little piece called 'On the Future of Movies'. In this article, written in 1974, Kael wrote on the growing need for filmmakers to 'break out of this humiliating, suicidal struggle with the entrepreneurs. There's only one way: They've got to help each other. It's a matter not of the lunatics taking over the asylum… but of the artists' abandoning the asylum to the lunatics who are the keepers.'[27] With characteristic audacity, Kael wrote of the need for filmmakers to start their own distribution company, noting that 'they might have to spend time on business problems, but, with any luck, much less time on dealmaking sessions.' She commented on the time and energy wasted by these artists 'preparing projects that they never get to shoot… The directors spend their lives not in learning their craft and not in doing anything useful to them as human beings but in fighting a battle they keep losing.' The amount of work and the inconvenience of controlling the funding and distribution of their own films might be a headache, she argued, but it would be relatively painless compared to the creeping, insidious contamination of studio interference, 'the self-pitying bosses, the indignity, the paralysis.'[28]

Kael made a strong case for the banding together of the major filmmakers and cited those she was hoping to rally, a list which today consists of many of the same lights (albeit dimmed), plus dozens more. Admittedly, back in 1974, there was a powerful new sense of creative potential in Hollywood which certainly isn't there today; but even so, Kael's argument may be more valid (and urgent) than ever. Instead of filmmakers endlessly compromising their vision and their talent and spending a year or more of their lives making empty dross like *Mission: Impossible* – on the off-chance it will be a big hit and fund more personal projects – might it not be smarter, in the long run, if they scaled down their ambitions (as Woody Allen does) and channeled their energies (and resources) into a collective enterprise? Needless to

27 'On the Future of Movies', *Reeling*.
28 'The artist can grow making his own mistakes; he decays carrying out the businessmen's decisions – working on large, custom-made versions of the soulless entertainment on TV. Privately, almost every one of the directors whose work I admire tells the same ugly, bitter story, yet they live in such fear of those spiteful, spying bosses that they don't dare even talk to each other. Hollywood is a small, ingrown community where people live in terror that "word will get back". They inhabit a paranoia-inducing company town, and within it they imagine these bosses to have more power in the outside world than they actually do.' *Reeling*, pg. 330-31

say, moviemaking is a medium that requires large numbers of people to work together, so logically, a major part of the creative process is in selecting just who those people are. Yet a director rarely gets to do this to any significant degree. This is the advantage of a repertory company of stock members who mesh together well, as Coppola was aware. Repertory companies can produce and stage their own works for the theater, but rarely if ever can filmmakers fund and distribute their own movies. Yet potentially, there is no reason why they shouldn't do exactly that. The idea is not new, obviously, and anything but simple, as Coppola can amply testify.

The truth is that similar collaborative endeavors have been attempted in Hollywood, on several occasions, but have never got very far. Recently for example (October 4th, 2001), *Variety* announced a collaborative enterprise identical in spirit to the one proposed by Kael, in which some of the most gifted and innovative directors would band together at USA Films (owned by Barry Diller and Paramount) to create their own mini-production company, or 'shingle'. With names such as Steve Soderbergh, Spike Jonze, David Fincher, Alexander Payne and Sam Mendes, *Variety* announced a 'major film venture' in which the directors would have 'complete creative control', along with the opportunity to own the titles in five to seven years. (Each of the filmmaker partners was committed to making three films over a five-year period.) Shades of the Directors Company, Diller's project never went any further than its announcement. As Sharon Waxman put it, 'Ultimately the rebels could not muster a united front';[29] the directors argued over whether or not to include David O. Russell in the group, while the fact that Sofia Coppola (Jonze's wife at the time) had not been invited caused still further friction, most of which was presumably less than creative. 'Artists' egos make mayhem of their best intentions,' might have been the headline, underlining a factor that Kael's essay failed to take into account – one that may well be the determining one, alas, and the primary reason the collaborative dream never seems to be realized.

There are only two true auteur/movie moguls in history, and they are Steven Spielberg and George Lucas. But Lucas and Spielberg seem content to create their own cinematic Disneyland, and so the two men who could conceivably beat the studios at their own game have opted to join them instead. On the other hand, if

---

29 *Rebels on the Backlot*, pg. xix, *Variety* quotes courtesy of Waxman, pg. ix. After the project collapsed, Soderbergh set up Section 8 at Warners; Payne went with New Line, Jonze with Sony Classics, Mendes with Dreamworks SKG; David Fincher made *Panic Room*.

all (or even some) of the more rebellious filmmakers joined together to distribute their own films, they could wield proportionally greater power than alone. Certainly, they would attract other artists into the fold, above all the people with the real pull: the stars, and once a few of the 'name' actors were on board, the bigger studios would be forced to string along. All that would be wanting, once the artists and the dollars were organized, would be the audience. And as any marketing expert knows, the public goes where it is told to go. Not only can you lead a horse to water, but you can be sure it'll drink once it gets there.[30]

Whatever was true thirty years ago is true today. Directors, writers and actors need to band together and apart from the studios, to develop their own personal projects. With the new technology, it's possible to fund, organize, shoot, sell, advertise and maybe even distribute movies, without either the assistance or the interference of studios. It is an unprecedented time of possibility: when standards of moviemaking are at an all-time low, independent cinema has never been stronger and the opportunities have never been better. With home computers and internet and ever cheaper, better technology for filmmaking (and digital video's improving standards), it is now perfectly feasible for filmmakers to make movies independently of corporate, committee-based funding, with a select group of like minds, getting the work to the public in the form it deserves. Those artists who achieve a firm grasp of the new, ever more accessible technology, and who join together with fellow artists on a shared enterprise with common goals (i.e., making good movies), will find – provided they stick to their vision and have the courage of their convictions – that Hollywood is their oyster. Like old *Brazil*, it will become a thing of the past. The old mill has peaked, and is beginning to run out of steam. Perhaps it's not a renaissance that is needed, then, but an out-and-out revolution? A coup in which heads will roll and bodies will burn. Like a steam-roller or a runaway train

---

30 Kael writes, '[I]t's a matter of picking up the pieces, and it may be too late. But if the directors started talking to each other, they'd realize that they're all in the same rapidly sinking boat, and there'd be a chance for them to reach out and try to connect with a new audience. If they don't, they'll never test themselves as artists and they'll never know whether an audience could have been found for the work they want to do. The artists have to break out of their own fearful, star-struck heads; the system that's destroying them is able to destroy them only as long as they believe in it and want to win within it – only as long as they're psychologically dependent on it... The system works for those who don't have the needs or aspirations that are in conflict with it; but for the others – and they're the ones who are making movies – the system doesn't work anymore, and it's not going to.' *Reeling*, pg. 330-31

that can only keep on the track for so long, Hollywood's accelerating momentum will eventually topple it over.

★

'The net effect was that the studios began to resemble large corporations. They became bloated bureaucracies, with a proliferation of so-called creative executives. The days when production at Paramount was run by two men, Evans and Bart, were long gone. The comeback of the studios would be accompanied by the reemergence of the producers through whose hearts Calley had driven a stake in the early 70s. They would crack the coffin lids, shrug off their shrouds, and rise again.'

Peter Biskind, *Easy Riders, Raging Bulls*

As F. Scott Fitzgerald famously observed, Hollywood is not so much a dream factory as a stealer of dreams.[31] Hollywood is a business, a corporation, and like any business that pretends to uphold the arts, it is a company of middlemen, a corporate parasite that drains and devours its host while pretending to serve it. Movies have been infected and contaminated by this parasite, and for the most part they are little more than two-hour, $100-million commercials for the vapid 'wonders' of America, propaganda fostering a dead dream on a sleeping mass. Over time, the artists who once made real movies (movies now made by corporate lawyers and agents and executives) have become infected by this parasite, as it filters down to them through the movies they are forced to make. Being in close proximity to this 'system' and working within it, they have become a part of it, and finally succumbed to it. In the end, the erstwhile auteur-filmmaker, now mere 'director', has become a middleman too, one more company executive peddling the corporate product. He's the public face, his name is on the product, and he gets to call it his own. But he's still peddling somebody else's goods.[32]

---

31 'The movies have taken away our dreams. Of all betrayals, this is the worst.'

32 Pauline Kael wrote of this middleman extensively, of how he 'functions as a book publisher, as a theatrical producer, as a concert manager, as a rock promoter,' but above all as a foil for the artist: 'the middleman in the movie world is probably more filled with hatred for the artists he traffics in than the middleman in any other area… The war of the businessmen against the artists is the war of the powerful against the powerless, based on the hatred of those who can't for those who can, and in return the hatred of those who can for those who won't let them. The producers' complaint about the hotheaded director who puts up a fight to try something different is "He's self-destructive. He's irresponsible. You can't do business with him." And they make him suffer for it.' *Reeling*, pg. 316–18.

Kael described how in the 60s and 70s, from merely controlling the selection and production of films, studios moved steadily into the realm of public responses via the (then little-understood) psychological tool of advertising. Studio executives devote their energies to a twin-pronged goal: on the one hand, shaping public taste/appetites until they conform to the product (so that a monstrosity like *Titanic* passes for greatness); on the other hand, manipulating and steadily corrupting the artists working within the industry, recruiting them to the commercial agenda and turning them into fully-functioning 'trash merchants.' If he is unable to quash or subvert the artist's vision, studio execs can always take consolation in their power to destroy the film itself. As Kael put it:

> 'The right of "final cut" – one of the great symbolic terms in moviemaking – gives them the chance to chop up the film of a director who has angered them by doing it his own way; they'll mutilate the picture trying to remove the complexities he battled to put in. They love to play God with other people's creations… When they've finished, they frequently can't do anything with the pictures but throw them away. That's their final godlike act – an easy act for them to live with because they always have the director to blame.' [33]

Kael cited studio men's unassailable conceit and their self-fulfilling prophecy, as comparable to the approach of a salesman who simply 'gives the public what they want.' By a standard bit of doublethink, he convinces his detractors – perhaps even himself – that it is not the supply which is shaping the demand but the demand which dictates the supply.

> 'The public has nothing to gain from believing this (and everything to lose), and yet the public swallows it… When they tell a director, "Listen, what you call crap is what the public wants," it's not just an objective comment; they want the public to want this crap, and they've made stark sure it will. Since they've cold-decked public opinion, since they promote and sell only what they like, when they say, "That's what the public wants," it's the truth.' [34]

In her 1974 essay, Kael prophetically pointed out how the steady derangement of American culture – and of society itself – was a direct result of the conglomerization of the arts, the rapid and irreversible

33 *Reeling*, pg. 319
34 *Reeling*, pg. 322-5

shift from a diverse variety of competing creative forms to a total centralization of media. What this means is that a once creative industry such as the movies (as well as all the other media) becomes chained to a corporate agenda and serves the function of propaganda instead of art. Creations become commodities, and what were once individual forms of expression become corporate means of social indoctrination. It may be that profit is the primary motive behind this agenda, but profit is not the only result. The 'unification' of the arts is the worst form of democracy and amounts to a kind of cultural totalitarianism directly (though not solely) responsible for the lowering of audience standards, and for subtly sabotaging its capacity to think for itself. As producer Michael Phillips (*Taxi Driver*) put it:

'In the 70s, the US domestic market accounted for eighty-five percent of the business. If an executive had a hunch, he would take a shot. It was a seat-of-the-pants business. There was no more than two, three million dollars on the line, and virtually nothing in releasing costs, because it was a pay-as-you-go process. You opened in one or two theaters in each of the major cities, saw how it went. Nurse it along. When the economics started to drive film distribution the direction of thousand- to two-thousand-print releases and big national buys of media and launch costs of ten, thirteen million dollars, the stakes were so high that each decision was fraught with sheer terror. Instead of a seat-of-the-pants process, people were grasping for a rational framework to make decisions, and the only rational process available was precedent and analogy. So the mentality of the sequel or the look-alike emerged in the 80s.'[35]

The paradox is that, at some level, there has never been more opportunity in the movie industry for up-and-coming talents, provided they can get with this agenda and suppress any of the troublesome creative tendencies that drew them to the medium in the first place. Studios love first-time talents, for obvious reasons: they are fresh meat to mold. As Kael wrote:

---

35 *Easy Riders, Raging Bulls*, pg. 404. As mentioned, Don Simpson helped pave the road to high concept hell. As Craig Baumgarten says, 'Don redesigned the way studios related to the material they produced… The 80s would become a period in which studios took charge of their movies. It wasn't like, Gee, we like it, or we don't like it, or why don't you try that? We began to issue blueprints. We came up with our own ideas.' Rob Cohen describes how, 'Don would dictate easily, twenty-to-thirty-page memos, single-spaced, that would go through the script from the beginning to the end, every scene.' Quotes from *Easy Riders, Raging Bulls*, pg. 402.

'The packagers offer themselves as the stars, and in many cases their pictures fail because they insist on employing nonentity directors who don't assert any authority... Movies have gone to hell and amateurism. A third of the pictures being made by Hollywood this year [1980] are in the hands of first-time directors, who will receive almost no guidance or help... It's not just that the decisions made by the executives might have been made by anyone off the street – it's that the pictures themselves seem to have been made by anyone off the street.'[36]

It's a lot easier for the entrepreneurs to push around a first-time amateur than a veteran filmmaker; the fact that the films these puppet-directors make fail to make the grade, artistically speaking – are often in fact, incoherent messes – is of little consequence to the studio-heads. What matters is that they conform to the studio demands and remain on schedule/budget etc, and that they make money when released, even if no one actually *likes* them.

As Kael lamented later in her life, 'It's reached a point where it's just about lethally impossible for somebody to do good work in the system. They're fought every step of the way.'[37] Perhaps her most poignant observation was how all the time, effort, money, sweat, blood and tears that went into making an endless stream of lousy movies could just as easily be directed into the making of real movies. This is a fact that doesn't seem to have occurred to the public, or to the artists caught up in this hideous process: the amount of work is the same, and probably costs would be lower and profits not much diminished (once the public adapted to a new supply). What would be different is that Hollywood might finally be able to claim to be serving its true function, and entertaining the public. One final Kael quote:

'In the past ten years, filmmaking has attracted some of the most inspired college students – the aces and prodigies who in previous eras would have headed into poetry or architecture or painting or playwriting. There they are, poised and ready to take off, and there is no place for them to take off to except the same old Hollywood vice – tighter now, perfected. And there are the high-fliers who have been locked out all along – the dozens of artist-filmmakers

---

36 'Why Are Movies So Bad? or, The Numbers', in *Taking It All In* pg. 15, 16 and *Reeling* pg. 316.
37 From an interview with Evelyn Renold, see *Conversations with Pauline Kael*, pg. 178.

who work in film not as a collaborative storytelling medium but as a highly individual art-from, more closely related to the graphic arts than to Hollywood… Right now, there is no way for their work to reach movie theaters and no way for them to heat up and fertilize feature filmmaking, which needs renewal. Everything is ready for an age of great movies, except the entrepreneurs and the public.' [38]

The obvious question is, why not give the public what it wants? Why persist on churning out lifeless product when it would be just as viable for real movies to be made? *Cui Bono*? As Rushing and Frentz write in *Projecting the Shadow,* movies are 'the instruments of domination as well as visionary art, they both reaffirm and subvert the status quo. Films can reveal that which is odious to consciousness, but they can also repress it.' [39]

If Marx were alive today, would he admit that movies, as much as religion, are the opium of the masses?

The Question of Independence and the Sundance Film Festival

'One line making the rounds in Hollywood… was that Andy Warhol had just upgraded his comforting prediction that everyone would be a celebrity for fifteen minutes to everyone in America would run a major movie studio for fifteen minutes.'

Jack Mathews, The Battle of Brazil[40]

---

38 Taken from 'On the Future of Movies,' *Reeling.*
39 Rushing and Frenz, pg 47.
40 In the same book, Mathews describes how, 'In recent years, with the conglomerization of Hollywood and its accompanying obsession with short-term profits and dividends, the faces of studio chief executives change about as often as those of game-show contestants. It is routine for the incoming administration to review the films committed by the outgoing one and, where possible, to toss off the unwanted projects' (pg. 23). In *Final Cut*, Steven Bach writes, "In one two-week period in the summer of 1984 the top managements of three major motion-picture companies changed personnel completely. Within three years of the *Heaven's Gate* debacle, with only one exception [Arthur Krim's Orion], the management of every major company in the motion-picture industry had changed. Not one production head in Hollywood today is where he was three and a half years earlier. Such instability preclude continuity and development not only in the industry but in 'the art form of the 20th century' itself, and one might fairly ask how discipline and responsibility can be expected from artists who know that the only continuities in the business are those of their own work and those derived from conglomerates who, for the most part, own Hollywood and are not, as we have seen, afraid to walk away." (pg. 417).

What exactly is independent cinema? Let's say, for the sake of argument, that an 'American independent movie' is a film that has been financed privately, if not by the filmmakers themselves (or his friends or family) then by private individuals (or even companies) not affiliated with any of the major or minor film studios. Already we have a slightly fuzzy definition; the only really independent movie would be one made by a wealthy individual who could afford to finance his own folly; one made with digital video for a pittance (a home movie, basically); or – as in rare cases such as *El Mariachi* – a movie shot so cheaply that the director was able to finance it solo by (for example) renting out his body for medical experimentation. Such cases, though perhaps on the rise, remain rare, and even these films aren't really independent by the time anyone's seen them. They've had to find a distributor, and have been picked up by a studio that splashes out on advertising to make sure that people like you and me hear of the film and get to see it. In the widest definition of the term, an independent film is simply one not funded or in any way influenced by any of the major studios. Tough call, indeed. The chances these days of a true independent film (like *Eraserhead* or *The Texas Chainsaw Massacre*) making it to your local multiplex are roughly on a par with those of someone becoming president (or even being in the running) without corporate backing. In a word, zero.[41]

On the other hand, a more general definition of an independent film is one not initiated by a studio but by a filmmaker (not necessarily a director) who then gets backing from various different sources – often as not Hollywood studios – who then each own a piece of the movie, even though none of them can lay claim to having actually funded it. This might be a more useful definition of independence – a film that has come about independently rather than as a studio endeavor – were it not for the fact that some of the greatest and most personal films ever made – such as *The Godfather* and *The Godfather Part Two* – were in fact studio projects.

By the common definition, *Pulp Fiction* and even *The English Patient* and *Shakespeare in Love* (or more recently, *The Passion of the Christ*) are considered 'independent movies' in so far as they

---

41 An exception such as *The Blair Witch Project* is duly noted, but *Witch* was perhaps a deceptive phenomenon, since it was a phenomenon precisely *because* it 'came out of nowhere' rather than despite it. The rumors that it was a 'true' document largely accounted for the public's morbid fascination with the film, and its success was the result of a massive hype campaign (initially independent and internet-driven, but that Hollywood soon got behind), rather than of any outstanding qualities of the film itself.

are financed and distributed by Miramax (or New Market, in the case of *Christ*), which is, or at least used to be, an 'independent' studio. But even before it was bought up by Disney, Miramax was already becoming one of the major players in the industry, so by what criteria is a company independent or not? How small does it have to be to be considered outside Hollywood? Strictly speaking, an independent company is one not owned by a larger corporation, just as an independent filmmaker is one not hired by a studio. But in the current climate and buying frenzy of the 21st century, everything is owned by something, or soon will be. A small, 'independent' company that is bought up by a major one becomes one with it, naturally – regardless of whether or not it keeps its indie label – just as Columbia became one with Coca Cola, then was gobbled up by Sony. Peter Biskind fairly succinctly sums up the current situation in his muckraking *opus magnus* (a loose and tell-all history of Miramax and Sundance), *Down and Dirty Pictures*:

> 'Increasingly it seemed that the small indie companies were being shuffled and reshuffled by the high rollers in the ongoing poker game of international capital for whom they had little intrinsic value and were no more than the jokers in the deck. Universal bought October, sold it to [Barry Diller, head of Paramount], who transformed it into USA Films, which in turn was gobbled up by Vivendi and returned to Universal, where it was merged with Good Machine to become Focus Features… At the beginning of the decade, the indie world was largely reactive; how it looked and felt, its focus and attitudes were determined by what studios did or didn't do. As the decade wore on, the two worlds reached out to each other – the studios starting their indie divisions and the indies responding with their Indiewood films – but it was a dangerous dance, at least for the indies…'[42]

For Spike Lee, '…the independent scene used to be all those repertory theaters all across the country. And those are completely

---

42 *Down and Dirty Pictures*, pg. 449, 477. As Biskind also points out, '…when the studios do acquire or create their own specialty divisions, they're often treated like orphans, starved and neglected.' Other 'independent' wings of major studios include United Artists Classics (MGM), Sony Classics, Paramount Classics, New Line/Fine Line (Warners), Searchlight (Fox), and Miramax (Disney). Genuine independent companies yet to be conglomerized include IFC Films, Lion's Gate, Newmarket, Strand and Artisan.

wiped out. What is an independent film nowadays? With Miramax owned by Disney and now October being bought by Universal, all the little people are being gobbled up.'[43] And of course even as the studios are buying up the independents, major corporations have already swallowed up the studios: Paramount was bought by Gulf & Western, United Artists by Transamerica, Columbia by Sony, Warner Bros. by Time Inc., and so forth.[44] As Robert Altman remarked, "There are really only two companies or three companies. By the time we finish this conversation, there'll be one less, probably."[45] Eventually there will only be one great corporation, with its own government, and its own movies (propaganda). Or perhaps this has already come to pass?

★

'Contrary to the popular belief that being publicized is an asset, in reality it is a handicap, both personally and professionally. Professionally you are plummeted into being a celebrity before you've made your bones as an artist. Personally undressing your life for the world to see is the quickest way to mayhem, unhappiness and ending up as an 8x10 glossy. Conversely, it is mystery that sustains your career and affords you some peace of mind.'

Robert Evans, The Kid Stays in the Picture

'Independent' means a million different things and hence nothing at all. In the end, there's really no way (in life or in movies) to be independent of everything. Still, the fact remains that, in the 80s and 90s,

---

43 Roger Corman echoes these sentiments. 'Probably the biggest change I've seen has been the ever-growing dominance over theatrical exhibition by the major studios. When I started in the late 1950s, every film I made – no matter how low the budget – got a theatrical release. Today, less than twenty per cent of our films get a theatrical release. The major studios have dominated the theatrical market. It started out about ten or fifteen years ago and has rapidly increased over the last five years to the point where we are dependent primarily on home video, pay TV and syndicated TV for our income.' Roger Corman interview by Andrew J. Rausch *Images*, #9, December 2000.

44 Edward Epstein describes in *The Big Picture* how the 'Big Seven' studios – M.G.M, RKO, Paramount, Columbia, Fox, Universal and Warner Bros. – have now been replaced by the 'Big Six': Time Warner, Viacom, Fox, Sony, NBC Universal and Disney, which are what Epstein calls 'global entertainment companies…that collude and cooperate at different levels to dominate filmed entertainment.' Movies actually account for only a tiny percentage of the total revenue of these corporations, but, as Epstein sees it, they are 'their principal source of prestige and satisfaction in Hollywood.'

45 Lee and Altman quoted in *Premiere* magazine, October 1997.

more and more films began appearing as if from nowhere, coming from so far left of field that they were off the field altogether, films which the industry only acknowledged when it had no choice but to do so. Although these films were not necessarily of a higher quality or even integrity than the Hollywood product, they were at least unfamiliar and challenging, even if only because we didn't know what to make them. They were refreshing like home-cooking is refreshing (even when less than perfect) after endless pizza deliveries. When a medium fails to change, it stagnates, and pretty soon it starts to rot; and only dead things rot. By the mid 80s, most Hollywood movies were rotting up on the screen, making so much noise that no one noticed they were staring at corpses. The films turned the audience into zombies, too. The new, independent films may not have been inherently more artistic than Hollywood movies but at least they were alive. They were coming out of an arena which was open to new ideas, out of everywhere and nowhere, springing up like weeds in a garden, offering the occasional new strain of flower. Obviously, the only thing to do apart from keep on weeding (and keep an eye out for those flowers), was to maintain an open garden.

Once upon a time, independent movies were dependent on repertory cinemas and art houses to be seen. Making a movie without studio backing was one thing, getting it to audiences another. In the 60s and 70s, before the days of video recorders and cable TV, there existed large numbers of privately owned theaters that showed old movies and had film seasons of specific directors, actors, genres, or 'themes'. These theaters, which showed whatever films they liked, attracted audiences of film buffs, as opposed to average movie-goers; as well as screening old classics and cult favorites, however, repertory theaters had the option of picking up new films that hadn't found a distributor, films made not by any studio but by independent filmmakers. As a result, filmmakers could get their work seen − without needing a studio to fund it or a distributor to buy it − through the benevolent intervention of a repertory theater owner (or two). Word of mouth could then help stir interest in the film, and the director could, if he was lucky, secure a wider distribution deal and thence a significantly larger audience.

Independent films, then, depended on the existence of independent theaters to show them, and as these began to disappear − with the arrival of home entertainment and the encroaching monopoly of multiplexes − the possibilities for independent filmmakers rapidly diminished. This left only one recourse for filmmakers to get their films seen: festivals. Initially, film festivals were an opportunity for a given city to showcase new movies and hand out prizes to the people who made them. They attracted audiences made up of critics, filmmakers and film buffs, with a smattering of regular film goers. If an independent film won a prize or received positive notices from critics, or if it sparked enough enthusiastic word of mouth, its chances of being noticed and picked up by one of the major studios were greatly increased. At the very least, the film and its makers would become known and talked about, and have a much better chance of making it to Hollywood (or at least getting their calls answered). But that was about as far as it went.

Originally, film festivals were primarily for audiences and critics, and only secondarily for filmmakers and the industry at large. All that changed with the arrival of the Sundance Film Festival. Sundance was largely actor (and occasional director) Robert Redford's vision, and its initial success was to a great extent thanks to the golden-haired movie star (who renamed the festival after his character in *Butch Cassidy and the Sundance Kid*.)[46]

Redford's intention was to support independent filmmakers and provide an alternate venue for their movies; naturally he also had a desire to make money and gain a reputation as the benefactor of indie film, but his vision seems to have been both genuine and inspired. By all accounts, however, Sundance quickly acquired a momentum of its own, and within a few years had grown into something far beyond the star's expectations or intentions (and beyond his input or control). What it became was a kind of forum for filmmakers to audition for Hollywood, an open auction for studios to snap up the latest hot picture and sign up its director while he or she was still green (and cheap).

As James Schamus (co-president of Focus Features) put it:

'The psychology of the American independent has supplanted the auteur psychology. There's no question to me that Sundance, as a culture, has dangerously infantilized auteurism, because the

---

46 In fact, Sundance '…was around long before Redford seized the reins. Way back in 1978 the Utah Film Commission brought you the awkwardly titled The Utah/United States Film Festival. It was held in Salt Lake City, the heart of Mormon country, as a way to lure tourists… In the early years it centered around retrospective presentations and seminars… Robert Redford founded The Sundance Institute in 1981…to actively engage aspiring filmmakers, with the festival becoming a forum for that newly unearthed talent… By 1991 the shebang had been officially renamed "The Sundance Film Festival" and developed a reputation for championing indie titles to box office success.' Stella Papamichael, 'A Brief History of Sundance,' http://www.bbc.co.uk/films/sundance/history_of_sundance.shtml

reigning assumption is that by the time you're seventeen or eighteen years old, you're pretty much an auteur if you're going to be an auteur, and if you're not, you're not. If you'd put that on someone like Coppola, I don't think he'd ever have been Coppola. What could that guy have said at the age of twenty? Your first independent film has gotta be your film, your voice. So now the pressure is really on from the time you're out of your diapers to be an artist. It's become a grim kind of joke.' [47]

Sundance became competitive in a way that film festivals were not supposed to be. Getting your film shown there no longer meant reaching an audience, it meant going on auction; if you were lucky, it meant a bona fide Hollywood deal. The indication of all this was two-fold. One, that the dearth of fresh new movies and bright new filmmakers in Hollywood was great enough to cause studios to leave their usual hunting ground and venture into a field previously considered beneath them – that of film festivals. Two, that the hunger and ambition of young filmmakers to cut a deal and 'sell out' to big studios was now not only acceptable but the norm, and a given from the outset. All of this quite inevitable corruption of intents notwithstanding, the fact remains that, in the early days especially, Sundance was an enormous boost to the independent scene, and more than any other single factor, it helped build a bridge between independent filmmakers and the general public. To this day it continues to provide a creative environment for filmmakers to learn their craft and develop their ideas in. The Sundance Laboratory, for example, attracts established filmmakers (such as Keith Gordon) to give instruction to fledgling ones still-forming, and it has helped more than a few filmmakers get their movie shaped, completed and distributed (two recent examples being Lisa Cholodenko's *Laurel Canyon* and Jordan Roberts' *Around the Bend*).

However mixed the Sundance blessing has proved to be for individual filmmakers, the specific cases of directors who in part owe their careers to that first big break at the festival is certainly impressive, and includes Michael Moore's *Roger and Me*, Richard Linklater's *Slacker*, Todd Haynes' *Poison*, Tarantino's *Reservoir Dogs*, Alexandre Rockwell's *In the Soup*, Robert Rodriguez's *El Mariachi*,

---

47 *Down and Dirty Pictures*, pg. 474. In the same work, Peter Biskind writes: '"Independents" had once been an umbrella term for filmmakers and companies outside the studio system that made all sorts of films, from art to porn. Sundance built a firewall between art films and the rest, appropriated the term "independents" for itself, and dismissed the others as junk' (pg. 76).

Bryan Singer's *Public Access*, David O. Russell's *Spanking The Monkey*, Kevin Smith's *Clerks*, Larry and Andy Wachowski's *Bound*, Todd Solondz's *Welcome to the Dollhouse*, Alexander Payne's *Citizen Ruth*, Neil LaBute's *In the Company of Men*, Darren Aronofsky's *Pi*, Henry Bean's *The Believer*, Todd Field's *In the Bedroom,* and Shari Springer Berman and Robert Pulcini's *American Splendor.*

Soderbergh's *sex, lies, and videotape*

'I think the reason a lot of suddenly successful people get screwed up is because they think they should feel better and be happier, and when they aren't, they think there must be something wrong with themselves, so they indulge in self-destructive behaviour... I think it's a bad idea to tie your self-image to your perceived success in the film business.'

Steve Soderbergh

The first real case of a fledgling filmmaker birthed into the mainstream by the midwifery of Redford's organization was Steve Soderbergh, with *sex, lies, and videotape*; it was a characteristically mixed offering to audiences, and a typically mixed blessing for Soderbergh.

Steve Soderbergh's mother was a respected psychic who practiced palm-reading and held seances at home while young Steve was growing up. Soderbergh's father, on the other hand, was a professor of education at Louisiana State University, and it was through him that young Steve first encountered film – when his father signed him up for animation class at the university, at the age of thirteen. After graduating from high school, Soderbergh worked as an editor for a former tutor on a TV show ('Games People Play'), then worked in Los Angeles as a freelance editor. After a while, Soderbergh lost interest and moved back to Baton Rogue, where a chance meeting with the rock band Yes led to his filming their 1986 tour. Three years later he made *sex, lies and videotape.*[48]

Judging by Soderbergh's debut film – a tawdry, creakingly Freudian 'exploration' of the perverted psyche of the average WASP male (James Spader standing in for the director), the public was as hungry for 'art' as filmmakers were for Hollywood, and equally indiscriminate about how they got it. As Soderbergh later remarked of the film,

---

48 The story of the film deals with a young man who interviews women with a video camera and uses the footage to masturbate to. In a nutshell.

'the fact that it got the response it did was only indicative of the fact that there was so little else for people to latch onto out there.'[49] *Sex* presented its credentials and telegraphed its meanings; it had 'art' written all over it. Mildly entertaining, the film gave little indication of the phenomenal talent that Soderbergh would eventually grow into, but it was slick and proficient and determinedly personal, and its sombre, confessional tone and queasy psychological undercurrents apparently satisfied the audience's crude criteria for 'art'.

After a decade of Hollywood brain-mashing, audiences were losing the capacity to tell art from pretension; the film made them feel uneasy and slightly guilty, and it was anything but comfortable, so it must be art. The combined will of critics, audiences, and the Sundance festival in toto was to find art and hail it; taking the lead from Soderbergh and acquiescing to the movie's suggestion of depth, that was exactly what they did. The movie was greeted as a masterpiece and Soderbergh as a new auteur; the critics had their darling, audiences had their highbrow entertainment and Sundance established its credibility and its 'cause' both. Soderbergh, on the other hand, had nowhere to go but down.[50] His choice to make *Kafka* for his next film seemed deliberately intended to destroy a career that had created itself out of next-to-nothing, as if to fulfil his own prophecy, perhaps. More importantly, Soderbergh chose to make a movie almost guaranteed to turn audiences off and critics against him, to minimize the damage of an unearned reputation before it became critical. In his own words, 'I decided I would go out in flames by making a film that really had a big red bull's eye on its chest.'[51] Franz Kafka was a dead Polish writer notorious (among people who had never read him) for his gloomy, existential indecipherability, and for a nigh-autistic self-scrutiny that bordered on self-loathing (not to mention that most un-Hollywood of traits, a complete indifference to his readers).[52]

Kafka was also a writer that no one in Hollywood – however familiar they might be with his name – had ever read; nor did they have

49 *Down and Dirty Pictures*, by Peter Biskind, pg. 41

50 And said as much when the film won Palme d'Or at Cannes: 'It's all downhill from here.' True to his word, his next five films, *Kafka*, *King of the Hill*, *The Underneath*, *Schizopolis* and *Gray's Anatomy*, were all commercial flops. By the time of his 'comeback' in 1998 (with *Out of Sight*), Soderbergh seemed to have been lost to posterity.

51 *Down and Dirty Pictures*, pg. 79.

52 Kafka requested all his works – at the time unpublished – be destroyed on his death; his friend Max Brody deliberated a long time but finally defied this wish. Had Kafka got his way, however, no one would ever have heard of Kafka.

any intention of reading him, ever. (Besides the trade papers, no one reads in Hollywood.) Soderbergh's choice to make a film about Kafka (not one adapted from any of his novels – as Welles had done with *The Trial* – but a fictional treatment of the writer himself) was essentially an act of defiance. It was Soderbergh saying, 'You want art? I'll give you art until you choke on it.' Which is exactly what studios, critics and audiences did with *Kafka*. The film received almost no favorable notices and sank without a trace, taking Soderbergh along with it, into the murky depths. At the time, Soderbergh's tale was the shortest success story ever told. It was also a harbinger of things to come.

By the late 80s and early 90s, studios were betraying a near frenzy to discover new filmmakers and back them, like race horses, in the hope of backing a winner and raking in both dollars and kudos. In consequence, most of the time – since there are always more losers than winners – filmmakers were disappearing almost as rapidly as they surfaced. Studios wanted to back a winner and, in their arrogance, they believed they could make a winner, too, that their belief and their dollars (and the public's susceptibility to advertising) was enough. In most cases, it wasn't. A filmmaker is not a horse, and his success and growth as an artist depend on more than good breeding, a healthy diet and a good jockey to ride him (or her). There are psychological factors, factors which studios are not only oblivious of but outright hostile to; any budding filmmaker who is suddenly hailed as a genius – thrust without warning from total anonymity to wealth and fame, Hollywood-style – is likely to have problems adapting. He or she is still the same person they were a week ago, after all, before being plucked out of the herd and anointed as the new Messiah. Unless he or she is temperamentally equipped (like Tarantino) to enjoy endless attention, flattery, adoration and a ceaseless stream of superlatives coming at them 24/7, they will probably lose the thread altogether. In desperation, they will be happy to go along with whatever the studio suggests and give it what it wants, just so long as the gods of chance continue to favor them. Either that or, like Soderbergh, they will react against the temptations and pull in exactly the opposite direction, consciously (or not) shooting themselves in the foot to get *out* of the running, back on safe (and sane) ground.

Consumer culture is about products being manufactured in order to be sold and consumed – as many and as rapidly as possible. The only criteria of success in such a culture is numbers: it is quantity, not quality, that counts. If a product is consumed, it is good; if not, it is bad and will be discontinued. In the 80s and 90s, not only movies but filmmakers themselves began to behave as they were treated, like products. The faster they could be 'manufactured' (discovered, backed and put to work), the better; and if most of them turned out to be faulty products, that was no big deal, they could be discontinued with equal speed and indifference, and there were plenty more where they came from. On such a factory line, the individual artist was likely to wind up feeling like meat in a grinder or grain in a mill: if he survived the process at all, it was in a vastly diminished form.

There were rare cases, however, of filmmakers who neither succumbed to the process nor tried futilely to resist it, but instead embraced the grueling experience of corporate movie production as a necessary initiation – albeit into a dark, satanic realm. Instead of being ground to dust, they allowed themselves to be refined into smarter, stronger, more enlightened filmmakers. These rare exceptions only proved the rule, true; but they also proved it could be broken.

Chapter Six - Bitch Goddess and Muse: Trash, Art and the Hollywood Trap

'We professional experimenters have inherited an old tradition. Some of us have been the greatest of artists, but we never made our muses into our mistresses… Our work, once it is finished, doesn't have the importance that most aesthetes give it. It's the act that interests me, not the result, and I'm only taken in by the result when it reeks of human sweat, or of a thought.'

Orson Welles in interview with André Bazin and Charles Bitsch, 1958

By temperament, writers tend to be introspective, and the nature of writing (and that of books in general) is of looking inward, of philosophical thought and reflection, in a word: the quest for meaning. Filmmakers on the other hand tend to be expansive personalities, and the nature of movies is likewise extroverted, outward-looking, drawn towards action, adventure, melodrama and superficiality. In a word, the quest for sensation. Audiences for movies (especially American movies) are not generally made up of literary people, or rather, the prevailing mood of audiences (even when made up of critics) is not so much a reflective, intellectual mood as a wide-eyed, 'surprise me' mood. It is this slightly infantile, sensation-seeking tendency − a mix of anticipation and wonder − that Hollywood works so hard to keep alive in audiences, and to provoke (if not satisfy) with its endless motion picture products. Since movies are naturally disposed towards impressing and delighting us (where books are more geared towards stimulating thought and reflection), it is natural for the majority of filmmakers to be likewise inclined, and for the showperson to be given at least as much respect, freedom and encouragement as the artist.[1]

When the director-showman takes prominence over the artist-writer, a filmmaker will be that much more in harmony with the prevailing order (hierarchy) in Hollywood, and consequently that much more likely to be a commercial success. Inseparably linked to this is the increased possibility that the filmmaker will lose his way as an artist and fall into the Hollywood Trap − a process commonly known as 'selling out'. On the other hand, the more the introspective, writer side

---

[1] The potential dichotomy of the two roles − or poles − can be seen at play in the work of writer-directors: what the writer composes, the director often dismisses.

of a filmmaker dominates, the closer the filmmaker is to his inspiration and creativity, and the less likely he is to be sidetracked by the allure and temptations of 'show business'; in consequence, his films (being equally introspective and reflective) are correspondingly less likely to be successful.

It may seem redundant to say that the more a filmmaker compromises his creativity, the more likely he is to be successful in Hollywood. But perhaps both these possibilities are really complementary side-effects of a filmmaker's overall preference for sensation-based material, as opposed to material based on content. Movies that are 'mindless' (that can still be great but are never going to be philosophic works) come that much closer to what audiences want from a movie: forgetfulness, visceral involvement devoid of any relation to their own lives. Filmmakers that enjoy 'mindlessness' (images, sound, and motion for its own sweet sake) are plainly going to advance in the Hollywood climate; but they are also likely to burn out that much quicker, when it comes to their own inspiration, purpose and integrity as artists.

Examples of this are legion and we will get to them presently. Examples of filmmakers unable to make 'mindless' movies even when they try, those who are compelled to make films primarily as a means to explore personal, philosophical questions, are, of course, extremely few, and rarely if ever are they successful in Hollywood. But such filmmakers tend to remain true to their inspiration and more or less immune to the insidious influences of commercial opportunism. Perhaps this is partially because they have fewer temptations to resist – it's easy not to sell out when no one is offering – but it may also be that such artists owe their allegiance to their muse, and are more interested in pursuing new ideas – and in the process of creation itself – than the rewards of financial (or critical) success. This in a nutshell is the difference between an artist and someone who, however gifted and inspired they may be as a filmmaker, is essentially and at heart, no more than a simple entertainer.[2]

---

2 The world's most successful and revered filmmaker, Alfred Hitchcock, was the epitome of the artist-as-showman, and made no bones about it. 'I don't care about content at all. The film can be about anything you like, so long as I'm making the audience react in a certain way to whatever I put on the screen... That's what I mean by pure film. The way you put it together to create an emotion... I'm a professional. I don't put my personal feelings into pictures. I don't indulge myself – I don't make pictures to please me. I make them to please audiences.' *Alfred Hitchcock Interviews*, pg. 70, 79, 113.

The Suburbia of the Unconscious: Richard Linklater's *Slacker* and *Waking Life*

'It's probably the theory of all our lives if you think about it. It's not very active, I've been criticized for like oh, you have a very passive protagonist; he doesn't do that much. I'm like, most people don't. Most people are receptors. We're receptors, we're like, breathers and receptors.'

Richard Linklater

Politically, the 80s were a dark decade in the US, with the aggressively regressive policies of Reagan and the fundamentalist right calling for a return to 'traditional' values. As always, this was reflected in (and by) Hollywood, which likewise adopted more stolid, cynical values, and began to cater to the conservative, rather than the rebel, within. The overall effort was to realize the impossible, to return to the optimistic complacency of the 50s and re-embrace the very same values that the counterculture of the 60s had worked so hard (and howled so loudly) to eradicate. Reaganomics offered the masses the comfort of a see-no-evil, hear-no-evil, speak-no-evil sleepy state of denial, as well as extra perks for the rich, and a new, shiny sense of pride and patriotism (free from self-analysis) for the rest of the public. Through all of this, the darker, more totalitarian undercurrents went largely overlooked.

The general American public had never really trusted the counterculture, and knowing the old traditional values were obsolete was no reason not to take refuge behind them when the alternative was sheer anarchy. In the 80s things went to the opposite extreme, to an almost grotesque degree and as a result – like a pendulum swinging forever back and forth – there was a growing hope (among those not-fooled by the New American Optimism) that the 90s would be a decade of revolutionary new ideologies and artistic renaissance. In the words of a quickly-forgotten pot-boiler flick, *Flashback* – with Dennis Hopper as a former hippie turned business entrepreneur – the 90s were 'going to make the 60s look like the 50s.' Of course they didn't, and politically the Clinton era was little different from that of Reagan and Bush save in the superficialities. Hollywood did not exactly embark on a new course of experimentalism, either, but persisted stubbornly in the slow transubstantiation of movies into tools of mass stupefaction (and vehicles for corporate advertising). Independently speaking, however, the new new wave that had kicked off in the 80s, and started picking up steam in 1989 with Sundance, was, by 1991, bringing to mainstream audiences new kinds of movies the like of which they had never seen before; at the same time, it offered expression to artists who had previously had no voice at all, and certainly not in Hollywood.

Slacker introduced audiences to what would become known as 'the neo-hippie,' at once making apparent that – whatever the general public might have believed about the counterculture – it was alive and well, and rapidly mutating in ways both unexpected and disturbing. Made on a shoestring in 1991 by Richard Linklater, *Slacker* was both about and from a generation of kids who were dropping out, tuning in, and turning on without ever bothering to announce their intentions to anyone, or even being fully conscious of it themselves. 'Slackers' represented not only a new facet of audiences but a new sensibility on the part of filmmakers, a sensibility resolutely and irredeemably disaffected, alien and independent.

Of all the American filmmakers to come to prominence in the 90s – with the possible exception of Hal Hartley (see Appendix) – Linklater is the most intellectually searching, stubbornly esoteric and open-minded. He is also the one who has so far come closest to breaking out the 'box' of Hollywood homogeneity and reinventing the medium to suit his own personal vision (most successfully with *Waking Life*). With *Slacker*, Linklater was a slacker from Texas who made a movie set in Texas about slackers in Texas. The narrative of the film was no more complex than a series of chance encounters-cum-dialogues between young suburbans drifting in and out of one another's lives on a summer's afternoon. The film was shot in real time in a blissfully simple blend of dream logic with ultra-mundane realism (a blend that Linklater would later perfect for *Waking Life*). A big part of *Slacker*'s charm was how it gave audiences the chance to see a director finding his feet in film; essentially it was a home movie that happened to capture (and helped define) a zeitgeist, a collective mood and attitude prevalent at the time, that of disaffection combined with intense curiosity. From Linklater's refreshingly schizoid perspective, sanity was just another word for small-mindedness.

In its own way, albeit on a far smaller, more makeshift level, *Slacker* was as much the voice of a generation as *Easy Rider* had been twenty years earlier; like Hopper's film, it opened the gates to a whole slew of independent (home) moviemakers, just waiting for their cue. By speaking to (and for) slackers everywhere, Linklater's movie challenged and gently goaded young people to find their own cameras and do the same. The irony of the film was that, while it helped a generation of drop-outs to find a clearer sense of identity *as* drop-outs, it also gave them the inspiration to *do* something and turn their apathy and indifference into creativity. The slackers of the film weren't losers in the usual sense. They were intelligent, lively, creative people who chose to do nothing as a considered (even strategic) response to a culture that offered nothing by way of career paths or role models, a society devoid of any values worth adopting or upholding. The *Slacker* ethos was the passive equivalent of Brando's *The Wild One*: whatever society had to offer was to be rejected, not angrily but knowingly, resignedly, it being a long-foregone conclusion that whatever was good enough for previous generations wasn't good enough anymore.

One thing slackers (Linklater foremost amongst them) were interested in was ideas. They were interested in questioning, not necessarily to find answers but for the simple enjoyment of going deeper. *Slacker* was archetypal cinema in the raw; it was about the quest for meaning and identity in a world apparently empty of both. Crude and awkward as the film was, it was a sharp and witty reminder that movies didn't have to be mindless fantasies divorced from everyday reality, bogged down by jaded assumptions and tired clichés about what kids really wanted. Movies could also be bona fide journeys into unexplored areas of human experience. They could take us on a field trip around the local neighborhood and, at the same time, venture into the suburbia of the unconscious. Real drama was right outside the front door. You just had to go and find it.

Zen and the Art of Selling Out: Quentin Tarantino's Adolescent Infatuation

'There's no way for pictures to be saved from premature senility unless the artists finally abandon the whole crooked system of Hollywood bookkeeping, with its kited budgets and trick percentages. Most directors are signed up for only one picture now, but after the deal is made the director gets the full de-luxe ritual: fancy hotels, first-class travel, expense money to maintain cool, silky blond groupies for traveling companions. The directors are like calves being fattened – all on the budget of the picture.'

Pauline Kael, 'On the Future of Movies'

The insidious temptations of the Hollywood life are well-documented. They are even said to account, as the above quote testifies and to a degree at least, for the tendency of movie budgets to run wild, as funds are swallowed up not by the film itself but by the on-going process of 'fattening the calf.' Sam Peckinpah was fond of referring to himself as a whore, yet he was so acutely aware of this possibility that in many ways he was the filmmaker who least deserved the description, and who least prostituted himself. Peckinpah was a maverick to the end; Quentin Tarantino, on the other hand, the world's first instant superstar director, was never cursed with such in-born integrity. An auteur with a love of junk culture who made popular movies for the masses, Tarantino lacked the rebel spirit of a great artist. Because of his tastes and temperament, Tarantino could thrive within the system; he could become the Steven Spielberg of the B-movie. Certainly, there were worse fates for an entertainer to suffer than that.[3]

Tarantino rose to unprecedented heights of popular success and critical acclaim with his first feature, in 1992 (*Reservoir Dogs*), and became both the beneficiary and the embodiment of the new wave of commercial independent cinema. He brought independent cinema to the mainstream by bringing the 'trash' aesthetic to it and, as a result, he had Hollywood eating out of his hand within a couple of years. Apparently the movie industry, waiting for a new wunderkind to groom and fatten with success, had chosen Tarantino. Starting with Sundance, where *Dogs* premiered, the publicity machine ground into motion, and within three years of his debut film, 'Quentin Tarantino' had become a Hollywood franchise. What took Scorsese and Demme almost a decade to achieve, Tarantino attained with two movies. Talented as he was, his rise to superstardom was way out of proportion with his actual accomplishments, however.

If *Reservoir Dogs* was meant as a kind of postmodern, urban-gothic, ultraviolent comedy, it came across as slick and shallow melodrama; what made it stand out above ordinary video-exploitation fare however was the quality of the dialogue. Tarantino may not have been a great writer, but he was definitely a writer, and the ecstatic reaction to *Reservoir Dogs* wasn't so much because Tarantino did it so well, but that he did it at all. *Reservoir Dogs* was a movie in which literally everyone wound up dead, and there wasn't a moment of regret or sympathy afforded for the characters. Tarantino wasn't interested in audience sympathy; his hip nihilism precluded it. He took a more ironic, detached approach; indifferent to invoking emotions, *Reservoir Dogs* was probably the coldest popular American movie since *Full Metal Jacket*, yet audiences responded to the freshness of Tarantino's approach, his cynicism and lack of sentimentality. *Dogs* was far superior to your average shoot 'em up – there was clearly a sensibility at work, and Tarantino was trying for something different, something fresh. The distancing effect the film

3 At least this way, he might go on providing his fans with the kind of bubble-gum they want. Judging by *Kill Bill Volumes 1* and *2*, this was the route Tarantino chose.

had on the audience was its most striking feature.

Audiences, especially hip, 'art house' audiences, love to play along with what they see as a filmmaker's games. They like to feel they're in on something that other people are missing, and a lot of people who hated *Dogs* no doubt felt square about saying so, or admitting distaste for Tarantino's predilection for sadistic violence. Violence was hip, and if you didn't think so, that just made you square. Tarantino was a man whose time had come and *Reservoir Dogs* was defended, even lauded, by people who might normally have known better but who didn't want to be landed with the squares. *Reservoir Dogs* was praised above all for what it pretended to be rather than what it actually was. Tarantino set out to make a kinetic, explosive, ferociously original, gritty, cynical and crackling comedy, the last word on the tough-guy movie ethic and the first word on a new kind of absurdist nihilism, and that was what people responded to. No one seemed to notice or care how shallow Tarantino's film was; the buzz was on and nothing could stop the rise of the new American auteur. Two years later, with the release of *Pulp Fiction*, Tarantino became the most famous film director in the world.

If we compare Tarantino's career with Brian De Palma's (for whom Tarantino expresses special admiration) we can put things into perspective. As we have seen, De Palma's first films, *The Wedding Party*, *Greetings*, *Get to Know Your Rabbit*, *Hi Mom!* (from 1968-71) were raw, amateurish, often inspired films independently funded (with the exception of *Rabbit*); they were rough-edged, clumsy, eccentric works that little by little attracted a cult audience but far from catapulted their maker to fame or wealth. With *Sisters*, De Palma took a step towards commercial filmmaking, then with *Phantom of the Paradise*, he literally exploded onto the screen. With *Obsession* and then *Carrie*, De Palma became a 'major-league player' in Hollywood, after a ten-year struggle. Tarantino, on the other hand, spent his formative years working in a video store watching movies; he never went to film school, spent his free time writing scripts (with Roger Avary), and one day decided to raise the money to make his own movie. The script for *Reservoir Dogs*[4] caught the attention of Harvey Keitel, who agreed to star in and co-produce the film on the strength of Tarantino's writing. With the blessing of one of the patron saints of independent cinema it was plain sailing all the way, and in a single bound, the young (twenty-nine), inexperienced film fanatic went from one of a legion of movie geeks to 'the most talented and promising American filmmaker of his generation.'[TM]

---

4 Tarantino abandoned hopes to film his first scripts, *True Romance* and *Natural Born Killers*, after much hassle and endless frustration, and wrote *Reservoir Dogs*.

Reservoir Dogs was probably the most profoundly overrated movie debut since Soderbergh's *sex, lies and videotape*, and if Tarantino had followed it up with a clunker, he might have disappeared as rapidly and totally as Soderbergh did after making *Kafka*. Instead, he came up with the hype phenomenon of the 90s and the 'true, new face of independent cinema' (for better or for worse) – *Pulp Fiction*. *Pulp Fiction* – the film that Peter Biskind called 'the *Star Wars* of independents' – was the first 'indie' movie to break the $100 million barrier and compete with the studio blockbusters, and it was with *Pulp Fiction*, more or less, that, as James Schamus put it, 'The independent film business became a hit business, just like Hollywood.' For Allison Anders, the film's 'victory was sort of the beginning of the end for the rest of us, because very few indie films can compete... It became a problem for non-genre, character-driven stuff...slow-moving tales with no violence, and no big stars...that kind of put an end to the dream that we had in the early 90s.'[5]

★

'Writers tend to approach the creation of drama too much in terms of words, failing to realize that the greatest force they have is the mood and feeling they can produce in the audience through the actor. They tend to see the actor grudgingly, as someone likely to ruin what they have written, rather than seeing that the actor is in every sense their medium. You might wonder, as a result of this, whether directing was anything more or less than a continuation of the writing. I think that is precisely what directing should be. It would follow, then, that a writer-director is really the perfect dramatic instrument; and the few examples we have where these two peculiar techniques have been properly mastered by one man have, I believe, produced the most consistently fine work. When the director is not his own author, I think it is his duty to be one hundred per cent faithful to the author's meaning and to sacrifice none of it for the sake of climax or effect... It is here that we see the cult of the director at its worst.'

Stanley Kubrick, 'Words and Movies'

Question: How can an artist – by definition at odds with the establishment – assimilate acclaim, adoration and affluence, without losing his edge? Answer: by being Quentin Tarantino and turning 'selling out' into 'manifest destiny'. Tarantino's rise was an indication, consequence and

---

5 *Down and Dirty Pictures*, pg. 194-5.

a primary cause all at once of the rapid and inevitable movement of independents (both movies and their makers) into the mainstream. As such, it's no coincidence that the destiny of the most commercially successful indie filmmaker in history was inextricably entwined with that of the most commercially successful indie company ever – Miramax. Miramax began as an acquisitions company rightly celebrated for picking up some of the more obscure and unique indie films, such as *sex, lies, and videotape, The Thin Blue Line, The Crying Game, Clerks* and Tarantino's *Reservoir Dogs*. Today it is a studio unto itself. After a bad year in 1992, Miramax co-chairmen and brothers Harvey and Bob Weinstein allowed their company (named after their parents, Miriam and Max) to be appropriated by Disney on the condition they retain their autonomy as an indie company, albeit one funded by a major studio. Following the huge success of *Pulp Fiction*, however, Miramax began slowly to move into production as well as acquisitions, becoming progressively less 'independent' and steadily more mainstream as a result, with films like *Good Will Hunting, The English Patient* and *Shakespeare in Love* (which won Harvey an Oscar for Best Picture). As Peter Biskind put it, '…the same time the indie world was being Miramaxed, Miramax itself was being Disneyized… Miramax became, as it were, a Trojan horse through which the studio values came to permeate much of the indie scene.'[6] Miramax's most valued general in this subtle and insidious takeover was Tarantino (Harvey Weinstein has often referred to Miramax as 'the House that Quentin built').

Tarantino's rise was evidence of the Hollywood Trap in action. The fact that Tarantino – the individual, as distinct from the franchise – came through the process (being hailed and anointed as the new Messiah of indie pulp cinema) with his talents intact was a remarkable, almost a historical, achievement. Yet, like his mentors at Miramax, Tarantino was motivated less by the higher goals of Art than by the considerably more adaptable ones of Trash/Commerce. Not that this is necessarily to question his integrity. As Ethan Hawke put it, 'The thing that's remarkable about Quentin is that he's as true to his own art as anybody. It's just that his taste is very commercial.'[7] Unlike most other auteur filmmakers,

---

6 *Down and Dirty Pictures*, pg. 375. Independent producer (Killer Films) Christine Vachon remarks how, 'People's expectations for [an independent] movie have really shifted. When they go see a so-called independent film they want to see *Shakespeare in Love*, they don't want to see something that is really challenging, that's in black and white, where the sound is difficult to make out.' (Ibid, pg. 165.) John Pierson also notes, 'The fact that these indie megahits now arrived with near regularity had a weird parallel to the audience herd mentality behind studio blockbusters.' *Spike, Mike, Slackers and Dykes*, pg. 203.

7 *Down and Dirty Pictures*, pg. 192.

Tarantino had no axe to grind, either with Hollywood or with the world at large. He was the least angry, the least subversive, of potentially great filmmakers, and Hollywood embraced him in a way it couldn't possibly have embraced Scorsese or Lynch at so early a stage in their careers. For all his ferocity, Tarantino was relatively harmless as an 'auteur'. He wasn't predictable, exactly, but he was amenable. His obvious love for the trashier aspects of movies made his sensibility both accessible to and compatible with the Hollywood agenda. Tarantino's success resulted from his affinity with the mainstream; despite all his posturing, he wasn't an outsider. His brash nihilism and irreverence appealed to a fairly broad spectrum of the public, and it was easily channeled into the more cynical goals of movie studios (specifically Miramax), who don't love trash for its own sake, but because it makes them money.[8] Tarantino was an artist second and an entertainer first. Like Hitchcock and De Palma, he was born to make movies for their own sweet sake. But he came into the business with a level of low cunning and street savvy that his antecedents lacked, these being characteristics that pertained especially to his generation.

Tarantino brought a burst of vitality and freshness to American movies. He gave a much-needed boost to the independent scene, and his success brought about a new respect for and attention to scriptwriting, specifically dialogue, which after Tarantino gained a new degree of ironic, true-to-life banality. Tarantino also helped solidify the 'seen-it-all', blasé, quasi-nihilistic approach to violence which first began with films like *Repo Man* and *Blood Simple*.[9] The flip side, inevitably, was that these innovations were rapidly assimilated and degraded by lesser filmmakers, and what had once seemed like a daring new development soon became another tired cliché. Tarantino, meanwhile, continued to renew his style and reinvent (through brazen pilfering and recycling) old genres with undiminished audacity and vigor, most recently with his bloodbath revenge-comedy epic, *Kill Bill*.

Kill Bill was how Tarantino (in the words of his star Uma Thurman)

[8] Tarantino is after all the man who said, 'I never feel I know a country until I've eaten at their McDonald's. Now, I'm joking, but it's also kinda true. McDonald's isn't culture, but there's something kinda sweet, cool that everywhere you go they know what a Big Mac is. It's little things like that, like Coca Cola and Big Macs and Madonna...that make us part of a world, whether we like it or not.' Is it any wonder the Hollywood establishment embraced a man who advocated trash culture so enthusiastically as this?

[9] Admittedly, the films of John Carpenter and George Romero (and later Sam Raimi and Peter Jackson) were early harbingers, but Tarantino brought it to the mainstream by successfully turning blood-and-guts into an art form and legitimizing the 'genre' of the splatter comedy.

'gave birth to himself as an action director'. Tarantino was equally succinct on the subject. 'I've always considered action directors the greatest movie directors in the world,' he said. 'If you can do action well, then you're the greatest. The whole idea on *Kill Bill* was to test the limits of my talent.'[10] *Kill Bill* was an impressive step forward for Tarantino the showman and action director, and the film was a masterpiece of superficiality and pointlessness, for which Tarantino attained new levels of virtuosity as a filmmaker. Blending countless different styles and visual/aural flourishes to create the apotheosis of the action flick, *Kill Bill* was mindlessness taken to the state of the art. On the other hand, the writing, once considered Tarantino's special strength, seemed to have become a mere function of the violence, and wholly secondary to the action. *Kill Bill* was easily as energetic a work as *Pulp Fiction*, but it was far less imaginatively written, and had even less depth to it. It was also a borderline sadistic work that so brazenly shirked moral responsibility (under the assumed immunity of 'trash') as to suggest an almost autistic lack of awareness (as to the real dimensions of pain and violence) on Tarantino's part. Were once ultra-violence was just one device in his arsenal, now it seemed to be the whole show. To this extent, the films marked a step back for Tarantino, the artist.

Tarantino is a self-styled, self-made director-superstar, the trash guru for a generation, and it looks like he is here to stay. His self-confidence is so overwhelming it borders on solipsism, and his affable, movie geek manner is deceptively innocuous: underneath it lurks a true megalomaniac, for nothing else could explain Tarantino's phenomenal success or his ability to sustain it. Megalomania is a loaded term, perhaps; it suggests pathology, conceit, tyrannical egotism, a whole host of unpleasant personality traits besides. But in the world of movie-making, a director who isn't capable of being a megalomaniac is probably either a producer's patsy – small fry to be pushed around – or else a fringe player like Sayles or Hartley, artists who have kept their movies on a 'family' basis. Otherwise, megalomania is practically a job requirement for superstar filmmakers. With this in mind, Tarantino has handled his success with a degree of style and grace, and if he has failed to explore new terrain as a writer or develop any moral depth as an artist, he has at least continued to evolve his gifts as a filmmaker. He may not have changed the face of an art form, but he has injected Hollywood movies with a whole new appreciation for trash, and in the process reinvigorated them considerably. Who can say that the

10 Quotes from the making of *Kill Bill* DVD extra feature.

showman's work is any easier than the artist's? Such virtuosity and passion may be its own reward. It's just too bad Tarantino can't invest his talents into something besides flying body parts and comic book philosophizing. There has to be more to movies than sympathetic killers; apparently Tarantino, like the rest of Hollywood, is still in thrall to an adolescent infatuation.

Popcorn and Bubble Gum: Robert Rodriguez and the Hollywood Trap

'There's a point in Hollywood when you realize you've become a whore. This was the point for me.'

Robert Rodriguez, *Rebel Without a Crew*

Robert Rodriguez (later Tarantino's protégé) started out as an inspired 23-year-old prepared to make the ultimate sacrifice for his art – selling his body for medical experimentation to get his film funded. Before he had turned twenty-four (at roughly the time Tarantino was breaking through with *Reservoir Dogs*), he was Hollywood's latest boy wonder. His story, familiar as it is, amply illustrates the prodigious pitfalls of 'overnight success.' In 1991, Rodriguez made *El Mariachi* for a cost of $7,000, with no crew, one camera, a handful of actors (most of them first-timers), and a script which Rodriguez threw together over a month spent in a Mexican hospital as a government guinea pig (for which he also earned most of the money needed to fund his film). Rodriguez's primary means of cutting down on costs was by following his script so closely, and planning the shoot so carefully, that he shot almost zero extra footage; what made it to the screen was more or less exactly what he shot (compare this to *Heaven's Gate*, for which 200 hours of footage was accumulated, by no means a unique example). Since there was no crew there were no fees, not even for catering; the actors worked for nothing, the film had no special effects besides an explosion and some bullet hits, and the Mexican police loaned Rodriguez the guns he needed. The film was shot almost entirely outdoors, on location, so there were no sets and little lighting costs. That left the price of the film stock and development costs, totaling roughly $7,000.

Once the film was finished, Rodriguez and his leading man Carlos Gallardo began to look for a buyer on the Mexican video market. Their intention was to thereby raise enough dollars to finance their next film, and so on, until they'd made a movie good enough to break into the mainstream. Hollywood had other plans, however. After a month or two in Los Angeles, just as Rodriguez was on the point of accepting his minimum offer for the film ($25,000 from a small video company), *El Mariachi* came to the attention of Robert Newman at ICM (International Creative Management), who wasted no time signing Rodriguez up. After that, everyone in Hollywood who saw the film loved it. In his journal (published as *Rebel Without a Crew*), Rodriguez insists from the start (to himself and anyone listening) that the film is nothing but a sketch, a quick, roughshod home movie he threw together to prove he could do it. The movie, he says, is no more than a warm-up for the real movie(s) to come. But the more people see the movie, the more the offers are coming in, the more Rodriguez's name is being thrown around. He is already being touted as 'the next Tarantino,' and the studios are getting interested.

Rodriguez's dream of selling his movie to make another movie – which he might then be able to use to get a job making a real movie in Hollywood – has been reduced to instant reality. He's already made a name for himself before he's even sold his first movie (a movie he assumed would sink without a trace, a movie he considered basically disposable). Rodriguez also keeps insisting (to himself and anyone listening) that if he made *El Mariachi* with $7000, he will make a movie ten or twenty times better with a real budget, proper actors, and a full crew. The first offer he gets (from Columbia) is to remake the movie in English, with Antonio Banderas in the lead (exactly how it turned out). At first, this is dependent on shelving the original, which, it is reasoned, would only compete with the Hollywood remake. Eventually, Columbia decides that *El Mariachi* is good enough to release as is and proceeds to do so; they commission Rodriguez, meanwhile, to do the remake anyway, figuring to cash in on both art crowds, with their subtitled independent cult movie, and mass audiences, with their big budget remake. Rodriguez goes along with this thinking and agrees to the terms. His dream has come true.

Reading *Rebel Without a Crew*, Rodriguez appears to adapt fairly well to the endless flattery and fawning of the Hollywood executives. His account is witty and ironic and highly entertaining. It's also a testament to one man's ability to delude himself, and to the negative effects that big business machinery can have on an artist, the deadening effects of 'encouragement' in Hollywood.[11] As in so many cases of 'exciting new talents' who fizzle out after their first movie, Rodriguez

---

11 Pauline Kael wrote that 'Hollywood is the only place where you can die of encouragement.' She meant something different, however, and was referring to how studios stall a filmmaker with endless procrastination and false obstacles, all the while keeping the *appearance* of being

endured endless encouragement expressly designed to inflate his ego, sap his will, and quash his desire for individual artistic expression. Such encouragement inevitably undermines an artist's sense of purpose and creativity, qualities that thrive above all on adversity, on not being given what they want too easily. Repeatedly assured he can do whatever he wants (he's a genius, after all), the artist no longer knows what he wants to do, and in confusion opts to toe the party line instead.

Released in 1992, *El Mariachi* was a sharp, crude, exciting movie that crackled with freshness and originality and talent to burn. Two years later, in 1994, Rodriguez made *Desperado*, the $7 million remake/sequel (it was a bit of both, and consequently neither) with Antonio Banderas, at a cost of no less than a thousand times that of the original. The film wasn't one hundredth as good. *Desperado* was an action picture with no redeeming features; gratuitous, senseless and poorly acted, it was an orgy of pointlessness strictly for audiences who want nothing more than 90 minutes of bodies riddled with bullets and resent the challenges of intelligent dialogue or plot. Seeing the shambles that he had made, it must have been painfully evident that *El Mariachi* was infinitely superior to the Hollywood remake, but would Rodriguez admit it? Would he admit – even to himself – that, in the immortal words of John Cassavetes (to Scorsese, regarding *Boxcar Bertha*), he had just spent a year of his life making a piece of shit? From what we have seen of those individuals who have succumbed to the first temptation of the artist (success), it seems unlikely.

After *Desperado*, Rodriguez teamed up with Tarantino for *Four Rooms* and *From Dusk Till Dawn*. The pairing promised an exciting new injection of energy into American movies, but instead the movies that appeared seemed more like evidence of a conspiracy of misjudgment, and of complicity in mediocrity. Tarantino's adolescent fascination for bad horror movies (and bad movies in general), his obsession with junk food culture, and his anti-art sensibilities – catering to the mindless, thrill-seeking side of audiences – brought out the very worst in Rodriguez, a man already inclined towards trashier modes of expression. Together they made about as healthy a mix as popcorn and bubble gum. With *From Dusk Till Dawn*, it was painfully, depressingly apparent that neither Tarantino nor Rodriguez were remotely interested in doing anything new or daring on the screen but only in indulging

on his side. (Their way of ensuring that the artist is not only jaded but decrepit by the time the opportunity finally comes around.) Rodriguez endured encouragement of a different kind: the 'You're a genius, now listen to what *we* think' variety.

their infantile tastes for B-movie excess and showing off their virtuoso capacities for mindlessness, even at the expense of their audience.

From Dusk Till Dawn (1995) wasn't an offensive picture, and it wasn't evidence of Rodriguez or Tarantino's having sold out and joined the crap game. It was more complex than that: the writer and director were taking Hollywood for a ride as much as their fans (the film was a moderate success, so movie executives may not agree). What the film was was an indication of what happened when artists – or talented showmen – achieved power and fame before having a chance to develop their sensibilities. Giving $20 million to a couple of chronic adolescents like Tarantino and Rodriguez was like letting kids loose in a candy store. Talent – especially young talent – has a natural tendency to be runaway, and when it is not only indulged but actively encouraged, chances are it will lose all sense of direction or purpose. Talent without sensibility and energy without discipline amount to one thing: disaster.

Both Rodriguez and Tarantino's movies take place inside a movie universe of their own heads, with little or no reference (or consequence) in the world outside their fanboy imaginations. There is nothing to say that this can't lead to good, even great, movies; Tarantino has made his share of trash classics already, and occasionally (with much of *Pulp Fiction* and *True Romance*, and parts of *Kill Bill*) he transcends his self-imposed limits and creates something of true substance, if not exactly depth. When there is heart to the story (such as Rodriguez almost found for the first *Spy Kids*, and then triumphantly, against the odds, with *Sin City*), the lightness and compulsive irony pays off, complementing the intensity of the material and providing a pleasing contrast to it. But when the material is already empty and weightless – as with *From Dusk Till Dawn*, *Four Rooms*, *Once Upon a Time in Mexico*, and the hoakier parts of *Kill Bill* – the movies sink into brainless violence and cheap, adolescent nihilism. They are exploitation cinema without the leavening fact of being cheap and makeshift; bloated, overpriced, Hollywood exploitation films whose multimillion-dollar cost can't hide the fact that they are just mindless B-movies.

If, as Orson Welles famously remarked, movies are the biggest train set a boy can have, the trouble with Rodriguez and Tarantino is their tendency (when presented with a big studio train set) to indulge the adolescent within, and make movies for their own amusement. When you have a ten or twenty million dollar budget and a bunch of stars, who cares if the script isn't worth a damn? When everything is handed to you on a Hollywood platter, and there's little left to prove as an artist, you may as well get your kicks and play the role of boy genius.

Rodriguez eventually recovered from the shimmering depths of *Desperado* and *From Dusk Till Dawn* to make smart entertainments like *The Faculty*, *Spy Kids* (Rodriguez's own personal franchise) and *Sin City*. But he continued to betray a glaring lack of artistry in sloppy indulgences like *Once Upon a Time in Mexico* (2002), a pointless and self-indulgent orgy – fully in keeping with the director's penchant for pointless orgies – that not even Johnny Depp could salvage. Though considerably less prodigious a talent than Tarantino, Rodriguez often gives the impression of a potentially brilliant filmmaker content to flitter away his talents making disposable trash movies, showing a wilful disregard (even a disdain) for weightier, more serious material; ironically enough, that was precisely what made him the perfect director for *Sin City*.

As Anthony Lane wrote, 'Rodriguez is pleased to flash his hipster credentials, proud of the hole where his heart is supposed to be.'[12] The triumphant irony of *Sin City,* which heralds both Mickey Rourke's resurrection as a movie star and Rodriguez's redemption as a pulp filmmaker, is how Rodriguez's very lack of a sensibility (heart) makes him perfect for the material. *Sin City* is to date the first comic book adaptation to do full justice to its source and capture the graphic, visceral, and hallucinatory highs of the comic book medium. Unlike other auteur filmmakers such as Richard Lester (*Superman II*), Tim Burton, or Chris Nolan (*Batman*, *Batman Begins*), Rodriguez both understands and respects the appeal of comic books for grown men with a predilection for macho fantasy. Rodriguez understands the whole wish-fulfillment fantasy appeal of superhuman violence and prowess – he celebrates it – as something most males never fully grow out of. What's especially refreshing about *Sin City* is that Rodriguez's grasp of the material precludes the usual, dreary need to impose a bogus 'human-ness' or realism onto two-dimensional characters and meet the demands of a standard movie format. There are no obligatory character arcs here, no vain attempts to deepen the material and make it accessible, sympathetic, to wider audiences. The movie exists in a genre and a universe of its own, and instead of adapting Frank Miller's stories, Rodriguez simply translates them; precisely and with an awe-inspiring fidelity to the source (and with a healthy lack of reverence), he transposes Miller's characters and scenarios – even his compositions

12 'Feelings,' from the *New Yorker,* April 4th, 2005.

and shadows – whole, into a new medium.

With an intoxicating blend of humility and enthusiasm, Rodriguez lets Miller's material guide his hand and eye, allowing it to find its own form. As a director, he is more like a mid-wife to Miller's vision than an auteur filmmaker, and the film is a perfect blend, a tale from hell's kitchen, made in movie heaven. Where Rodriguez more or less spurns the need for artistic vision, Miller has sensibility to burn. Miller is all sensibility, with the talent to match, and since he used film noir as a take-off point for his mythic melodrama of pain and machismo, with the help of Rodriguez (the pulp filmmaker *par excellence*), Miller's *Sin City* translates almost effortlessly into the medium that inspired it. The result is something both more and less than a regular action fantasy, more *because* of being less, blissfully uncontaminated by the usual dull concession to realism or morality. Unlike *Kill Bill*, however, the extreme sadism that Miller's characters display doesn't appear to be shared by the director, and so the violence stays where it belongs, as comic book extremism and part of the fantasy – as the only way for these characters to express themselves. Despite their relentless pulpiness, despite being walking clichés caught inside a demented fantasy of post-modern medievalism, Miller/Rodriguez's characters develop, improbably, into flesh and blood beings, with hearts that bleed and not just bodies. This is especially true of Rourke's Marv, a superlative characterization whose sad eyes and beaten face raises the movie above its pulp roots, and into something tragic and grandiose. It would be a beautiful and poetic irony if, through the humility and self-effacement he displays with *Sin City*, Rodriguez developed his true calling as a film artist. He may just have found his soul exactly where we'd expect it to be – inside a comic book.

★

'There's a pecking order in filmmaking, and the director is at the top – he's the authority figure. A man who has never been particularly attractive to women now finds that he's the *padrone*: everyone is waiting on his word, and the women are his for the nod. The constant, unlimited opportunities for sex can be insidious; so is the limitless flattery of college students who turn directors into gurus. Directors are easily seduced. They mainline adoration.'

Pauline Kael, 'Why Are Movies So Bad? or, The Numbers'.

In general, artists are loath to collaborate. They feel their 'genius' will only be diminished or contaminated if put at the service of a more collective goal, and for the greater part, they're right. But film is different to the other arts, and of necessity a collaborative medium, so a big part of being successful as a director or producer (though not necessarily a writer) is an ability to get along with other people. There's no way for an artist whose self-esteem precludes respect for his or her collaborators (and his or her fans) to survive as an artist when he or she's already started to think and act like a whore.

Creative personalities thrive on adversity, restriction, strife, and above all challenges. There can be nothing more essential for an artist than feeling passionately committed to what he or she is doing. Any kind of obstacle that exists, the scepticism, discouragement, incomprehension, rejection or plain hostility of others – especially people in positions of power – exist to prove an artist's vision and commitment. After all, if he or she has to fight to get his movie made, there's that much more of a chance it will be worth making (and if it's worth fighting for, chances are it's worth seeing). There is a difference between opposition and interference, however. When studios actively oppose an artist, he or she's still in with a fighting chance; they can wheel and deal and find ways to express him or herself despite the worst attempts to thwart them. He or she may even find that adverse circumstances force him or her to use their ingenuity and imagination in ways in which they might otherwise not have dreamed. But when the studios manifestly interfere with what an artist is doing, the artist is probably already sunk. (There are exceptions to this, of course, as with Terry Gilliam's *Brazil*.)

The question of opposition or interference is especially dynamic in the film industry, obviously. A writer or a painter doesn't have to fight to overcome resistance in order to create his or her masterpiece – their battle begins only once it's done. For filmmakers, there is a wholly different battlefield to contend with, and both the rewards and the punishments are vastly increased once an artist ventures into the fantasy world of movie production. On the one hand, it is difficult almost to the point of being paralyzing for an aspiring 'auteur' to ever get his or her film financed, completed, sold and released to their satisfaction. On the other hand, if by some miracle of will and dedication he or she succeeds in accomplishing this Herculean task, the chances of their becoming a household name, or at the very least a minor cult-figure, are enormously favorable.

An independent filmmaker who makes it in Hollywood has plenty of reasons to be proud. He or she can (rightly) tell themself that only through a mixture of talent, devotion, persistence and – that most elusive and magical of virtues – luck, could they ever have made it at all. At the same time, they might be forgiven for feeling all the more determined to remain in the limelight now that they have made it there. So early in the game as this, with this hungry artist's willingness (even eagerness) to compromise, the temptation begins. As Kael observes, 'Stardom is success made manifest, success in human form, and, naturally, the yes-sayers are, in general, the biggest stars.'[13] When an artist like Tarantino or Robert Rodriguez hits the big-time with his very first feature and is surrounded by people with nothing on their minds but pleasing him and telling him what a genius he is – it is understandable if, in a rush of gratitude, he feels magnanimously obliged to please, in return, these fawning figures around him. The first temptation is to believe the outrageous flattery and praise with which, like a race-horse, he is being greased and primed for the show. The second temptation is an almost irresistible desire, perhaps even a duty, to perform, in order not to disappoint his newly acquired fan-cub. And when the budding auteur is inundated with endlessly varied 'suggestions', 'recommendations', 'pointers' and 'tips' as to the 'direction' his 'career' should take, the unprepared artist is likely to find himself, before he knows it, converting into a (reluctant but grateful) merchant of trash, merely in order to get along.

There is a process to be observed here, a process (Kael called it 'fattening the calf') that no doubt has been perfected over the decades and is now more or less the primary purpose and *raison d'être* of Hollywood. It is a process designed and directed towards the harnessing and suppression (the suppression by harnessing) of 'dangerous' 'unpredictable' new talents as they are breaking into the business, in order to keep them from rocking the boat of movie production by reminding the public of what movies might still be: art. This is an unconscious, 'natural', or at least mechanical, process by which Hollywood, that dark, satanic mill, turns daring, subversive, vital new visionaries into torpid, soulless and tasteless merchants, salesman whose merchandise is a form of propaganda for the corporations that own them. This is the basis for a fuller understanding of the Hollywood trap, and its workings are in evidence all around us.

13 *Reeling*, pg. 322.

David Lynch, Genius High and Low

'Success is a beguiling devil and you're not smart enough to know what that means, and then some part of you sees the guns getting loaded and the rope getting prepared.'

David Lynch

One such (fortunately only temporary) victim of the trap was David Lynch. A curious fact is that filmmakers experience and exhibit highs and lows in ways that artists working in other mediums generally do not. Where a musician or a novelist may be seen to deteriorate or evolve over a period of years, even decades, filmmakers tend to burn out in a matter of a movie or two, occasionally, though far more rarely, resurrecting with equal swiftness. Witness for example Robert Altman, a unique case of a director whose talents seemed to come and go as if with the waxing and waning of the moon. Altman followed near-masterpieces such as *McCabe and Mrs. Miller* or *The Long Goodbye* with shapeless and self-indulgent messes like *Brewster McCloud* and *Images*; sometimes 'good' Altman and 'bad' Altman co-existed, side by side in the same movie, as with *Short Cuts* (mostly good) or *Prêt à Porter* (mostly bad). Altman is a unique case, however; far more typical is the decline of a once-visionary filmmaker into a grotesque parody of himself, a process perhaps most clearly evidenced by the rise, fall and rise again of David Lynch.

Like all good visionaries, Lynch came out of nowhere, with *Eraserhead* in 1977; he then gradually disappeared into creative oblivion some fifteen years later with *Wild at Heart* and, finally, the execrable *Twin Peaks: Fire Walk With Me*. In 1998 he made *Lost Highway*, a film that, by consisting of two distinct parts, offered a clear delineation between the two sides of the director, the artist and the hack. The first part of the film was haunting in its brilliance; the second part (unfortunately far longer) was a depressingly inept retread of the tacky TV-style sensationalism of *Wild at Heart* and *Fire Walk With Me*. Though presumably he had not intended it thus, Lynch laid his cards on the table with *Lost Highway* for all to see; the only question remaining was – will the real Lynch please stand up?

From the start, David Lynch was a writer–director in the fullest sense. His most personal movies (*Eraserhead, Blue Velvet, Mulholland Drive*) hatched whole from his unconscious, untarnished by external influences, as if traveling directly from the filmmaker's psyche to the screen. It was when Lynch began to collaborate, first on *Twin Peaks* (with Mark Frost) and then with the novelist and film critic Barry Gifford (for *Wild at Heart*, based on Gifford's novel, and later *Lost Highway*, which they worked on together), that the purity of Lynch's vision began to dissipate. Significantly, Gifford, also a critic, had panned *Blue Velvet* mercilessly on its release, leading one to wonder what strange forces drew the two writers together in the first place. *Lost Highway* was a work half inspired by genius and half miserably contrived, and there could be little doubt where Gifford's influence was most pronounced.

Except for the world of film, writers rarely collaborate. A book, fiction or otherwise, is normally a one-person enterprise, as private and individual an endeavor as painting or sculpting. Unlike filmmaking, writing is a meditative, introspective act, closer to prayer than partying. (Incidentally, Lynch likes to meditate daily, even – or especially – while filming.) A writer needs to be isolated and centered in himself in order to tap into his inner reserves of creativity, and to hear the voice of the muse. It is a particular kind of discipline that – as most writers with their monastic lifestyles will testify – can be almost religious in its focus and devotion. Obviously, all of this is lost once a writer embarks on a collaborative piece. For writers who are primarily entertainers, this can work beautifully. For those who are primarily artists on personal journeys of self-discovery, it rarely turns out so well.

Trash can be fun; it can even be art. But did ever a movie try so hard to pass for fun as Lynch's *Wild at Heart*? One of the most grotesque and joyless films ever made by a former genius, *Wild at Heart* was awarded the Palme d'Or at Cannes and was greeted with salivating ecstasy by critics, some of whom had mercilessly trashed Lynch's previous film – his masterpiece – *Blue Velvet*. Perhaps the same critics who had been unable to get their heads around the twisted brilliance of *Blue Velvet* wanted to make up for their failure by praising Lynch's follow-up film (for which the perversities were all on the surface and easy to get to grips with)? If *Wild at Heart* had been made by an unknown director, it might have shown promise, but it would certainly have been recognized as vulgar trash fit mostly for the exploitation market. The film, which came out a mere four years after *Blue Velvet*, indicated a director who had become a mere shadow of his former self. What happened in the interim? *Twin Peaks* happened. Apparently Lynch – whom Pauline Kael touted as 'the first populist surrealist'[14] – in his attempt to revolutionize American TV, got swallowed up by it instead. David may have slain Goliath, but no artist ever took over an industry without selling his soul to it first.

Twin Peaks captured the imaginations of millions of viewers and turned Lynch from a cult filmmaker and still-forming genius into a national celebrity, celebrated above all for his twisted sense of humor and his ability to mix the grotesque and macabre with the mundane and the absurd. Popular as the series was, and however much it served to popularize (and sanitize) the surreal, it was still, at the end of the day, an American soap opera: superficial, gaudy, melodramatic, sensationalist, glib, and basically soulless. By choosing to adapt his visionary talents to a medium that simply demanded their taming and sanitizing to meet with network standards, Lynch essentially pimped his genius for the sake of greater dividends. Perhaps he was genuinely driven by a creative desire to subvert and undermine the collective American psyche by infiltrating its favorite pastime; but if so his naiveté bordered on hubris.

Twin Peaks was eventually cancelled mid-season, no less (not so much due to poor ratings as to the network's discomfort over Lynch's increasingly bizarre plot turns); his characters were left hanging in dark limbo. Apparently Lynch was in that same limbo. When he returned to filmmaking it was with *Wild at Heart*, a slick, shallow romp through weird, wild, wonderful Lynchsville USA that played like a cheap commercial for the director's once-prodigious talents, now vanished into the void. What was even more disturbing, however, was Lynch's apparent cynicism in exploiting his audiences' goodwill and pandering to their baser needs for sex, violence and gratuitous weirdness. A filmmaker can't denigrate his audience without denigrating himself, and the most depressing thing about *Wild at Heart* was how Lynch seemed to be exploiting his own talent, and turning into a parody of himself.[15]

Wild at Heart appeared to be made by a wholly different person than *Eraserhead*, *The Elephant Man* or *Blue Velvet*. It was made by someone whose sensibilities had been sabotaged by too much exposure to corporate thinking. Lynch directed the film not like an artist but like a whore – taking no pleasure in what he was doing, just going through the motions and trusting (or praying) that no one would know the difference. Exploitation and prostitution are closely related: both infer a gratuitous use (either of oneself or the 'client') devoid of respect for whatever is being used. With *Wild at Heart*, Lynch was treating his talent

---

15 As Kael writes, 'As soon as an artist ceases to see himself as part of the audience – when he begins to believe that what matters is to satisfy the jerk audience out there – he stops being an artist. He becomes a businessman, marketing a commodity – his talent, himself.' *Reeling*, pg. 327.

like a whore treats their body, and he seemed to be eradicating whatever was left of it in the process. Implicit to the film's glib violence and pseudo-surrealism was a cynical assumption that audiences wouldn't be able to tell the difference between vision and cheap fantasy, between the workings of the subconscious and mere commercial opportunism. Lynch had turned his audience into a 'trick', dragging it down to the lowest level, pissing on it and calling it rain.

Evidently, there was a basic conflict in the artist's psyche at work. The conflict was between exploring the unconscious realms and developing creativity, regardless of audiences' expectations (as he had done with *Eraserhead*), or else working at a conscious, contrived level to exploit audiences' tastes and pursue a more cynical, commercial course. The latter approach, though it might lead to popular success and even critical accolades (as with *Wild at Heart*), left creativity more or less in the dust. Lynch had successfully fused the two approaches – those of abstract surrealism with generic entertainment – for his two best films at the time, *The Elephant Man* and *Blue Velvet*. In between the two he made *Dune*, which saw the auteur swallowed up and spat out (undigested) by a monster industry that apparently had no place for him. If Goliath slew David, however, the fault was as much Lynch's as producer Dino DeLaurentiis'. Lynch knowingly took on an impossible project, and was undone as much by his own ambitions as by any interference from the studios. (DeLaurentiis later funded Lynch's *Blue Velvet* and gave the director final cut.)

Dune was an involuntary, perhaps even forced, movement towards commercialism and populism on Lynch's part, and in the process – as is so often the case – the artist's vision was derailed. But when Lynch returned in triumph in 1986 with *Blue Velvet* – easily the most visionary American movie of the decade – the film banished any lingering doubts as to whether his gifts were compatible with audience tastes. Until then, it had still been open to doubt. Impressive as *Eraserhead* was, it fell short as entertainment; *The Elephant Man* was rousing stuff, but it was Lynch as director-for-hire, Lynch light; *Dune* was an outright disaster, after which it looked like Lynch might wind up as one more genius-casualty of Hollywood. *Blue Velvet* set the record straight. As personal a work as *Eraserhead*, it was as accessible and as entertaining as any Hitchcock thriller, and it established Lynch at the very front rank of American filmmakers. Then came *Twin Peaks*, and by the time of *Wild at Heart* four years later, Lynch's awesome talent seemed to have putrefied into something grisly and obscene. After a critical mauling over *Fire Walk With Me* and a cool reception for *Lost Highway*, Lynch seemed cowed;

for his next film, *The Straight Story*, he was treading water. The title referred not only to the lead character, the real-life Alvin Straight (an old man who, lacking an automobile, rode his lawnmower across the US to visit his brother), but also to Lynch's approach to the material. As if exhausted by the effort of sustaining his trademark weirdness – and perhaps leery of his reputation as the master of the bizarre – Lynch did the movie 'straight,' almost devoid of Lynchian touches, but also mercifully free of the tacky sensationalism to which he had sunk for his last few works.

In retrospect, this was a regeneration period for Lynch. When an artist becomes recognized for a certain style, and audiences demand works that conform to their expectations, he finds himself in a no-win situation. Whatever he does – unless he simply repeats himself – is going to confound people and be greeted with confusion, disappointment or outright hostility. This is the price of recognition, and it is a price that many, even most, artists (especially filmmakers) cannot afford to pay. Instead, they end up creatively bankrupt. The problem is further aggravated when audiences require a filmmaker to be 'weird' – i.e., unexpected – since there is simply no way to meet such expectations except by confounding them. As Lynch himself said, around this time, '...when you start thinking about what certain people might say...the work isn't talking to you anymore: this worry is talking to you. And you become paralyzed. So the trick is: you've got to forget making a hero or a fool of yourself and just try to get into that world. And if you can do that, and you feel good about the decisions that you make, then you can weather whatever good or bad storm comes along.'[16]

Caught in the glare of public fascination and critical adulation – in the period between *Twin Peaks* and *The Straight Story* – Lynch was visibly floundering. The problem was that, with *Twin Peaks* and *Wild at Heart*, he was best known for his shabbiest work, being embraced for his populist qualities more than his visionary ones. Since Hollywood took its cue (and measured a director's worth) from the public – and

---

16 Chris Rodley, pg. 79. Later in the same work, Lynch says, 'I think, for me, it's more like respect for the work. That, to me, is success. All the other things make me feel completely dishonest. It's really the reasons why you do stuff... You should really be like a monk. I haven't quite got that down. There must be some part of me that is weak, and it's like dancing towards a flame. It is a weakness, in a way... [Success is] a dangerous, dangerous thing. It plays tricks on you, and it can make you a really ugly human being. Or it can be just what you need to heal certain things and make you relax and be able to do what you're supposed to do. Successes are complicated things, psychologically... Failure's the only solution!' (pg. 105-7)

to a lesser extent the critics – it was this Lynch that studios were interested in funding, not the twisty, impenetrable Lynch of *Eraserhead* and *Blue Velvet* but the schlocky, nasty Lynch of *Twin Peaks* and *Wild at Heart*.[17] Ironically, Lynch's struggle to break free of the downward pull of commercialism came about despite his continued effort to work in TV, when he shot what was intended to be a pilot for a new popular surrealist show, *Mulholland Drive*. Lynch's backers (ABC TV) found the material he was shooting too weird and disturbing (the same reason *Twin Peaks* had been cancelled) and dropped the project like a hot potato, leaving Lynch upstream without a paddle. Stuck with an hour or so of footage and nothing to do with it, determined to continue the project, Lynch secured extra funding from Pierre Edelman (at the French company Studio Canal Plus) to shoot another hour or so of scenes and turn *Mulholland Drive* into a feature film. A huge critical success, the film constituted Lynch's comeback in more ways than one. Above all, it saw the return of a unique cinematic talent to former heights of creativity. The irony was that it was only when ABC rejected Lynch as too 'artistic' that Lynch returned to his first love, that of celluloid. Against the odds, and much to everyone's surprise, the medium embraced him warmly, as it would a much-lamented lost lover, restoring Lynch's wandering talents to him.

Mulholland Drive was Lynch's best film since *Blue Velvet*, and it proved that his vision hadn't died, but had only been sleeping. Where Lynch goes from here remains to be seen. The principal thing is that he is back, and that, when it comes to filmmakers, being down doesn't necessarily mean being out. Recently Lynch said, with characteristic humility, 'I just hope that I get a chance to keep making pictures in the atmosphere of freedom to make mistakes, and to find those magical things. Then I don't care what else happens. I would like the people who invest in the pictures to make some money, and be happy they went along.'[18] After a sojourn with the Bitch Goddess, Lynch returned to the source and found his creative wellspring as fresh and flowing as ever. It was a lesson to filmmakers everywhere, a lesson as obscure and mysterious as Lynch's best work, and as supremely poetic. Under the dictates of Mammon, art and commerce may never mix, but only by the blessing of god. Talents abused soon dissipate into nothing; and

---

17 If the studios had been able to cut *Lost Highway* according to their taste, doubtless they would have removed the first forty minutes of creepy, hypnotic atmospherics, and left the violent, pointless orgy that was the remainder of the film; it was at least halfway 'coherent', and had lots of sex and violence.

18 Rodley, pg 190

whoever opts to serve the Bitch Goddess Success will be sucked dry in no time. The artist who honors his muse, on the other hand, will be find his inspiration eternally replenished.

The Gospel in the Mouth of the Monster: Martin Scorsese's Obsession

'The thing to keep in mind through all the discouragement is that you simply have to continue. It's like in *The Red Shoes*, when Anton Walbrook asks Moira Shearer, "Why do you want to dance?" and she says, "Why do you want to live?" '

Martin Scorsese, 2003

Like Lynch, Martin Scorsese has shown a tendency to come and go. As a movie 'genius', Scorsese is a some-time visionary with an authentic religious obsession only sporadically compatible with his artistic one. The first decade of his career, between *Mean Streets* and *The King of Comedy*, is perhaps unequalled in subversive brilliance by any other American filmmaker besides Coppola. The series of failures and setbacks that constituted the last half of that decade, from *New York, New York* to *King of Comedy*, almost destroyed Scorsese's will to create, however. Almost, but not quite. 'I realized then, you can't let the system crush your spirit,' Scorsese said later. 'I really did want to continue making pictures. I'm a director, I'll make a low-budget picture, *After Hours*. I'm going to be a pro and start all over again.'[19] He did, but though his spirit may not have been crushed, his vision had been severely dimmed. The following decade, from *After Hours* to *Cape Fear*, was at best a pale reflection of what had come before. The decade that followed that, from *Age of Innocence* to date, roughly (*The Aviator* being Scorsese's latest Hollywood extravaganza), has offered only scant moments of the passion and intensity that once suffused the director's work and made it unique to American film. Scorsese really burned out in the years between *New York, New York* and *King of Comedy*, and even the technical brilliance evidenced in 'Life Lessons' (*New York Stories*) and *Goodfellas* couldn't cover up the essential fading of his vision. But it wasn't until *Cape Fear* that Scorsese fully succumbed to the pressures of being a world-class film artist, and fell into the Hollywood Trap.

An artist driven by his private demons is permitted, perhaps even obliged, to immerse himself in his vision and allow it to swallow him up, at least for the time it takes to bring it into expression. With *Cape Fear*, however, Scorsese took his compulsion for self-immolation to new depths, and self-immolation became self-abasement. *Cape Fear* was religious pulp in the worst sense, a monumental display of self-deception that, by attempting to exalt pulp to spiritual heights, reduced religion to a bloody pulp. The ways and means for an artist to justify his spending valuable time on trash are indeed legion. For the self-respecting artist working in Hollywood, the art of self-deception is arguably the most essential 'art' of all, without which he will be a bitter old man or a gibbering wreck in no time. For the successful artist in Hollywood, integrity is far less essential than the capacity to hoodwink with the appearance of integrity. The hoodwinking starts with studios, steadily extends to critics and audiences, and finally comes round to the artist himself. Hoodwinking the self is not easy, but it is entirely necessary for the artist to survive, or rather succeed, in Hollywood.[20]

Actually, Scorsese had been around a lot longer than most film directors by the time he made *Cape Fear*, and certainly knew the ropes by then. If we take into account the fact that a director must always stand by his works (even the very worst of them, in public at least), Scorsese was probably aware how low he was sinking with *Cape Fear*. It wasn't the first time he'd sold out; seven years earlier he made *After Hours* out of desperation when *The Last Temptation of Christ* was cancelled; then there was *The Color of Money*, his first sequel, his first big budget, star-studded mainstream production, his first major box office success, and his first wholly impersonal movie since *Boxcar Bertha*. The film's success gave him the clout to get *Last Temptation* made, however, and Scorsese was savvy (and cynical) enough to know that, in Hollywood – where there is no such thing as a free lunch – no points are given for integrity, and no artistic reputation is good enough to compensate for a lack of commercial success. The only freedom in Hollywood is the freedom that is earned, and it has to be earned over and over again. If, by making *Cape Fear*, Scorsese was selling out big-time, he would have known that he was capable of buying his integrity back again afterwards with the money earned. That was just the nature of the business.[21]

20 This may sound overly cynical, but there are times when cynicism is the only viable approach, and dissecting the Hollywood infrastructure is definitely one of those times. Those who doubt this should watch a double bill of *Taxi Driver* and *Cape Fear* and remind themselves that both films were made by the same man.

21 His next film, *Age of Innocence*, dull as it was, was at least a wholly personal and heartfelt work, and he might never have made it without the commercial success of the previous film.

Scorsese was such a consummate film artist that he could put his heart (if not his head) into just about anything, and he stormed through *Cape Fear* with near-psychotic energy. Scorsese's cinematic virtuosity seemed almost like an apology, however, a way of compensating for the banality of the material; his frenetic style was like a smoke screen, so thick and viscous that it kept audiences (if not critics) from noticing that there was no fire at all. Yet for all Scorsese's flourishes and technical trickery (there was hardly a scene in the film that didn't have an ostentatious touch to it), *Cape Fear* was a sluggish, turgid film, with no room for nuances or playfulness. Like its monster Cady, the movie was relentless, unstoppable, abrasive, and – for all its literary quotations and spiritual pretensions – shockingly stupid. The theme of Scorsese's movie for once wasn't redemption, however: it was closer to the Old Testament in spirit. *Cape Fear* was about purification – trial by fire – with Cady as the avenging angel come out of Hell (prison) to punish and prove the corrupt (dysfunctional) family and force them to look at the evil of their ways.[22]

The film seethed with biblical quotes for every occasion, and when Scorsese (and scriptwriter Wesley Strick) couldn't stick them in Cady's mouth, they stuck them on his body instead. (Cady was 'the word made flesh', covered from the waist up by tattoos.) But all these quotes and references and subtexts didn't add up to meaning when the film itself was so utterly at odds with them, and if Scorsese believed that *Cape Fear* was about the purification of a sinful family by Max Cady, then he was taking the point of view of the psycho, aligning the film with Cady's own twisted vision. Apparently Scorsese wanted to have it both ways. He wanted to have a studio hit and make another personal movie about street saints; so he put the gospel in the mouth of the monster. *Cape Fear* wasn't about anything, it was just another monster movie with pseudo-philosophic dialogue. Apparently this was the only way Scorsese could reconcile himself to the film's brazen absurdities, but it didn't seem to occur to Scorsese that, by giving this dialogue to the

---

22 De Niro played Max Cady with such broad strokes that it seemed like an inadvertent parody, and if *Cape Fear* hadn't been such a high-strung, brutal film, it might have passed for camp. When Cady boasts to the lawyer, 'I can out-fight you and I can out-philosophize you!' – or when he sentences the fallen family to 'the third circle of hell!' – he's about as credible a psychopath as Wily E. Coyote. When he's not killing dogs and raping women, Cady seems content to go around leering, puffing on his enormous phallic cigar and quoting Nietzsche, Henry Miller, Dante and the Old Testament prophets. Cady was an intellectual's worst fantasy of a psychopath – not only was he tougher and meaner and crueler – he was better read, too.

monster and claiming that was what the film was really about, *Cape Fear* was probably the first horror movie in which the monster got to explain the film's subtext. If *Cape Fear* had come clean and been an overtly supernatural horror movie, it might even have worked; as it was, there was no way. Comparing the film with *Taxi Driver* – Scorsese's last depiction of a psycho deluded enough to think he was on a destroying mission from God – made it clear just how far Scorsese had sunk into the quagmire of his metaphysic.[23]

Cape Fear wanted to be a straightforward thriller in which the psycho was just the psycho, and in which the family overcame and destroyed the psycho and all was well. In any case, that was the film Steven Spielberg must have envisioned when he talked Scorsese into remaking the (much darker) 1962 original. But Scorsese, unable to work up any enthusiasm for such a paltry challenge, tried to turn it into one more take on his personal obsession, to turn Max Cady into himself. In the process of personalizng pulp, the artist got trashed. This might have seemed inevitable from the moment Spielberg first talked Scorsese into doing a remake for his Amblin company – with friends like that, who needs movie executives? – but Scorsese was so wholly wrapped up in his own obsessive-compulsive filmmaking (while at the same time so basically unsure of himself as an artist) that he let himself be swayed into something he knew wasn't right for him. In order to save face, he had to convince himself that it *was* what he wanted to do, that he could use it as a vehicle for his own ideas, and make it 'searingly personal'. Scorsese may have expressed his ideas with *Cape Fear*, but he messed up the movie in the process; what the film expressed was the frustration and despair of an artist trapped by an empty idea. If it was about a religious man wrestling with his faith, that was only because, for Scorsese, movies *were* his religion; and even

23 Pauline Kael was especially succinct on this matter in her review of *The Color of Money:* 'Scorsese tried to turn Eddie Felson into himself; he even tried to turn Rupert Pupkin...into himself... Maybe he insists on making everything "searingly personal" because it's his only way of getting into a subject. Does he lack the imagination to become involved in other characters – characters with their own distinct individuality? I'd rather put it this way: his obsessiveness may be so strong that his imagination doesn't operate freely... But his obsessiveness has plunged him into some serious binds – like the pyschodramatic morass of *New York, New York* – and so he doesn't go all the way with it anymore. He pulls back, or maybe he no longer has anywhere to go. The showmanship he exhibits here may be the only ground where he feels confident. When he plays with camera angles, he can feel like the master he's being called. 'Scorsese's Showmanship,' *Hooked*, pg. 227-8.

when he was doing something that wasn't worth a damn, his faith pulled him through.[24]

Of all the American filmmakers who came to prominence in the 70s and 80s, Scorsese has probably survived the best. He survived the debacle of *Last Temptation* and the excessive accolades of *Raging Bull*; he survived *Cape Fear* and the string of misguided projects that came after, culminating in the grand pulp folly of *Gangs of New York*, a film that so desperately aspired to being a masterwork that critics – if not audiences – glumly acquiesced and called it one. *The Aviator* was a partial return to form, but only a partial one, and the only film of the past twenty years that Scorsese really seemed to put his heart and talent into (besides his segment of *New York Stories*, 'Life Lessons') was probably *Bringing Out the Dead,* a film the critics largely ignored.

Based on the evidence, it's a safe bet that Scorsese will never again regain his former heights as a film artist (the heights of *Mean Streets* and *Taxi Driver*, or even *King of Comedy*); but he's by no means out of the running, as seems the case with so many others (such as Jonathan Demme, and even Coppola). Scorsese has come as close as any auteur ever has to being assimilated by Hollywood while still retaining his individuality, and that may in part be why he's so damn obsessed. It's not easy for an artist to serve god while in the employ of Mammon – there's no way to serve two masters at once – but Scorsese is so addicted to filmmaking that he simply can't give it up now, any more than he could give up breathing. Instead, he is left to barter and trade, bribe and cajole, wheel and deal his way from movie to movie, all alone in the Hollywood jungle, with cannibals on every side. It's no wonder he holds so tightly on to those rosary beads as he steps into the mill one more time. In Hollywood, the artist is the most endangered species there is.

Brian De Palma: Artist Enslaved to the Mainstream

'The thing you can determine from me and my career is that I never gave a damn what anybody thought.'

Brian De Palma, 1998

24 'Religion and the whole concept of the actual practice of Christian ethics in modern society is a theme that I'm always attracted to and is something that goes through my mind and my heart every day. It's a constant part of my life. But you know it's also a way of simplifying things because one does not always want to talk about your personal life to journalists or television, so it's also a way of deflecting things. That's all it is kid, movies and religion, thank you!' Martin Scorsese, in a BBC online interview. See http://www.industrycentral.net/director_interviews/MS01.HTM

Was there ever an auteur more amenable to selling out, more seemingly compatible with Hollywood, than Brian De Palma? If we discount Spielberg, who falls short of the criteria for personal filmmakers – and Lucas, who falls short of the criteria for filmmakers, period – then of all the movie brats who came to prominence in the 70s, Brian De Palma must be the most extravagantly shallow visionary showman currently working in America. By rights, he ought to have been the one most warmly embraced by Hollywood, and yet bizarrely, the reverse is the case. Life is full of paradoxes, and the sad paradox of Brian De Palma is that, hard as he may try to sell out and become an A-list Hollywood director – and despite his stubborn allegiance to the mainstream – he remains a fringe filmmaker. Judging by De Palma's best efforts to sell out, Hollywood (and the public) just isn't interested.

It may be fitting in its way. De Palma started out as an underground filmmaker with a predilection for social satire and subversion, and though few of his later films have provided much evidence of this, De Palma's sensibility and temperament is actually far more radical and unorthodox than any of his peers, including Scorsese, Altman, and Coppola. Perhaps it is this fact that lies at the heart of the mystery, and explains why, throughout his career and with only brief and momentary exceptions, De Palma has been shunned by the Bitch Goddess Success?[25] Commercially speaking, De Palma's career has peaked twice, between 1976 (with *Carrie*) and 1980 (with *Dressed to Kill*), and then again, even more briefly, with *The Untouchables* in 1987 (we won't mention *Mission: Impossible*, since no amount of box office dividends can counter the dull fact of the film itself). Artistically, on the other hand, he has peaked and continues to peak at regular intervals, usually in diametric opposition to his commercial success. In 1982, for example, he made *Blow Out*, his best film at the time and a commercial flop. Like Powell's *Peeping Tom*, Antonioni's *Blow Up*, and Coppola's *The Conversation* (all of which inspired De Palma's film), *Blow Out* was a film whose text grew out of its subtext rather than vice versa, whose depths were all on the surface, and whose theme was one with its plot. In the tradition of cinematic games, it was a puzzle, a film about filmmaking, a movie about movies. Audiences just didn't get it.[26] Then in 1989, De Palma made his masterpiece, *Casualties of War*.

25 Relative to his peers, of course, Spielberg, Lucas, Scorsese, Coppola et al. Relative to the average, middle-class person, and even to most aspiring filmmakers, De Palma has been hugely successful. But compared to his aspirations and talent, clearly he has not.
26 'No one would answer my phone calls after *Blow Out*. It was a very bad time... You've gotta realize that when you've made a movie that may be commercially disastrous, it may also be the best work you've ever done.' *Brian De Palma: Interviews*, pg 88.

The film was not a great success, and was more or less overlooked by critics, considering that it was easily one of the best American films of the decade. Following closely the script by David Rabe, De Palma for once kept his customary flourishes and self-serving directorial set-pieces to a minimum; he respected his material and, intent on doing it full justice, he was both confident and generous enough to take a back seat and let the script and the performers carry the show. *Casualties of War* wasn't 'A Brian De Palma Film' in the usual, bombastic way, but it gave intimations of what De Palma was really capable of as an artist. In the ten years since *Dressed to Kill*, he had evolved in leaps and bounds, into the most technically proficient of directors.[27]

After *Casualties of War*, De Palma made a mixed bag of movies, only a couple of which were worthy of his talents. *Carlito's Way* reunited the director with Sean Penn and Al Pacino, and although a rather routine gangster story, De Palma's talent for creating set-pieces with minimum fuss and maximum delight were truly formidable. When it came to suspense sequences – such as the poolroom shootout, the final hit on Sean Penn's weasel lawyer, and the climactic chase at Grand Central Station – De Palma was without peer. Aside from this film, the director bracketed *Raising Cain*, a return to small-scale, personal (and negligible) filmmaking, with the twin fiascoes *Bonfire of the Vanities* and *Mission: Impossible*: mega-budget, star-studded exercises in futility of which it was hard to say which was more regrettable – the amount of time and dollars poured into them or the talent wasted. De Palma seemed unfazed by regret, however, and *Mission: Impossible*, at least, was a hit, though it seems doubtful if anybody understood (or liked) the film.

Of all the major, maverick American directors, De Palma was the most adaptable and seemingly 'impersonal.' He didn't appear to resent (or lament) the studios' demands upon him, merely to regard it as part of the deal. Yet his increasingly sinking status over the last fifteen years (since *Casualties of War*) as a studio hired hand means that his reputation has suffered accordingly, and of all the directors to come to prominence in the 70s (Coppola, Scorsese, Lucas, Spielberg), and even compared with the auteurs of the 80s (Lynch, Stone, Demme), De Palma's reputation is now undoubtedly among the worst. (Two obvious exceptions would be Friedkin and Bogdanovich.) Even in the first part

27 His technique was as flawless as Hitchcock's, but like Hitchcock, De Palma was only as good as his material; he didn't have the visionary qualities of a Scorsese or a Coppola, and with a mediocre script (as with *Wise Guys*) he appeared no more than a competent hired hand, a hack (just like Hitchcock was a hack on *Dial M For Murder* or *Torn Curtain*).

of his career, De Palma was variously dismissed, reviled, scorned or condemned by critics as an empty showman, an untalented plagiarizer, a tasteless schlock-meister and a sadistic misogynist. To have offended so many different people was no easy feat, and De Palma, whatever critics had to say about him, was a genuine individual. He was the most willfully irreverent and playful of auteurs, and he seemed to possess almost incalculable reserves of untapped talent. But De Palma's charm was one with his failing: he didn't appear to take his own art seriously.

Recently, though De Palma's peaks have been less impressive, they have still matched those of most other filmmakers currently working and certainly surpassed those of his peers. Yet the films have been almost unanimously dismissed by the critics (critics who once took the time to revile him). Three times in succession, De Palma has made a film of uneven but seductive brilliance and suffered the ignominy of being ignored.[28] *Snake Eyes* was a smart, suspenseful thriller boasting a powerful performance from Nicholas Cage, a dazzlingly complex structure and a virtuoso shooting style that surpassed most if not all of De Palma's contemporaries. Admittedly, it was badly marred by a formulaic ending, but even so, in a period when halfway decent movies were increasingly hard to find, *Snake Eyes* was completely passed over as another mindless Hollywood action film.

Then came *Mission to Mars*, a sumptuous piece of filmmaking that displayed the director's technique to be nearing a state-of-the-art perfection bordering on cinematic grace. *Mission to Mars* had a richness of texture, a visual beauty, and an emotional sweep to it that few movies (much less sci-fi movies) can compete with. Depicting the zero gravity environment on the ship and the heartfelt cavorting between Tim Robbins and Connie Nielson, De Palma showed his passion and genius for moviemaking, his sheer love of the medium, and put audiences briefly in movie heaven. Audiences didn't seem to care, however.[29] Though once again a rather hackneyed ending reduced the overall power of the movie, nothing could account for its vitriolic reception by critics, the same critics (we might add) eulogizing over films like *Dances*

28 'They have an almost preprogrammed idea of "what De Palma is", and then they just walk into a screening and measure it against that immediately, without ever opening their eyes and watching what's on the screen.' *Interviews*, pg 171.
29 For a summer sci-fi movie, *Mission to Mars* had genuine depth of feeling (in the central husband and wife relationship), as well as an emotionally overwhelming scene in which one of the main characters dies. Apparently audiences didn't want to be moved by a sci-fi blockbuster, however, much less upset by it, and in part this may explain the film's appalling reception.

with Wolves, Titanic, Silence of the Lambs, Saving Private Ryan, Gosford Park and *Gangs of New York*.

Finally, De Palma made *Femme Fatale* – probably his most personal work since *Casualties of War* – and the film barely registered on critics' radar at all. *Femme Fatale* had many of the weaknesses of De Palma's worst 'personal' (Hitchcockian) thrillers (*Body Double, Raising Cain*), the improbable storyline, overblown set-pieces, and a penchant for voyeurism more in keeping with an oversexed adolescent than a man in his sixties; but it also had the soaring visual highs and the gleeful irony of his best earlier works (*Phantom of the Paradise, Carrie, Dressed to Kill*). It was dazzlingly shot, cunningly scripted, subtly moving and wickedly entertaining. But no one seemed to care, and the film was never even properly released in Europe.

As Auric Goldfinger tells James Bond: 'Once is happenstance. Twice is coincidence. The third time, Mr. Bond, is enemy action.' De Palma's artistry appeared to be under attack. Though none of these films could exactly be called enduring works of art, they were all superior pieces of entertainment, fresh, exciting movies from one of the country's foremost auteur filmmakers, one of the very few of who still seemed to be evolving and experimenting with his gifts. There seemed no obvious reason why audiences wouldn't go see these films and enjoy them, except that critics (for reasons equally mysterious) were almost unanimously telling them not to. As a result, De Palma has been unable to get his films funded in his own country, and has resorted (like Jarmusch) to seeking European backing. The sad irony is that, never was a filmmaker less inclined to small, intimate, independent filmmaking than De Palma, who – like Gilliam, Stone, Michael Mann or James Cameron – makes visual spectacles on a grand scale and has little or no interest in doing it on the raw. (Was ever a filmmaker less likely to do a Dogme film than De Palma?[30])

Like Hitchcock (and Tarantino), De Palma has a disregard for content, and even substance, a predilection for style. Though he often writes or co-writes his films and is extremely gifted with plotting and dialogue, his all-consuming passion for trying out and developing new cinematic techniques – for pure cinema, as Hitchcock called it – tends to give his films the appearance of superficiality. For De Palma however,

---

30 That said, De Palma did make *Home Movies* in 1980, a slight but endearing comedy that he shot with his students as part of their NY film course, using some of his regular actors (Keith Gordon and Nancy Allen from *Dressed to Kill*, Kirk Douglas from *The Fury*, Garret Graham from *Phantom*). The film was shot for next to nothing, and barely got a release at all, but it has endured, a little-known gem for the director's followers (what there are of them), and one of his most enjoyably personal films.

style, taken to such a level, is substance. Like Hitchcock, De Palma has
the skill and the ingenuity to cast a spell with his camera that precludes
(or makes redundant) any questions of depth or content. Unlike
Hitchcock, who was eventually 'understood' and fully appreciated by
critics and became the living exemplary of his medium, De Palma has
not been so lucky, but has become the victim of critics' inability to
look beyond the content and fully appreciate the style with his films are
imbued. As the director laments, with ample justification:

> 'There's a whole school of de Palma criticism that says I'm
> absolutely terrible, that I've never had an original idea in my life,
> that I'm just a poor man's Hitchcock. And, actually, I do get all
> the knocks Hitchcock used to get before critics decided he was a
> genius. They say this isn't literary material, that my themes aren't
> serious. I can give the answer Hitchcock gave. Like, "What is the
> content of a still life? *Nada!* But artists paint them anyway." ' [31]

Can there be any fate more galling than that of an artist enslaved to
a mainstream that refuses to acknowledge him and give him his due?
Does Hollywood have it in for Brian De Palma? Or is it just that,
by choosing to focus on the more superficial aspects of his trade and
thereby limiting his creativity (the man who made *The Untouchables*
and *Mission: Impossible* is plainly not the artist who made *Blow Out*
and *Casualties of War*), De Palma has offended his muse, and so jinxed
himself? Perhaps, by trying to satisfy two mistresses at once, he has been
faithful to neither, and incurred the wrath of both? Like Orson Welles
before him, he is in danger of becoming that most tragic of animals: an
artist cast out by his own medium.

The Auteur Syndrome: Evans' and Coppola's *The Cotton Club*

> 'The artist's worst fear is that he'll be exposed as a sham… Deep
> down we're all living with the notion that our success is beyond
> our ability.'
>
> Francis Coppola

Besides Orson Welles, there may never have been a Hollywood
filmmaker so briefly in tune with his muse and yet so inclined to hubris

31 *Brian De Palma: Interviews*, pg 85.

as Francis Coppola. Apparently, uncommon talent instills unreasonable ambition. Like Welles in his time (with *Citizen Kane*), Coppola can rightfully lay claim (with his two *Godfather* films) to have made the Great American Movie and so realized the ultimate ambition: to top all the rest. The two *Godfathers* are complete and irrefutable proof of the alchemy of movie art, of the fusing of countless different elements and facets of genius – performances, camerawork, lighting, set design, costumes, etc – into a nigh-impeccable and seamless whole that is greater than the (already impressive) sum of the parts. Alchemy.[32]

The Godfather was a story and subject of such tragic depth and significance that it seemed to take on a life of its own. As if by the in-dwelling spirit of 'Corleone', it summoned together the individual ingredients needed to do full justice to its heart-rending and universal tale of the road to perdition; and Coppola was the man who summoned the winds and rain and moved the Earth (or Hollywood) to make it happen. With *The Godfather* and *The Godfather Part Two*, Coppola became more than just a great filmmaker, he became a sorcerer, conjuring up the images of the collective unconscious and capturing them on celluloid forever. A true visionary, he wove his tapestry from the collective dreams of a nation as it prepared to face its demons. Yet what is more remarkable is how he imbued this tragic, archetypal myth-story with an intimacy and simplicity (and a veracity) drawn directly from his own personal feelings about family.[33] *The Godfathers* (and the experience of directing *Apocalypse Now* that followed) took everything out of Coppola, however, and after the 70s, he no longer had much stomach for plundering the fire of the gods. Coppola went on making movies, because that was what he knew how to do, and nothing he did could detract from what he had already achieved. Or could it?

The Cotton Club started out as a Robert Evans 'comeback' project with which Evans hoped to redeem himself after a string of bad luck and worse publicity suffered during the 80s. As well as producing

32 'Where the process gets at its best, where it's relaxed and fun, where every single moment becomes an opportunity, you don't even remember who thought of anything.' Coppola, quoted by Michael Sragow, 'Godfatherhood,' *New Yorker*, 24/3/97.
33 By casting his sister, Talia Shire, as Connie Corleone (Michael's sister), having his father conduct the score and write incidental music, and drawing countless details of the Corleone family life from his own Italian-American family memories, Coppola turned the Corleones into his own blood. What made the films so powerfully affecting was the way the characters never for a moment seemed like fictional Hollywood creations, but lived and breathed – and suffered and died – in the world which Coppola (and writer Mario Puzo) created for them, a world as rich as any fictional world ever invented.

it, Evans planned to make his debut as a director, and having paid $350,000 for the rights to the book (by James Haskins), Evans set about securing a budget before he even had a script. He passed around a poster he put together (using the tagline: 'Its violence startled the nation; its music startled the world') at Cannes, selling the future flick as '*The Godfather* with music.'[34] His first investor was the Arab arms trader, Adnan Khashoggi, who several years later became infamous for his involvement with the Iran-Contra affair. Khashoggi invested $2 million into the project, $1 million of which went immediately into hiring Mario Puzo – now a rich and successful author – to write a script. Unfortunately, when Khashoggi read Puzo's script, he backed out of the production. Evans managed to secure funding elsewhere, this time for a full-budget estimated at $18 to $20 million, from the Doumani brothers, owners of the Tropicana Hotel and El Morocco Casino in Las Vegas. Evans then succeeded in getting Richard Gere – fresh from *An Officer and a Gentleman* – to star in the film, and as a result of Gere's involvement Orion pictures offered $10 million to distribute the film. After weeks of work from Puzo, the script was in terrible shape, however; the Doumanis hated it so much they threatened to pull out of their agreement, while Gere was starting to have doubts too. In desperation, Evans called his old nemesis, Prince Machiavelli himself (Evans' pet name for Coppola). 'I have a sick child,' he said. 'I need a doctor.'

As a personal favor to Evans, Coppola offered to look at the script free of charge, and soon after he arranged a meeting at his Napa valley estate with Evans, Gere, Gregory Hines and producer Dyson Lovell. The ideas Coppola presented at the meeting impressed everyone (particularly Gere, but also Evans), and Evans gave Coppola a quarter of a million dollars to rework the script based on his suggestions. Coppola came back with a script that (according to a dismayed Evans) had nothing to do with Coppola's original pitch. Evans had no choice but to pay Coppola another quarter million to do it again and to do it right this time. All of this money was coming out of Evans' own pocket, since the Doumanis refused to authorize the Coppola rewrites. Coppola, meanwhile, was under pressure of his own, receiving increasingly ominous predictions of doom concerning

34 Evans' idea was a historic treatment of the famous cotton clubs of the 20s, which were largely run by gangsters and that only whites were allowed to enter (mostly white celebrities), despite the fact that all the musicians playing there were black. 'Godfatherhood,' *New Yorker*, 24th March 1997.

his beloved studio, Zoetrope, which was in the process of going down the tubes forever.

When the Doumanis finally got a look at Coppola's script (despite Evans' best efforts at damage control), they were so appalled they withdrew all further funding from the movie. In desperation, Evans made a deal with a variety show promoter, Roy Radin, and together they formed a holding company in Puerto Rico worth $35 million, money that was supposedly coming from the Puerto Rican government. The company's first project was to be backing *The Cotton Club*, but soon after the agreement, Radin was shot in the head, his body found rotting in a canyon outside LA.[35]

According to Evans' account of the ill-fated production, it was around now that, little by little, Coppola began to insinuate himself into the production and, backed by Gere (understandably more enthusiastic about starring in a Coppola film than Robert Evans' directorial debut), took over as director. By Evans' account:

> 'Coppola summoned the department heads, the three investors and me to his office at Astoria Studios. With his wife Ellie beside him, he slowly panned each and everyone before him. He knew the moment was right, the next nail was ready to be hammered in my coffin. Suddenly he thrust his finger in my face. 'It's not *The Godfather*, Evans. I've had it! Fed up with you. Tired of your second guessing. Tired of everything about you. The family's packed, we're outta here. You do it or I do it. You stay, I leave.' Shocked? I thought I was hallucinating… No mistake about it – this was an ingeniously conceived, ten-year-festering come shot, a royal fucking from Prince Machiavelli himself.'[36]

Evans is almost certainly embellishing his role as fall guy here, however, and according to Coppola, Evans begged him to take over. 'I always thought it was for him to direct,' Coppola said. 'Then he said that it was too big for him to direct, and that I had to. I refused many times, always offering to help him – to spend the first few weeks backing him up on the set. I didn't realize that he needed me to get the money, and he never said that. He was never honest with me.'[37]

35 Though Radin's death was eventually established as having nothing to do with Evans or the movie, it was for a long time known as '*The Cotton Club* murder,' much to everyone's chagrin, most especially Evans'.

36 *The Kid Stays in the Picture*, pg. 345.

37 Schumacher, *Francis Ford Coppola: A Filmmaker's Life*, pg. 343.

Whatever the case, Coppola agreed to direct the film for $2.5 million, a slice of the profits and complete creative control. Evans consented, whereupon Coppola proceeded to fire most of the team that Evans had assembled and replace them with his own people; Evans had no choice but to sit back and pay for it all. Exasperated by his increasing lack of control, or even input, Evans decided to stay away from the set altogether, reassuring the Doumanis that he could reign Coppola in if and when it became necessary. This was something Evans must have had every reason to doubt, however, and doubtless the Doumanis had their doubts too.[38] In the end, as was inevitable from the beginning, Coppola took over the film completely, and what had once been Evans' baby became Francis' monster.

However unreliable Evans' version of events may be (he has had a long-standing feud with Coppola, ever since they butted heads over *The Godfather*), it is probably not entirely devoid of facts. Judging at least by the finished product – all-too clearly the result of a director's runaway megalomania, loss of perspective or judgment, and the resulting collapse of anything resembling teamwork – Coppola does seem to have been largely at fault. Coming from the same team that made *The Godfather*, *The Cotton Club* was an inverse example of the collaborative process, of how utterly wrong it can go when there is a lack of unifying vision to fuel or direct it. The film wound up costing around $50 million, and was a sprawling, unsightly cacophony of a movie with almost nothing going for it. It was final, shocking proof of the dissolution of Coppola's talents as a filmmaker.

However shaky Evans would have turned out to be as a director, it's hard to imagine that he could have made a worse film than Coppola's, or anything quite as soulless, tacky and vapid as that which audiences were landed with in 1984. Evans at least believed in his movie when he started it. Coppola appeared to have taken over mostly for mercenary reasons. He may even have been on a strange power trip, paying back Evans for whatever affront Coppola considered him guilty of.[39] Whatever his motives, there can be little doubt that, in the absence of a personal vision or a strong producer presence to direct

38 According to Fred Doumani, Evans '…abnegated all responsibility. Most of the fighting should never have happened. But Bob Evans went to New York, worked out of his townhouse, visited the set for about one hour and never went back again.' Schumacher, pg. 357.
39 Specifically, one imagines, for ever having dared to suggest that he, Evans, had saved *The Godfather* from mediocrity by forcing Coppola to reinstate the scenes he had removed for his first, two-hour cut of the film.

the director, Coppola simply lost his way. In a *Playboy* interview with William Murray, in July 1975, Coppola said the following:

'There are a handful of directors today who have total authority and deserve it. And then there are a lot of other directors who really ought to be working with strong producers and strong writers, but they all think they're Stanley Kubrick. The auteur theory is fine, but to exercise it you have to qualify, and the only way to qualify is by having earned the right to have control, by having turned out a series of really incredibly good films. Some men have it, and some men don't. I don't feel that one or two hits or one or two beautiful films entitle anyone to that much control. A lot of very promising directors have been destroyed by it. It's a big dilemma, of course, because, unfortunately, the authority these days is almost always shared with people who have no business being producers and studio executives. With one or two exceptions, there's no one running the studios who's qualified, either; so you have a vacuum, and the director has to fill it.'

With *Apocalypse Now*, Coppola had certainly attempted to fill that vacuum, and to become a one-man renaissance with his very own studio. But in the end, the vacuum swallowed him up. It seems unthinkable that anyone capable of making the original two *Godfather* movies – films of scope and grandeur filled with devastating insights into the corrupting effects of power – wouldn't have a certain tendency towards excess ambition and ruthlessness, and all that this entails – megalomania, extreme competitiveness, and a lack of generosity when it came to sharing credit with others. Such qualities may help cement a director's legend – as in Coppola's case – but they will almost invariably take a corresponding toll upon his vision. Generosity and selflessness are as essential to the nurturing of vision as small-mindedness and greed are antithetical to it.

Significantly, Orson Welles betrayed a similar voraciousness when it came to taking credit for *Citizen Kane*, and at one time even took his co-writer Herman Mankiewicz's name off the shooting script entirely. According to Pauline Kael (in her exhaustive essay on the making of the film, *Raising Kane*), Mankiewicz was as essential a creative force in the genesis of *Kane* as Welles, so it's ironic that Welles later touted the supremacy of the writer in the filmmaking process, considering that he was never able to give full credit to his collaborator for the film that made his name (and did little for Mankiewicz's standing).

There is a tendency for 'geniuses' to need to be given total credit for the work they do in order to maintain the illusion of divine inspiration, as if only lesser mortals require collaborators. Yet in Coppola's case, the fact that he has always been extremely generous in giving his co-writer Mario Puzo credit for The Godfather films would seem to give the lie to this.[40] Still, like Welles, Coppola's career, post-Apocalypse, has been so disappointing that he may have felt increasingly insecure and a growing need to defend at any cost his genius, even as his talents deserted him. Perhaps Coppola's reluctance to share credit extends specifically to producers, or perhaps even solely to Evans, for whom, for reasons never fully divulged, Coppola seems to have a basic distrust, even animosity. If so, he may have had his revenge on The Cotton Club; but then, so did Evans.

Throughout the shoot, Evans was barred from seeing the film's rushes and only saw any footage towards the end of the shoot, when Coppola showed a rough edit to some four hundred company members, in an attempt to boost everyone's seriously flagging spirits. Evans was appalled by what he saw; in its present state, he considered the film almost unreleasable. In this, at least, he was justified. But the lines of communication were down; as Schumacher writes, 'The macho posturing between the two became so ridiculous that, according to one account, they actually considered fighting a duel, not with guns but with fists.'[41] What's more, Evans was legally barred from the film. Orion had agreed to furnish an additional $15 million to finish the production, but only on one condition: Evans was to have no further control over production, distribution or advertising of his once beloved baby, The Cotton Club. Coppola's mood can't have been much better. On February 19th 1984, Zoetrope Studios went up for public auction, and was bought by the businessman Jack Singer for just over the minimum bid of $2.2 million. Overnight, Coppola's dream came to a final end and his beloved Zoetrope became Singer studios (Coppola did manage to negotiate the rights to continue using the name Zoetrope, however, even if the studio itself was now history.)

In despair, Evans filed suit against the Doumanis, Coppola and

40 Even in the case of the second film, when Coppola was working with a largely original story conceived by himself, the film began with the title 'Mario Puzo's The Godfather.'
41 Schumacher, pg. 359. Schumacher also notes how, 'Robert Evans had reached the limits of his own patience with the project. For months, he had watched his authority over the picture gradually stripped away to nothing, even though he was expected to help find more money to keep it running; he had not received a penny in salary for his efforts, and his percentage in the film's profits was looking like so much ink on paper. His personal credit was in serious jeopardy.' (ibid)

Orion, attempting to regain at least some control over the film he had initiated, almost four years previous. Several more law suits followed, coming from various different quarters and making *The Cotton Club* – with its murders, shady backers, producer-director in-fighting and plethora of court hearings – one of the most ill-fated and controversial movie productions in Hollywood history. As a result of his suit, Evans was again granted control over marketing and distribution of the film, and his name was to appear on the credits; he was denied any say in postproduction, however. Evans then reached an agreement with the Doumanis, abandoning all his interest in the picture in exchange for a cash settlement and the cancelling of a $1.6 million debt to the Doumanis (for which Evans' home was collateral). As Schumacher writes, 'Evans could not have expected more. The court case had restored some of his bruised reputation, and the settlement had restored some of his cash. By Hollywood standards, it was a sweetheart bargain.'[42]

Coppola meanwhile (with debts of his own to contend with) had nearly half a million feet of film to edit into a two hour movie. Having seen the rough cut, Evans knew it was in bad shape, and spent fourteen hours composing a thirty-one page critique full of suggestions on how to salvage the work. He sent it to Coppola via the Doumanis, and Coppola ignored every one of Evans' suggestions. 'He would rather see the picture do three hundred thousand and not three hundred million than have Evans get credit for being the saving grace,' wrote Evans.[43] Coppola released the film in the form he wanted, and that is the film we have to this day: a creative disaster from start to finish and a complete failure in every regard. Would Evans' suggestions have salvaged the movie? It seems doubtful; but on the other hand, there's a fair chance they might have improved it, and that Coppola, determined to do his own thing, blocked Evans not out of artistic integrity, but out of creative conceit and artistic hubris.

If so, Coppola's words came back to haunt him, as words so often do. He had become a victim of 'the auteur syndrome', of the vacuum at the center of movie production, and of his own incapacity to fill it. The Bitch Goddess had wreaked her revenge.

---

42 Schumacher, pg. 363. Like Coppola, Evans' judgment seemed drastically to fail him in the 90s, and he wound up producing works like *Sliver* and *Jade*, eulogizing over the genius of 'Maestro Friedkin' (whom he laughably referred to as 'an explorer of the art of film'), and touting future cinematic geniuses who were never heard of again. (Evans on George Gallo: 'As far as Gallo's concerned, I don't think, I know: he's the Coppola of the 90s.' George who?) For all his flailing after former greatness, the closest Evans came was by writing his memoirs.

43. Evans, *The Kid Stays in the Picture*, pg. 354–357.

Chapter Seven - God and Cosmetics: Hollywood 'Morality' and the Vow of Chastity

'Creation 101 years/or how edison destroyed god – when the camera projected at 24 frames, man looked and saw himself on the screen. He saw himself big. It wasn't until the cinema that man actually saw who he thought he was and or who he wanted to be. And until that point in time man had thought of god in mainly simple, comfortable terms, we had to visualize him. God to us was big and he had no competition. Now that we are the same size as god, we don't need him, he is worthless to us, we can sit in the movie house/temple on Sundays. God will commit suicide. The virgin mary is bardot. God has left us here with 32 Elvis movies all dubbed in German.'

Laird Henn (formerly Harmony Korine), *Digital Babylon*

Dogme 95 and the Aesthetics of Asceticism

'Dogme 95 is a rescue action! In 1960 enough was enough! The movie was dead and called for a resurrection. The goal was correct but the means were not! The New Wave proved to be a ripple that washed ashore and turned to muck. Slogans of individualism and freedom created works for a while, but no changes. The wave was up for grabs, like the directors themselves. The wave was never stronger than the men behind it.'

Dogme 95 Manifesto

The idea of bringing a monastic discipline – an ascetic aesthetic – to movies, complete with political rigor and a manifesto, was not unprecedented, but it was an audacious move all the same. In Paris in the 1920s and 1930s, André Breton, Max Ernst, Jean Cocteau, Salvador Dali and others wrote their own manifesto and formed their 'secret society' of surrealists, an artistic movement as political as it was artistic. There is a natural tendency for artists to group together into elitist factions. They are, after all, a band apart from ordinary people, and by temperament and calling set against the society they are forced to inhabit. Of course, it is necessary for an artist to set himself against something, and after family (the enemy of the adolescent), society as a whole is the logical adversary for a rebellious nature. Artists both thrive and depend on outsider status, and that status is strengthened by opposing an exiting consensus, be it social, political or artistic. This is a more or less reactionary position, but a radical one, and an original, impulsive reaction against an existing system of thought (and the rejection of it) can often lead to creative regeneration, inspiration and a new 'wave' – even a revolution.

Artistic revolutions are safer and generally more effective than social ones. Since it is not a political system or institution that is being challenged but an abstract aesthetic, a way of thinking, any changes brought about by the 'revolution' don't need long-term success, but only need to be noticed. The mere fact that the artistic 'revolution' occurs is enough, since the arrival of new concepts forces the medium to evolve, in order to accommodate them.

In the case of Dogme 95, the Danish avant-garde (Lars von Trier[1], Thomas Vinterberg, Søren Kragh-Jacobsen and Kristian Levring) were filmmakers and not politicians, and they chose as their symbol of a tyrannical, totalitarian system (to defy and if possible destroy) none other than – Hollywood. This was never overtly stated – the 'enemy' was wisely not named – but it was implicit in the terms used.[2] The Dogme

1 Lars Trier was raised by Jewish, 'radical, nudist Communist parents' who, as Trier put it, allowed everything besides 'feelings, religion and enjoyment.' At eleven, young Lars was given a Super-8 camera and soon went to work. He spent his teens making movies, and signed up at the Copenhagen film school in 1980; his student films won prizes at the Munich Film Festival in both 1981 and 1982. Trier, now von Trier (having added the 'von' for aristocratic affect) graduated in 1983 and made his first feature, the low-budget futuristic thriller *The Element of Crime*. It was released in 1984 and won a technical prize at Cannes. *Epidemic* came out in 1987, a film in which von Trier played a director trying to raise money to make a movie about a lethal virus unleashed in Germany. Then in 1988, von Trier made *Medea*, for Danish TV, and completed his 'European trilogy' with *Europa*, in 1991 (the film was retitled *Zentropa* for its American release). *Europa* came in third place for the Special Jury Prize at Cannes, and in his acceptance speech, von Trier, angry about coming in third place, gave thanks to 'the midget' (referring to jury chairman Roman Polanski). He worked on a miniseries for Danish TV, *The Kingdom*, in 1994, and in 1995 his mother gave Lars her 'deathbed revelation' when she informed him that he was not really Jewish. Von Trier converted to Catholicism and, partly in emulation of the Danish filmmaker Carl Theodore Dreyer, he co-authored the Dogme 95 manifesto with Thomas Vinterberg. Von Trier's next movie, *Breaking the Waves* (1996, not a Dogme film) became an art house hit and this time earned von Trier second place on the Cannes Grand Jury. After making *The Kingdom II* in 1997, and after Vinterberg's *Festen* (*The Celebration*) brought Dogme 95 to the attention of the world, von Trier unveiled his own Dogme work, *The Idiots*, in 1998, to much controversy and acclaim.
2. The Vow of Chastity: 'I swear to submit to the following set of rules drawn up and confirmed by DOGME 95: 1. Shooting must be done on location. Props and sets must not be brought in. 2. The sound must never be produced apart from the image or vice versa. (Music must not be used unless it occurs where the scene is being shot.) 3. The camera must be handheld. 4. The film must be in color. Special lighting is not acceptable.
(continued overleaf)

95 manifesto was a rejection and defiance of genre conventions, and more generally of the homogenized Hollywood style of moviemaking that reduced everything to an 'immoral' stimulation of the senses, and a deadening of intellect and imagination. Dogme's mix of vision and cunning (or opportunism) was in voicing a till-then unspoken dissent in the general pubic towards the commercialization of movies; it was also addressing, more or less covertly, a corresponding need for new inspiration in filmmakers. (Not specifically American ones, however, and the very pertinence of the challenge to US sensibilities tended to make it unacceptable to them. American filmmakers, as the ones most in need of embracing the Dogme aesthetic, were the least inclined to do so.)

Had Dogme 95 been no more than a manifesto, it would never have made it outside Denmark. There was nothing especially original about the 'rules' – Cassavetes in the US and Godard in France had already 'invented' the raw, documentary style of filmmaking and had never felt the need to make an itinerary of their methods. The most remarkable thing about the Vow of Chastity was its audacity and its seemingly arbitrary choices as to what constituted 'pure' cinema and what didn't (black and white was forbidden, for example). The Dogme brothers astutely chose to announce their new aesthetic in tandem with unveiling the first experiment in it, *Festen* (*The Celebration*); the following year, von Trier delivered *The Idiots*. These films were the best, indeed only, testimony to the validity of the manifesto.

Both films had strong story ideas, well-written scripts and accomplished performances, and would have stood out even if they had been shot in a more conventional fashion. As it was, the hand-held cameras, digital photography, absence of musical scores, and stripped down location shooting gave audiences the unshakable impression (however much they knew otherwise) of watching dramatic documentaries; interestingly, this impression did not reduce the intensity of the drama but increased it, the unstaged realism adding a new sense

---

5. optical work and filters are forbidden. 6. The film must not contain superficial action. (Murders, weapons, etc, must not occur.) 7. Temporal and geographical alienation are forbidden. (That is to say that the film takes place here and now.) 8. Genre movies are not acceptable. 9. Film format must be Academy 35 mm. 10. The director must not be credited. Furthermore, I swear as a director to refrain from personal taste! I am no longer an artist. I swear to refrain from creating a 'work' as I regard the instant as more important than the whole. My supreme goal is to force the truth out of my characters and settings. I swear to do so by all the means available and at the cost of any good taste and any aesthetic considerations. Thus I make my VOW OF CHASTITY.'

of urgency. The films caused a stir at Cannes and throughout Europe, and finally in the US (where *The Idiots* was censored for its orgiastic sex scenes); within less than a year, Dogme 95 looked set to take over Hollywood. That never happened, of course, yet clearly the time was ripe for a re-evaluation of cinematic values.

The over-produced, underwritten, bloated SFX blockbusters that Hollywood continued to churn out (*Hollow Man*, *The Saint*, *Con Air*, *Batman Forever*, *What Lies Beneath*, *Godzilla*, *Armageddon*, etc) were beginning to collapse under their own weight. Worse, audiences were starting to show their disgust by hooting at the screen, walking out, or even – on rare occasions – demanding their money back. Hollywood's worst nightmare was creeping into the realms of possibility: quality control for movies! The old formulas weren't working anymore. How many times could you re-do *Jaws*, *Star Wars* or *Independence Day*, without using up the formula? Each time the result was a little shabbier and emptier, copies of copies of copies, until audiences found themselves staring at films like *The Avengers*, and the penny started to drop. Hollywood couldn't dumb down audiences as fast as the product itself was degenerating; audiences were 'wising up'. There was a limit to how many times they would allow their intelligence to be insulted and their time wasted without balking, or choking.

Dogme 95 wasn't a solution to any of this, but it was at least a response. By offering up the opposite extreme, and offering it up as entertainment, it presented a stark and troubling (though also inspiring) contrast to Hollywood's 'business-as-usual'. Dogme 95 succeeded where Tarantino's paltry Band Apart had failed, by bringing filmmakers together and having them banish their egos momentarily for the sake of something greater than their own glory. Pleasing audiences and achieving financial success naturally went hand in hand. Tarantino and his sidekick Rodriguez (and those other indie filmmakers he tried to band together for *Four Rooms*) may have had something on their agenda besides spoon-feeding the public, but the desire for acceptance and admiration was still primary. Vanity outstripped commitment to creative innovation, and stunted these artists' growth.

By willfully defying the unwritten rules of commercial cinema and popular entertainment (supplanting them with written rules all their own), Dogme 95 pledged its allegiance to the creative process and to evolving new variations of it, new twists, and popularity and audience acceptance be damned. By forgoing director's credit, Dogme 95 demanded the ultimate sacrifice – that of fame and recognition – making it clear that the gains of Dogme filmmaking – the spoils of conquering new artistic terrain – were not those of ego-gratification but pertained to the greater glory of 'art'.[3] Such an audacious appeal, backed as it was by living examples and practitioners, couldn't fail to stir the vanity and curiosity of artists everywhere. It was a call to arms and a challenge for filmmakers to prove themselves, to test their dedication and integrity as innovators and explorers of the medium. It was also a means for otherwise proud individuals, being anything but group-orientated, to join a collective cause without forsaking their customary and much-valued autonomy and isolation. Dogme was not an organization but an abstract, an ideal that could be tested by applying it (i.e., making a Dogme movie). In the process, artists could test themselves by facing the challenges of the Chastity Vow.

Von Trier subsequently made it clear that the Vow of Chastity was meant for one film only, and that the 'movement' of Dogme 95 was as much a stunt or subterfuge as anything. It was the means to attract attention (publicity) to the idea of 'pure' filmmaking and bring the current state of the art into relief, into new perspective. The idea of making a Dogme film was for filmmakers to strengthen and develop their talents by deliberately restricting them, to stimulate their imagination and hopefully regenerate their creativity by forcing them to view their craft through a new lens, and so rediscover it at a purer, more simplified level. By stripping the art form down to its basic core, filmmakers could effectively start over, rediscover their virginity, so to speak, and in the process, regain the curiosity, excitement and enthusiasm of amateurs exploring a new mode of expression. One film was enough, because the point of Dogme 95 wasn't to create a new formula but to free filmmakers from their tendency to follow formulas and get stuck in a routine approach to their craft, making films by numbers rather than from the heart and gut.[4]

The idea was sound, but despite its enormous success in getting noticed across the globe – and despite a few diverse recruits in the US who rose to the challenge[5] – the Dogme goal has yet to be attained,

---

3 Of course, this was a symbolic gesture, since the director of a Dogme film was always identified, one way or another, and even wound up getting extra attention by forgoing titular credit.

4 Von Trier says, 'All these rules are designed for me to give away control… If you see the rules, they are more or less designed for me not to do what I have been doing for a long time.' *Digital Babylon: Hollywood, Indiewood & Dogme 95*, by Sharl Roman, pg. 50.

5 Harmony Korine – writer of *Kids* and director of *Gummo* – made the first American Dogme film, *julien donkeyboy*, in 2002, followed by *Chetzemoka's Curse*, *Amerikana*, *Camera*, *Reunion*, *Resin* and *Security, Colorado*.

and no regeneration or revolution of the medium has occurred. It's true that Steven Spielberg expressed a childlike (or childish?) desire to make his own Dogme movie, but so far he has been content to go on slumming with the Toms (Cruise and Hanks). If Spielberg or Oliver Stone or Tarantino, or even Woody Allen, had taken the bait, thrown caution (and consistency) to the wind and made their own contribution to Dogme 95, it's likely that other Hollywood filmmakers would have followed suit; maybe there would even have been a chain reaction, a freeing up of the form and a new influx of experimentalism and innovation, similar to that of the late 60s and early 70s. But Hollywood engenders its talent above all with a mix of timidity and self-importance, a poor combination for a filmmaker when it comes to reinventing the self. [6]

Clint Eastwood and the Art of Unraveling

'At this particular time in my life, I'm not doing anything as a moneymaker. It's like I'm pushing the envelope the other way to see how far we can go to be noncommercial.'

Clint Eastwood, 2005

Once upon a time Clint Eastwood was no more highly regarded as a film artist than Charles Bronson, and was similarly dismissed as a one-trick action pony whose popularity was as prodigious as his range was limited. Today he is venerated as a rock and a legend, a Hollywood survivor and pioneer, a veritable one-man movie industry. As a filmmaker, Eastwood has proved unreliable at best, responsible both for some of the most dubious, formulaic and mindless action films and some of the best movies ever to come out of Hollywood. His career now spans forty years, from his emergence as the lethal, silent Man With No Name in Sergio Leone's *A Fistful of Dollars* (in 1964) to his recent triumph with *Million Dollar Baby* in 2005. In between, he has acted in almost fifty films and directed twenty-eight to date (most of which he appeared in, and counting his current work, *The Flags of Our Fathers*).

Like Cary Grant, Eastwood never got much credit for doing what he did, however well he did it, mostly because he made it look so damn

6 Reinvention of the self may be the *sine qua non* of the creative journey, but it is sheer anathema to Hollywood. A director who has finally got the system to work for him has no desire to rock the boat he thinks he's now helming. Of course, that may be precisely what the system *wants* him to think, and when an artist decides he is at the top of his game, the game is already as good as over.

easy. Unlike Grant, however, Eastwood never had much of a range, even within the parameters of the one character he did play. Eastwood's strength was in embodying the cool, strong, silent, sardonic center around which chaos and destruction invariably unfurled. Eastwood has often quoted a Hollywood director telling Gary Cooper, 'Don't just do something, stand there!' As an actor, Eastwood just stood there, and the less he did, the more hypnotic he was. In terms of sheer cool and screen magnetism, Eastwood was without peer, and he was the most popular film star of the 70s. He wasn't any worse an actor than Cooper, and he could hold his own in the flinty, squinty, tough guy department against fellow hard men Lee Marvin, Steve McQueen and Charles Bronson. He might not give much competition in the nice guy department to Redford or Newman, but he shared their sexiness, smoothness and charm. Such traits combined with his virility and volatility into a screen presence no other actor could compete with. The 70s were Eastwood's time as an actor, his commercial prime and the period in which he found his meatiest roles and gave some of his best performances. They were also when he began to cut his teeth as a filmmaker.

Eastwood's first directing experience was *Play Misty For Me*, which he convinced Universal to let him direct, without fee and on the condition that he took the leading role (a disc jockey terrorized by an obsessive female fan). Eastwood was nervous about directing a feature with so little experience and persuaded his mentor, director Don Siegel, to take a small role in the film as a bartender, to provide Eastwood with moral support. Siegel was so terrified by his first acting role that Eastwood soon forgot his own anxiety, and the next thing he knew, he was a director. The film was thin and creaky, but it held together well enough and delivered the goods. (Today it might be seen as a prototype for *Fatal Attraction*.)

Soon after this debut, Eastwood formed his own production company, called Malpaso. The name Malpaso was Spanish for 'wrong step' and inspired by a piece of advice Eastwood received about *A Fistful of Dollars,* that it would be a '*mal paso*' and that he would live to regret it. The film made him a star, of course, and Eastwood has continued to take '*mal pasos*' ever since. Eastwood's name for the company was a private joke and piece of poetic irony, but it was also an indication of how the actor-director relied on his instincts to make decisions, and how little he valued the 'guidance' of outsiders. Eastwood enjoyed such phenomenal success playing archetypal Western and urban heroes essentially because he *was* the archetypal, self-determining male, doing what his gut told him to do and backing down for nobody. He was the

American dream in a dusty poncho with a squint and a cheroot – a ruthless killer of mystical prowess – whose instincts (if not his creative choices) have proved almost infallible throughout his career.

Eastwood followed *Play Misty* with *High Plains Drifter*, a crude, surrealist pulp Western classic for which he successfully aped his maestro Sergio Leone's style. On *Drifter*, Eastwood's amateurism was as starkly, touchingly apparent as it had been on *Misty*, but he was now on considerably safer ground, and the movie was one of the seminal Hollywood revenge fantasies of the period. It was also a model of 'economic' (in terms of plot and dialogue as much as budget) filmmaking. From the outset Eastwood possessed an ability to cut corners and reduce superfluous spending – be it on repeat takes, overpaid stars or unnecessarily lavish production – as rare in Hollywood as it was cost effective. His movies consistently came in under budget and ahead of schedule, and rarely if ever did they suffer the usual logistical difficulties or 'creative differences' that plagued most Hollywood productions.

Although Malpaso was Eastwood's own company and oversaw all levels of production, it was basically a subsidiary of Warner Bros., the studio which has funded all but a few of Eastwood's movies for the duration of his career.[7] Eastwood's presence in a movie alone was enough to guarantee a profit for the studio, at least so long as he didn't stray too far from type.[8] In the late 80s, Eastwood began to display a growing interest in less conventional, more experimental film projects, and in 1988 he made *Bird*, a film about Charlie Parker, a dead black jazz musician and heroin addict (in which Eastwood didn't star) that the studio was considerably less enthusiastic about supporting. Not even Clint Eastwood is guaranteed a green light in Hollywood, and much of his career has evidenced (even to the casual observer) an ongoing compromise between his own creative interests – jazz, for example – and his commercial obligations to the studio, as a box office 'giant'.

As early as 1973, Eastwood made the wafer-thin, melancholic whimsy

7 Woody Allen had a similar kind of relationship with Arthur Krim at United Artists, and later Orion, who gave Allen *carte blanche* to do whatever films he wanted on a one-a-year basis, confident that once in a while the director would deliver a high-prestige hit, such as *Annie Hall*, *Manhattan*, *Hannah and Her Sisters* or *Bullets Over Broadway*. Allen's films always recuperated their costs on the overseas market anyway, where he is considerably more popular than in the US.

8 As in Siegel's *The Beguiled*, in 1971, in which he plays a wounded civil war soldier who hides out at a girls' school and has his leg amputated by jealous females (one of his few commercial failures from the period), or later with *Bronco Billy* and *Honkytonk Man*.

Breezy, with William Holden as an aging businessman who falls for a young hippie waif (Kay Lenz). The film was a mistake creatively, and a complete flop commercially, but it demonstrated early on Eastwood's need to break out of the mold and make films with something besides violence as their primary *raison d'être*. His next film as director gave the lie to that however. *The Eiger Sanction* was a mean-spirited and mediocre revenge thriller that at least allowed Eastwood to indulge his passion for mountain climbing (as ever, he did most of his own stunts), and was the kind of film that audiences and studios expected from him. At such a level (commercially), it 'delivered'. In 1976, Eastwood made *The Outlaw Josey Wales,* his first mature work as a director.[9]

In 1980, after directing *The Gauntlet* and enjoying his biggest hit to date with *Every Which Way But Loose,* Eastwood made *Bronco Billy* – perhaps the first of his films to betray the actor's desire to play with his image and subvert the iconography of the Western hero. Though *Josey Wales* is by far the more revered film, *Bronco Billy* was probably Eastwood's first inspired work as a director. Though it's little more than an appealing whimsy, coming from the biggest box office action hero at that time, it was a minor revelation. It was also a flop. The public didn't want to see Eastwood as a down-on-his-luck circus owner struggling to keep a sorry band of losers together, they wanted to see him curl his lip and kill people; ever one to respect his audience's wishes, Eastwood made *Sudden Impact* in 1984, his fourth excursion as *Dirty Harry* and a hideous, rancid thing to behold.

Besides *Honkytonk Man* (in which he played a country and western singer dying of tuberculosis, one of his finest films, and also a flop), the 80s were not a good time for Eastwood creatively. He seemed too old to convincingly play the crusading urban avenger anymore, his heart no longer in it. But his attempts at self-satire (*City Heat*) were strained, and his excursion into Western terrain (*Pale Rider*) shaky at best. After he

9 Eastwood fired the film's original director, Philip Kaufman, and took over the reigns himself, so ironically, from Kaufman's point of view, the auteur-to-be Eastwood represented the interfering studio sabotaging the director's 'vision' (in this case appropriating it as his own). Also telling is that Eastwood's career as an actor is marked, and severely marred, by his choice never, or almost never, to work with directors of any real authority or vision, or even much by way of talent. In 1974, Eastwood gave Michael Cimino his first gig directing his own script, and the result (*Thunderbolt and Lightfoot*) was not only one of Eastwood's best films but also one of his finest performances. But for most of his career, from the mid-70s on, Eastwood either directed himself or hired one of his crew to stand in as director (for example, Buddy Van Horn, who took the blame for several of Eastwood's worst movies). One result of this is that, for most of his career, until recently at least, Eastwood has failed to develop much as an actor.

made *Bird*, however, Eastwood suddenly enjoyed a critical reevaluation as a 'serious' director (as ever, the reevaluations began with the French). The film was sombre and self-conscious, and considerably less a work of art than it wanted to be; but it showed another side to Eastwood, one that at least aspired to being an artist. With *Unforgiven* in 1992, for which he won the Academy Award as Best Director, his canonization was complete; since then, his career has continued to regenerate itself. However excessive the praise for *Unforgiven*, it signified a willingness on behalf of the critics, and the industry at large, to give Eastwood his due as one of the foremost artist-entertainers ever to make his home in Hollywood. Eastwood was not someone critics took seriously until he forced them to do so, and it was Eastwood's presence as a movie personality, his sheer authority, determination and adaptability within the business, that finally called attention to the work itself.

Eastwood is a filmmaker with a need for total control over the shooting process, with little patience for the waste – or perceived waste – of repeat takes and extended shoots. This approach to filmmaking has given Eastwood's films a certain solid, workmanlike uniformity and a lack of 'flourishes' which at worst makes for dreary and lifeless works made with apparent sloppy indifference.[10] As a director, Eastwood was self-taught and self-made. He started out as a movie star before he knew much about acting, and embarked on a career as a director before he knew more than the basic rudiments of directing. He created his own production company in the same spirit, and with the same uncanny self-confidence he resolved to learn simply by doing it. His career has been one of trial-and-error characterized by an enviable indifference to the opinions or judgments of others, and today Eastwood seems to make movies not for himself, exactly, but without much of an eye towards audiences (and certainly not for the studios). Eastwood has always been more a craftsman than an artist – witness his inconsistent judgment of material – and he is motivated perhaps most of all by the pleasures of developing his craft. If so, it is his strength as much as his weakness.

It seems unlikely that Eastwood can't tell the difference between a poor script and a good one (between a *Space Cowboys* and a *Mystic River*), but it can't be that he doesn't care, either. Probably he simply likes to work, and continues to do so regardless of whether he has the

---

10 Besides *The Eiger Sanction*, Eastwood also directed *Firefox, Sudden Impact, Tightrope, The Rookie, Pink Cadillac, Space Cowboys, Blood Work*. It's hard to think of any other American filmmaker whose oeuvre betrays such an appalling contrast between works of depth and artistry and works of complete, dreary ineptitude.

right material or not. Eastwood's artistry as a director is similar in nature to his strength and presence as an actor. It stems from cool detachment and a nonchalance bordering on indifference. There is an underlying perspective in his films of the everyday, a matter-of-factness that grounds the work in the real world and gives it substance and grace.

Eastwood has cited John Huston's advice to filmmakers – 'Treat every scene like it's the most important scene in the picture' – and this sums up his approach to making movies: take it one step at a time. 'If you can just take each scene at a time and really get the very best out of it, it'll dovetail together and be very nice... Don Siegel used to call it unraveling. Let's just see how this scene unravels... I like to see what the instincts bring to it. After a while, we can fiddle with it.'[11]

Hitchcock, an obsessive director whose approach to film was as far removed from Eastwood's as it's possible to imagine, was oft-quoted as saying, 'It's only a movie'. For Hitchcock, movies were everything, however, so the remark was perhaps more a mix of self-effacement and bluff than anything. With Eastwood it is different. Never driven to make movies by creative obsession or personal vision, Eastwood's talents have never been in danger of burning out. On the contrary, they have slowly – painfully slowly in fact – developed and reached maturity. Now that Eastwood is in his 70s, he has begun to do his best work. His case is almost unique among filmmakers.

Mystic River, his most powerful film so far, was an urban melodrama soaked in darkness, with a depth of personal pain and tragedy almost reminiscent of Shakespeare. *Million Dollar Baby*, his most recent work, though less showy overall, contains Eastwood's best work to date, both as director and actor.[12] Eastwood's sensitivity as a filmmaker has evolved notably in the last few years, even since *Mystic River*, in which he discovered a gift for observation and empathy previously undeveloped. *Million Dollar Baby* carries audiences along on a wave of trust and affection for the characters, and for Eastwood himself (who has his best role in years

11 Eastwood quoted from '*Mystic River*. From Page to Screen', DVD extra.
12 A melancholy, sardonic, unsentimental love story worthy of John Huston, the film begins as an archetypal tale of a reluctant veteran trainer (boxing manager Frankie) and his enthusiastic apprentice (Maggie, played by Hilary Swank). The scenes roll effortlessly on from each other, developing mood, atmosphere and character until the story becomes incidental to the detail, in what is (for Hollywood) a remarkable simulation of life. With little fuss and no fancy footwork, Eastwood creates a unique world of characters, a world that seems to exist in its own time and space, self-contained and complete. (The film at first seems to be a period piece, only gradually revealing itself to be contemporary.)

here, and gives probably his most touching performance). The final shot
– a ghostlike Frankie eating lemon pie through the misty window of a
roadside canteen – is purest movie poetry; if *Million Dollar Baby* should
turn out to be Eastwood's last film, it's hard to imagine a more fitting and
memorable epitaph for the movies' greatest icon-turned filmmaker-poet
than this. Every great legend knows when it's time to disappear.

Kevin Smith, Auteur Lite

'Independent cinema kinda allows anybody to pick up a camera
and tell their story. I don't think of myself as an artist at all, but
I think I'm just kind of pigheaded enough to want to do my
stories my way, without any involvement, without any tips from
somebody else.'

Kevin Smith

After Jarmusch in '84 and Linklater in '91, the next hipster with a
camera to wing his way into Hollywood was Kevin Smith, who made
Clerks in 1994. If Linklater's *Slacker* was the voice of a generation, *Clerks*
was the belches and farts. Crude from conception on, *Clerks* was a
fluke, an all-round 'bad' movie with nothing going for it save its bawdy,
irreverent humor and a complete indifference to credentials (of which
it had none). The success of *Clerks* confirmed that a truly independent
movie – provided it had enough personality to get noticed – could find
an audience by sheer dint of being independent. In fact, independence
was the only real virtue that *Clerks* possessed. With its terrible acting,
non-existent storyline, brainless characters and lewd, adolescent
dialogue, it was painfully obviously the work of amateurs, yet it passed
(sort of) for a 'real' movie. The fact that audiences, and even critics,
greeted it with something like awe and gratitude was an indication of
how impoverished the American movie scene had become. Hailing
Clerks as a good movie was less a response to any qualities possessed
by the film itself, and more a statement of solidarity with independent
filmmakers and the alternate movie scene at large.

Like Tarantino, Smith was a movie geek made good. His success
depended on the support of a large and dedicated fan base of nerds,
eternally devoted to one of their own who had made it into the nigh-
impenetrable ranks of Hollywood filmmakers. Even more than Tarantino,
Smith was a geek of the people, completely, brazenly free of pretensions
as a filmmaker. Yet like Tarantino, Smith appeared to have a special knack
for getting along with studios, specifically Miramax, to whom Smith (like

Tarantino) has been faithful since his career first began.

Of course, Smith's continuing success in Hollywood – or at least his ability to do his thing – has been largely contingent on his willingness to cater to audience tastes and appeal to their more basic demands for entertainment. This is another thing Smith has in common with Tarantino, though in Tarantino's case it has meant a predilection for hip, shallow violence, and in Smith's it has resulted in lots of boob and fart jokes. Smith did branch into mature, personal filmmaking (as opposed to prepubescent personal filmmaking) for his third film, *Chasing Amy*, revealing himself to be a talented writer as well as prankster. But Smith chose not to pursue his path as a New Jersey Woody Allen for the slacker generation, and returned instead to poop jokes – albeit with a metaphysical twist – for the mind-bendingly silly religious farce, *Dogma*. The film got Smith and Miramax into hot water with Catholics, but only strengthened their standing in Hollywood as maverick creative forces willing to take on the Vatican in defense of their art (and their right to tell fart jokes). Smith's talents went straight to hell for his next movie, one expressly 'for the fans' – *Jay and Silent Bob Strike Back* (with Smith as Silent Bob). Though the film may have reassured his fans that Smith hadn't lost any of his commitment to scatological humor, it didn't reassure critics that he cared much about his growth as a filmmaker. In fact, Smith seemed to be regressing.

Then came *Jersey Girl*, for which Smith went beyond regression and magically transformed himself into a maker of sentimental Hollywood 'feel-good' trash. It's hard to imagine how the prankster behind *Dogma* (much less the artist who made *Chasing Amy*) could have spawned a grotesque artifact like *Jersey Girl*, but there was no denying the evidence. *Jersey Girl* is a film that might have been made by Chris Columbus (on a good day), or better yet, by no one at all, by a group of Hollywood executives, eagerly joining the dots of a summer feel-good rom-com. Smith's shameless attempt at more 'traditional' (i.e., clichéd) romantic comedy more or less single-handedly destroyed his hitherto untarnished reputation as the light side of indie cinema, putting him in the doghouse with fans and critics alike. It's rare to see a filmmaker commit artistic suicide so efficiently and so brazenly as Smith did with *Jersey Girl*, and at this point, if he is going to avoid the fate of John Hughes, the director has no option besides complete resurrection as a filmmaker. Smith's lowbrow tastes, and his resolution to stick close to his roots as a suburban slacker-filmmaker (both of which evaporated into nothingness with *Jersey Girl*), have proved inseparable from his charm; although they've also been restrictive to his talents (about as restrictive as a clown suit on a gymnast), without them, there doesn't seem to be anything left at all.

Like Tarantino, Smith has an abiding love for comic books and superheroes, and his wide-eyed appreciation for the 'redeeming' qualities of trash culture and pop mythology (as displayed in the best scene in *Clerks*, in which the characters discuss the morality of *Star Wars*) is above all what has given his movies their special buzz. Smith's films are exuberantly in-the-moment, providing the instant high of soda pops and comic books, and the goofy, guilt-free pleasures that make movies the number two American export.[13] The lack of moral weight to Smith's films (excepting *Chasing Amy*) is perfectly complemented by an absence of sophisticated film technique or production detail. His films are like live-action cartoons in which real-life characters get to live out the fantasy of being – if not superheroes, imaginary beings. Smith's imagination is rich and fertile ground, and his visual style (that evasive film sense) is surprisingly developed for a director who is essentially dialogue-dependent.

Maybe Smith originally wrote the character of Silent Bob for himself so he wouldn't get caught acting in his movies but could join the party in front of the camera. It turns out (in *Chasing Amy*) that Bob is silent not from lack of depth but from a reluctance to speak up until he has something worth saying. He's a thinker not a talker. Judging by *Chasing Amy*, Smith is a writer more than a joker, but he may be so used to trying to get attention that pratfalls and flatulence are what come most naturally to him. He might be better off doing a Silent Bob, however, and waiting till he has something worth saying.

Making Waves: Charlie Kaufman's Dangerous Mind & the Art of Insecurity

> 'I embrace the notion of failure. The only way to do something interesting is not care if you fail… To me, failure is a badge of honor. It means you took the chance.'
>
> Charlie Kaufman

It may not be a coincidence that the two greatest pioneers of American film – Welles and Coppola – shared a common regard for the writer as the single essential creative force in movies. Neither is it a coincidence that, of all the key contributors to the cinematic process, it is the writer

---

13 The number one export being arms. America gives goofy, guilt-free trash highs better than it does anything else, besides waging war on underdeveloped countries.

which the Hollywood system as presently maintained values least. Since audiences have shown time and time again their preference for shallow spectacles like *Independence Day*, *Titanic* and *Spiderman 2* (and even shallow religious spectacles like *The Passion of the Christ)*; and since none of these films possess anything resembling an imaginative story or intelligent dialogue – are in fact shockingly stupid sub-literary creations – it is assumed by the people who run studios that good writing is not only inessential to a film's success, but may even be detrimental to it. Yet it's doubtful if there is a single great film that didn't start out as at least a decent script; and while a mediocre director can make a good film out of a great script, the most talented filmmaker in the world will be at pains to make the proverbial silk purse out of a sow's ear.

Hollywood's policy on writing and writers is self-justifying and to some extent self-fulfilling. The less the writer is valued in Hollywood – the less 'perks' (be they the perks of respect, freedom or a decent paycheck) he is offered – the less writers are going to be attracted to work there, or even inclined to write screenplays at all. They know that however good their work is, chances are it will be destroyed by studio rewrites. Since only mediocre and unoriginal scriptwriters end up in Hollywood, Hollywood can feel justified in thinking that scriptwriters are basically mediocre creatures – not really artists at all – and that any script written by one person can certainly be 'improved' by the input of ten more (often not even real writers but studio executives convinced that a screenwriting program is all they need).

Such a policy denies the basic fact that the writer and his script is the primary creative element needed before a movie can even begin to approach final form through the various contributions of producers, director, technicians and actors, all of whom (logic would insist) are in service to the script/story/idea that brought them together in the first place. In Hollywood before the script – before even the idea – there is the 'concept' (be it ever so high). A director, producer, actor or even studio executive might hit upon a concept that he or she is confident would a) make a great movie and b) make lots of money for everyone involved. At which point, the actor/producer/director/executive then hires a writer to turn his or her concept into an idea, a treatment or story, and finally a script. The process proceeds in much the same way – one imagines – that an interior designer fills out an apartment according to the precise instructions and taste of the homeowner. Such a process reduces the writer to another craftsperson, basically interchangeable with a hundred other writers or craftspeople; and like the lighting cameraman, assistant director, or key grip, he is basically a second-class citizen. By this approach, movies are freed from any dangerous proximity to works of art, or from being mistaken for the results of creative inspiration springing from the dangerous minds of individual artists. Instead, they come about via the commercial calculations of studio executives, lawyers, and other business types, who have now earned the right to consider themselves 'creative people', too.

Into this dark and Kafkaesque world came Charlie Kaufman.[14] Charlie Kaufman was some kind of prodigy: a one-off. A romantic visionary with a genuinely subversive streak, Kaufman somehow managed to conquer Hollywood, achieving autonomy, respect and popularity without once compromising his vision. Kaufman was a freak whose worldview by all rights ought to have been incompatible with mainstream cinema, but he was blessed with street-savvy and canniness; he knew his audiences and, equally vitally, he understood the corporate mentality of Hollywood. As a result, he was able (with *Being John Malkovich*, *Adaptation* and *Eternal Sunshine of the Spotless Mind*) to get his vision across more or less intact to the public, and to somehow keep studios happy, too.[15]

Kaufman – whom Jim Carrey called 'the voice of our generation' – is the first writer to attain auteur status in Hollywood without having to turn himself into a director to get it. There are plenty of writers in Hollywood who have made a name for themselves by being associated with hit movies and getting ever plumper salaries for their pains (Joe

---

14 Kaufman is refreshingly close-mouthed and evasive about his personal history. Possibly, he was born in New York in 1958, and followed high school in Connecticut with a brief stint at Boston University, before transferring to NYU to study film. He may have moved to LA in 1991, and may also have worked on various television shows. Finally on safe historical ground, Kaufman's screenplay *Being John Malkovich* was made in 1999 by Spike Jonze and Kaufman entered reluctantly into the spotlight. As to why Kaufman gives away so little about himself, at least compared to your average Hollywood celeb, he has this to say:

'There's something corrupting about talking about yourself like it means anything. I have a regular life, mundane, just like everybody else. I just want to be a person who writes screenplays. Your work is your work; people respond to it or they don't. I really just like my stories to speak for themselves. And also, I'm just shy.'

From 'The Best and the Brightest – Charlie Kaufman,' by Mike Sagar, *Esquire*, Dec, 2002.
15 But it didn't come easily. 'For years I was not able to show anybody anything I'd written, which is not conducive to getting anything produced. I had an enormous struggle with that, and I had to get over it… I'm never expecting anyone to get it, and I become especially interested if it feels like there is no possibility of it getting made. I think that everybody has very tired and predictable thought patterns and stories to tell. To push against that to me seems interesting.' Kaufman in interview with Nicola Christie, 'The Weird Voice of a Generation,' *Daily Telegraph*, 30th April 2004.

Eszterhas, David Koepp et al.). But they have invariably attained such status not by proving their individuality and creativity as artists but, on the contrary, by proving themselves capable of writing the formulaic, crowd-pleasing generic dreck that Hollywood values so highly, and that generally results in hit movies. Kaufman wrote scripts that were idiosyncratic, unpredictable, eccentric, slightly perverse, twisted and wholly personal. His scripts were soaked with original ideas and insightful, lively dialogue; they were so visionary and unique that – like Tarantino's early scripts – there was no way for a director to film them without staying true to them, without allowing Kaufman's vision to come through. The result has been that four of the five movies made from Kaufman scripts (two by Spike Jonze, two by Michel Gondry, the exception being *Confessions of a Dangerous Mind* directed by George Clooney) have belonged as much, or more so, to Kaufman than they have to the directors who filmed them. So who is the auteur here?

Kaufman first came into audience consciousness with *Being John Malkovich*, probably the closest thing to a comedy of schizophrenia that had ever slipped into mainstream American movies at the time. *Malkovich* was about conflict of interests, about separate and mutually exclusive desires, about vying for supremacy inside a single (divided) psyche. The film played on the awareness that everybody wants to be something (or someone) that they aren't. Woody Allen's famous quip, 'My only regret is that I wasn't born somebody else,' probably applies to ninety percent of moviegoers, at least on a bad day; with *Malkovich*, Kaufman played on this awareness and made comedy of it. He made an art form out of insecurity.

The next Kaufman film to come out was the messy, unfocused *Human Nature*, directed by Michel Gondry. Shapeless and not very funny, the film was barely released and had to settle for cult status. *Adaptation* and *Confessions of a Dangerous Mind* came out around the same time; one (*Adaptation*, directed again by Spike Jonze) was successful, the other, *Confessions*, directed by George Clooney for Soderbergh's Section Eight, was not, despite a superb lead performance from Sam Rockwell.[16] Most recently, the fullest expression of Kaufman's literary genius so far, came *Eternal Sunshine of the Spotless Mind*, starring Jim Carrey and Kate Winslet.

Exhilaratingly original as Kaufman's ideas are, it is his insights

16 Kaufman was less than thrilled with the finished product. 'I was cut out of the process. [Clooney] followed the script in a plotty way, but, to me, that's the least important part. I didn't say anything when the film came out, because I didn't want to hurt it. But, recently, someone in an interview said to me, 'I loved *Confessions of a Dangerous Mind*,' at which point either I could say, "Oh, thank you," or "Well, I didn't…"'[Clooney]'s not my

into human nature and his willingness to put his own insecurities in service of his story that distinguishes him in Hollywood. The labyrinthine depths of *Eternal Sunshine* weren't in its premise, nor in the complexities of its unfolding, but in the mind of Kaufman himself. As with *Adaptation,* though far less ostentatiously (and more effectively), Charlie Kaufman put himself whole into the movie. *Eternal Sunshine* was filled with Kaufman's personal ache, his romantic loneliness, his sexual inadequacies and emotional longings; yet his ironic detachment made the self-exploration anything but self-indulgent, and instead wildly entertaining. Kaufman's gift was to let audiences under his skin without making them feel sordid or uneasy about it. As a comedy, *Eternal Sunshine* was dark and faintly disturbing, but the undercurrents of self-loathing only enhanced the humor. As a sci-fi mystery, it was blissfully light, playful and erratic, indifferent to scientific credibility. As a romantic drama (its real aspiration), it soared: Kaufman's genius allowed the movie to have its heart and break it. It offered audiences a whole different kind of 'feel good'.

Eternal Sunshine was as close to a shamanic comedy as Hollywood was likely to get. It was all about choices, above all the choice to have a choice at all. The consensus position, according to Kaufman, was choosing not to have a choice. Collectively, we choose to forget, to stagnate, to stay inside the loop, to live the same experiences over and over again, never suspecting that we have been here before, done it already, seen it all a thousand times over, that we are doomed to an eternally repeating cycle of futility from which even the 'Game Over' of death is no escape, just a brief pause to stick another coin in the slot. All this, and Jim Carrey too. Like *Being John Malkovich, Eternal Sunshine* felt uncompromised. It felt real. Where *Malkovich* had John Cusack, however, *Eternal Sunshine* had Jim Carrey, in an admirably restrained performance, whose presence alone made the movie a major multiplex release that millions of unsuspecting humans – hoping for another Carrey gibberfest like *Bruce Almighty* – were then subjected to. What the untutored masses – most of whom had never heard of Philip K. Dick, never mind Alexander Pope – made of the movie we can only guess. (Just because it was a hit doesn't mean audiences understood it or liked it.) If it was possible for the average moviegoer to enjoy *Eternal Sunshine,* it was because it was entertaining enough, at a superficial

enemy. I just wouldn't work with him again. Or Soderbergh, or any one of those guys… I'm not scared of Clooney. I don't need him.' Charlotte O'Sullivan, 'Charlie Kaufman: An Extranormal, Extraordinary Scriptwriter,' *The Independent*, May 7th 2004.

level, for its rather sinister subtext to pass largely unnoticed. The sugar coating was thick and sugary enough for Kaufman's bitter pill to go smoothly down. This in a nutshell is how Kaufman and his dangerous mind have conquered Hollywood. His art is in disguising his art as wacky, freewheeling entertainment. Studio heads may not be able to make head or tail of his ideas, but they can't escape the fact that they're brilliant. Even more importantly, they sell.

Against all the odds, Kaufman proved that there is space in the Hollywood system for a writer to do his thing and do it his way, and to get rich and famous into the bargain. Kaufman is the exception that proves the rule, however. He is a fringe artist who somehow wound up center stage in the middle of the mainstream. He might have proved the rule, but he is also busy setting a precedent. However much he has been swimming against the current, the current has been steadily changing to accommodate him. Kaufman doesn't just make waves, he surfs them.

Art and Punishment: Gus Van Sant's *Elephant*, and the Two Steves, Soderbergh and Spielberg

'...this art, cinema, if it is, I know it can and has been, has stolen and destroyed far more than it has fulfilled me. It has helped to reinforce my disdain for the simple-minded viewer. The brainwashed slug who believes in nothing. The director must have faith in god because he who truly understands the power makes the life abound.'

Laird Henn (formerly Harmony Korine), *Digital Babylon*

When Gus Van Sant returned to his indie roots and made *Elephant* in 2004, he pulled so far away from anything resembling conventional Hollywood entertainment that the film was like punishment. It was as if Van Sant was flagellating himself for his former transgressions (those of *Good Will Hunting*, *Psycho*, and *Finding Forrester*), but if so the punishment was also leveled against audiences for daring to have enjoyed his Hollywood films. Van Sant's early indie feature, *Drugstore Cowboy* (1989), was a smart, nihilistic comedy with brains and guts and integrity, but it was also a rip-roaring road movie in the best Hollywood tradition. It was an almost perfect fusion of artistic sensibility with the demands of entertainment. Even *To Die For* – glib and gaudy as it was – was a superior piece of trash art that blended Van Sant's quirky taste with audience's more conventional ones to form a seamless comedy thriller. After *Cowboy* and the avant-garde misfire *My Own Private Idaho*, Van Sant looked set to become one of Hollywood's more interesting auteurs, but he was badly burned by the experience of making *Even Cowgirls Get the Blues* and took refuge in the wholly conventional and surprise-free 'feel good' Hollywood hack work of *Good Will Hunting*. After that he came a total cropper with the stupefyingly misguided remake, his 'art' movie *Psycho*, and returned with his tail between his legs to formula filmmaking with *Finding Forrester*. Presumably it was around now that Van Sant began to feel he had lost his sense of roots or direction as a filmmaker, and chose to do the Dogme thing, to get back to basics. But *Elephant* was indie cinema in the worst imaginable way, an art movie that did away not only with the trappings of mainstream genre, but all the pleasures of movies too. Van Sant was so determined not to fall back on ordinary dramatic devices or emotional manipulation that he drained his film of any substance or bite.

The story dealt with a Columbine-style massacre at a US high school, and Van Sant (who also wrote the script), determined not to reduce so 'tragic' a subject to melodrama, ensured that nothing came between the audience and the subject matter. In this case what that meant was no story, no interesting dialogue, no characters, and no narrative drive. Nothing happened in the film until the shooting began, and then it was for no obvious reason, since the killers hadn't been developed any more than the rest of the characters. The explosion of violence would have come as a relief after the mind-numbing tedium of the previous hour, but Van Sant denied us even the satisfaction of a dramatic finale and seemed to deliberately flub it instead. In the end, the film played like an assemblage of all the scenes that didn't make it into the finished film: a total misconception from start to finish. But *Elephant* was an art film by an independent director returning to his roots, and so of course it was greeted with laudatory notices and hushed tones of respect as a 'serious' and respectful treatment of a modern-day tragedy. The fact that the film was a miserably lifeless affair and boring beyond belief (BBB, the mark of a true 'art film') was of little consequence to the critics. After all, one cannot judge 'art' by the same vulgar criteria as one judges mere 'entertainment.'[17]

Steven Spielberg seems to share a similar misperception, one common to Hollywood thinking in general, namely, that artistic integrity is measured by intentions rather than results. What's more, he seems to

[17] A film released soon after *Elephant*, Matthew Ryan Hoge's *The United States of Leland*, was a remarkable treatment of a similar subject that critics wasted no time in savaging. Certainly, it's hard to imagine two films taking a more different approach, and all the reasons *Elephant* failed more or less coincide with what makes *United States of Leland* so affecting and effective a movie (see next chapter). In a bizarre twist, however, Hoge himself has expressed unrestrained admiration for *Elephant*.

believe that it is maintained on a point-by-point basis, like a batting average, and that provided he intersperses tacky commercial outings with 'worthy' films carrying weighty moral themes, he is upholding his status as 'an artist.' Critics may even go along with this, conveniently ignoring the simple fact that, although artists can have good days and bad days, they cannot choose when to be artists and when not, or turn off the 'integrity' when it suits them to do so. The fact that Spielberg's masterpiece to date (*Jaws*) also happens to be one of his most brazenly commercial movies more or less sums up this dilemma.

When Spielberg is being a dedicated showman and can forget all about scoring points for integrity and 'seriousness' as an artist, his gifts truly shine, and he can stand alongside the brightest lights of the field. Of course, *Jaws* (the film that Soderbergh claims 'was the first time I started thinking about how movies get made'[18]) happened when Spielberg was in full swing of discovering his genius, carried away by the creative euphoria of making movies, and it's no wonder if he did his very best work while operating at such high levels of enthusiasm. But even with his more recent films, it's clear that Spielberg is far more taken by the excitement of moviemaking than by any of the themes, stories, or novels which he wrestles to bring to the screen as an 'artist.' His most fully enjoyable work of recent years was *Catch Me If You Can*, a piece of fluff that at least freed him up to enjoy himself. His best recent work, scene-by-scene, has been in the darker, more visceral sections of *Saving Private Ryan*, *AI*, *Minority Report* and *War of the Worlds* when he was able to forget about the 'message' and focus his attention on delivering maximum visual jolts to his audience. When not hampered by his impoverished perception of 'art', Spielberg's imagination is a marvellous thing to behold.

From the outset, Spielberg's movies reassured and comforted audiences with their fond allegiance to the ordinary, everyday security of suburban, middle-class life. When the unexpected, strange or alien entered into this idyllic tableau, it did so not – as in a horror movie – by bubbling up from under the surface (forever destroying the illusion of normality), but rather – as in a fairy tale – like magic rain from above, transforming the mundane without challenging the assumptions on which it was founded. Spielberg was the perfect film artist for the shop-happy, New Age-daffy 80s and 90s. He allowed audiences to have their space cake and eat it, and gave them magical fantasies that were really rose-colored embellishments on more mundane fantasies – those

18 Waxman, pg. 97-8

of living in a safe, happy world with a loving spouse, good neighbors and perfect children.

Spielberg's movies were anything but subversive. Instead of warning signs from the unconscious, they were lullabies for the conscious. An entertainer first and foremost, Spielberg was only secondarily an artist.[19] Spielberg made movies somewhere on the borderline; he was less than an authentic film artist, yet more than merely a showman (like his pal George Lucas[20]). Perhaps the most revealing – and rewarding – overview of Spielberg's oeuvre would consist of a history of the blunders committed throughout his nonetheless dazzling film career. For no other auteur filmmaker of equivalent stature has juxtaposed such a wealth of talent with such atrocious judgment. Spielberg seemed to epitomize the privileges and pitfalls of genius, as if unequal to his own prodigious gifts.[21]

As previously mentioned, this is a predicament far from restricted to Spielberg – who after all embodies and represents the industry as no other filmmaker does – but is characteristic of Hollywood as a whole. Compare the case of *Elephant* to the reception to *Ocean's 12*, Steve Soderbergh's vastly superior sequel to *Ocean's 11* released in 2004 as

19 Even with *Schindler's List*, Spielberg shied away from any psychological insights as to the Nazi phenomenon itself. Never for a moment did the possibility arise that what happened in Nazi Germany could happen anywhere, or that the Nazis (or the principle nasty Goeth, played by Ralph Fiennes) were just twisted versions of ourselves. Had Spielberg had the sensibility to treat the Nazi subject unflinchingly, *Schindler's List* would have undone all his previous work and exposed it as insubstantial. Impressive as it was, *Schindler's List* was an evasion of greater, more disturbing truths, and far less of a departure for Spielberg than critics would have had us believe.

20 In some ways the reverse of Spielberg, who has artistic technique to burn but little real vision, Lucas has or had the inspiration of a true artist, but is lacking either the technique or the passion to bring it to fruition; only Irvin Kershner managed it for him, one time, with *The Empire Strikes Back*.

21 To give an example: *Close Encounters of the Third Kind* – by the express wishes of the director – was re-released in a markedly inferior version in 1980, termed rather ambivalently *The Special Edition* and missing several crucial domestic scenes (showing Roy's mental breakdown) and a key scene depicting the US military's badgering of UFO witnesses. Instead, a pointless and lackluster finale sequence showing Roy's entry into the mother ship was tacked on at the end. This version superseded the original, which became all but impossible to see. Spielberg not only allowed this but actively encouraged it, apparently considering his original cut to be too 'dark'. (He has since repented, however, and made efforts to retain prints of the original version on laserdisc and DVD.) This has to go down in cinema history as the first case of a filmmaker willfully butchering his own work. It is a case of 'studio mentality' meddling with the artist's vision, with an added twist in the tale: the studio mentality belonged to the artist himself!

a 'break' from his more 'serious' film projects (the disappointing *Full Frontal* and the downright awful *Solaris*). Though it was one of the most sheerly enjoyable movies of the year, *Ocean's 12* was received with a certain degree of scepticism and even scorn by many critics. After all, Soderbergh had recently been hailed as the new king of indie cinema with his twin successes, *Erin Brockovich* and *Traffic*, and that he should frolic so shamelessly with movie conventions and 'squander' his talents on so frivolous a project was seen to cast doubt on his integrity. Some of these critics seemed not to notice (just as they'd been blind to *Elephant*'s lack of grace or substance) that *Ocean's 12* was a strikingly innovative piece of filmmaking, easily the most assured and joyful work Soderbergh had done, and one of the best-made American movies of recent years. Thin and inconsequential as it was, in terms of the styles used, its blissfully unruly camerawork (by Soderbergh himself) and its graceful mix of digital and film stock, the film was genuinely ground-breaking. As mindless hokum, it offered the kind of highs that Hollywood – once the uncontested king of mindless hokum – had lately proved so miserably inept at providing.

The joys of *Ocean's 12* were similar to those that Spielberg had given audiences with *Jaws* three decades earlier: flawless editing, dazzling technique, witty dialogue and the special delights of seeing a top-notch cast on peak form, bouncing off the fourth wall and having a ball doing it. Above all it offered the buzz of seeing gifted people do what they do best without taking it too seriously. Admittedly, the film came undone in the last half hour, tangled up by Soderbergh's overly audacious, slightly childish desire to subvert the rules of the genre and veer off into postmodernist self-satire, and throwing intelligibility out the window. But even so, the film was satisfying at such a deep level as entertainment that it blurred the already vague and intangible lines between trash and art (just as *Jaws* had) and left audiences not caring which it was. Anything this much fun had to be good.

The sad and absurd fact is that critics, and even audiences, may not know how to appreciate good, mindless entertainment, any more than they know how to appreciate art. Soderbergh himself – like his almost-namesake and rival for the Hollywood throne Spielberg – may not be that well equipped to discriminate, either. Apparently he was the only one who didn't have fun making *Ocean's 12*; maybe he's happier when he can do his Tarkovsky, or hang with Antonioni and get to feel like a real artist?

★

'In this business, the only thing you can count on is that people will act expediently in their own interest, so I try to set up circumstances in which my needs and their needs are close enough so that there's not going to be a problem.'

Steve Soderbergh

When an artist insists he creates for himself, that doesn't mean he makes movies in order to bliss out on them afterwards, but rather that he has to create for his own peace of mind. This is a far cry from the self-indulgence of a grown man investing millions of dollars in his latest train set.[22] When Spielberg made *Always* in 1989, the film gave irrefutable evidence, if any were still needed, of the lack of unifying vision or artistic integrity to his method. Presumably Spielberg believed just as wholeheartedly in this lachrymose crap as he had in *E.T.* – and would later believe in *Schindler's List* – and this alone was proof of a profound flaw in his thinking. In his worst films, Spielberg seemed almost paralyzed by his own ill-judgment, incapable, as his passion deserted him, of bluffing his way through, until not even his trusty technique could save him. Having abandoned both his judgment and his sense of direction, Spielberg wound up investing time and energy in projects palpably unworthy of his gifts. Apparently the child in him – not the guileless innocent that made *E.T.* but the sentimental brat who remade *A Guy Named Joe* as *Always* – couldn't resist the temptation of squandering his gifts making empty escapism that, in the end, wasn't even entertaining.[23]

22 George Lucas commented on making *Raiders of the Lost Ark:* 'I'm really doing it so I can enjoy it. Because I just want to see this movie.' Such 'artistic' motivation showed in the finished film. On the other hand, by far the best of the Indiana Jones films, *Indiana Jones and the Temple of Doom* (1984), was also the most controversial. Spielberg was criticized for subjecting his younger viewers to scenes of barbarity, even though the film's violence was neither gratuitous nor mean-spirited, and fully in keeping with the movie's lurid intensity and gleeful perversity (otherwise absent from the director's work). There was some speculation at the time – perhaps not overly fanciful – that Spielberg's involvement with *The Twilight Zone: the Movie* (1984), and the catastrophic deaths of actor Vic Morrow and two Vietnamese children (resulting from gross negligence on the part of Spielberg's collaborator John Landis), may have accounted for the somewhat grisly mood in which *Temple of Doom* found its director. If so, it was a mood that brought the best out of his talents.
23 'It might be argued that self-deception is central to Spielberg's achievements, as central to them as deceiving the public, because the two activities ultimately amount to the same thing. Audiences wouldn't be nearly so susceptible to accepting the seriousness of Spielberg's "grown up" projects if he weren't so adept at doing con jobs on himself.' Jonathan Rosenbaum, *Movie Wars*.

E. T. (1982) was Spielberg's most personal film since *The Sugarland Express,* but it was also one of his most technically flawed films. Fuzzy, slack and rather sloppily put together, it lacked the precision and mechanical grace of his other best works, perhaps because he was shooting from the heart for once, and the story was more important to him than the telling. *E. T.* was not a film for the cynical, and its fairy tale naiveté was the real thing; it was shameless and mawkish but also pure and simple, as if springing from the mind of a child. Spielberg's touch was so assured – and so ingenuous – that he drew tears from a stone, and audiences were ready and eager to be regressed: the film became the most successful movie of all time, ousting Lucas' *Star Wars* from the number one spot.

When the entertainer made a bid to become an artist, however, the result, as often as not, was that he ceased to entertain us.[24] *Schindler's List* (1993) was a good film on a great subject that was hailed as a great work per se. Yet, perhaps afraid his audience would choke on their popcorn, Spielberg pulled back from the material; trying for a gentler, more delicate vision of horror, he gave them an armchair holocaust. Spielberg's point of view (being hooked into his Jewishness) was inadequate for a full perception of the holocaust, and so he made a nice little tale about the exceptions that disproved the rule: the good Nazi and the gutsy, resourceful Jews who survived to tell their terrible tale. Though actually the story of one man and 1100 Jews, *Schindler's List* was greeted as a film about 'the Holocaust' and herein lay its primary failing. For Spielberg encouraged this perception at every level by touting his movie as a lesson in history, an experience which audiences should feel obliged to partake of if they cared about history at all. But a movie can only be judged by its merits as a movie, not by its historical significance (and certainly not by its good intentions). With films like *Ghandi, Cry Freedom,* or *Philadelphia,* the 'virtuousness' of the intentions was all there was, landing like a blunt club on audiences' skulls. Unlike these films, *Schindler's List* did possess genuine vision – it came from the heart – but it was marred by the same virtuousness. This kind of self-importance invariably sabotages even the best of movies.

Another critically lauded historical epic, Spielberg's *Saving Private Ryan* (1998)[25], was a powerful glimpse into the horrors of war and a *tour-de-force* of cinema that suffered from the same basic problem, a film

---

24 Spielberg's brief and misguided excursion into literary adaptation – *The Color Purple* and *Empire of the Sun* (1985 and 1987) – were, outside of his total failures (1941, *Last Crusade, Always, The Lost World*), his least interesting films. Spielberg has yet to realize (if he ever does) that, just as all art is entertainment, really great entertainment – like *Jaws* – can pass for art.

25 Or, as John Waters tagged it, 'Saving Ryan's Privates'.

that, in its bid for moral depth and social significance, reduced itself to asinine sentimentality. When a German soldier's life is spared by the compassionate Miller's intervention, and then the same man shoots down Miller at the climax, Spielberg sacrifices not only all credibility but all artistic integrity to make his 'point'. Beyond a clumsy attempt at irony, the only reasonable message to be derived from this shabby little vignette is that Miller should have let his men shoot the Nazi when they had the chance. Since this can hardly have been Spielberg's intention, it shows how utterly lost he is when it comes to organizing his deeper meanings. Spielberg lacks the intelligence for making observations – much less judgments – about the 'heart of man'. He is a consummate entertainer but a lousy philosopher, and when it comes time to explore the depths of his own, presumably troubled psyche – the work of every artist worth his salt – Spielberg isn't even a good dilettante.

The trouble is that, for Spielberg, film technique is everything and dramatic integrity next to nothing. A filmmaker of enormous talent, Spielberg has yet to grow into a genuine artist because, for all his technical skills, he lacks the one essential attribute: creative sensibility. His films, even the best of them (*Duel*, *The Sugarland Express*, *Jaws*, *Close Encounters*, *Schindler's List*, *Indiana Jones and the Temple of Doom*, *Catch Me If You Can*, *War of the Worlds* and, if we stretch it, *Saving Private Ryan* and *Minority Report*), are devoid of hidden depths: they are precisely and exactly what they appear to be and nothing else besides. Spielberg, like Hitchcock before him, makes no bones about the nature of his work. His movies are there to entertain audiences and help them pass the time. Unlike Hitchcock, however, Spielberg's honesty and ingenuity does not veil a darker, more complex agenda at work; when Spielberg attempts to delve into 'deeper' waters and mark new, more 'adult' territory for himself, he generally comes a cropper.

Graham Greene had a whimsical habit of dividing his books into serious novels and mere 'entertainments', yet anyone who makes it through his oeuvre may be surprised to find that some of his best works are categorized as entertainments (*The Confidential Agent*, for example), while some of the 'serious' novels can be pretty heavy going (*The Comedians*). An artist sweating blood to get his point across doesn't necessarily make for greatness, nor does effortlessly doing what he does best make for insignificance. Spielberg offered up a similar, even more questionable, conceit with his films by moving from simple, mindless entertainments like the *Indiana Jones* and *Jurassic Park* films to 'worth' (often painfully so) works like *The Color Purple* and *Amistad*, films which he seemed to consider it our duty to sit through, as works of historical importance and not just more movies.

There is a problem here that Spielberg has failed to take into account, and this failure alone exposes him as a flawed artist at best. Social conscience and creativity do not make comfortable bed fellows, and a great movie is almost never an overtly moral one.[26] A great work of art such as Dostoyevsky's *Crime and Punishment*, however anarchic and subversive it may be in spirit and execution, contains a moral underlayer that is inseparable from its power to affect us. Such 'morality' is distinct from social conscience, however, relating rather to a sense of compassion and humanity; truly moral works are usually condemned as immoral by the consensus, and only recognized by those other artists (and critics) who respond intuitively to the artist's vision. It is a vision of morality that co-exists with an awareness, and an experience, of the things which constitute immorality. Something that Spielberg, with his apple pie suburban view, can claim little knowledge of.

Recently, Spielberg has returned to the safe terrain of the genre he is perhaps most at home in − sci-fi − with the unwieldy and pretentious *AI*[27], and the rather pedestrian *Minority Report* and *War of the Worlds*. *Minority Report* (2002) especially proved Spielberg's lack of depth or vision by attempting to fuse his sensibilities with those of Philip K. Dick, the reigning master of schizophrenic literature of the twentieth century. Over and above Kafka and the existentialists, Dick diagnosed the malaise of our times − fragmentation of the self − and his writings encapsulated the symptoms, both good and bad. His books feed on paranoia, uncertainty, the terror and potential derangement (but also empowerment) of realizing that nothing is what it seems. For Dick, the author of reality was

26 De Palma's *Casualties of War* and Fritz Lang's *M*, two exceptions which come to mind, perhaps serve only to prove this rule.

27 *AI: Artificial Intelligence* (2001) gave Spielberg an opportunity to ape the master: every filmmaker's Maestro, the late, none-too-great Stanley Kubrick. Kubrick was a filmmakers' filmmaker and, to a lesser extent, a critics' filmmaker, but he was never really a filmgoers' filmmaker. At least after *Dr Strangelove*, his films were alienating in the extreme, dazzling exercises in film technique devoid of anything resembling dramatic human interest. Spielberg's *AI* was long and rather boring, portentous without really portending anything. The subject was treated with a solemnity very nearly fatal to genre filmmaking, and there was none of the lightness and excitement of Spielberg's previous forays into science fiction. He allowed his awe and reverence of Kubrick to inhibit his more kinetic gifts, and only a few sequences (involving Jude Law as a gigolo robot fuck-doll on the run after being framed for murder, the future being depicted as a sort of high-tech pleasure dome of vice and squalor) had any real kick to them. Spielberg was at home with the imagery of decaying cities and hyper evolved machine entities, but when he was required to write his own mythology, he needed to take a few tips from his pal George Lucas (a truly inept filmmaker but a passable mythmaker). *AI* wanted to be post-*Blade Runner* sci-fi realism and at the same time a pre-World War II fantasy (this is the same man who gave audiences *Always*), but the mix turned out to be absurd and slightly grotesque.

the mind itself, and as such anything was possible, our responsibility total. But the only sane reaction to such a realization was complete madness, and Dick's vision eventually led to religious acceptance. His writing was inspirational in the deepest sense: through paranoia came awareness. This was a concept as far beyond Spielberg's comprehension as rocket science is beyond raccoons, so why was he drawn to adapt Dick?

Probably it related more to a desire to keep abreast of the times than any actual affinity for Dick's writings, and all Spielberg did for the film was adapt his technique to a suitably gritty, slightly surreal, rawer, edgier template. *Minority Report* started well but in the last half hour crumbled into a by-the-numbers action whodunit melodrama with zero philosophic depth. There were scenes (the sequence in which Tom Cruise has his eyes replaced to avoid the eye-scan security, with Peter Stormare as the black-market surgeon) unlike anything in the Spielberg canon, possessed of a bizarre, otherworldly, surreal intensity. The sense that anything might happen is not a common feeling in a Spielberg film, and if he had stayed true to the spirit of Dick's vision – that of madness, despair, defeat, oppression, dementia, and visionary excess – he might have created a work of rare brilliance. But Spielberg wasn't enough of an artist to suppress his personal feelings and do justice to so twisted a vision. Despite its source material, reality was never really questioned in *Minority Report* Even family values came out unscathed.

Over the years, Spielberg has privately (not that privately, obviously) lamented being denied the kind of critical recognition granted other filmmakers, such as Francis Coppola and Martin Scorsese, his friends and peers. Lately, he has had less of a reason to lament, however, which may say less about Spielberg's development as an artist than it does about the state of the movie industry in general. Spielberg has kept abreast of movies – of the trends and formulas, of technical advances and popular tastes – in a way that his peers (Coppola, and even Scorsese) have not, and the times have proved more accommodating to his brand of talent, and his particular 'sensibility'. While Scorsese and Coppola have peaked and settled into rather complacent moviemaking, Spielberg approached maturity late; he may even have yet to reach the pinnacle of his talents.

A filmmaker possessed by genius tends to be ruthless, obsessive and more than likely half-deranged in his unflagging commitment to his vision. These are not qualities easily associated with Spielberg, who may be too socially well-adjusted to ever isolate himself enough to become a true artist. If Spielberg seems essentially unsure of his own gifts, it is perhaps no bad thing. Yet it is a curious conundrum – the entertainer beloved by millions who lacks faith in his own lovability, the would-be artist, hailed by a generation, who deep down lacks faith in his art.

Spielberg has often claimed to be a *mensch*, a regular guy, and the mantle of master filmmaker and genius auteur sits uncomfortably upon him. He lacks the irony, the self-awareness, and the perversity, to assume the role slyly, sardonically, as Hitchcock did before him (and as Polanski did for a brief spell, before disaster struck). He also lacks the inner conviction, the introversion and the vision to simply immerse himself in his work and ignore the hoopla, as Kurosawa or Ford once did. He lacks the charm and panache of Welles and the cunning and cynicism of Tarantino; as a director-superstar, Spielberg is a poor show. In interviews, his lack of personality confirms what we may have already suspected – that here is a man who puts everything into his movies, and leaves nothing for himself.

With great artists, audiences respond to the greatness in their work because they feel – palpably – that it is as close as they can get to the greatness of the men behind it. With entertainers, or craftsmen, audiences know – instinctively – that the only thing that distinguishes such showmen from themselves – the ordinary Joe – is the mastery of their craft. They are working a trade like any other, and beyond the works which he has given the world, the pleasure and excitement of his images in our consciousness, what there is to Spielberg is what he has always maintained there was, and no more. Just a guy named Steve.

Shakespeare Never Did This: Sex, Sensibility, and the Dancing Midget Art

'In 1960 enough was enough. The movie had been cosmeticized to death, they said; but since then the use of cosmetics has exploded. The supreme task of decadent filmmakers is to fool the audience... predictability (dramaturgy) has become the golden calf around which we dance... The result is barren. An illusion of pathos and an illusion of love. To Dogme 95 the movie is not illusion. Today a technological storm is raging of which the result is the elevation of cosmetics to God. By using new technology anyone at any time can wash the last grains of truth away in the deadly embrace of sensation. The illusions are everything the movie can hide behind.'
— Dogme 95 Manifesto

The Vow of Chastity played upon – while subtly mocking – the common association of virtue with art and the (basically Christian) equivalence of goodness with abstinence, or sacrifice. Christianity demands a lack of sensual pleasure or physical indulgence and a reduction (or purification) of the sexual function to purely procreative ends, viewing (pro)creation to be of God, sexual pleasure to be of the Devil. The fact that they co-exist, and even accompany each other (are in fact inseparable), is seen as evidence of how sneaky the Devil can be rather than an indication of God's mysterious and contradictory ways.

A similar kind of relationship – both symbiotic and antagonistic – might be said to exist between 'Dogville' and Hollywood, or art and commercialism, as seen by the common public. It is this assumption that von Trier and his gang were playing on. Creativity, like sexual passion, can be channeled in more ways than one. For example, it can be directed towards engendering new life-forms that advance the evolutionary design (whatever *that* is) and increase 'God's glory.' This would equate with procreation in the 'pure' sense. On the other hand, sexuality can be 'deviated' into 'lower' channels of self-gratification – placed in the service of Mammon – and so give rise to impure thought-forms that fill the chambers of Babylon and corrupt the beauty of Creation, blaspheming it by their mere existence.

Dogme mocked such dualistic, Puritan, and totalitarian thinking, while at the same time using it to further their own, specific ends.[28] The message of the Vow of Chastity was clear: the ways of Hollywood were decadent and corrupt, a despoilment of the sacred medium of film, and a profanation of all those who practiced them. The 'simple' pleasures and 'harmless' joys of movies were no longer either simple or harmless. The surface – style – had become everything, the underlying content nothing. Movies were eye candy that bypassed the brain entirely, or rather, that never went deep enough to reach it, never made it past audiences' bedazzled retinas and besieged eardrums. Such movies not only gave them nothing to take away (besides pretty images of destruction), but left them diminished and stupefied by the experience. If the art of movies had been reduced to 'pure' entertainment, and if entertainment had sunk to the level of advertising (and if advertising depended on the steady erosion of audiences' thinking faculties and imagination via a bombardment of the senses), it was time to reevaluate the nature (the dichotomy) of both 'art' and 'entertainment' – of cosmetics and of God.

The public has always displayed a basic failure to appreciate the potential harmony between art and simple entertainment, and critics have done little to amend this. No doubt this failure arises first of all

---

28 As von Trier's *Dogville* shows, his Catholicism is genuine, if postmodern, and of the more apocalyptic variety (a very different kind to that practiced by Mel Gibson!). Sometimes the old God of fire and vengeance is the only God suited to circumstances. Irony and self-mockery is a lot more effective when backed up by lightning bolts.

from an education system in which Shakespeare and other classics are forced on young, untrained minds as 'art', by teachers whose enthusiasm has been dimmed – if it ever burned at all – by years of dreary curriculums and lifeless presentations. From an early age, we associate art, if not with punishment, then with a tiresome and obligatory subjugation to weighty themes and flowery phrases, having little or no bearing upon our daily lives. It is no wonder if, later in life, when audiences discover the pleasures of Cary Grant, Howard Hawks, Charlie Chaplin, Buster Keaton, Preston Sturges, Humphrey Bogart, Alfred Hitchcock, or John Huston, the last thing that occurs to them is that they are in the presence of 'art'. Movies are fun, shamelessly so, and surely nothing 'good' for us could be so easy to enjoy. Shakespeare was never like this.[29]

As a result of this built-in prejudice (a prejudice no one schooled in the West is entirely free of), there is the persistent tendency to denigrate works that are *too* pleasurable, too delightful, too much fun, as being somehow less than 'art'. Such a prejudice is similar in nature (perhaps even related) to the in-bred Christian terror that everything that gives pleasure is somehow suspect, meant as a test. Art is what makes us *work* to understand it. It is lofty, obscure, complex, dark. It makes us better people by stretching and straining our capacities to fathom ourselves, by educating and edifying us, as if sent – like The Bible, and Shakespeare – from Heaven above. Certainly it is not anything we are going to get from a Preston Sturges or Jim Carrey movie; nor would audiences know what to do with it if they did.

Movies in general have had a difficult time being considered – or even aspiring to be considered – as art. This is not only because of their dependence on commercial factors, but also because of the natural tendency of the medium itself: *to be light*. Cary Grant may have been one of the three or four finest male screen actors who ever lived – and perhaps the greatest movie star of all time – but he was never really considered to be an actor of any great depth, because he made it look so *easy*. The same went for Hitchcock (who favored Grant as his leading man): his art was in seducing audiences so that they were unaware of being seduced, oblivious to his artistry, and fully open to the experience *of* it. As a result, for much of his career, he went unrecognized. The problem is that, since audiences are not made up of artists, and have little cognizance of how art 'works' – what it 'is' – they tend to need art that draws attention to

29 The irony is that Shakespeare was exactly that—Hollywood half a millennium before its time. Until academia and education got their hands on him and turned him into "art," he was seen as one of the great entertainers.

itself in order to recognize it. This despite the fact that, for a true artist in service of his story (it may be argued), the last thing he wants to do is draw attention to the means by which he is telling it.[30]

The antithesis of this rule is someone like Stanley Kubrick, a virtuosos filmmaker whose storytelling abilities finally atrophied into non-existence, but who continued to be hailed as a great artist even after he lost all sense of the rules of good entertainment. In the Hollywood heyday, the Golden Age of the 30s and 40s, when films like *Gone with the Wind*, *Casablanca*, *The Maltese Falcon*, *Rebecca*, *The Lady Eve*, *Bringing Up Baby*, *Stagecoach*, *Only Angels Have Wings*, and *It's a Wonderful Life* were coming out of the studio system like hamburgers off a grill, it was evident that the restrictive formula of genre entertainment – just as the Dogme rules would – were actually *inspiring* individual artists to do their best work within the limits set for them, transforming genres and transcending the imaginary line between art and 'mere' entertainment. Not that the public gave a damn; so long as they were entertained, the production values luxurious enough and the stars beautiful enough, they would keep coming back for more. That demand and that indifference has remained basically the same; the only major difference is that audiences—needing their spectacles and their stars to keep abreast of the times – require ever-increasing levels of sex and violence – of *sensation*.

The question of what makes art is still unanswered, however, and probably the primary justification for the Academy Awards ceremony is to provide the public with an easy, lazy answer on a yearly basis. Where once audiences were gently guided towards an acknowledgment and appreciation of art, however, now it is their own tastes that often dictate what is decreed as art. These days any film sufficiently popular is likely to be showered with awards and favorable notices. Perhaps this is due to an upholding of the first rule of commerce: the customer is always right? In any event, audiences no longer need to know about art, so long as they know what they like. There is no longer any clear distinction made anyhow.

---

30 This is perhaps the meaning and essence of the Dogme decree, 'I swear as a director to refrain from personal taste! I am no longer an artist. I swear to refrain from creating a "work" as I regard the instant as more important than the whole. My supreme goal is to force the truth out of my characters and settings. I swear to do so by all the means available and at the cost of any good taste and any aesthetic considerations. Thus I make my VOW OF CHASTITY.' Ironic that, with Dogville, von Trier pulled so hard in the other direction and practically forced the viewer to be aware of the artist telling the story and the means by which he did so. His intent, partially, appears to have been to test the audience's ability to forget—or ignore—such ostentation and be drawn into the story despite everything.

If art and the new medium of movies gave rise to Hollywood, which then gave rise to the movie-going public (and to individual artists aspiring to serve both the public and their Muse), the situation has gradually, inevitably, reversed itself: the worm has turned and the tail is now wagging the dog. Now it is the public that calls the shots; studios answer to the blind, insensible mob, as it calls out for ever more empty sensation. 'Art', that once inviolate abstraction, has become a dancing midget for the public's amusement. The public, meanwhile, sits tight, smug and secure in the knowledge of having brought about art's total debasement, and in having revenged itself for all its former punishments (those awful school days!).

If Mel Gibson makes a Sunday school snuff-splatter extravaganza about *The Passion of the Christ* – and does it in ancient Aramaic, Hebrew, and Latin with subtitles for the masses to respectfully chew upon – what matter that he strips the Gospels of all power and poetry, down to a sadomasochistic simple-mindedness bordering on pornography? The public (in their pious Christian hordes) attend the show, and see that it is 'good', the numbers rack up, and from such grotesque and sordid million dollar masturbations – Lo! – as by the hand of God itself, 'art' is born from flesh of Gibson's folly. What threat is Shakespeare anymore, when he can be reduced to *Shakespeare in Love*? That is what the public decrees to be art! Tired of being brow-beaten into submission by empty academics, the public has pulled to the opposite extreme and determined that the criteria for art will no longer be decided by a stuffy elite but only by sheer weight of numbers. The ultimate triumph of the mass sensibility over the artistic one is this: whatever makes enough money and opens 'big' enough will be deemed great.

When the average moviegoer begins thinking like a Hollywood executive, the war between art and commerce is effectively over.

Chapter Eight: Hollywood Be Thy Name: The Story So Far and One Possible Ending

'The two aims of the party are to conquer the whole surface of the earth and to extinguish once and for all the possibility of independent thought.'

George Orwell, *1984*

When Lars von Trier shot *Dogville* with his Hollywood cast – on a skeleton set that offered even less illusion of 'reality' than the average stage production – he provided the actors with a curious amenity (besides those of food, hot beverages and clean toilets), and a special kind of solace from the madness of the shoot. On the edge of the set was a small, makeshift cubicle, no bigger than a public toilet, with a single seat inside it and a hidden camera pointed at the seat. Whoever sat on the seat would see only a red light to indicate that the camera was filming, and was encouraged (though not obliged) to 'confess' – or perhaps vent? – any and all doubts, anxieties, hopes, and frustrations regarding the film and its director.[1]

The trailer for *Dogville* consisted of a brief assemblage of these 'confessions', of the various actors (Nicole Kidman, James Caan, Paul Bettany, Ben Gazzara, Lauren Bacall, and von Trier himself) commenting on the movie they were making, or their feelings about von Trier's methodology. It was a fittingly unorthodox trailer for a movie that was nothing if not an exception to the rules of melodrama. *Dogville* was a comment upon itself, a movie that asked what movies were and why – and how – they were made, and what they were really for. What the trailer suggested – as did *Dogville* itself, at an oblique level – was that the process was everything, the end product next to nothing. Movies, as just another aspect and manifestation of living, could not have a function or purpose any different from that of life itself: an on-going process of self-discovery.

It is curious to consider that, if the means by which movies – at least good ones – are made relates to self-discovery and a deepening of awareness, the end of movies (entertainment) is the very inverse. Most of us go to see movies to forget ourselves and escape the ceaseless pressure of living, caught as we are in a universe that demands constant change. To greater or lesser degrees, every moviegoer seeks such a refuge from reality

1 Interviews pg. 89

via the pleasures of artful entertainment, and every artist filmmaker aspires to provide such a refuge, in the process evolving his or her own personal understanding of 'reality.' This apparent paradox is perhaps reconciled if we consider that the audience-perspective that is seeking refuge belongs to the mass mentality, while the artist-filmmaker's desire to confront and transform reality pertains to individual thought. Every artist is isolate, just as every moviegoer belongs to a collective of moviegoers (regardless of whether he stays at home and watches them on DVD).

Movies are group efforts. Yet it is almost axiomatic that any great art work, including a movie, is the product of a single individual's sensibility and vision. The difference between moviemakers and other artists − writers, painters, sculptors, et al. − is that the filmmaker not only has to maintain his own levels of inspiration and creativity, but to inspire a whole team of others as well. Any great movie is a combination of dozens of separate artists and technicians bringing their best to the project. It is the fusion of countless different individual elements into a cohesive unit, both on set, as a team, and on celluloid, as a finished work. The director is the man who makes that happen. He is the band leader, the circus ringmaster, the squad captain and symphony conductor who draws together all the different factors − both human and otherwise, those of time, money, location, and subject matter − to enliven his vision, give birth to it, make it a reality.

If we consider all this, it's easy enough, to see how great filmmakers burn out so quickly and how, when they do, it is so painfully apparent and usually so final. When a writer's inspiration begins to fail him, he can stop writing and wait for it to return; at worst he can fake it and churn out a fair imitation of his previous work. When a director's vision fails him, his confidence and enthusiasm go with it; his energy levels drop and there is no way for him to disguise it from his cast and crew. Everyone feels it, and will respond with a corresponding drop-off of commitment and energy. A director who is uninspired cannot hope to inspire others, and so his sad apathy will finally extend all the way to the audience, as they struggle through the finished film (assuming he ever manages to finish it). Terry Gilliam is succinct on the subject:

'In films, you have to deal with so many different things, so many different kinds of people: money, talent, time. It's the closest thing to being in the real world, and it's a totally false world. That's what I like about it, and I also hate it for that same reason. You're so divided in a million different directions, you begin to lose yourself in it. You're supposed to be the calm eye of the hurricane, and everybody's coming to you. It's like you're the Wizard of Oz. As long as they believe in you, and the power of the Wizard of Oz, then the film gets made. The minute you lose their confidence, the film starts falling apart. Then you become an actor, playing the role of the director.'

Hollywood is set up in such a way as to abolish, as far as possible, such a dangerous dependence on the vision and commitment of one man. It rejects the idea of the artist as impractical and unrealistic to the business of moviemaking. In a way, it is right to do so. Studio movies are made by groups of technicians in the pay of a studio; they are scripted by writers-for-hire who follow the studio's guidelines every step of the way and directed by agreeable 'professionals' unhampered by personal vision (either seasoned hacks like Richard Donner or inexperienced technical whizzes fresh out of music videos or TV commercials). This way, although there may be little or no chance of creating a work of art, there is also less risk of the production going off-course or over-budget on the whim of a single individual. In such a set-up, the director is there merely to shoot the scenes, to organize and command the crew, and to ensure that the film gets done. Quality is of minimum concern, and even less relevant is the integrity of any 'vision'. The director is certainly not there to inspire anyone, except to do their job and earn their wage; whatever talents he may have are placed in service not of the movie but of the studio that funds it. This is Hollywood in a nutshell: a system and a process that more or less precludes the possibility of 'art,' and does everything it can to prevent personal vision from interfering with the smooth running of the machine.

Yet within this machine – ensconced inside the system, locked into the process – rogue artists and visionaries continue to do their vision thing. In part – until recently at least – this was a simple, if tragic, matter of artists depending on the system that was striving to destroy them in order to make movies on a scale equal to their vision. But there was another factor at work: an overweening pride and ambition on the part of these artists who, with a mix of self-importance and creative zeal (a dangerous combination), aspired to the ultimate hubris. Perhaps this was why von Trier set up his confessional booth, as a means to keep tabs on his ego and make sure it didn't run away with him. Like Prometheus, artists tend to overreach themselves and pay the ultimate price. In their attempt to prove their godlike prowess by stealing the forbidden fire and bringing it to the masses, they are cast out of the company of the gods, and sentenced to the lower depths. So a god becomes a mere mortal, and a once visionary artist becomes a common merchant.

Merchant of Dreams: George Lucas's Plastic Empire

'In 1946, weekly movie attendance was a hundred million. That was out of a population of a hundred and forty-one million, who had nineteen thousand movie screens available to them. Today, there are thirty-six thousand screens in the United States and two hundred and ninety-five million people, and weekly attendance is twenty-five million. And what is the main cinematic experience? The tickets, including the surcharge for ordering online, cost about the same as the monthly cable bill. A medium popcorn is five dollars; the smallest bottled water is three. The show begins with twenty minutes of commercials, spots promoting the theater chain, the previews for movies coming out next Memorial Day, sometimes a year from next Memorial Day. The feature includes any combination of the following: wizards; slinky women of few words; men of few words who can expertly drive anything, spectacularly wreck anything, and leap safely from the top of anything; characters from comic books, sixth-grade world-history textbooks, or "Bullfinch's Mythology"; explosions; phenomena unknown to science; a computer whiz with attitude; a brand-name soft drink, running shoe, or candy bar; an incarnation of pure evil; more explosions; and the voice of Robin Williams. The movie feels about twenty minutes too long; the reviews are mixed; nobody really loves it; and it grosses several hundred million dollars.'

Louis Menand, 'Gross Points'

In the case of George Lucas, a more apropos myth than that of Prometheus might be the tale of Midas, the king whose touch turned everything to gold, making ordinary contact with the world impossible. Midas became the richest man on Earth but was unable to enjoy his riches, unable to even eat, since he couldn't eat gold. He became, like Tartarus (another myth), cursed to have earthly pleasures always within sight but forever out of his reach. The Midas/Prometheus syndrome is perhaps emblematic of our times and of our fascination with, and worship of, celebrities. Men like Howard Hughes, Elvis Presley and Michael Jackson were all in their way victims, both of their own lust for glory (gold) and superiority (divinity) and of the public's equally neurotic need to give it to them. For these tragic public figures, as for Midas, a gift became a curse, as whatever 'genius' they once possessed was swallowed up by the insatiable demands of celebrity. When it comes to leading God's favorite children (artists among them) astray, fame is indeed the devil's trump card. (See *The Devil's Advocate* for a dramatization of this law.)

As the most visible embodiment of this grim tradition, George Lucas is a figure of legendary, nigh-godlike dimensions who is yet almost wholly devoid of creative abilities or even rudimentary human virtues. Baldly stated, Lucas is the most inept filmmaker ever to attain the status of movie giant, yet his reign is supreme. The three *Star Wars* 'prequels'– occasional pleasures of *The Revenge of the Sith* notwithstanding – embody everything that is wrong with Hollywood, with pop culture in general, and, if we stretch it, the world at large. Here is a mystery to ponder upon. Lucas may have the power, and even the vision (in the most basic sense), of a cinematic genius, but he has none of the talent to match. He is a prince with the sensibilities of a toad, so utterly out of touch with anything beyond his masturbatory fantasy world that he can no longer be considered human in the usual sense. His films seem to have been made by a committee of androids, or by a computer program designed to simulate human sentiment yet with next to no idea of what drives human beings (or good melodrama). The result is a fantastically elaborate, multi-million dollar puppet show in which the CGI creations (such as General Grievous in the last film) have infinitely more personality than the actors, and in which even Ewan McGregor and Samuel Jackson are reduced to soulless action figures. That is the Lucas touch.

As a 'world class director,' Lucas' staging of scenes is roughly on a par with a sixth grade school play. Actors walk on, speak excruciating lines, go through the necessary motions, and walk off again, or die, or fade away, making way for the next creakingly unconvincing characters to do their thing. Lucas' grandiose vision grinds along with all the relentless purpose of a combine at harvest time; his 'touch' with actors is so numbingly awful that the movies play like a read-through of the script before shooting. Costing millions of dollars in special effects, sets and costumes, the results are mind-boggling in their wastefulness; uncalculated amounts of time, energy, ingenuity and talent are swallowed up by the black hole of Lucas' talent, leaving audiences with a sloppy, vapid, apathetic rendering of what remains a potentially devastating tale of power and loss. The tragedy of the tale pales in comparison to the tragedy of its (non-) execution. Lucas lacks any aspirations beyond that of a slightly autistic prepubescent, desperate to create his own universe to hide in. Is this not Hollywood in a nutshell?[2]

What happens when fame, success, obscene wealth and power, and complete 'artistic' freedom are granted to a filmmaker with no discernable talent? Power corrupts and absolute power corrupts absolutely. George Lucas has come as close to absolute power in Hollywood as anyone has ever dreamed of; though his 'vision' has remained more or less intact in the thirty years since he dreamed up his space saga (devouring Joseph Campbell and Carlos Castaneda books and splicing them with 'Flash Gordon' TV shows), his ability to do justice to it has not. Whatever creativity Lucas once possessed has now been absolutely corrupted. Yet in the last of the films, the soaring, intergalactic mythos that young Lucas dreamed up all those years ago can still be glimpsed from time to time, albeit dimly. The pay-off to all that went before (not just to the last two – redundant – prequels, but retrospectively adding a whole new layer of pathos and tragedy to the original movies), *Sith* contains by far the richest and most challenging ideas of the series; if only Lucas had handed the reigns over to someone with the necessary talent to do justice to them (as with *Empire Strikes Back,* written by Lawrence Kasdan and directed by Irvin Kershner, the only film in the series that approaches a work of art), the film might have been a genuine classic. It would have justified the hopes, expectations, and devotion of millions of fans who had grown middle-aged waiting for it. Instead, what they got was final, uncontestable proof that, if Lucas has any talent at all besides marketing, it's a talent for bowdlerizing his own inspiration and reducing grand tragedy to artistic travesty.

Anakin/Darth Vader, as conceived in Lucas' story, could have become one of the great tragic, mythic embodiments of Luciferic despair in the history of movies. Instead, we get Hayden Christensen, whose suitability for the role seems to hinge upon having as little charm (or acting ability) as Mark Hammil (Luke Skywalker, Anakin's offspring, whose birth in this movie coincides with Anakin's transformation into Vader). In one of the film's less hackneyed examples of Lucas-speak, we're told that fear of loss is the route to the dark side. Anakin's ominous dream

2 Watch *Revenge of the Sith* with the sound down or wearing headphones and you might be fooled into thinking it was a great fantasy film. It's conceivable that, by dubbing most if not all of the lines with intelligent, thought-provoking dialogue delivered by well-directed actors, the film might be saved from the crushing mediocrity of Lucas' writing and direction. It would probably fare best, however, under the treatment that Woody Allen gave *Kagi-no-Kagi,* turning it into *What's Up Tiger Lily.* Whatever was done with Lucas' film, however, we'd be stuck with the inglorious, strangely moving spectacle of his billion dollar folly.

of his wife Padme's death during childbirth leads him to embrace the dark side, in the hope of gaining sufficient power to save her. But when Anakin gushes to Padme, 'We can rule the galaxy together!', she is understandably non-plussed (as is the audience, hearing this comic book crap). Anakin's conversion to 'evil' (which the opening scrawl helpfully informs us 'is everywhere') is so swift and complete that, within a few scenes (his eyes glowing yellow to signal his malevolence), he has turned his power on his beloved Padme and brought about her premature death. The fact that it was Anakin's visions of Padme's death, his fear of losing her, that drew him to the dark side and ensured the visions came to pass (and the possibility that it was the Sith who sent Anakin his dreams, for this very reason) is never touched upon in the film. Lucas isn't interested in developing the darker undercurrents of his mythos, only in expostulating it; and this he does, with painful deliberateness and an almost frightening lack of artistry.

How can we reconcile Lucas' interest and affection for such mythic concepts with his complete indifference to exploring them? In the first three films, the mythos was a thin but satisfying backdrop to the action, a casual, organic underlayer for the fairy tale, leading to an action yarn that children, teenagers, and adults could all enjoy in their varying ways. Those movies (even the lifeless and mechanical *Return of the Jedi*) carried audiences along with humor, suspense, and a genuine sense of exhilaration and romance – attributes the second trilogy is almost wholly lacking. Lucas became so immersed in his 'vision' – and in the self-importance of mythmaker – that the story weighs his movies down. There is no lightness or sense of play to the action anymore, only the dreadful pressure of expostulation, of seeing the damn thing through to its end. If any of the last three *Star Wars* films had been the first, there never would have been a *Star Wars* franchise at all, because no one would have cared enough to come back for more. Looking back, thirty years on, it might not have been such a bad thing.

Lucas created, or adapted, some beautiful archetypes. The fallen avatar-turned scion of darkness; the twins separated at birth but reunited by destiny; the Force; Han Solo, the heroic scallywag (easily the best character in the series, and there is nothing in the prequels to compensate for his absence); the mythic order of the Jedi Knights; the wise old Master Yoda – all elements of a rich, dreamlike fable to answer audiences' unconscious need for myth and fantasy, both in life and in movies. Now they are just more plastic figurines to clutter up the toy store shelves, and all the richer, more soul-stirring elements have been lost in the shuffle of mass-marketing.[3]

George Lucas isn't really to blame for all this, any more than Anakin or Adolf Hitler are to blame for what *they* turned into, taken over by their base natures and the lust for power. The Machine is stronger than any individual. By responding to a correspondingly dark need in society, Anakin, like Hitler, and like Lucas, became the reflection of a collective dementia. The Republic had to create its Dark Lord to become the Empire, and a world that turns a crass and shallow dream merchant like George Lucas into the most powerful cultural force in movies – that world gets the entertainment it deserves. Lacking insight into his own mythos, Lucas has proved blind to the implications of his own vision. By hitching his creativity to Hollywood's combine, he moved inexorably over to the dark side. He may have conquered the world, but he paid the traditional price for it. Now everything Lucas touches turns to plastic.

True to the Muse: Keith Gordon's Life on the Fringe

> ' "The critic is a soldier in an army put to rout, who deserts and goes over to the enemy." And who is that enemy? The audience.'
> Jean-Luc Godard, quoting Jules Renard

The shadow of George Lucas is Keith Gordon, an artist as marginalized as he is gifted. The inverse consequence of a system, culture, and public that creates legends out of merchants is a talented filmmaker condemned to obscurity and 'failure'. Theoretically, this imbalance is what critics are there to correct; in practice it rarely works out that way, and less and less so as film criticism devolves into mere PR. Inevitably, critics have next to no effect on behemoths like the *Star Wars* or *Matrix* franchises, since fans are going to see those films anyway. All the slings and arrows in the world cannot stop a juggernaut. When it comes to helping a small film find its audience, however, critics do help, or at least used to. Unfortunately, movie critics these days appear less and less inclined to stick their necks out or go against the current of the consensus. It is now more or less *de rigueur* for critics to slam Brian De Palma, for example, and to praise Stanley Kubrick, Wes Anderson or Alexander Payne. Critics, even when they are immune to the more blatant pressures of marketing, hype, studio and/or star seductions, and

---

3 Whatever happened to Jedi mind control? Along with a dozen other ideas, rich in potential, that might have been developed throughout the series, it was tossed off and forgotten, apparently lacking in sufficient potential for product tie-ins.

popular tastes, allow themselves to be swayed – however unconsciously – by critical consensus. They are only human after all. Film criticism has always suffered from accusations of elitism and of being out of touch with (or indifferent to) public likes and dislikes; but lately critics seem to have succumbed to the pressure and adjusted their standards accordingly, betraying the very faculty that made them critics to begin with. Critics can sell out, too, and for exactly the same reasons as filmmakers: wealth, fame, and mass appeal. In a word, the desire to be liked.

This may be a simple matter of resignation (and realism) on the part of critics, however. As Keith Gordon discovered with the release of his fourth feature, the power of critics to sway the mass is negligible at best.

'One of the most depressing but fascinating things about *Waking the Dead* was there were cities where we got nothing but rave reviews and there were cities where we got nothing but bad reviews and it had almost no effect on the box office. That's the one thing you think with independent film: 'Well, reviews are going to make all the difference.' But we could not have gotten better reviews than we got in Los Angeles. And it still didn't make any money in Los Angeles. We couldn't have gotten worse reviews than we did in Philadelphia and it didn't do that much worse in Philadelphia.'[4]

Among critics, Pauline Kael was a noted exception; in her willingness – at times her perverse determination – to go against accepted critical opinion, she took delight in trashing revered filmmakers and adulating ones she felt unjustly neglected. In the latter case, Kael often took her support of a beloved filmmaker to absurd degrees, undermining her own credibility in the process, such as when she praised Peckinpah's *The Killer Elite* (and even *Convoy*), or eulogized Brian De Palma's *The Fury*. But it was the spirit with which Kael championed individual films and filmmakers that gave her such a persuasive and influential voice in movies, and her passion undoubtedly helped many films find the audience they deserved.[5]

4 See Peter Tonguette, 'Keith Gordon on Keith Gordon,' http://www.sensesofcinema. com/contents/04/33/keith_gordon.html.
5 In 1967, Kael was responsible more or less single-handedly for rescuing *Bonnie and Clyde* from critical and commercial oblivion with her review of the film (her first for *The New Yorker*). It was a move that also helped to make her own name in the business, as the guardian angel of the New Hollywood. As Robert Towne put it, 'Without her, *Bonnie and Clyde* would have died the death of a fuckin' dog.' *Easy Riders, Raging Bulls*, pg. 41.

This current essay is admittedly something of a personal aside on the part of the author, an expression of despair, not so much for the state of movies but for the state of film criticism. When a film like *Silence of the Lambs* or *American Beauty* is unanimously hailed as a work of art, when even *Spiderman 2* is greeted as an outstanding piece of entertainment while the latest Brian De Palma is ignored, the rot goes deep. And when a film as rich, complex and audacious as Keith Gordon's *The Singing Detective* is more or less roundly dismissed by critics and so denied the audience it deserves (and that audience likewise deprived of a movie it would probably enjoy), critics have a lot to answer for.

Keith Gordon is a director whose consistently thoughtful, sensitive, and wholly original work has gone almost entirely overlooked by audiences. In a different world – a world where George Lucas produced but was never allowed to direct, and in which critics knew what they were talking about – Gordon would by now have established himself as one of the dozen or so most gifted and challenging filmmakers working in America. Instead, he is almost unknown, and despite having made five of the most interesting independent movies of the past seventeen years, he remains almost criminally ignored by Hollywood and its money men. Since his debut in 1988, Gordon has averaged a film every three-and-a-half years. In his own words, 'I'm now a full time fundraiser. That's the great reality of independent filmmaking in America – my job is raising money, and I direct as a hobby.'

Gordon's approach to life as an independent Hollywood filmmaker is nothing if not pragmatic, and he has shown the wisdom to keep a low profile in more ways than one:

'I've been lucky enough right now, and I live simply enough… I mean, not to say that I live like a monk – I live in a nice house – but I learned a lesson growing up with parents in the business that you don't trust what the future's going to bring economically. So I haven't run out and bought a Porsche, I don't buy Armani suits. I try to, when I make some money doing a movie, to put it in the bank, so that if it's three or four or five years before the next one, that's OK. And because of that I've been able to do this thing of really pursuing the things that excite me and do the things I love and have it be less about how much money can I make and more about how much do I care about this story and how much creative freedom can I get. I mean, I'd much rather lose a zero off of my salary and have more control of the film than make a film for a studio and be paid a million dollars but have somebody else reedit it.'[6]

*

'Once you've proved you aren't the next George Lucas, then your stock goes down... It doesn't get easier, it gets harder, 'cause with each film you define yourself more, what your limitations are. If you haven't had a financial success, you get smaller and smaller.'

Richard Linklater

Gordon's love of movies began when he was seven years old and his father took him to see *2001: A Space Odyssey*. Unable to fully understand the film, but aware that something was going on that he couldn't grasp, Gordon soon developed an almost obsessive interest in movies (as well as a perhaps excessive regard for Kubrick). In his mid-teens he began acting in school plays and in 1978 (at seventeen), he was persuaded to audition for a part in *Jaws* 2. To his surprise he got the role, which led to a part in a TV mini-series 'Studs Lonigen'. Then, in 1979, after a meeting with Brian De Palma, he landed the lead role in De Palma's student project *Home Movies* (filmed at Sarah Lawrence college). By this time, Gordon was determined to be a filmmaker himself, and working with De Palma (on what was essentially a film studies production) provided him with the perfect opportunity. As Gordon put it many years later: 'Working with De Palma was a major education...it was the world's best film class for me, as an actor and an aspiring director.'[7] In effect, De Palma became Gordon's teacher and mentor, a fitting relationship considering that Gordon became something of a De Palma surrogate (his teenage alter ego) both in *Home Movies* and the following year in *Dressed to Kill*. Gordon continued the process of learning by osmosis (and relentless questions) with another master director, John Carpenter, when he was cast as the psychotic car-lover in Carpenter's Stephen King adaptation, *Christine*, in 1983.

Soon after, in 1985, he wrote the script for the haunting cult film

6 Tonguette, 'Keith Gordon on Keith Gordon.'
7 Cynthia Fuchs, 'Interview with Keith Gordon,' www.popmatters.com.

Static, directed by Mark Romanek and co-produced by Gordon.[8] In the late 80s, having played Rodney Dangerfield's son in *Back to School* in 1986, Gordon withdrew from acting and in 1988 made his directorial debut, an adaptation of *The Chocolate War*, the engrossing but infuriating novel by Robert Cormier; the film, though well-reviewed, was not a commercial success.[9] It took Gordon four more years to make *A Midnight Clear*, based on the book by William Wharton. A subtly affecting, heart-rending wartime tale told with remarkable assurance and restraint, the film was once again well-reviewed but soon disappeared without a trace. Though according to Gordon it was his most successful picture to date, it was severely injured by a release date coinciding with the Rodney King riots. As Gordon put it, 'Even if you do everything right, it can fail.'[10] *A Midnight Clear* is a beautiful, poetic work, haunting and surreal; an overwhelmingly affecting character portrait full of richly observed, subtly memorable moments and marvellous performances (Ethan Hawke and Gary Sinise are among the ensemble cast), it is probably the best anti-war film since Kubrick's *Paths of Glory*. But, like all Gordon's subsequent films to date, it slipped under the radar to become one of the most under-appreciated American films of recent years.

Gordon's third movie, in 1996, was also an adaptation. *Mother Night*, taken from the book by Kurt Vonnegut, dealt with an American spy (Howard Campbell, played with devastating pathos by Nick Nolte) who poses as a Nazi and broadcasts their propaganda on the radio, sending coded messages to the Allies. *Mother Night* was above all a character

8 *Static* relates the tale of a young inventor who begins building a mysterious device in a small town. The curiosity of the town inhabitants grows steadily to fever pitch, especially when the young man promises that his invention will banish all their troubles forever and make everybody happy, free from fear. When he finally unveils it, however, it appears to be an ordinary TV set. The young man insists that his device can pick up transmissions from heaven, but no one besides him is able to see anything but static. In desperation, the young inventor kidnaps a busload of old-age pensioners; the police surround the bus and open fire and a stray bullet hits the gas tank. The bus explodes and everyone is killed. The young man has indeed shown them 'heaven.'

9 Cormier's novel (in a rare case of the artist knowing less about art than the businessmen) was initially rejected by several publishers largely due to its gratuitously pessimistic ending, in which evil and despair prevails. For *Chinatown*, this may be a legitimate finale, for a young adults' novel about the price of conformity, it was not, and left the reader with a message of, as Gordon put it, 'You can't fight city hall.' Cormier refused to change his ending, however, and the novel was eventually published to great success. Recognizing the nihilistic nature of the book's ending, Gordon made some subtle but perceptive changes, much to the frustration of many of the book's younger fans.

10. Tonguette, 'Keith Gordon on Keith Gordon,' © 2004.

study about a man who loses his identity from the lack of an adequate frame of reference. Campbell (Nick Nolte) is neither American nor German, neither Nazi nor Ally; he is simply a playwright who takes on the ultimate challenge, a challenge that proves to be beyond him (not beyond his talents but beyond his moral strength). There is a scene in the film when Campbell first realizes he has lost his will, and simply stops on the New York sidewalk and stands motionless, as the crowd and the hours pass by, devoid of reason to move. Interestingly enough, the scene evoked a moment from Brian De Palma's equally neglected *Home Movies*, in which Keith Gordon, then an actor, sits on his suitcase in the middle of the train station, day after day, having become 'an extra in his own life.'

Like *Midnight*, *Mother Night* was largely overlooked, perhaps due in part to its ambivalent view of Nazism. Like the book, the film refrained from judging its characters, preferring to deal with Campbell's conscience (or lack of it) rather than the moral question of Nazism itself. It's conceivable that the film was punished for its refusal to toe the party line, but whatever the case, once again Gordon found himself being marginalized for the very qualities that made his films so outstanding: their subtlety, sensitivity, and intelligence. Gordon described *Mother Night* as follows:

'The real deep theme is of personal responsibility. The idea that you have to be careful about what you pretend to be because what you pretend to be is what you are, to me that's completely timeless. World War II was just a convenient device. The thing about World War II is that it heightens everything. You're taking something that's always seen in the blackest of blacks and the whitest of whites, and showing that even there behaviour is a very grey thing. The most dangerous thing to do is to deny the dark side of yourself, to not take responsibility. Howard's crime is not so much that he acts like a Nazi, it's that he doesn't think about and take responsibility for his actions in any direction. I like the fact that neo-Nazis are ironically the comic relief in the film, because again it makes you reconsider who everybody is. In a perverse way they're the most honest people in the story. Everybody else has triple identities, but these are the only persons who really are true to something they believe in. Which is in no way defending them, but it gets into the complexity that these perverse, pathetic guys are not the danger. The guy standing on the street corner screaming is not what's dangerous. It's the Howard Campbells, the people who should know better, who have a chance and are smart enough to stand up and say no – those are the people who bear responsibility. There'll always be an

Adolf Hitler in every society at every moment, screaming that if we just kill these people or those people it'll solve all of our problems. They're not to blame – they're just nuts. It's the people that listen who make it go one way or the other.'[11]

With remarkable fidelity and affinity for the material, Gordon and scriptwriter Bob Weide uphold the spirit of Vonnegut's novel and perfectly capture its sad, ambivalent, and ironic view of life. As a director, Gordon seems to have a natural affinity for the schizophrenic experience, for isolation, despair, and the twists and turns of the broken human spirit. None of which exactly makes for a roaring success in Hollywood, or for 'the next George Lucas'. Yet such empathy is above all what makes Gordon's work so unique and affecting, and what makes him such a remarkable creative presence in today's movie climate.[12]

It also perfectly suited him for his most recent film, *The Singing Detective*, released towards the end of 2003, and easily his most ambitious work to date. Based on a screenplay by Dennis Potter, the film was produced by Mel Gibson's Icon Pictures and shot in 35 days for $8 million. Gibson (who also plays a role in the film, gleefully out of character as the psychiatrist) was instrumental in initiating the film as an 'independent' project; the script had been floating around Hollywood for ten years, ever since Potter wrote it, and it's largely thanks to Gibson that it finally got made. The film is a strange animal, all right, a work sans genre, and at times Gordon seems to have overreached himself, grasping for effects he isn't quite able to achieve. The various styles, moods, and genres give the film a slightly garish, amateurish feel, yet in the end (perhaps consciously on Gordon's part) this very awkwardness works in the film's favor. *The Singing Detective* is a remarkably ingenuous work, fresh and daring, almost childlike in its lack of pretension, and easily one of the most original American movies of the last twenty years. Above all, it showcases Robert Downey Jr.'s raging, embittered psoriasis-afflicted pulp writer, inside whose head the whole movie (more or less) takes place, and Downey gives an inventive, powerful performance, what may be the apotheosis of his enormous talent. Praise for Downey notwithstanding, on its release Gordon's film met with a wall of critical resistance, a veritable consensus of contempt. This may have been

---

11 See http://mondofausto.com/interview-gordon-vonnegut.htm
12 His fourth feature, *Waking the Dead*, made in 2000, once again suffered from the whims of fate and bad timing when the company that funded it, Gramercy, went bankrupt just prior to its release. Of all Gordon's films, *Waking the Dead* is probably the least known (which is really saying something).

due in part (in the UK at least) to a fondness for Potter's original TV series; but it was perhaps due even more to the basic incompatibility of Potter's idiosyncratic, scathing vision with mainstream (critical) tastes.[13] Whatever the case, the movie once again tragically failed to find its audience.

As with his previous adaptations, Gordon respected the source material without revering it, and as a director, he has a rare gift: the ability to fuse his own sensibility and talents with his subject at a fundamental level. In the case of *The Singing Detective*, it was a somewhat less seamless fusion; Potter's vision (his bizarre blend of musical fantasy with bleak psychological realism) was so startlingly original it required another sensibility at least as strong and eccentric to fuse with. Gordon doesn't quite possess (yet) the surrealist gifts to make Potter's vision his own, or to take it to the next level (David Lynch might be the only director capable of that). He's a proficient director in every way, and seems to be blessed with a natural rapport with actors (perhaps why so many good ones want to work with him). Yet Gordon isn't a visionary director, and this was a visionary script. Fortunately, he had a visionary actor at a career peak to take up the slack, and Downey carries the day.[14]

The Singing Detective isn't a masterpiece; it's flawed and fractured and at times thin, even facile and occasionally redundant (most especially in the pseudo-noir sequences). But it's an imaginative and fearless piece of cinema, an admirably eccentric work that manages to do something like justice to a brilliant piece of writing. Full of inventive delights and heartfelt touches, it leaves most other recent American films in the dust. Yet it flopped badly, both in the UK and the US, being so poorly reviewed that many people (myself included) gave it a miss, wary of the stench of failure. As it happened, the bad smells came not from the film but from critics too corrupt and jaded to recognize a work of art when they saw it. There's no accounting for taste, and no sense in getting riled over a lack of it on the part of critics or the public. *C'est la guerre*, and in a war, everyone must take sides. Hollywood has helped create a world where *Titanic* did not sink and George Lucas is the unchallenged Emperor who rules the

13 A similar fate had befallen Herbert Ross' adaptation of *Pennies from Heaven*, with Steve Martin, which was also a commercial flop and seemed to baffle critics and public alike, though in this case, Kael was there to champion the film.

14 Downey was just out of jail for drug abuse (and still on probation) when he made the film, and it's impossible to imagine any other actor of his age group bringing such intensity, humor, and depth to the role.

15 Actually, according to Premiere's 2005 'Power List,' Peter Jackson (*Lord of the Rings*) is now officially the Emperor of Hollywood, closely followed by Steven Spielberg. Poor George must settle for 11th place.

waves.[15] Movies are founded on mass appeal, and the mass is characterized by its lack of discernment, after all; the critics (those who have joined the enemy at least) are little more than servants to that mass. In the end, success and adulation, however desirable, are besides the point. Like Hal Hartley, Keith Gordon may thrive in obscurity, and his talents can develop all the better for being mostly unsung (this piece notwithstanding). Audiences (as well as Gordon) can be grateful he's allowed to work at all, and that there is at least one American filmmaker who has stayed true to his Muse.[16]

One From the Heart: Matthew Ryan Hoge's *United States of Leland*

'It's a more difficult and dangerous world to live in where we accept the fact that some people who do bad things have good in them. You can't define a life by one action. We all have some of that bad in our goodness; the line is always sort of blurry.'

Matthew Ryan Hoge

With his famous mix of wit and wisdom, Oscar Wilde once quipped how 'no good deed goes unpunished'; perhaps the same perverse law applies to fresh and original works of cinema? In Hollywood, there is apparently no sin greater than artistic integrity, and in being denied access to the collective consciousness of 'mainstream' audiences, Keith Gordon is far from alone. Such works as Steve Kloves' *Flesh and Bone*, Alexandre Rockwell's *Sons,* Finn Taylor's *Dream with the Fishes*, Henry Bean's *The Believer* and Nick Cassavetes' *Unhook the Stars* are among the most enjoyable and memorable movies of recent years yet they are works that have come and gone (like Gordon's work) with barely a twitch of acknowledgement from the mass mind of critics and moviegoers.[17] However lamentable this situation may be, however, it has to be said that there is a special pleasure in discovering rare movie gems that no one

16 His most recent work, in 2005, was slated to be *Billy Dead*, starring Ethan Hawke, for which Gordon attempted to finance through an 'initial public offering' (IPO), via which the public was invited to buy shares in the finished film, so providing the budget. Unfortunately, there was insufficient interest, and Gordon was forced to abandon the project. Gordon was also commissioned to write a script for a Cruise/Wagner production of Isaac Asimov's novel, *The End of Eternity*, though this at present 'seems pretty much dead' (Gordon to the author). Gordon expressed no regret to me over this, however, and I can't help but think it may be just as well, since Cruise and Muse do not easy bedfellows make.

17 Other interesting works largely ignored by public and critics alike include *The Alarmist, The Boiler Room, Jesus' Son, Palookaville, Kissed, Bodies: Rest and Motion.*

else has a clue about. At the same time, the relative obscurity of these works only confirms a growing suspicion, namely, that Hollywood and its audience are already too far gone to ever recognize works that truly come from the heart. The most recent example of this sad but no doubt inevitable fact is Matthew Ryan Hoge's *The United States of Leland*.

So far in the present work, I've been using the term 'auteur works' loosely, to describe films possessed of a strong, usually directorial personality (for example when Scorsese made *Taxi Driver* or De Palma did *Casualties of War*, both from scripts written by others). In a stricter sense, however, an auteur work must really be written and directed by the same person, and so imbued with a unique sensibility from its inception onward. Auteur directors who bring a strong visual, aesthetic, even thematic sense to their films are common enough, and by such a wide definition even James Cameron and Peter Jackson may be considered 'auteurs.' But filmmakers who possess a unique philosophical or literary (for lack of better words) sensibility – whose personality is felt almost as strongly through their films as a novelist's is felt through his books – have always been extremely rare in movies.[18] Because of the depth of feeling and layers of meaning which they possess, works of this kind often seem to have been based on novels even when they aren't. Perhaps this is because the ideas have been fermenting that much longer inside the mind of the filmmaker, or perhaps it's because they are drawn more directly from his or her personal experiences; whatever the case (and be it *Flesh and Bone, Dream with the Fishes,* the recent *Around the Bend*, or *The United States of Leland*), the result has been some of the finest films ever made in America, but also some of the least known.

Like Richard Kelly's *Donnie Darko* (another recent auteur work), *The United States of Leland* is about a young adult who suffers from an excess of empathy, and how it leads him both to wisdom and madness, in more or less equal proportion. Ostensibly, it's about a senseless murder (Leland kills the retarded brother of his girlfriend, after she dumps him for another boy), and the equally senseless search

18 Novel ideas, flesh and blood characters, genuine human interactions, depth psychology, emotional poignancy – what we might call heart – these are all qualities that only arise when a movie is made, not out of a lust for fame or Hollywood glory – nor even out of a simple love for images – but from something that burns within the artist's breast and demands to be expressed. Such filmmakers must, one supposes, be first of all writers, and that they choose to express their thoughts and feelings by writing and then shooting a movie is secondary; if they couldn't make their movie, such artists would always express themselves somehow.

for a reason why, a search that invariably turns up answers deeper and more disturbing – and more mysterious – than the original question. Although Hoge – whose first film this was – doesn't have any obvious visionary gifts as a director (unlike, say, Richard Kelly), he does an astonishing job drawing together the various elements of his screenplay into a cohesive whole, creating an Altmanesque patchwork of lives in distress.[19] Hoge has a phenomenal gift as a writer: the ability to create scenes, characters and dialogue strong enough to carry his personal, philosophical concerns without ever being bent out of shape by them. Hoge is clearly writing from the heart, and unafraid to put his psyche whole into the movie. Yet his touch is unobtrusive and discreet, with none of the usual angst and indulgence common to first-time auteurs (*Pi, Welcome to the Dollhouse*, etc, etc). Hoge's restraint is especially remarkable because, by choosing to concentrate on story and character and letting the personal stuff seep through in its own good time, instead of diminishing the intensity of his vision, he allows it to come slowly to life through the course of the film. By the end, it packs such a wallop that it may take a day or two to recover. This kind of restraint – and such an assured creative instinct – is almost unique to first-time filmmakers, most especially ones this ambitious.

The United States of Leland presents an impressively rich and complex array of human problems – neurosis, fear, grief, confusion, rage and sorrow – yet it never gets bogged down by them, it never feels indulgent or morose (as in the case of Paul Thomas Anderson's *Magnolia,* for example), and it never seems forced or contrived. Its only motive (like *Leland*'s?) seems to be to release some of the unbearable pressure of empathy, in the face of an overwhelming universal sadness. And because it's a gesture made in earnest – without airs or expectations or ulterior motives – the film connects; it connects to something close to the essence of being human – our shared loneliness, and the isolate despair

---

19 All the performances are flawless, none more so than that of Ryan Gosling playing Leland. Gosling brings to the role just the right qualities of isolation, strangeness, and sweetness to hold Hoge's vision together; another actor – one less endearing and unsettling – and Hoge's deceptively complex character portrait might have fallen apart. With Gosling in the role, the full richness and heartache of Hoge's psychological tragedy is expressed. Besides Gosling, there are remarkable performances from the entire cast, which includes Martin Donovan, Don Cheadle, Jena Malone (from *Donnie Darko*), Chris Klein, Michelle Williams, Ann Magnuson, Lena Olin, and a perfectly cast Kevin Spacey as Leland's absent father, the cold and self-obsessed writer-genius Fitzgerald. (Spacey no doubt hand-picked the role for himself, since he also co-produced the film for his company, Trigger St.)

of being an island, a nation unto ourselves. As Leland says, all the tears in the world can't make what has happened unhappen. But the tears come anyway.

In essence, Hoge's vision touches upon something profound: how the most apparently monstrous evil can come out of an excess of goodness, how the burden of empathy – of deeper seeing – can lead to the most desperate of acts, to suicide, for example, or murder. Like a distress signal from a lost soul afloat in a sea of lost souls, it suggests both complicity in despair and the possibility of release from it; like an aria, it appeals to audiences to let down the shields and the blinds, for just a moment, and look. Audiences could not have cared less, however. Hoge's film appeared out of nowhere, and vanished back from whence it came soon after, under a barrage of critical incomprehension and outrage, and several attempts to boycott the film (by parents of autistic children, claiming it glorified murder – having never seen it, of course). I can think of no other recent film that was so unjustly overlooked as this, nor greater evidence of the nigh-pathological obtuseness of American film critics. (These are the same critics, mind, who hail a smug and asinine work like *American Beauty* as a work of moral depth, social relevance, and psychological poignancy!)[20]

Audience and critics' indifference notwithstanding, however, make no mistake about it: *The United States of Leland* attains the highest goal of art; by expressing the bottomless pain of a single individual, it eases the sadness of the world. That Hoge isn't recognized and acclaimed as a brilliant new film artist – along with Paul Thomas Anderson, Alexander Payne, and the rest of the new indie lights – is perhaps evidence of just how unwilling people are to be reminded of that sadness. Hoge made a masterpiece from the heart, and was duly punished. The world (and Hollywood) rode right over him.

Hollywood Will Eat Itself: Remake-'itis' and Sequel-mania

'The independent film movement, as we knew it, just doesn't exist anymore, and maybe it can't exist anymore. It's over.'

Steve Soderbergh

---

20 As Hoge expressed it at the time, 'some of it is the subject matter which people can't get past, but it's sort of sad to me that sincerity is not a virtue, you know? That being earnest in your storytelling and trying to tell a story that means something in an earnest way isn't appreciated. People, particularly critics, sort of prefer an ironic distance and not getting emotionally close to characters who are asking difficult questions about human nature.' (Ergo, the ecstatic response to *American Beauty*.)

The population of the USA has more than doubled in the last sixty years, an exponential explosion of humans that has been the primary cause of the rise of consumerism and of the current frenzy of excess we call modern living. Less self-evidently, the rise of human beings may also account for the steady degeneration of Western culture apparent to anyone who tries to have a good time at 'the arts' these days. More humans means more consumers – a bigger mass demanding more products to consume. The worse planetary conditions become, the more distraction and 'entertainment' the mass needs to forget their awful predicament. This doesn't necessarily mean more artists, however; nor, most crucially of all, does it mean more ideas.

Hollywood movies – barring the occasional blip, such as occurred in 1999[21] – can be said with a minimum of subjectivity to have steadily declined in quality and originality since roughly 1976; this despite the fact that the overall output of movies has increased, and the public infatuation with all things Hollywood has reached an all-time high. Hollywood has become a place of glamour, wealth and excess, however, rather than a source of creativity or innovation. Since the late 70s, sequels to successful movies – almost invariably inferior[22] – have been favored by studios. In the 80s and 90s, the mania for recycling old material was taken even further into cannibalism when Hollywood began remaking old movies for new audiences, again almost always at the loss of whatever made the original movies 'worth' remaking.[23]

Initially, remakes were confined to old movies that Hollywood decided needed revamping for modern (i.e., teenage) audiences; but before long, studios were desperately redoing movies from no more than a decade or two ago, movies that were never considered classics but had the right ingredients for easy, crowd-pleasing genre entertainment. Sam Peckinpah's *The Getaway* was a negligible movie the first time around on which Peckinpah whored his talents; two decades later it became a mediocre and gratuitous Roger Donaldson remake with Alec Baldwin and Kim Basinger (an 'item' at the time; probably designed expressly as a vehicle for the hot couple, the movie tanked). Still not satisfied,

21 The year of *Fight Club*, *The Matrix*, *The Insider*, *Three Kings*, *Being John Malkovich*, 1999 produced more great or borderline great movies than the rest of the decade combined.
22 Although the rule of 'second is best' does also seem to apply, as with *The Empire Strikes Back*, *Superman II*, *Mad Max II*, *Indiana Jones and the Temple of Doom*, *The Evil Dead 2*, *Ghostbusters II*, *X2*, all of which were markedly superior to the originals.
23 As John Huston once pointed out, it makes little sense to remake a classic if it's already been done right the first time; more logical by far would be to redo movies that had a potential unfulfilled the first time around..

Hollywood began to plunder the archives of old TV shows, cartoons, even video games, for material for 'blockbuster' movies with which to attract undiscriminating audiences. *Sgt. Bilko, The Saint, The Avengers, Charlie's Angels, The Flintstones, Scooby Doo, The Mario Bros., Tomb Raider*, some of the most indefensible and irredeemable big budget turkeys (many of which were financially successful) started out as dud ideas that only a studio executive could love.

Also up for grabs were recent foreign films that could be bought up and done over with Hollywood stars, free of those pesky subtitles. (The American public has a built-in resistance to non-American movies – or non-American anything – and to reading in general, most especially at the movies; at least this was what studios assumed; the runaway success of Gibson's *Passion of the Christ* seemed to contest it.) A recent foreign art house hit such as *Abre Los Ojos* (a visionary and sophisticated Spanish film by Alejandro Amenábar) was remade – through the intervention of Tom Cruise and his director-in-pocket Cameron Crowe – as the asinine *Vanilla Sky*, a grotesque anti-vanity vanity piece for the star.[24]

Hollywood – like a polymorphous predator of all things 'art' (including its own trash) – devours and defecates at an increasingly rapid pace in order to maintain the illusion of being a living organism, a productive – even 'creative' – industry. Lately, this remake-mania has taken on a decidedly ironic thrust, as Hollywood begins to remake once-low-budget independent 'sleeper' hits such as *Dawn of the Dead, The Texas Chainsaw Massacre* and *Assault on Precinct 13* as slick, expensive, ultraviolent Hollywood spectacles, expressly for young audiences who have probably never heard of the original films and hence are unaware of being served last week's leftovers warmed over. Usually the result (as with *Vanilla Sky*) is to strip the original work of the very qualities (its raw simplicity, spontaneity, and invention) that made it interesting to begin with. Remaking a B-movie as an A-movie (or an indie classic as a big studio dud) more or less sums up the situation regarding the current (and indefinitely

---

24 After Tom Cruise saw *Lock, Stock and Two Smoking Barrels*, the debut film by Guy Ritchie (later Mr. Madonna), he reportedly shouted 'It rocks!' and proceeded to buy up the rights to remake it as an American movie. So far this has not come to pass, but it illustrates the sort of thinking that characterizes Hollywood (which Mr. Cruise so admirably embodies): that art is there not to be appreciated but to be acquired, in fact can *only* be appreciated if it is acquired. Usually the work in question (as with *Abre Los Ojos*) is completely destroyed by the 'makeover', which is motivated by the collector's vanity, his conceit of being an artist rather than merely a collector (and destroyer) of other people's work. There are exceptions, such as Chris Nolan's *Insomnia*, which deftly adapted Erik Skjalabjoerg's original into a haunting Al Pacino vehicle.

continuing) famine in Hollywood, its desperation to harvest a new crop of cinematic material even if it has to plunder the local farmers' land to do so.

Of course, studios wouldn't give even half the money these remakes cost to the original directors to make new films with (fair enough when you look at Hooper's, Carpenter's, and Romero's recent work, but still). The total dearth of good new material in Hollywood is all-too-apparently the reason it is starting to feed off the carcass of independent cinema. *The Dawn of the Dead* remake was a respectable horror movie and one of the more enjoyable studio films of the year; but even so it seemed largely pointless. Why not make a new zombie movie with an original script? How hard can it be? The answer is that Hollywood is both temperamentally disposed towards recycling old material and deeply averse to working with new ideas. Ergo, cannibalism comes naturally to it.

Most if not all of these remakes were made by directors we have never heard of before and who, often as not, we will never hear of again.[25] Who are they? Where do they come from? Most likely, they come from music videos, MTV, TV shows and commercials, and if so it shows. Essentially, what is happening is that these remakes/updates/sequels/adaptations are studio movies in the fullest sense, put together by a group of executives who decide – presumably after going down a long list of potential cultural carcasses to cannibalize – that 'Scooby Doo' would make a great movie. They then set about finding someone (usually six or seven or a dozen 'someones') to write a script, and someone (preferably someone who has never made a movie before and will be grateful for the opportunity and do exactly as he is told) to direct the film. This is what is known as a 'package movie'.

Actors in Search of a Script: The Curse of the 'Package Movie'

'The people who make movies need to be able to take themselves more seriously than the people who make popcorn do. The situation would be simpler if everyone was certain that

25 *The Dawn of the Dead* remake was directed by Zack Snyder, that of *Assault on Precinct 13* by Jean-Francois Richet, and the new *Texas Chainsaw Massacre* by Marcus Nispel. Coming remakes include the British classic *The Wicker Man* and Sam Raimi's cult indie fave, *The Evil Dead*.

the movies making money today have no more creative integrity or cultural significance than a beer commercial. But no one is certain. People fear that they've lost the key to the distinction. Hence the anxiety.'

Louis Menand, 'Gross Points'

Package movies are films that consist of a director, a producer (or five), one or more name actors, and a story, of sorts, though often no finished script to speak of. One recent, more or less random example is *The Mexican*, a film about a gun that starred Julia Roberts and Brad Pitt. The script that was finally shot only had one scene in which their two characters appeared together, a lame fight scene and anything but the dream coupling of Hollywood's beloved 'beautiful people'. The rest of the movie didn't even exist, but evidently, some shrewd studio executive had convinced Julia Robert's agent that Brad had committed, then told Pitt's agent, 'We have Julia!' whereupon both stars, eager to work together, agreed to the project despite the conspicuous absence of a script. The studio heads probably didn't care much, either, since any movie with Brad and Julia was bound to turn a profit. It did, but only barely; the film was one of the most brazen con jobs in recent Hollywood history, a history choc-a-bloc with brazen con jobs.

Perhaps the most depressing thing about studio package movies is not the waste of money or the exploitation of directors' talents, but the sight of gifted actors floundering hopelessly in a sea of witless dialogue, trapped inside a meandering storyline and stuck with material utterly unworthy of their talents. The desperation shows in their eyes, as they plead with audiences to forgive them for ever committing to such trash. Actors are notoriously lacking in discrimination or intelligence when it comes to choosing their movies, however. Could anyone who saw *The Score* doubt that the film was greenlighted wholly on the basis of its cast – Edward Norton, Robert De Niro and Marlon Brando, three generations of leading method actors together in the same movie!? But why did these three greats ever agree to work together with such a mediocre script and a director (Frank Oz) best known for impersonating a pig?[26] Ed Norton made no bones about his reasons, admitting that he would have done this one for the poster alone, and to get to see

---

[26] Frank Oz was originally the voice behind Fozzie Bear and Miss Piggy on 'The Muppet Show.' He went on to direct such dubious comic hits as *Dirty Rotten Scoundrels*.

his name alongside his legendary method ancestors; but what was their excuse? *The Score* cost many millions of dollars in actors' salaries alone, but it gave them nothing at all to do for their money. How much more interesting would it have been (it couldn't have been less) simply to have filmed the three actors for a few weeks with a digital camera, had them improvise or just be themselves, anything at all, and edit that into a movie? A digi-Dogme mistakist movie starring Brando, De Niro and Norton might have been a disaster, but at the very least it would have made an interesting artifact. Instead, we got *The Score*, a movie that never should have been made, that faded away into non-existence while audiences stared at it in disbelief, and that left nothing behind but the poster.[27]

The Hollywood Draft: How the Movie Business Devours Its Young

'There are few first novels in filmmaking, efforts that go into the drawer or up in flames, because there are no – or very few – second chances. Or, to put it another way, indie film is almost exclusively a cinema of first films.'

Peter Biskind, *Down and Dirty Pictures*

It may be observed – by close analysis of all these package movies, remakes, and adaptations – how Hollywood operates. In Hollywood, there is a kind of draft system, whereby up-and-coming new 'talent' is called up for service to the hallowed Hollywood cause – that of profits. Most of those who are called into service go down their very first time in the field and never get up again, leaving only a soulless package-movie to mark the spot where they died.[28] Some of them

---

27 Another example: In 2005, Sean Penn and Nicole Kidman – two actors at the peak of their craft with remarkable track records to date – for some reason agreed to make *The Interpreter* for Sydney Pollock, a director who peaked twenty years ago with *Tootsie*, and who has long since settled into making torpid, star-driven redundancies like *Out of Africa* and *Random Hearts*. In fact, *The Interpreter* was Pollock's most satisfying movie in years, but even so, why would Penn and Kidman agree to such a routine project except for the opportunity to work together? It seems a tragic waste of a potentially explosive pairing. But then, waste is what Hollywood is all about: just as wealth is gauged by the rich capitalist by how much he throws away (uneaten food and unworn clothes), Hollywood can display its power and abundance by abusing its brightest lights, sticking them under bushels to burn.

– such as Simon West or Michael Bay, two recent 'hot' directors with zero artistic aspirations – display sufficiently sensationalist 'technique' and possess an adequate degree of egomania to become 'A-list' directors, even though they may never make a single personal movie. These men (and they are always men) are Hollywood's pride and joy, cut from the cloth that Hollywood has manufactured, as much products of the studio system as the movies that they, in their turn, produce for it.

On the other hand, Hollywood is especially proud and triumphant when it can recruit a recently emerged independent 'auteur' (a personal filmmaker still struggling to break through) and send him or her into the field for their second or third movie. This way, Hollywood can redirect creative potential down channels of crass commercialism, and for the cynical exploitation of the masses. It is in such deviation of artistic potential and debasement of an individual's once-pure creative intent (via the vulgar but reliable temptations of sex, money, and power) that Hollywood's true *raison d'être* lies. This is, after all, its only possible 'victory' in times of creative bankruptcy such as now, and it revolves around a kind of points system, one relating not only to dollars – how much profit can be made by turning a low-budget independent flick (or artist) into a mainstream smash – but also, more crucially, to power. How many so-called artists can be corrupted with a whiff of success in their nostrils is a means for Hollywood to consolidate its power as a whole, as an entity. Likewise the countless individuals locked into blind, greedy service of the system (not just studio executives, but actors and directors too) can thereby feel secure in their choice of Mammon over the Muse.

As Orson Welles told Kenneth Tynan in 1967:

'The advertisers are having a disastrous effect on every art they touch. They are not only seducing the artist, they are drafting

---

28 Back in 1980, Brian De Palma had this to say on the subject: 'See, the problem in this business is that, in order to grow, you have to make lots of pictures. And fail a lot of times. We're going through a wild budget syndrome at the moment, where a young director will make a big score on some small-budget picture, and then whatever he says and does is right. The problem with this is that your failures won't be half-million-dollar ones but $30 million ones. And those can be devastating. The critics start reviewing your budgets, and the distribution companies, who have lost a lot of money, become reluctant to let you experiment. I had the advantage of being able to fail many times on miniscule budgets early in my career, and I wasn't wiped out. With most directors, ten-to-one their first couple of pictures were disasters.' *Interviews*, pg. 72

him. They are not only drawing on him, they are sucking the soul out of him. And the artist has gone over to the advertiser far more than he ever did to the merchant... Among the advertisers, you find artists who have betrayed their kind and are busy getting their brethren hooked on the same drug. The advertising profession is largely made up of unfrocked poets, disappointed novelists, frustrated actors and unsuccessful producers with split-level homes. They've somehow managed to pervade the whole universe of art, so that the artist himself now thinks and functions as an advertising man.'

Forty years after Welles made this ominous remark, the examples are legion. After Danny Cannon came to the attention of the business with his mildly interesting indie crime thriller, *The Young Americans* (with Harvey Keitel), the next thing we heard was that he was directing Sylvester Stallone in the big budget folly of *Judge Dredd*. Cannon's next film was the gratuitous slasher sequel, *I Still Know What You Did Last Summer* (the title says it all); Cannon has not been heard from since, and is currently working in American TV. When Doug Liman made the quirky, imaginative *Go*, he was a filmmaker worth watching. Within a few years, he was making *The Bourne Identity* for Matt Damon (a superior Bond imitation with an amnesiac Bond) and it was plain the gig was up. Ditto Peter Greengrass, who went from the gritty *Bloody Sunday* to *The Bourne Supremacy*, a sequel that made the most of the director's talents while simultaneously shackling them to a largely pointless action thriller.[29]

Perhaps the most unequivocal example of this dark process is that of Lee Tamahori, the New Zealand director who grabbed audiences by the throat with his ferocious independent domestic drama, *Once Were Warriors,* a masterpiece of raw and ruthless filmmaking. Tamahori went Hollywood soon after, made the disappointedly lackluster *Mulholland Falls,* followed by the rip-roaring adventure yarn *The Edge* (from a script by David Mamet). At this point, Tamahori still had a fighting chance of finding his feet in Hollywood; but then along came a serial killer flick with Morgan Freeman (a franchise unto itself), and that was the end of Tamahori.[30] He was then recruited to make a Bond movie, one way

29 Greengrass is currently attempting the impossible and adapting Alan Moore's and Dave Gibbons' *Watchmen* into a movie.
30 *Along Came a Spider.*

Hollywood buries its recently dead. Here lies the artist formerly known as Lee Tamahori.[31]

Auteur No More: Chris Nolan's Shallow Bat Magic

'It's that kind of thinking – you're in a desperate situation, you gotta have a job, you're offered a lot of money... It affects you... The key to that kind of system is, 'What's his price? How can he be had? How can we get him interested?' And there are a lot of people a lot smarter than I am who think about nothing else twenty-four hours a day. I'm smart enough to know they might find some way to get me. You just try to keep on a different road.'

Brian De Palma

It at least took Hollywood a few movies and almost ten years to bury Lee Tamahori; Chris Nolan, on the other hand, looks set to go under after only three movies, swallowed up by the shadow of *Batman*. A mere seven years ago, in 1998, Nolan made his obscure debut with *Following*, breaking through onto the indie scene in full glory two years later with the much-celebrated *Memento* (which took over a year to find a distributor in the US, but finally became a hit in 2000). *Memento* led to Nolan's signing up with Soderbergh and Clooney's Section Eight and making *Insomnia* in 2002, a more or less mainstream Al Pacino thriller that artfully subverted the cop genre and became one of the most powerful auteur works of recent years (albeit based on a Norwegian movie of the same name, and from a script by Hillary Seitz). Then, in 2005, along came a dark knight; though only time can say for sure, judging by *Batman Begins*, Nolan's development as an auteur filmmaker has ended with only his fourth picture.

31 Further examples: Jean-Pierre Jeunet, one half of the seductively original team behind *Delicatessen* and *City of Lost Children,* went Hollywood to make the laughable *Alien Resurrection*, proving that European auteurs are not immune to the allure of tinsel town, and in fact, make up some of the very worst causalities, perhaps because they are unprepared for just how vision-killing Hollywood can be. Occasionally it does work out, however. After *Abre Los Ojos* (and even as Cruise was vomiting out *Vanilla Sky*), Alejandro Amenábar made *The Others* with Cruise's ex-amour, Nicole Kidman; the film was an almost perfect vehicle for the director's talents. After *Y Tu Madre Tambien*, Alfonso Cuarón went all the way into the Labyrinth of the Penumbra to face Hollywood Dementors and made the third *Harry Potter* film; though it may not be the high point of his career, his input did save the franchise from terminal mediocrity, and sorcery-loving kids everywhere can be grateful to him for selling out. *21 Grams* was Alejandro González Iñárittu's follow up to *Amores Perros*, and an American classic.

Memento was based on a short story by Nolan's brother, Jonathan, and was a measured work of quiet intensity. It concerned Leonard Shelby (Guy Pearce), a one-time insurance agent suffering from short-term memory loss. As the character explains over and over again, he is 'unable to make new memories'. His memory functions much like a goldfish in a bowl, like a tape that is continuously rewound and erased to make space for new memories. The twist is that Leonard is on a revenge mission, seeking his wife's killer. A revenge drama about 'the futility of revenge,' as Nolan put it, *Memento* was a canny meditation on the nature of perception, memory, delusion, belief and emotional need, and the real fascination of the movie had less to do with the plot than with observing, and gradually coming to grasp, the nature of Leonard's condition. A clinical study of dementia dressed up with guns and car chases and *femmes fatales*, the film achieved a haunting, hypnotic quality as rare and precious in movies as it is central to their essence. Though it was anything but leisurely paced, *Memento* had some of the trancelike fascination of *Vertigo*. It was film noir eating itself, a postmodern, Surrealist puzzle *par excellence*.

Nolan followed *Memento* with *Insomnia*, for Section Eight, seamlessly fusing a mainstream, star-studded genre piece with his own unmistakable cinematic vision. In the course of the film, Will Dormer (Al Pacino) went from being a good cop to a bad cop, and in the process (less than half an hour into the film), *Insomnia* mutated into something way beyond your average Hollywood police drama. The film positively reeked of Patricia Highsmith and the psychology of complicity – a post-modern, post-*Memento Strangers on a Train*, it fulfilled the promise of every cop 'n' killer doppelganger/shadow Hollywood chase revenge movie ever made, and though it wasn't as tricky or as ingenious as *Memento*, it was an even more affecting work. With moral depths closer to Dostoyevsky than *Die Hard*, *Insomnia* took the basic components of an Al Pacino policer and rearranged them, subtly and with disturbing ambiguity, into poetry; in the process, it completed its own journey of transformation from a bracing psychodrama into full-blooded Shakespearean tragedy.

All of these attributes made Nolan ideally suited for his fourth movie, *Batman Begins*, a movie which hurled him into $180 million blockbuster terrain. Watching the film, it's easy to imagine how Nolan and his co-writer David S. Goyer started with a vision, determined to create a rich and imaginative reworking of the all-too-familiar *Batman* mythos that would be acceptable to Warner Bros. and justify the enormous budget with a big action summer smash hit to resurrect the franchise. Along the way, all Nolan and Goyer's best intentions were waylaid, shackled to a Hollywood franchise based on a beloved comic book character that (for most audiences) was always going to be closer to action hero cliché than mythological Jungian archetype.

Using what we can only suppose passes for indepth psychology in Hollywood, Nolan made a valiant but vain attempt to inject dramatic authenticity into the old familiar tale; but since he was contractually bound to cut to the chase and deliver the goods (Batman franchise product no. 5), the philosophy felt rushed, cursory, contrived. There isn't a single scene in the film that exists for its own sweet sake, or that is allowed to play at a leisurely pace and unfold at a natural rhythm, so developing some depth. It's all there to keep the motor turning and get the movie where it's going: Batman kicks ass. The characters and the story – the archetypal/psychological undertones that Nolan works so hard to get in there, finally even Nolan himself – are steamrollered by a big blind machine of a movie, moving relentlessly forward with no more purpose than any other Hollywood blockbuster – thrills, spills and big summertime profits. Audiences expecting another Hollywood action flick may have been pleasantly surprised to find a little more depth, realism, character development and archetypal resonance to *Batman Begins* than your average comic book movie. Those expecting to see the latest auteur work from Christopher Nolan, however, can only have left the theater wondering what the hell happened. The answer was simple: another auteur down.

It's easy enough to see how an artist like Nolan might have been drawn to a dark, complex myth like Batman. It's also easy to imagine how he might take the plunge – all the way into the Hollywood Trap – fired up by a sincere and passionate desire to bring something new to the franchise, and by the genuine though misguided belief that he could succeed where others have failed. On the film's release, Nolan remarked how, 'Over sixty-six years, there have been all kinds of things that were tried with Batman and didn't stick. Somehow they didn't feed into the elemental mythology of what Batman is. For me, it would be the mark of great success for this film if there are a couple of things that do stick.'[32]

Not exactly the loftiest of goals, admittedly, but with his sights set suitably low, Nolan attained his objective. *Batman Begins* comes closer to understanding the Batman myth – and to translating it into a Hollywood blockbuster for teen-heavy audiences to thrill to – than any other Batman movie to date. A couple of things even 'stick' (the

---

32 'Caped Fear,' by Tom Russo, *Premiere* magazine, June 2005.

bats, for one, and Batman's first time out, when he leaps from a rooftop and winds up clinging to a drain pipe). But after $180 million and two years' work, capturing on screen a couple of moments of pop mythology already immortalized by two classic graphic novels isn't really what I'd call a 'great success.' In the end, the Hollywood machine is more powerful than any creative individual, and its will is not for 'elemental mythology' but for a big, dumb action blockbuster. Hollywood's will all but annihilates Nolan's desire for a subtle, nuanced psychodrama and leaves audiences with a slightly smarter big dumb action blockbuster. How could a filmmaker as intelligent and sophisticated as Nolan ever believe he could transform a Hollywood franchise with a little vision and some good intentions? Probably, he never thought he could, and felt compromised right from the start. But if he winds up doing two more Batman flicks, he may as well kiss his gifts for subtly nuanced psychodramas goodbye, because Hollywood will squeeze him dry. Whatever's left of them will be used up raising big dumb blockbusters out of the quagmire of terminal mediocrity.

Hollywood isn't solely to blame for scuppering Nolan's vision and reducing it to its crudest elements, however, because that's exactly what most audience members *want* from a superhero flick. People don't go to a superhero movie for psychological realism or archetypal drama; they go to see an escapist action fantasy of self-empowerment, to see good conquer evil in as stylish and rousing a manner as Hollywood's shallow magic can conjure. Mythic underlayers are all very well, so long as they embellish the action and give it an extra kick; when they threaten to impede it, however – or prove too disturbing and thought-provoking to allow for the woozy bliss-out of escapist fantasy – then those underlayers are quickly glossed over. In *Batman Begins*, the supposed depth and realism is all on the surface, providing an artsy sheen to the mindless action and making it a lot fresher and more vital than the last couple of *Batman* duds. Nolan succeeds in that, but big deal. In the process, he undermines his talent, and turns into a former artist reduced to comic book mythologizing. If that was what Nolan was aiming for, he hit the bullseye. But he never for a moment transcends the pulp roots of the material (as Frank Miller did with *Dark Knight* and *Year One*); he just squanders $180 million transplanting them from one medium to another.

There is a common assumption that comic books adhere to a lower standard – aesthetically and dramatically – than other art forms, an assumption that Hollywood is temperamentally disposed to go along with (having congenitally lower standards of its own). Judging by the glowing reviews of Nolan's film, any treatment of a superhero story that isn't basically sub-literate is greeted as if it were Shakespeare, and any summer blockbuster that is halfway coherent, that is possessed of a rudimentary amount of integrity and fidelity to its story and characters, and that doesn't actively insult audiences' intelligence, is seen as a virtual revelation. *Batman Begins* is good 'sophisticated' action-fantasy fare for teenagers, and as a dumb Batman flick smartened up by an auteur sensibility, it delivers the goods. But coming from an erstwhile artist of psychological subtlety and depth – and one of the leading talents in American movies supposedly on his way to maturity – it's a real bummer. Apparently Nolan couldn't resist getting his hands on that big Hollywood train set, even when the tracks were laid down and he knew exactly where they would take him. *Batman Begins* may not have insulted the audiences' intelligence, but it sure as hell dumbed Nolan down.

Sam Raimi Is Swallowed by the Mainstream; Michael Mann Gets Lost in the Slums

'The great thing about show biz: there's always something more important going on than real life.'
Julia Philips, *You'll Never Eat Lunch in This Town Again*

Along with Nolan, Sam Raimi is probably the most unequivocal example of an independent director being swallowed up by the mainstream and waylaid by his desire to play with ever bigger train sets. Like all good independent filmmakers, Raimi started out by funding his first feature, *The Evil Dead*, more or less solo. (As is customary, he made a horror movie, which offers the best cost-to-profit ratio. The film is still a cult classic today.) Raimi then experienced his first taste of studio interference with only his second feature, the much-manhandled *Crimewave* (co-written with the Coens); he then made a successful and superior sequel with *The Evil Dead 2* (heavier on comedy than horror this time), and went halfway Hollywood with the trashy, brain-dead *Darkman*. He made a third, largely gratuitous *Evil Dead* movie, *Armies of Darkness*, then brought his visceral comic gifts to full expression with the exuberant quasi-spaghetti Western, *The Quick and the Dead*, with Sharon Stone.

The small-town tragedy *A Simple Plan* was Raimi's best film to date and his first sincere work; restrained but intense, the film suggested Raimi's gifts would develop into a mature sensibility. He followed with *The Gift*, however, Hollywood hokum written by his *Simple Plan* star,

Billy Bob Thorton, which reduced Raimi to Hollywood hack status. Then, his fate changed forever. Somehow, Raimi landed the job of directing *Spiderman*, a project James Cameron had once been involved in and one of the most expensive and greatly anticipated Hollywood blockbusters of recent years. Against the odds, Raimi brought his baroque, visceral talents to joyous expression; he was the perfect director to bring the beloved comic book hero to the screen and do justice to his pop-mythic appeal, thereby pleasing both younger viewers and adults who'd grown up with the comic. *Spiderman* was probably the best movie in the comic book subgenre to date.[33]

Spiderman was as huge a summer hit as was predicted, and Raimi was already signed to do two more sequels (along with the stars, Tobey McGuire and Kirsten Dunst; the third is due out in 2007). *Spiderman 2* was almost unanimously greeted by critics as superior to the first film and as one of the outstanding works of its kind; it was even hailed as one of the best films of the year. The film I saw, however, evidenced the total disintegration of whatever talent and integrity Raimi once had as a borderline artist–entertainer. Witless, poorly staged, woefully plotted, the film inflicted audiences with excruciating dialogue, sloppily directed scenes and lackluster performances, making it one of the most disappointing sequels in a Hollywood history rife with disappointing sequels. Yet critics praised the film, and audiences seemed to respond to it, so I can only cite it as evidence of the dumbing down of both movies *and* audiences – a process which critics seem happy to accelerate.[34]

It's easy enough to imagine the process of rationalization by which an ambitious and inexperienced filmmaker persuades himself that temporary compromise and refuge in mainstream studio movie production will be the means to greater freedom and creativity to come. It's even easy to see how established directors who had yet to make it to the 'A-list' (such as Raimi and Linklater), or to enjoy the special rewards and challenges of mega-budget moviemaking, would also be tempted, in the end, to bite the bullet and jump aboard the Hollywood band wagon. What's a little more

33 Bryan Singer – another independent film auteur turned franchise man – was doing similarly stand-up work with *X-Men* and *X2*.

34 Of course, some critics praised *Pearl Harbor*, but this was presumably more a result of the Mafia-style tactics of studio publicity departments than of anyone actually liking the film. Studios routinely resort to bribery, and even subtle threats, to ensure that at least some of the mainstream publications praise their movie. Hollywood's handling of critics, whom it seeks to put on its payroll or silence completely, is maternal in the darkest sense: 'If you have nothing nice to say, don't say anything at all!' Unfortunately this topic – rich in sociological relevance – is beyond the scope of the present work.

difficult to understand is why filmmakers who have already attained the highest levels of success and freedom possible within the system (without being Lucas or Spielberg) would be drawn to make increasingly shallow extravaganzas at the cost of developing their talents and creativity. Martin Scorsese has done his share of big budget movies, but his strength as a filmmaker is so clearly on the street level, when working with more intimate, psychological material (such as *Bringing Out the Dead*), that it's a mystery why he persists in investing years of his time and energy in basically flimsy (however 'personal') projects like *Gangs of New York* and *The Aviator*. (If anyone could benefit from doing a Dogme, it's Scorsese.)[35]

Oliver Stone's best film may still be his first, the gritty, gonzo *Salvador*; his smallest film, *Talk Radio*, is also one of his most intense and effective. And although *JFK* and *Natural Born Killers* were rare cases of a director's vision being equal to the scale of his production, his more recent, bloated, self-important, basically empty melodramas, *Any Given Sunday* and *Alexander* (with a Kubrick-like seven-year hiatus between them), served to emphasize Stone's worst traits as a director. Spielberg, whom we have already put under the microscope, is a man who seems incapable of committing to make a movie unless he can turn it into an event, be it a social, historical, or merely a technical 'SFX' event. But what are we to make of Michael Mann, who started out with a big vision hidden inside simple genre fare, then evolved into a filmmaker of such consummate skill and grace – with the romantic *The Last of the Mohicans* and the epic crime saga *Heat* – that he transformed genre into art?

When Mann made *The Insider* – in 1999, one of the few films of the decade to invite the term masterpiece – he looked set to become one of the two or three most exciting filmmakers in Hollywood. Then he made *Ali,* with an absurdly miscast Will Smith (could Will Smith ever *not* be miscast?), a film that ended up (exactly as we knew it would) as a dull and worthy biopic with nothing but Jon Voight's toupee to relieve the tedium. *Ali* saw Mann's talents beginning to unravel from over-ambition – the most common downfall of the potentially great director. Perhaps aware of this, he took refuge in the unremarkable genre flick *Collateral* (with a non-smiling Tom Cruise), a seemingly willed regression and a return to the generic terrain in which Mann

---

35 Who knows, maybe he will? In a recent interview for *The Aviator*, Scorsese claimed: 'I'm getting to a certain age where I don't see myself doing any more big films within the context of the Hollywood system. I think I will be doing smaller films in future because I can take more risks.' 'Scorsese: this is my last big movie,' by John Hiscock, *Daily Telegraph*, December 10th 2004. We can only hope.

had first developed his gifts as a filmmaker, but which (we had hoped) he had since moved beyond. The artist had gotten lost in the slums. They were slums that Hollywood had spent a fortune developing for just this very purpose: creative ghettos for lazy auteurs turned glorified hacks to hide in. The best laid plans of mice and Mann.

Fight Club, Three Kings, and the Alpha & Omega of Art

'Reality is something none of us can stand, at any time.'

Alfred Hitchcock

That same ghetto claimed David Fincher (let us hope temporarily) when he chose to follow his anarchic opus magnus *Fight Club* with the wholly routine *Panic Room*, a superlative piece of suspense filmmaking as devoid of depth or creative vision as *Fight Club* was filled with it. *Panic Room* existed solely as an opportunity for Fincher to unleash his virtuoso camera and take the 'art' of directorial ostentation to new levels of emptiness. To go from *Fight Club* to *Panic Room* was like abandoning acts of corporate terrorism to work in a bank; at least, it would have appeared as drastic a retreat, were it not clear from Fincher's choice of material that – as one of the new breed of directors, the anti-auteur school for whom content is in service of style – Fincher had only played the role of anarcho-terrorist required of him by *Fight Club*. As a filmmaker, Fincher was excited by ideas in an abstract and professional capacity rather than a personal one. *Fight Club* may have seemed like a profoundly personal movie, and conveyed a unique, idiosyncratic, wholly subversive vision; but the vision did not belong to Fincher so much as to Chuck Palahniuk, the author of the book on which it was based.

Admittedly, the *Fight Club* film was in many ways more intense, provocative, subversive, and entertaining than the book had been, and both Fincher and the scriptwriters (Jim Uhls and Kevin Andrew Walker, as well as Brad Pitt, Edward Norton and Helena Bonham-Carter in the lead roles) did a more than admirable job bringing it to the screen. But, judging by these people's previous and subsequent work, it was the ideas in the novel that inspired them and brought a level of passion and commitment lacking in their other work. True, they may have had a basic affinity with these ideas, but that didn't mean they had any *personal* tendencies towards acts of subversion. Like all great movies, *Fight Club* was the result of specific sensibilities and talents, including those of producer Art Linson and the studio personnel who supported the project, at least at first, for reasons we may never know (most especially Bill Mechanic, who put his job on the line to see the film made). All these factors came together at precisely the right time and, under ideal or close to ideal circumstances, worked together to deliver what was essentially Palahniuk's vision whole to the world, in a new medium.

Fight Club was a love it or hate it enterprise. It went straight to the heart of the schizophrenic nature of society, not only exposing it but positively wallowing in it. It took delight in trashing consumer culture and Western values and spitting in the face of the collective zeitgeist. It was only natural that it invoked the most intense reactions of both admiration and loathing in audiences.[36] *Fight Club* was not a movie that ingratiated itself easily. Probably the most virtuoso and passionate nihilist work ever made, it went beyond nihilism, beyond a mere denunciation of values, into an orgiastic celebration of their absence. Though it was smug and self-satisfied in its contempt for society, and even for humanity itself, it never stooped to moralizing about it. It was a reactionary work (in that it posited only negative responses to a negative situation), even at a pinch a 'fascist' one (it appeared to advocate blind force as a solution). But those were superficial (political) readings of a film that was at heart purely anarchic, hence beyond political readings. *Fight Club* advocated chaos as the only response to an irredeemable (dis)order, and entropy as the inevitable answer to an evolutionary plan that had all-too-plainly come off the rails.

Fight Club was deep, but it brought its depths to the surface and put them out in the open; at times it seemed simple-minded, facile, even asinine. As a sociological study of a culture on the brink of collapse, it hardly offered much by way of revelatory insights. It was far too extremist to qualify as a serious inquiry into society's ills. It was a fantasy work, and as such, closer to a nihilist's *It's a Wonderful Life* than to *The Battle of Algiers*. As much as *The Matrix* though in a totally different manner, *Fight Club* took audiences through the looking glass and stripped them of the luxury of objectivity or distance, of discerning between right and wrong or, for that matter, real and unreal. It provided audiences with the schizophrenic experience from the inside out, adeptly – with low cunning and artistry – turning the act of moviegoing into a simulation of schizophrenia.[37]

---

36 As a general rule, viewers under twenty-five responded freely and easily to the movie's 'destroy all values' nihilistic message. Older generations, on the other hand, could only react with dismay, and even disgust, to a film that pissed all over their chosen way of life.
37 This was acknowledged, finally – after many hints of what was to come – when the movie stopped and the narrator informed us, 'It's called a changeover. The movie goes on, and nobody in the audience has any idea.'

The ideas behind *Fight Club* were so fresh, vital, and unique – so alive – that it was as if the *ideas* themselves created and directed the means of their expression, as if the ideas had made the movie, as a vehicle to travel into the public psyche. Idea is king in any art form, and even, at times, in the world of business too. An individual artist inspired by an idea – an idea which, out of laziness or conceit, he considers his own – is inspired above all to communicate the essence of that idea, and to this end sets out to create a vehicle for it. That essence – if the artist is successful – is what audiences leave with. Not only the movie (book, painting, etc) but the artist himself, then, is the means by which ideas – the alpha and omega of art, there in the beginning and there in the end – cross over into the world of form. *Fight Club* embodied this, just as *The Matrix* embodied it; they were works that transcended the means of production and attained unprecedented artistic ends.

Something similar happened when David O. Russell went Hollywood and made a studio action/war movie for Warner Bros. called *Three Kings*, starring George Clooney. Against incredible odds, Russell succeeded in making a subversive, eccentric, thoroughly individual movie, probably the most politically subversive mainstream movie since *Natural Born Killers*, as only his third movie.[38] *Three Kings* didn't flinch from dragging audiences through the mud (or milk) of recent history and rubbing their all-too-clean noses in some nasty home truths. Like all action movies it was a brutal, ruthless movie, only this time with a purpose. By the time he made the movie, Russell had already picked up more tricks with three movies than most filmmakers learn in a lifetime, and he was canny (and goofy) enough to know that audiences don't come to the movies to be politically corrected, they come to be entertained. Hollywood had been exploiting and propagating the national war engine for so long that, by 1999, audiences were starting to distinguish between noisy entertainment and lousy propaganda; *Three Kings* catered to that new awareness.[39]

38 In 1994, David O. Russell made the dark, user-unfriendly incest story (it was difficult to say whether the film was a comedy or not), *Spanking the Monkey* with Jeremy Davies. He followed with the unruly and exasperatingly overwrought kitsch family farce, *Flirting with Disaster*, with Ben Stiller and Patricia Arquette. Russell's latest film was the bizarre existential comedy, *I Heart Huckabees*. He also made a documentary on George Bush Jr.'s war in Iraq.

39 Tarantino introduced the possibility of a post-modernist, smart-ass slant to action movies – most especially with the Scott-directed *True Romance* (Scott being the man responsible for that dourest of military-industrial movie products, *Top Gun*) – but it was not until someone at Warner Bros. took a chance on David O. Russell's script for *Three Kings* (1999) that the rough beast (the thinking man's actioner) was born.

Peter Biskind may not have been exaggerating when he described *Three Kings* as 'the most important film of the last decade, because it showed that an indie director could ram a major film with leftist politics and a daring aesthetic through a studio.'[40] Certainly *Three Kings* was successful, historically so, in reworking the action movie, transforming it in one fell swoop into an artistic, almost surrealist, enterprise; perhaps even more remarkably (and subtly), it reintroduced the possibility of counter-propaganda into the arts. *Three Kings*, a subversive, thinking man's action movie, was clearly an animal whose time had come, a living, breathing manifestation of the movie zeitgeist.[41] And that same year audiences were pummeled and perplexed not just by *Three Kings* but by *The Matrix* and *Fight Club* too.[42] For an all-too-brief moment, Hollywood appeared on the verge of being taken over by visionaries – by *ideas*.

Idea-wise, *Fight Club* rammed an even more daring aesthetic – and an infinitely more radical 'politic,' not leftist but anarchist and even terrorist – through the studio system than *Three Kings* did. Unlike *Kings,* however, it was not primarily the vision of a single individual (Russell wrote the script as well as directing *Three Kings*); yet in a way, the film was all the more remarkable for having been the result of a group enterprise. The cast and crew of a movie is made up of individuals, too, and every once in a while a collective vision thing occurs. Although it is considerably rarer, there seems no reason why the process of zeitgeist – ideas finding a form through works – can't operate equally through a group of people as through a single visionary. Though considerably less an 'auteur' work than *Three Kings*, *Fight Club* was a much greater movie, not because of any single factor but because the ideas behind it were strong enough to cross over, from one medium to another (from novel to film).

40 *Down and Dirty Pictures*, pg. 477.

41 Russell suceeded in giving audiences what they wanted, while slipping through the ideas that he needed to get across. Doing so cost him dearly, however, and by his own admission he has no intention of ever trying it again. Although he pulled the film off successfully (and it may be his best work to date) he paid the price of grape in the wine press: '*Three Kings* was my bottom,' he says. 'It was so stressful and so unpleasant that I said, "I will never, ever do that big a movie again… I don't want to make that bargain anymore."' *Down and Dirty Pictures* pg. 419.

42 To give credit were due, it should be mentioned at this point that neither *Three Kings* nor *The Matrix* were projects that Warner Bros. was naturally disposed to making. It is not only filmmakers who have to fight the studios, but the executives who sufficiently believe in them and their ideas. In this case, it was primarily thanks to Lorenzo di Bonaventura that the two films were eventually greenlighted.

These ideas just naturally – organically – found the means (the people, money, locations, etc.) to do so, and in the process, brought the best out of them all.

From such a perspective (admittedly a somewhat esoteric one), Hollywood is no more the enemy of art – of ideas finding original expression – than is the artist. Both are means to an end, an end which is going to be attained one way or another, with or without our co-operation. Ideas will out. The difference between Hollywood and artists is more a difference of degree than any intrinsic distinction of nature. Artists 'have' ideas; ideas come through them, and so they are said to be 'full of good ideas.' Hollywood does not 'have' ideas (except bad ones), ideas do not pass easily through it, so it appears empty of them. Yet Hollywood exists as a barrier and an obstacle for artists who wish to express 'their' ideas; as such and despite itself, it serves to make those ideas (and the artists themselves) stronger, by the very act of opposing and resisting them. Because the more an idea is repressed, the more it will grow in urgency and intensity in order to get through.[43]

This process continued even after the film was released, since US critics almost unanimously reviled the film and denounced it for its irresponsibility, either unwilling or unable (or both) to contemplate the deeper, more provocative questions raised by the film. Even as sophisticated a filmmaker as Paul Thomas Anderson rejected the film on grounds of its irresponsibility. Anita Busch, at the *Hollywood Reporter*, noted how:

> 'The ultragraphic violence of Fox 2000's *Fight Club* has drawn more gut anger from the industry than I've ever heard. And for good reason. The film will become Washington's poster child for what's wrong with Hollywood. And Washington, for once, will be right... The film is exactly the kind of product that lawmakers should target for being socially irresponsible in a nation that has deteriorated to the point of Columbine.'[44]

---

43 This thesis, which I suppose relates to Rupert Sheldrake's 'morphogenetic fields' and Jung's 'collective unconscious', is supported by the fact, well documented, that powerful new ideas such as inventions tend to surface simultaneously in various parts of the globe, and through different individuals who are not in communication. The idea exists then, somewhere in the 'ether', independent of the channels (humans) through which it surfaces.

44 Waxman, pg. 295-6. P.T. Anderson on *Fight Club*, pg. 297.

As ever, the policy was to kill the messenger and conveniently ignore the message. *Fight Club* diagnosed society's condition; it didn't create it. And what it diagnosed was a society that was beyond the pale. If *Fight Club* – unequivocally the best, most subversively brilliant big studio movie, since *Taxi Driver* – embodied everything that was wrong with Hollywood, then clearly Hollywood was beyond the pale too, because in that case, there was nothing right with Hollywood. *Fight Club* stated, as plainly as possible while remaining a thrilling piece of surrealist satire entertainment, that the only thing to be done to 'improve' consumer-crazed society was to dynamite it. Hollywood – foremost offender in said culture – was never going to embrace such a message, or advocate a film that had brought it to their tender and sensitive ears. Apparently, this included most critics too.

But just as *Fight Club* was almost certainly a far better movie as a result of the amount of corporate/studio incomprehension (admittedly never resulting in interference) which it had to overcome, it was also somehow 'proven' by the critical/social disapproval that greeted it on its release. Like any 'revolutionary' idea, it had to face and overcome such resistance in order to find its true form, and later, its proper audience. And of course, the exact same structure (in this case, 20th Century Fox) that had opposed the film – the artists behind it and their right to do it as they saw fit – had also greenlighted the project in the first place.[45] No doubt this was the fact that rankled worst of all. Ditto with a society that had created the necessary conditions to give rise to such a film, and that had born a generation that would embrace its message and be grateful for it. Such is the way of Hollywood, as a microcosm for the society that spawned it, a conglomerate divided, destined to fall. *Fight Club* was the final proof, on the eve of the millennium, that the system – like Babylon, like Tyler Durden himself – was self-destroying. All that remained was to stand back and watch the towers fall.

---

45 As Biskind notes in *Down and Dirty Pictures*, however, Bill Mechanic, 'was swept away by Rupert Murdoch's broom in a "regime change"'. (pg 447) It was an ironic end to the story, because Mechanic had himself threatened to quit his job if Fox didn't back *Fight Club*; Fox capitulated and made the film, only to fire Mechanic soon after its release, when it was far from a hit. Predictably Rupert Murdoch loathed *Fight Club*. It was a huge success on its DVD release however, and became a cult favorite.

The End of Hollywood and the Lobotomization of an Art Form

'The truth is that there is no terror untempered by some great moral idea. To me style is just the outside of content, and content the inside of style, like the outside and the inside of the human body. Both go together, they can't be separated.'

Godard, 'The Future of Cinema,' from *Digital Babylon*

When Francis Coppola finally agreed to make *The Godfather Part Two*, it was (as with the first film only more so) only with great reluctance. In fact, no sequel would ever have come about at all had not Paramount (specifically Charles Bluhdorn of Gulf & Western, who owned Paramount) so avidly desired it. Bluhdorn was so intent on making the movie – on having Coppola make it for him – that he agreed to Coppola's most outlandish conditions: an unprecedented fee as the film's writer-director and, most amazingly of all, a complete boycott on studio interference, to the extent that – for perhaps the first time since Welles had made *Citizen Kane* – no one at Paramount was allowed to see the film's rushes during the shoot (according to Coppola, they weren't even allowed to look at the script).[46] Like Welles before him, Coppola had total freedom to realize his vision, and this he proceeded to do, making what is sometimes considered the greatest Hollywood movie of all time.

And yet – and here is the most significant, little-noted fact to the legend – Coppola would never have decided to make the movie at all if Paramount hadn't talked him into it. Without the studio's eagerness for a big, money-making, high-prestige sequel, no *Godfather Part Two* would exist today. The same can be said of the first film, of course. It can also be said of Sam Peckinpah's enduring masterpiece, *The Wild Bunch*, a movie Peckinpah suggested to Warner Bros. only when he couldn't get anything else funded, knowing it would meet their demand for a simple-minded action film. Who knows how many of the greatest movies ever made came about only when artists were forced to compromise their vision to satisfy a studio? There are no figures, so far as I know, but I'd wager it is quite a few. Neither Peckinpah nor Coppola would have made the best films of their career if they had had complete freedom to do as they pleased. They might have made films that would have been equally great, perhaps – we will never know – but I am inclined to doubt it.

---

46 Another one of Coppola's conditions was that Robert Evans, by then involved in his own production with *Chinatown*, had nothing at all to do with Coppola's movie.

Hollywood is to filmmakers what a wine press is to grapes: it gets the best out of them, but crushes them in the process. Creativity co-exists with adversity. The two forces are complementary, to the point that they increase and flourish in direct proportion to one another – provided of course that adversity is never strong enough to quash creativity altogether (or vice versa). In a perfect world, art simply would not be. What would artists have to push against or testify to? What would there be to communicate, when relieved of the internal pressure of rage, sorrow, hatred, despair, confusion, and frustration that living in an oppressive, soul-destroying world-system creates? In a state of complete and unchallenged joy, freedom, peace and stability, who but a madman would be moved to create anything at all? It is the very imperfection of the world that drives artists to perfect their gifts and communicate their frustration with such a world.[47]

Communication is undoubtedly the key. This is why the elevation of style at the expense of content so prevalent today is a gross disservice to movies; it is also a fundamental misperception of the nature of art to think that the two could ever be separated. If content is what is conveyed by a given work of art – the ideas that are contained therein, passed on like a virus, traveling from one host to another – then style is the means by which it is communicated. Logically, from such a view, style must follow content, and not vice versa. Yet, in a visual medium, things are not so simple. An image can be the essence of a (non-intellectualized) idea, and as such may itself be a kind of style – free of content without being empty of it. In other words, in movies, style and content are really the same thing. A sunset is pure style; the medium, as Marshall McCluhen put it, is the message. So it is really less a question of which takes precedence than of whether the two are fully fused and in service to each other. Style is empty; content is what fills it.[48]

---

47 This may inevitably bring to mind Orson Welles again, and the speech he wrote for his character Harry Lime in *The Third Man*. Lime justifies his evil by commenting that the greatest artistic renaissance occurred in Europe during a time of war, disease, and bloodshed. He compares this fact to Switzerland and its centuries of peace and prosperity, drolly remarking that the only 'art' to have arisen was 'the cuckoo clock.' (Actually, as Welles later pointed out, the cuckoo clock isn't even a Swiss invention.)

48 Coppola has always been especially insightful on this subject. 'I worry about content… I worry about story… The talent for writing a good tune is especially admirable when we think how long composers have been arranging and rearranging those few notes into something that sticks as a melody. A story must be like that–a specific talent to come up with the sequence of events, the unfolding of information that captures us and has us eagerly awaiting the outcome, as though we were children.' Lillian Ross, 'Some figures on a Fantasy: Francis Coppola,' *The New Yorker*, 8th November 1982.

What this comes down to, in practical terms, is that the script – the writer – must come first and be given primary place in the filmmaking process (and within the Hollywood hierarchy) for any profound or lasting change in the quality of movies to come about. This is probably all academic, however, it being far too late to propose such a restructuring. Hollywood is as Hollywood does. Digital video, combined with pending global ecological collapse (so popular a theme in Hollywood blockbusters of late), seem set to do away with studios, moguls, box office figures, trade papers, Hollywood, and maybe even California too, within the next decade or so. But being academic doesn't make it any less pertinent. We have started the thesis, so let us finish it.

A lot has changed since Bluhdorn corralled Coppola into making *The Godfather Part Two*, since Scorsese gave Columbia *Taxi Driver*, and since Steven Spielberg fulfilled the studios' dreams with *Jaws*. There is nothing inherently wrong with the 'package' method of making movies, provided it starts with a solid idea, and provided the people who are making the package respect it and seek out the very best creative people to bring it to full form.[49] But this no longer happens in Hollywood, or at least, when it does it is about as rare as lightning striking twice in the same place. The package now revolves around stars and concept, in a word, marketing. If a movie can be sold, then who cares if it is any good?[50]

Who can say which film was worse – to use two fairly recent examples – *Hollow Man* or *What Lies Beneath? Hollow Man* was a shamelessly trashy, purely exploitative work, but for this very reason it was dimly amusing at times. (It at least offered up the pleasure of Kevin Bacon's hammily demented Sebastian.) *What Lies Beneath* offered no such solace, leaving almost nothing to be said about this dreary, mechanical thriller save that it was a criminal misuse of its stars and a total waste of the audience's time. What these movies did reveal, however, was that Hollywood was losing the most basic rudiments

49 Robert Evans negotiated the rights to Ira Levin's *Rosemary's Baby* with producer William Castle (who intended to direct the film), and put together a team consisting of director Roman Polanski and actors Mia Farrow, John Cassavetes and Ruth Gordon. He did something similar with *Chinatown*. At his best, as Evans is at pains to point out in his book, the producer is the man who assembles the team that creates the classic.

50 'The key to the system is marketing. In 1975, the average cost of marketing for a movie distributed by a major studio was two million dollars. In 2003, it was thirty-nine million dollars.' 'Gross Points,' by Louis Menand, the *New Yorker*, February 7th, 2005.

of moviemaking: the capacity to provide slick, empty entertainment. Hollywood ought to have *some* reason to exist besides sheer, cynical, commercial opportunism; but if it once did, then it has gotten lost in the crush. How hard can it be for talented workers like Paul Verhoven or Robert Zemeckis to provide audiences with solid suspense products? Yet these movies failed at every level, not just as thrillers but as halfway amusing send-ups (such as *Basic Instinct*). Devoid of even the barest trace of artistry or inspiration, they were lifeless, spiritless, hopeless; in a word, corpses. Yet the slick production values and star names were enough, apparently, for audiences not to feel conned. They may have come out dissatisfied and hungry for a movie, but they weren't demanding their money back.[51]

At the base of the problem of why movies are so bad is one single factor: the almost total disregard for good writing in Hollywood. Most Hollywood movies fail because, despite the talent and money involved, the quality of the script is so appallingly low that there is nothing (short of genius) that can raise them above the level of soulless dross. A mediocre director with average performers can still make a watchable movie if the script is good enough. A lousy script, like that of *Hollow Man* or *What Lies Beneath*, will never make more than a mediocre movie, no matter how gifted the 'artists' involved may be. *What Lies Beneath* and *Hollow Man* (along with two dozen other movies released this year alone) offer resounding, depressing and uncontestable proof of this law. Every year, every month, Hollywood provides ever more evidence for the prosecution. The trouble is that these moronic scripts are just the kind of scripts that Hollywood studio executives love: empty, formulaic and entirely devoid of innovative or visionary qualities. Essentially they are an amalgam of previous movies: 'pure' generic fare, clotheshorses to hang the dirty, greasy rags of special effects and star vanities on to. It's not that good writing isn't recognized or valued in Hollywood; it's that it is in the process of being eliminated altogether. It is seen as an unnecessary 'inconvenience', an obstacle on the greased slide to movie hell. The kind of 'pure filmmaking' that studios have long dreamed, wetly, of achieving is now within reach. It may be the end of real entertainment for moviegoers, but for these specific few 'dreamers' who run the show, it's nothing less than a *coup d'art* – the lobotomization of an art form.

---

51 With *The Avengers*, this terrifying precedent may have been set.

Phone Booth: How the Script Saves the Day and a Director Reinvents Himself

'I feel that only the literary mind can help the movies out of that cul-de-sac into which they have been driven by mere technicians and artificers... In my opinion the writer should have the first and last word in filmmaking, the only better alternative being the writer-director, but with the stress on the first word.'

Orson Welles

On the other hand, a film like *Phone Booth* – written by independent cult horror guru Larry Cohen and directed by one of the premier Hollywood hacks, Joel Schumacher – is proof that, if the script is strong enough – the ideas behind it fresh and topical enough – a movie will find its proper form. There are ample cases of technically adequate, less-than-visionary film directors rising to the occasion provided by a solid script who then sink to the lower depths of tastelessness when stuck with a stinker. Adrian Lyne, for example, gave the world *Flashdance, 9½ Weeks*, and *Indecent Proposal* – some of the worst movies ever to ooze their way into the public consciousness. Yet Lyne also directed the creepy, paranoid classic *Jacob's Ladder*, from a script by Bruce Joel Rubin, and the lyrical, haunting *Lolita* – written by Stephen Schiff – arguably an improvement over Kubrick's cool and detached treatment of 1962. In both of these cases the script carried the day, bringing Lyne's talents (talents we might otherwise have assumed not to exist at all) to the fore.

There are many cases of filmmakers whose passion and focus – and therefore talent – comes and goes according to the script they're working with and just how much it inspires them. It's understandable that Lyne, when working with dross like *Flashdance* or *Indecent Proposal*, would do a sloppy, lackluster job of it. When blessed with a *Jacob's Ladder,* on the other hand, he knuckles down and puts all he's got into it so as to do justice to the material. Perhaps more common is when a basically schlocky but capable director – Taylor Hackford, for example – gets a decent script and, without ever really doing justice to it, makes a superior piece of entertainment by not screwing it up too badly. *Devil's Advocate* is easily Hackford's best film, but it is still visibly the work of the man who made *Against All Odds*.[52]

With such modern classics as *The Lost Boys, Flatliners, Falling Down, Batman Forever* and *Batman and Robin*, Joel Schumacher has often been seen as the living embodiment of a soulless Hollywood hack churning out soulless Hollywood trash. In the last few years, however – starting with the gritty bit of psycho-camp *8mm* in 1999 – he has embarked on a process of creative regeneration almost unique in the annals of hack filmmakers. In fact, as a director, Schumacher has reinvented himself as few filmmakers – not Scorsese, not Coppola, not Altman – ever do, making him a kind of reverse burn-out. Schumacher started out as a shop window dresser whose specialty was ladies' lingerie, became a costume designer for Woody Allen (*Sleeper* and *Interiors*), and slowly evolved into a Hollywood director of vague promise (*The Incredible Shrinking Woman* in 1981, *St. Elmo's Fire* in 1986) before sinking to the depths with *The Lost Boys* and *Flatliners*. At this point, and also with subsequent works *Falling Down* and two *Batman* stinkers, Schumacher appeared to settle into the groove as one more empty studio hack with no visible talent. Then, as if by sheer will power (once he'd sunk about as low as he could go with *Batman and Robin*), he gradually mutated into a gifted filmmaker and – dare we say it? – an artist. Did anyone notice this amazing transformation? Apparently not; apparently, once a shop window dresser, always a shop window dresser. Schumacher can reinvent himself all he wants, few critics seemed willing to give him credit.

After *8mm*, Schumacher made *Tigerland* (2000), a Vietnam movie that never set foot in Vietnam and a powerful, inspired piece of filmmaking, with Colin Farrell's affecting performance as the rebel-soldier Bozz marking the arrival of a major new talent. Schumacher's handheld camera and his assured work with actors – his respect for the material and his obvious confidence as a director – gave the film a bracing, documentary-style authenticity. Schumacher's work here exhibited the

---

52 The same might be said for Tony Scott – the man who made *Top Gun* – who, when given a Tarantino script to sink his teeth into (*True Romance*), proved to be an exhilarating filmmaker. His choice of material is generally pedestrian, however, and though Scott gives above-average genre entertainment with action flicks like *Enemy of the People, Spy Games* and *Man on Fire*, he is not likely to ever be mistaken for an artist. Scott's older brother, Ridley, though overall the more gifted of the two, has proved equally dependent on his material (and an even less reliable a judge of it), alternating the formulaic mediocrity of *Someone to Watch Over Me, Black Rain, GI Jane* and *Hannibal*, with borderline works of art such as *Alien* and, more recently, the superb *Matchstick Men*. His in-between stuff, *Thelma and Louise, Gladiator, Black Hawk Down*, though dubious, is at least slickly made and entertaining.

kind of 'searing urgency' that directors like Ridley Scott and Spielberg were busy winning awards for, and as a complete work, *Tigerland* wiped the floor with *Saving Private Ryan*. Yet despite a largely favorable critical response, the film never found an audience.

Then came *Phone Booth*, the first Hollywood classic of the digital age. Shot in ten days and in 'real time' (its eighty minute length covers eighty minutes of action), *Phone Booth* bordered on Dogme in its simplicity and ruthlessness (as it happens, Schumacher is an admirer of Lars von Trier and the Dogme movement). With its admirably limited and exact goals, the film attained every one of them with unerring accuracy, precision and economy. *Phone Booth* was an almost perfect genre piece that transcended its self-imposed limits and entered smoothly and inconspicuously into the realm of art. Too inconspicuously, as it happened. A tiny masterpiece of suspense and psychological drama, impeccably directed, acted (that feral Farrell again), shot, edited and scripted, it was the purest piece of suspense entertainment Hollywood had produced in years; it was almost totally ignored by the critics.[53]

One reason the film never got the attention it merited was the timidity of the studio, who held back the film's release date when news of a real-life sniper killing at random in the US put the nation in a state of fear and paranoia – or so the media would have it. The studio was no doubt afraid that, having weirdly overlapped with reality, *Phone Booth* would seem in bad taste for making entertainment out of real-life 'tragedy'. Had the studio possessed the courage and cunning to back their movie – the wit to realize that so unlikely a 'coincidence' gave it extra credibility and topicality – and released it as planned, the film would have probably stirred up some controversy and received the attention it deserved. As it was, it pretty much passed audiences and critics by, a fact doubly regrettable considering what a lousy year it was for movies.

It's ironic, to say the least that, with auteur after auteur being dumbed down and swallowed up by franchise-happy Hollywood, a rare and revealing case such as Schumacher's has gone almost entirely unremarked upon. But what *Tigerland* and *Phone Booth* briefly showed was a filmmaker evolving out of franchise jobs and into accomplished, occasionally brilliant personal work. For a brief time,

---

53 What was especially impressive about the movie was that the 'villain' (the sniper played by Keifer Sutherland, though we only see him briefly at the end), was not merely sympathetic but also quite admirable, in his way. The movie didn't indulge in the kind of perverted admiration that made *Silence of the Lambs* such a crock, but it treated its villain with respect. It was smart and open-minded enough to let the audience judge for itself.

Schumacher became one of the most exemplary filmmakers working in Hollywood, because if the man behind *Batman and Robin* could successfully transform himself into an artist, there was hope for hack filmmakers everywhere.[54]

The *Matrix* Sequels: How a Franchise Crashes and Burns and Makes a Billion Dollars While It's At It

'There's an expression, 'Where your attention is, that will be lively.' That's a truthful and magical expression. You could think about that for a long time. It's like the focus and the desire form this bait, and the fish – which are the ideas – are the lovely things that start swimming up there. You can catch the fish, but it's understood not to be a sure thing each time you go looking for them.'

David Lynch

Above all, what made *Phone Booth* special, beyond Cohen's script or Schumacher's and Farrell's input, was the fact that it had something to communicate. This, plainly, can't be said of most Hollywood productions, which are palpably *not* idea-driven. In fact, they are not even plot, dialogue or character-driven. They are star and/or effects-driven, even when there are no 'special' effects to speak of. A romantic comedy is driven by the desire to make us cry and laugh, and the success of *Rocky, Rambo* and its ilk depends on getting the audience on its feet and cheering the hero; these are also 'effects', special to Hollywood, which can manipulate audiences like no other industry outside of advertising.

Hollywood movies are products that promise to provide a specific

---

54 More recently and less encouragingly, Schumacher's *Veronica Guerin* (2003, produced by Jerry Bruckheimer), was a so-so thriller based on the murder of the Irish journalist who took on the Dublin drug world in the 1990s, with Cate Blanchett miscast in the title role. Schumacher's work was slick but unimaginative, and the film was serviceable at best. Considerably worse was *The Phantom of the Opera* (2004), a showy, bloated spectacle with little to recommend it. Possibly his work with Colin Farrell was only a momentary blip of brilliance in an otherwise consistently mediocre career, or possibly, Schumacher is aspiring to two careers simultaneously: one as a Hollywood hired hand, the other (his real vocation?) as a rough-and-ready, guerilla-style filmmaker. If so, we can only hope his latest work – an adaptation of *The Crowded Room*, based on a multiple-personality serial killer – falls into the latter category.

service, though of course they don't come with a guarantee. George Lucas' *Star Wars* prequels, starting with *Phantom Menace*, are the recent apotheosis of the empty, lumbering movie event, over-burdened by production values and special effects, almost devoid of ideas to convey (and whatever paltry ideas they do contain, they are bereft of any style or grace to communicate). Audiences come away from these movies dazed by the inconceivably costly display of arrogance and stupidity, benumbed and bewildered by the awe-inspiring paucity of imagination. They have every right to be, because one thing there is never a shortage of is new ideas.

At a slightly more sophisticated level, the recent *Matrix* sequels were as guilty as George Lucas of betraying the faith and good will of their audience, palming them off with an empty simulation of former delights. *Matrix Reloaded* and *Matrix Revolutions* were films which more or less unanimously disappointed but which still rang up huge profits due to the fact that audiences felt compelled to see them even after they knew how bad they were going to be. The *Matrix* sequels not only displayed an almost wanton disregard for audiences and their right to a coherent, intelligent fantasy (like the first movie) but – far worse – seemed to disparage the very ideas which had made the original film special and which, audiences had understandably assumed, were the *raison d'être* of the sequels. As it happened, the movies had an altogether different *raison d'être*, one belonging to Joel Silver and Warner Bros. considerably more than to the Wachowskis. Moolah.[55]

The plain and probably inevitable fact of *The Matrix* fiasco was that, by the time of the sequels, four years after the original, Joel Silver and Warner Bros. had taken over the enterprise and left poor Keanu in the cold. Judging by certain scenes, particularly in *Reloaded* (the Merovingian and the Architect, for example), the Wachowskis had plenty of ideas still to work with. But for some reason they had delegated them to the back burner, focusing almost entirely on action, special effects and quasi-religious hyperbole. It's even possible that Warners edited the movies that way in order to deliver the necessary action and spectacle to justify the

---

55 'Marketing costs for the *Matrix* sequels exceeded a hundred million dollars. The reason that those movies had such enormous grosses, despite terrible reviews and negative word of mouth, is that each opened on eighteen thousand screens simultaneously worldwide. As [Tom] Shone says [in *Blockbuster: How Hollywood Learned to Stop Worrying and Love the Summer*], "By the time we've all seen that it sucked, it's a hit."… These are all ways of preselling the picture, before the reviews can unsell it.' 'Gross Points,' by Louis Menand, the *New Yorker*, February 7th, 2005.

expense and the hype, and that the Wachowskis' best material wound up on the cutting room floor. If so, we will never know.

With *Reloaded*, much of the movie was like watching an animated video game. The effects had taken over and no longer required any justification, so far as plot or character went. The movie was cotton candy: exploding cars and flying bullets with some *Dune*-like religious undertones and a few Braudrillardian nods to keep the fans happy and hoodwink them that this movie was as deep as the first. But somehow the message was hijacked. The artists who made the first movie had been infiltrated and replaced by the agents of the Hollywood matrix, by Joel Silver and the rest of the Time-Warner executives. If anything, *Revolutions* was even worse, a disaster of a film in which nothing made any sense.[56]

The Wachowskis appeared to be so out of whack with their own vision, their own ideas, that the sequels did away with plot almost completely; all that remained was the predictable race against time/war against machines bit, interspersed with weird interludes that made no sense within the greater 'structure', of which there was none, finally. Anyone who wrote down the plots of *Reloaded* and *Revolutions*, step by step, would quickly see that they didn't make any sense and/or were mostly superfluous. The whole Keymaker/Merovingian plot of *Reloaded* and the battle with the machines of *Revolutions* were just arbitrary excuses for action sequences, while the various trips to the Oracle didn't actually further the story, as such, but only served as catalysts for more action, contrived rationale for the characters to run around shooting each other and blowing things up. Those scenes which did have the kind of depth and drive of the first movie – the meetings with the Merovingian and the Architect in *Reloaded*, Neo's getting lost in limbo and his trip to Hell in *Revolutions* – weren't tied into each other enough to seem integral to the 'plot' and appeared almost redundant, lost fragments from different, and far more interesting, movies.

The drop-off of intelligence and originality in the sequels was so severe that no one could fail to observe it. People even began to wonder if the Wachowskis had actually written the first movie at all. Had they stolen the idea from somewhere or someone else? It seemed a distinct possibility. As an explanation for what happened to *The Matrix* franchise, however, it was too simplistic. Things are always more complex in Hollywood. More likely, as is so often the case, the

---

56 For example, the question which the Architect brought up in *Reloaded*, as to Neo being part of the matrix program, was totally forgotten by the time of *Revolutions* a mere six months later. Neo was the One and he saved Zion – and of course died doing so, in good Hollywood-martyr fashion.

Wachowskis took credit for ideas which were simply bigger than they were, ideas that they didn't have a clue – when it came to the crunch – how to develop it into two more movies. Or perhaps they were taken over by agents of the matrix? Anything is possible in Hollywood.[57]

The ideas in the first movie were wholly incompatible with the world of big money deals and commerce, but it was the same world the Wachowskis landed in after the movie's huge success. What did Hollywood know about unplugging? Hollywood was everything that the matrix stood for, everything that *The Matrix* had so artfully exposed as hollow and corrupt. By the time of the sequels, the franchise was backed up with *Matrix* ice pops, coffee mugs, TV sets, the whole relentless machinery of marketing behind it. It had become the very thing it had once been set against. No wonder the movies had lost their bite.[58]

The Wachowskis dangled challenging, mystifying questions in front of audiences, with the implicit promise that all the questions would be answered in the end. They weren't, and instead audiences' worst suspicions were confirmed, and the questions became meaningless, just obligatory mystification to embellish the empty spectacle and make us think there was something deep going on underneath. There might have been, if the Wachowskis had taken their own ideas seriously enough, and if they had taken the time to find satisfactory answers. Maybe Joel Silver and Time-Warner didn't let them? More likely, since Silver and co never understood the *Matrix* idea to begin with (being plugged in up to their bad toupees), they never realized that the sequels didn't make any sense. They may still not know; since the movies made a profit of over a billion dollars, it was easy for them to ignore the reviews and tell themselves that the fans were happy.[59]

---

57 Incidentally, for our sole excursion into gossip in the present work, we might mention in passing how Larry Wachowski showed up at the *Revolutions* premiere dressed as a woman, proudly parading his new, post-*Matrix* identity. Unplugged, or what? (See Waxman, pg. 215.)

58 'Blockbusters today aspire to be "tent-pole franchises" – centerpieces for multiple spin-off products, from lunchboxes to soundtracks, comic books, children's books, arcade games, and computer games. *Batman* earned three times as much from merchandise as it did from ticket sales; the makers of *Jurassic Park* sold a hundred licenses for a thousand dinosaur products. Blockbusters today are commercials: they're commercials for themselves. They also *include* commercials, in the form of product placement.' Menand, 'Gross Points', *The New Yorker* 7th February 2005.

59 Legend has it that a lot of Hollywood people felt the same way about the first movie, were surprised when it turned out to be a hit, and utterly baffled when kids and academics discovered the 'hidden' meanings. The sequels were bigger, more expensive and easily as difficult to understand as the first movie; ergo they must be better!

Audiences are encouraged not to care about 'sense' – or about content at all – and to be satisfied with style. Any doubts they were harboring would be drowned out by the cacophony and embarrassment of the $200 million folly, and all dissidents would be beaten into submission – not by critics but by 'fans' (those kids determined to repress their disappointment and bitterness by insisting that the movies rocked, whatever anyone said). Free your mind? Money speaks, the scum rises to the surface. The *Matrix* sequels conquered the whole Earth (especially Japan) and temporarily extinguished the possibility of independent thought in audiences everywhere. Ironic that they served the exact same agenda that the heroes of these movies were supposedly fighting to destroy. Hollywood doublethink at its best.

The Thoughts of God, Or: 'What We Have Here Is A Failure To Communicate'

'For the first time a person can improvise alone in camera in much the same way so-called free jazz came to be. A natural progression with an audience who doesn't care to see any true cinematic progression. Film as art is an idea whose time has come to pass.'

Harmony Korine, *Digital Babylon*[60]

With the *Matrix* sequels it wasn't just a question of a failure to communicate, it was that the Wachowskis didn't seem to care whether they communicated or not. They had disconnected from the source of their inspiration and had done a lousy job of faking it. The gaping vacuum of decent new ideas – or even an engaging or believable storyline – was covered up by mindless spectacles of violence and mayhem in the good, Hollywood tradition. (One thing Hollywood seems never to run short on is images of destruction.)

If, as I have attempted to argue, ideas struggling to break through into the world of form are the reason that art exists at all – and the reason movies were invented – what becomes of a medium when it disconnects from the source of its existence and denies its primary function? When it assumes an alternate, debased function wholly at odds with the first? The answer is, the same thing that happens to any

60 'There has to be a certain system for me. Even if it's chaos, there has to be a way to anticipate the chaos, to reorganize it, and then make sense of it. People always speak of "truth in cinema", but that's a fallacy. It's all subjective. The truth is, if I didn't have film, I'd be a lost soul.' Korine, *Digital Babylon*, pg. 59.

vessel when the current ceases to flow: like a limb drained of its life-blood, it shrivels up and dies; at which time, it has to be removed from the circuit. No one knows where ideas come from, but one thing is for sure: they don't come from Hollywood.

Since it may be argued that what the world, and the individuals who make it, needs more than anything right now is ideas – fresh inspiration to overcome the mess we've landed in – it is odd that movies should be so impoverished these days so far as answering this need goes. If Hollywood is not part of the solution, it is part of the problem. Movies have stolen our dreams, our power to imagine. The price of this is that Hollywood itself is slowly dying from a lack of new dreamers to feed off, and from its own incapacity to imagine. The nature of a factory is that nothing new comes out of it, only endless copies of what came before. This is why independent cinema – and Dogme and Korine's 'mistakist' art, and whatever else that is new and raw and unassimilated – is the only real answer. Hollywood was always for the masses. Now it is of the masses too. And the masses, blind and insensible, can only ever consume; they can never create.

Perhaps movies were meant as training tools to help us to imagine, visualize, to think and communicate in images? If so, the moment they abandoned this function and began to serve an opposite agenda – that of stealing our dreams and selling them, in recycled form, back to us – they effectively became obsolete, childish things to be put away, along with all the other broken toys. The next step would seem to be this: for the individuals who once made up movie audiences to make the leap – a leap of courage and imagination – and turn away from the magic mirror of the movie screen and abandon the forgetting chamber forever. It would mean renouncing the ways of the mass – the passive consumer-observer who lines up to be pleasured and entertained, like a babe on the teat of the universe. It would mean facing up to the anything but comforting illusion we have created and meeting the challenge (that of individual creators) of conjuring up our own illusions. Most of all, it means making our own myths, myths not to escape into but to live by.

Maybe this, finally, is behind the romantic glorification of the independent filmmaker, the maverick artist and the rebel genius: not that he gives us great works to enjoy but that he sets the only example worth following, inspiring us to live fuller, truer, richer lives? As indie producer Peter Broderick states, 'There is only one reason to be an independent filmmaker, and the reason is quite simple. It's because you have no choice. If it's not total compulsion, it doesn't make sense.'[61] The example given by the artist is this: to tap into our individual source of inspiration and become a thoroughfare for the thoughts of God. The balance is due to shift, and Hollywood, audiences, and the current crop of independent filmmakers all know it. The age of entertainment is over. There is no time left for us to kill, because time is killing us right back.

In the future, the ratio of doers to watchers – artists to audience members – will slowly (or perhaps rapidly) reverse. The many will create, and only the impoverished few will retain the dull luxury of passive observation, the luxury of movies. It is all in the nature of things. The less that new, vital ideas are allowed to come through, the more they pile up in the collective unconscious, unexpressed, repressed, angry and impatient to get through, to be *heard*. And consequently, the stronger and more urgent they become. Hollywood, like all systems of corporate control based on fear and greed, corruption and oppression, is the Dragon that proves the Hero. That's the greater myth wrapped around all the little ones. The uprising only comes when the tyranny of totalitarianism has become truly intolerable, for nothing inspires humans to move, to seek change, so much as unbearable conditions indefinitely sustained.

Creativity that isn't a means of survival is really just dilettantism. If artistic expression comes about as the necessary means to maintain sanity, chances are it is a sincere and profound expression. That's the lesson of Dogville, at least: complacency is the only real evil in this world. And it's the lesson of Hollywood too. In the end, it's the lesson of everywhere. We all need to confess our individual sins and make our vows, to write our personal histories in lighting and leave an imperfect image of our perfected selves in the dust, to mark the spot where art got the best of us, where reality succumbed to vision, and our lives turned into fiction.

There's only one system that can support humanity, and that's the ecosystem. All the rest is just crutches and ballast. True independence means finding our roots and getting out there on our own two feet. Metaphorically speaking (to stick to the subject), it means finding a camera and shooting your own movie, and proving to yourself that it can be done and that you don't need Hollywood to do it for you. It means taking your dreams back. It means each of us takes responsibility for his or her own actions, and so the gods or monsters that rule our realities don't have to do it for us.

There's no refuge left for the artist, anyway. Hollywood is going the way of Atlantis, and Judgment Day has come and gone in Dogville. All that leaves is the open road of independence. What choice do we have but to go to it?

Appendix - The New Avant-Garde: Honoree Mention For Films and Filmmakers That Didn't Make It Into the Book[1]

Hal Hartley: Integrity Through Obscurity

'My films all, in one way or another, try to demonstrate that it is usually a fairly lonely individual effort to reclaim this power – the power to feel without illusions.'

Hal Hartley

The most outstanding example of a philosophical filmmaker working in independent American cinema in the 90s is probably Hal Hartley. Briefly, Hartley studied painting at Massachusetts College of Art, Boston, in 1977-78, but soon after branched out into Super-8mm filmmaking, making made several shorts (*Kid, The Cartographer's Girlfriend, Dogs*) that allowed him to fund his first feature. Shot in 1989 for $75,000, *The Unbelievable Truth* came out around the same time as *sex, lies and videotape,* and was greeted with similar, if more subdued, enthusiasm as evidence of a renaissance in independent American film. *The Unbelievable Truth* had none of the slick, shallow professionalism of Soderbergh's film however; it was raw, crude, clumsy and amateurish, and yet its intellectual probings into urban neurosis – unlike those of *sex* – were genuinely thought-provoking (if somewhat glib), its satirical approach to the angst of modern city life refreshingly sharp and insightful. There was no doubt that here was an authentic creative sensibility at work, and that Hartley was a filmmaker to be watched. His next film was *Trust* in 1990, his first with Martin Donovan, an immensely appealing actor and master of the deadpan delivery that would become Hartley's signature style.[2]

Gauche and self-conscious in his stylistic approach to dialogue and framing, Hartley apparently deliberately opted for stilted, wooden delivery from his actors, emphasizing the literary bent of the lines. Despite this almost anti-cinematic approach, *Trust* held itself together, primarily thanks to Donovan as the hand-grenade-carrying computer worker who quits his job in order better to nurture his self-destructive 'genius'. The film saw the continuation of Hartley's Spartan, intellectual,

1 With apologies to those (like Michael Moore) who didn't make it into the final version of this appendix.

2 Donovan appeared in most of Hartley's films but disappeared from sight for his last couple of features, *Henry Fool* and *No Such Thing*; his presence was sorely missed. Hartley's style of filming was so sparse and dry that it badly needed the input of an actor as appealing as Donovan to breathe life into the films.

heavily ironic and resolutely eccentric approach to filmmaking, and appealed to a certain (limited) audience made up of people tired of big, dumb, unreflective movies. Hartley's films reflected and satirized the writer-director's own neurotic self doubts and his distaste for society, with its corrupting, soul-suffocating dictates. Rarely did a filmmaker's voice come through so strongly as this. Hartley was closer to a playwright than a moviemaker per se, but he opened up his 'plays' and made them cinematic. Of course, talk is cheap, and the films' heavy reliance on dialogue and on deliberately static scenes of human interaction was as much a response to Hartley's budgetary limitations as a deliberate creative device.[3] But the limitations worked in his favor, and Hartley rapidly established himself as the foremost – and practically the only – postmodernist, ironic-philosophic filmmaker in independent movies.

Hartley peaked in 1991 with *Surviving Desire*, the pinnacle of American intellectual cinema to date. *Surviving Desire* was about 'a man's ability to delude himself. A sketch of how a man can re-dress lust and possessiveness as respect and admiration; love and romance.'[4] Only an hour in length and not eligible as a feature work, *Desire* remains Hartley's masterpiece, the fullest synthesis of his philosophic concerns with his comedic, vaguely absurdist humor and his stark, austere film style. Not since Woody Allen peaked with *Annie Hall* had an American filmmaker brought existential angst and esotericism to the romantic comedy as audaciously and gracefully as Hartley did. With its university literature professor (Donovan again), as obsessed with Dostoyevsky as he is with one of his female students, *Surviving Desire* was a bibliophile's dream of a movie: intellectually searching without being dry or pretentious, deep without being self-indulgent, an almost perfect fusion of the pleasures of movies and of literature, pleasures that Hollywood

3 'Aesthetics and economics have a lot to do with one another in this field and I see no need for that to be a drag. In my part of the world, at least, it is hard to make work that is not comfortably within the mainstream unless you make it for almost no money. Ok. I'm not going to roll over and die. I'm going to figure out how to make work that interests me, in a way that interests me, for small amounts of cash. So, I have this tiny little camera that makes pretty impressive images. But the images are not anything like the things I aspire to when shooting motion picture film. So, I have to look. I actually experiment. I try to find what it is this new medium does well and how those things that it does do well can cause me to change my habits of the new avant-garde working.' Quote from 'True Fiction Pictures, Hal Hartley in conversation with Kenneth Kaleta,' as yet unpublished. © 2002 Hal Hartley and Kenneth Kaleta. See http://www. possiblefilms.com

4 'True Fiction Pictures, Hal Hartley in conversation with Kenneth Kaleta.'

generally considered mutually exclusive.

Hartley followed *Surviving Desire* with *Simple Men* in 1992, and the film marked a considerable advance in the director's assurance and technique.[5] Two years later, he made a partial foray into the mainstream with *Amateur,* a quasi-thriller about an amnesiac (Donovan) who hooks up with a former-nun-turned-nymphomaniac (French star Isabelle Huppert). Despite the typically off-the-wall premise, Hartley was somewhat at sea in his first attempt at 'genre' filmmaking as the title suggests, and his tendency to satirize and intellectualize the story led to a film that was neither fish nor fowl, neither a fully satisfying melodrama nor a pure Hartley creation. The following year he made *Flirt,* a compendium of three short films, all using the same script but shot on different locations with alternate casts, in three different languages. More of a stunt/experiment than a genuine feature, the film garnered Hartley some of his best notices but sunk at the box office. It took him two more years to make his next feature, and when he did he was reduced to roughly the same budget he'd had on *Trust,* six years earlier (around $700,000).

Though one of Hartley's best films, and despite winning a prize for best original screenplay at Cannes, *Henry Fool* (1997) seemed to pass by largely unnoticed. Amid a slew of smart, superficial, Tarantino-worshipping *wham-bam* indie films flooding the market, *Henry Fool's* humbler, more introspective qualities seemed to belong to another medium. Hartley's most recent film, *No Such Thing* in 2002, partly funded by Coppola's American Zoetrope, was a 'monster' movie with a Hollywood cast (of sorts) led by Sarah Polley, Helen Mirren and Julie Christie, but despite this, the film came and went without generating much interest. Since then, Hartley seems to have disappeared from sight, content to work on stage (on his play *Soon*) and leave off filmmaking for the time being. To this day, his films remain mostly unknown to mainstream audiences.

As Hartley himself describes it:

'My job is all about finding the right balance between exuberance and restraint... I have everything I need to make work. In the big picture, I guess I'm not so recognized. But a lot of the recognition I do have is a pain in the neck too. I think a certain degree of obscurity helps protect and strengthen one's freedom

---

5 Hartley also made two enormously entertaining shorts in this period, *Theory of Achievement* and *Ambition,* both 1991.

of movement and the approach to one's larger aims. In any event, I don't think anyone is ever awarded facilities and recognition. One pays for everything. I'd rather pay for things that are more immediately useful to me.'[6]

With or without Hartley's continuing output, and beyond the reach of the films themselves, Hartley's unique brand of irony and esotericism, his eccentric, postmodernist reinvention of cinematic conventions, seem destined to live on. He is a true original of the cinema; his sensibility is every bit as fresh and iconoclastic as Tarantino's, and in his own way he is just as talented a filmmaker (and a considerably better writer). Yet his influence on American movies (especially when compared to Tarantino's) has been subtle at best. Of course, Hartley is an introspective artist type, while Tarantino is an action-based entertainer. If Hartley's introversion and abstraction (as a person as well as a filmmaker) have kept him from 'breaking through' into the collective consciousness of Hollywood or of wider audiences, they have also kept him clear of the trappings of 'success'. By never making it, Hartley has made sure not to lose it. His best work may be yet to come.

*

'Films and paintings are all things you can control. To take an idea and translate it into something material is a beautiful process. It's thrilling to the soul! Who knows why? And that, to me, is the best thing you can be doing.'

David Lynch

Although it looks unlikely that Hollywood as an institution – as a policy – will ever again support the kind of ambitious personal projects that it did in the first half of the 70s, for Bogdanovich, Altman, Coppola, Scorsese, Malick et al., there is still a thriving pool of talent currently working more or less with its blessing and backing, and despite remaining basically on the fringes. Since the 90s and the rise of Tarantino and Miramax, independent filmmakers have had increasing opportunity to make wholly personal films without compromise, on small to medium budgets, at least part of which has come from studios eager to invest in them, even if too conservative and unadventurous to support them outright. With few exceptions, all of these original talents began by

6 'True Fiction Pictures, Hal Hartley in conversation with Kenneth Kaleta.'

making a small, independent film, through their own ingenuity and determination, followed by a less small but still independent work that caught the attention of the industry, and then accepted an offer to make a mainstream but still personal work, so graduating from avant-garde artist to Hollywood filmmaker. In most cases, this happened without the filmmaker having to overly compromise his integrity in the process. What follows is a brief resumé of some of the leading talents currently working in American independent cinema.

Richard Linklater

Linklater followed *Slacker* with the chaotic cult favorite, *Dazed and Confused*, in 1993 – his tribute to 70s college days – then returned to minimalist filmmaking with the excruciating *Before Sunrise*, in 1995, a movie that took true-to-life-ism to extremes and successfully recreated the tedium and discomfort of two strangers small-talking. In 1996, Linklater made *SubUrbia*, a film that came and went without a trace; he then disastrously attempted a big budget Western with *The Newton Boys*. In danger of losing his way, Linklater found his feet again with two back-to-back digital experiment movies, *Waking Life* and *Tape*. A labor of love, *Waking Life* (2002) weaves a tapestry out of the threads of human perception. A dreamer wanders through his dream, seeking clues to determine if he is really dreaming, and a way to wake up. Every time he wakes, however, it is into another dream. *Waking Life* is to all intents and purposes a scripted documentary and a return to the original terrain of *Slacker*, using a narrative based wholly on the free association of characters. Each player in *Waking Life* – a projection of the dreamer's unconscious – is basically a mouthpiece for Linklater's personal perspective. Yet despite the limitations of an idea-based movie devoid of action, *Waking Life* is a filmmaking triumph. Linklater takes his thesis all the way, treating it with utmost seriousness while staying loose enough to play around with it. Linklater's passion for philosophical themes pulses through the movie and keeps it alive. Since his rejection of the rules of melodrama (i.e., plot) cancels out any conventional element of suspense, the film relies on an alternate form of tension: that of ideas. And Linklater's ideas are as volatile, stimulating and provocative as any in mainstream movies, making *Waking Life* fluid, non-linear; unfolding like colors on a painter's palette, it is amazingly visceral entertainment for a movie that is all talk and no action.

With the cheeky, feel-good kids' movie, *School of Rock*, in 2003, Linklater surprised everyone by rising to the ranks of A-list director.

His least personal film, it was far and away his most popular, and despite its basically asinine premise, was well-received by critics willing to indulge Linklater's temporary lapse of taste. He returned to organic filmmaking with the quick, cheap *Before Sunset*, a mercifully superior sequel to *Before Sunrise,* in which we got to see how much Ethan Hawke had aged (and how little Julie Delpy had), and how much Linklater had matured as a filmmaker. In 2005, Linklater seems to be splitting himself into two – a Hollywood player for the sloppy and redundant remake *The Bad News Bears*, and an indie visionary for *A Scanner Darkly,* based on the Philip K. Dick cult classic novel. Shot with Keanu Reeves and painted over by computer animators à la *Waking Life, A Scanner Darkly* promises to be Linklater's most interesting work to date.

Todd Haynes

Todd Haynes made his debut with the underground style, Anger-esque *Poison,* three short films assembled into a feature. The film won a prize at Sundance in 1991 and led to Haynes' second film, *Safe,* with Julianne Moore, an arty, esoteric, all but inaccessible film that deliberately alienated audiences with its stark, monotonous story and depressed, dissociated scenes. By simulating the state of environmental sickness, *Safe* created an almost unbearable mood of tedium and despair; anything but an audience pleaser, the film won some favorable notices but did next to no business. Haynes followed it with his first big budget movie, *Velvet Goldmine* with Ewan McGregor, an overly ambitious, only partially successful recreation of the Glam Rock era of 70s Britain. The film fared poorly with both critics and audiences and might have ended a lesser director's career, but Haynes pushed on, and with the help of Clooney and Soderbergh's Section Eight, made *Far From Heaven*. The film turned out to be Haynes' breakthrough, a brilliantly designed, soulful and heart-rending 1950s melodrama in the style of director Douglas Sirk. The film was no doubt beguiling in its affectedness to younger audiences, those who had never heard of Douglas Sirk or probably ever seen a 1950s movie, but it won critical eulogies and a host of awards. Ironic that Sirk was only later recognized as an auteur due to his ability to hide a personal vision inside a mainstream melodrama – his films were basically high class soap opera. One of the most avant-garde of the new indie directors, Haynes had come into his own as an artist by channeling the ghost of one of the most 'conventional' of 50s Hollywood filmmakers.

Todd Solondz

Another Todd who broke through in the early 90s but has yet to enjoy the same degree of acceptance by Hollywood was Todd Solondz. Solondz's first film was *Welcome to the Dollhouse* (1995), a raw and original black comedy, in 1998, followed by *Happiness*, a multi-character suburban drama that included the tale of a paedophiliac father's (non-sexual) relationship with his prepubescent son. *Happiness* was inevitably a controversial work but generally well-received by all but the moral majority; with its sensitive portrayal of its subject, it revealed Solondz's gift for exposing the darker, more aberrational aspects of American society (and the human psyche), his deft irony and wit helping to balance out an essentially misanthropic view. *Storytelling* took a similar approach, with its scabrous, surgical dissection of family values, but was slightly less popular with audiences. Solondz's most recent film was *Palindromes* (2005), featuring Ellen Barkin and Jennifer Jason Leigh.

Sean Penn

Since his breakthrough role as Spicoli in *Fast Times at Ridgemont High*, Penn has attained a nigh-unprecedented degree of respect, autonomy, and creative clout in the Hollywood community. From the start, Penn (anything but a media darling and a risky box office prospect at best) was a runaway talent who, with his eclectic, sometimes perverse choice of roles, seemed more in danger of being burned up by excess talent than ever sinking into formulaic mediocrity. A genuine Hollywood maverick, Penn's films so far as a writer-director (*The Indian Runner, The Crossing Guard* and *The Pledge*) have been stubbornly noncommercial, complex psychological dramas driven by personal themes and concerns antithetical to either audience or studio tastes; character studies with subtly nuanced performances, they possess emotional-psychological depths almost unheard of in mainstream American movies. Penn's best qualities as an actor – his lack of sentimentality and fierce authenticity, slightly abrasive honesty, assurance bordering on arrogance and poetic sensitivity – all come through in his writing and direction, making his films as soulful and intriguing as is Penn the actor. None of them have been financial successes, however, and despite showcasing Jack Nicholson's best performances of the last thirty years, they have been largely passed over. Not so Penn, who with his Oscar-winning turn in Eastwood's *Mystic River*, is slowly approaching iconic status. Hollywood may actively punish individual thought and action wherever it finds it, but when the offender is too tough or stubborn to submit – as in the case of both Eastwood and Penn – it settles for canonization instead.

Atom Egoyan

This remarkable Canadian filmmaker, like his countryman David Cronenberg, is the most independent and eccentric of auteur filmmakers, and unlikely to ever reach a mainstream audience, despite being something of a critics' darling (the closest he came was with the haunting, lyrical death poem, *The Sweet Hereafter*). Egoyan broke into movies with *The Adjuster*, followed by the intricate, beguiling psychological drama *Erotica,* and his most popular work to date, *The Sweet Hereafter*, with Ian Holm. More recently, he made the ambitious, only partially successful *Ararat*, a deviation from Egoyan's esoteric subject matter into more political terrain. Like Hal Hartley before him, Egoyan seems to make his films inside the rich vacuum of his own sensibility, almost entirely unconcerned or uncorrupted by current trends or popular genres. Yet his films all have a curiously distinct tone and personality to them, their mood falling somewhere between bewilderment, obsession and despair. Rather like Kubrick, his films are cool and precise in execution, yet unlike Kubrick a flawless surface masks untold depths of emotion. Also unlike Kubrick, Egoyan has a natural affection for and insight into human follies, as well as a seemingly in-born sense of beauty. He is, as one friend put it, 'a true poet of the cinema'.

Neil LaBute

Neil LaBute, the first Mormon filmmaker, made his debut with *In The Company of Men*, a scabrous, misanthropic comedy about two bored office workers who decide to seduce and dump a deaf-mute colleague and so avenge themselves on womankind. LaBute's conception of human nature was as unremittingly bleak as Todd Solondz's, but unlike Solondz, LaBute didn't offer any leavening sweetness or even much by way of ironic detachment. LaBute's vitriolic dialogue and stubbornly unsympathetic characters made for a cinema of self-loathing that, presumably for LaBute at least, aspired to catharsis. LaBute divided audiences down the middle – those who loved it and those who hated it – but one thing his films definitely didn't bring to mind was the Christian idea of 'love-thy-neighbor'. *Your Friends and Neighbors*, LaBute's follow-up film, was also unrelentingly personal, but with its larger cast (including Ben Stiller, Catherine Keener, Jason Patrick and LaBute's regular Aaron Eckhart) and wider spectrum of neuroses to cover, it was considerably more accessible as entertainment, however dark. LaBute went halfway into the mainstream for his third film, *Nurse Betty*, for which his scathing view brought a refreshing degree of honesty and ruthlessness to an otherwise fairly routine Hollywood comedy romance, with Renee Zellwegger. The limitations of a studio picture, and being confined to someone else's script, brought LaBute's talents as a director to the fore. Next he returned to his own material and filmed the stage play, *The Shape of Things,* a contrived and creakingly acted, basically absurd but oddly absorbing film: LaBute's talent for creating irredeemably nasty characters and placing them into suitably repugnant scenarios has a fascination all its own. Most recently, LaBute strayed off course entirely for the generic folly of *Possession,* since which he seems to have been laying low, biding his time perhaps, before his next attack on humanity?

Paul Thomas Anderson

In 1996 Paul Thomas Anderson made *Hard Eight* – which few people saw but which allowed him to make *Boogie Nights*, a sleeper hit that briefly resurrected Burt Reynolds' career and made a star out of Mark Wahlberg. With its affectionate and ironic treatment of the 1970s porno industry, *Boogie Nights* was a hazy, sleazy, wholly engrossing ensemble piece that defied convention and showed its writer–director to be a uniquely gifted filmmaker with an almost fully-formed sensibility after only two pictures. The blend of violence and humor, pathos with detachment, was a million miles away from the aforementioned Tarantino school of *wham-bam* filmmaking, and approached a kind of documentary purism, like anthropological melodrama. Anderson's next film, *Magnolia*, aspired to be just that; lacking the appealing roughness and humility of *Boogie Nights*, *Magnolia* was a sprawling, only partly successful imitation of Altman, and suggested Anderson was a filmmaker with aspirations possibly beyond his talents. As if aware of that possibility, Anderson scaled everything down for his next film – and gave a nod to commercialism by casting Adam Sandler – the short, snappy, inventive romantic comedy, *Punch-Drunk Love*. Though his most conventional film to date, it was also his lightest and most enjoyable, and no less unique for being something of a concession to genre filmmaking. Even working within the parameters of the romantic comedy, Anderson has a natural affinity for human complexity, and with his pleasantly restrained style together with his predilection for realistic detail and the seamier side of life, Anderson effectively (and perhaps consciously) echoes the early 70s filmmaking style.

Wes Anderson

Another Anderson to ascend to glory in the late 90s was Wes Anderson, who made the all-but unseen *Bottle Rocket* with a then-unknown Owen Wilson. This was followed soon after by the eccentric school-time comedy, *Rushmore*, starring Jason Schwartzman (evoking Dustin Hoffman's Benjamin in *The Graduate*) as Max, and with Bill Murray in vintage form. Over a period of months the film gathered slow but steady momentum, mostly through word-of-mouth, and went from an obscure indie flick to the 'must-see' movie of the year. *Rushmore* was a film that everyone was talking about and that almost everyone professed to adore. A gentle, bizarre character piece, it had no sliced-off ears and no hyper-kinetic violence, but was possessed of such a unique personality that it was like a genre unto itself, a freak of the cinema.

This was even more true of Anderson's follow-up, the ambitious, and mesmerizing *The Royal Tennebaums*, a film which actually managed to give a career-topping role to Gene Hackman, creating a world of characters so individual and vibrant as to constitute a veritable alternate movie reality. *Tennebaums* was probably the most completely unique cinematic vision since Hal Hartley hit his prime, but it was especially remarkable as an auteur-vision for its lightness of touch and its bittersweet optimism. Anderson's vision wasn't anaemic, like Spielberg's; it was full of pain and anxiety. But the suffering was out on the surface, and even the angst and despair was part of the comedy. Like Hartley, or Woody Allen at his best, Anderson knew how to turn personal pain into the universal balm of irony, and made mischief of his own existential concerns. Certainly, *The Royal Tennebaums* is one of very few films of recent years to come out of Hollywood distinctly resembling a work of art.

His most recent film, *Steve Zissou and the Life Aquatic*, despite a strangely affecting central performance from Bill Murray, was something of a disappointment. Almost willfully aimless and enervated, the film's humor and character vignettes, which made *Tennebaums* such a treat, never really take off, and it floats along in pleasant, dreamy and occasionally dreary indifference to plot or narrative drive – a stoned Murray does not an engine make. Over all, the film suggests a tendency towards auteur self-indulgence, the kiss of death to many a young movie 'genius'. Still, like the rest of Anderson's small oeuvre, it's a unique work that never for a moment feels compromised.

Alexander Payne

Alexander Payne's first film was *Citizen Ruth* with Laura Dern, a film that garnered praise and won prizes without making it to the multiplexes. Payne followed with *Election*, starring Reese Witherspoon and Mathew Broderick, a smart college comedy that brought the director into the mainstream. No less a Hollywood star than Jack Nicholson appeared in Payne's next film, *About Schmidt*, a touching, lightly amusing, perfectly observed comedy of anxiety and melancholy in which Nicholson gave a revelatory performance as an ordinary 'schmoe'.[7] In 2004, Payne made his fourth film, *Sideways*, a slight but poignant road movie that captured critics' (and even the public's) imagination and sympathy, with its wryly observed depiction of the woes and follies of the everyman. A wholly human comedy, *Sideways* was about as un-Hollywood as you could get without actually being avant-garde. It was a movie about nothing in particular, with no bubbling psychological undercurrents or layers of psychosis to justify its threadbare story, nothing but the mundane comedy of anguish, timidity, regret and self-loathing suffered by its central character. Paul Giamitti in the lead role gave a perfectly understated performance as the mildly obsessed, quietly desperate, failing writer Miles, whose passion for life has been siphoned off until all that is left is a nigh-fanatical penchant for vintage wine.

Of all the best independent filmmakers to emerge in recent years, Payne is the least showy or impressive, the least obviously talented, and the one who comes closest to capturing the essence of mundane human experience. His focus as a director seems almost perversely self-effacing and diffident, wholly directed towards bringing the best out of the actors and material, and apparently indifferent to parading his own talents as a director. Payne's talent is for downplaying his talents in service of the story. If he shows a paucity of style, it may only be because he has such a high regard for content. In this day and age, where every filmmaker strives to top the rest with the audacity of his technique, Payne's modesty is practically unheard of.

---

7 Devoid of leering grins and cocked eyebrows, Nicholson seemed like a totally different actor. Penn got Nicholson to act again for the first time since the early 80s; but Payne got him to do *character* acting.

Sofia Coppola

What's interesting about Sofia Coppola's career as a director – post *Godfather Part Three* – is how markedly it differs from her father's work. It is characterized by a humility and an almost deliberate inconsequentiality, diametrically opposed to the grande follie of her father in his heyday, before he crashed and burned with *One from the Heart*. Perhaps she learnt from observing his mistakes close at hand, and from suffering directly as a result of them?[8]

Her first film, *The Virgin Suicides* – partially funded by Coppola's American Zoetrope and starring Kirsten Dunst – was a haunting, heart-rending tale, melancholy and dreamlike; with its eerie, lazy grace reminiscent of Peter Weir's *Picnic at Hanging Rock*, it was a remarkably assured debut film. Her next film, *Lost in Translation*, for which she enjoyed widespread recognition, was equally graceful a work yet so slight and self-effacing that it seemed almost not to be there at all. Of all the (few) recent films directed by women, *Lost in Translation* was most manifestly the work of a female sensibility.[9]

Lost in Translation wasn't a great movie by any stretch of the imagination, but it was a unique one, a movie that seemed refreshingly free of the need to impress audiences by doing much of anything, that was content simply to be. James Cameron and Oliver Stone might take a leaf or two out of Sofia Coppola's book – there's more to art than hubris. Real wisdom is having nothing to prove.[10]

8 For *The Godfather Part Three* – a film that never should have happened, a film that in a sense (an archetypal, Platonic sense) never *did* happen – Coppola cast his daughter, Sofia, as Michael Corleone's daughter in the film (a last minute decision prompted by Winona Ryder's sudden illness); by doing so he exposed her – at the tender age of eighteen – to a barrage of critical vitriol that ought rightly to have been reserved for Coppola alone. Sofia survived the experience; not only that, she went on to become a director herself, one whose work surpassed her father's current work in quality (and also in critical reception). It was a fitting revenge, perhaps, though doubtless Coppola was as happy for his daughter's triumph as a filmmaker as he had been distraught by her ruin as an actress.

9 Excepting *The Piano*, a real woman's art movie made by a woman, and mostly for women. Jane Campion is the only other major American female director besides Coppola currently working in Hollywood (at least since Kathryn Bigelow has faded away). But Campion has lately gone the same creatively self-negating route as Bigelow (and so many male auteurs), with the shallow and sordid serial killer movie, *In the Cut*.

10 I may have been premature in suggesting that Sofia Coppola hasn't inherited her father's excessive artistic ambition; her latest film is a treatment of the life of Marie Antoinette (2006).

Bibliography

Belton, John. *American Cinema, American Culture*. New York: McGraw Hill, 1994.

Biskind, Peter. *Down and Dirty Pictures*. London: Bloomsbury, 2004.

Biskind, Peter. *Easy Riders, Raging Bulls*. London: Bloomsbury, 1998.

Carney, Ray. *Shadows*. London: BFI Publishing, 2001.

Cowie, Peter. *Coppola*. London: Faber and Faber, 1998.

David Puttnam (with Neil Watson). *Movies and Money*. New York: Vintage Books, 1998.

Epstein, Edward Jay. The Big Picture: The New Logic of Money and Power in Hollywood. New York: Random House, Inc., 2005.

Estrin, Mark W., ed. *Orson Welles: Interviews*. Jackson, Miss: University Press of Mississippi, 2002.

Evans, Robert. *The Kid Stays in the Picture*. Beverly Hills: Dove Books, 1995.

George Orwell, *1984*. London: Penguin Books, 1990.

Gottlieb, Sidney, ed. *Alfred Hitchcock: Interviews*. Jackson, Miss: University Press of Mississippi, 2003.

Grimes, Larry E. *"Shall These Bones Live?"* In *Screening the Sacred: Religion, Myth and Ideology in Popular American Film*, ed. Joel W. Martin and Conrad E. Ostwalt, 20, 25. Boulder, Col: Westview

Kael, Pauline. *Conversations*. Jackson, Miss: University Press of Mississippi, 1996
  – *Deeper into Movies*. London: Calder and Boyars, 1975.
  – *Hooked*. London: Marion Boyars, 1992.
  – *Movie Love*. London: Marion Boyars, 1992
  – *Reeling*. London: Marion Boyars, 1977.
  – *Taking It All In*. New York: Holt, Rinehart and Winston, 1984.
  – *When the Lights Go Down*. London: Marion Boyars, 1980.

Knapp, Laurence E., ed. *Brian De Palma: Interviews*. Jackson, Miss: University Press of Mississippi, 2003.

Mathews, Jack. *The Battle of Brazil*. New York: Crown Publishers, Inc, 1987.

Philips, Gene D. and Rodney Hill, ed. *Francis Ford Coppola: Interviews*. Jackson, Miss: University Press of Mississippi, 2004.

Phillips, Julia *You'll Never Eat Lunch in This Town Again*. New York: Random House, 1991.

Pierson, John. Spike, Mike, *Slackers and Dykes: A Guided Tour Across a Decade of American Independent Cinema*. New York: Hyperion, 1997.

Rodley, Chris, ed. *Lynch on Lynch*. London: Faber and Faber, 2005.

Rodriguez, Robert. *Rebel without a Crew*. London: Faber and Faber, 1995.

Roman, Shari *Digital Babylon: Hollywood, Indiewood, & Dogme 95*. Hollywood: Lone Eagle Publishing Company, 2001.

Rosenbaum, Jonathan. *Movie Wars: How Hollywood and the Media Limit What Movies We Can See*. Chicago Review Press, 2002.

Rushing, Janice Hocker and Thomas S. Frentz. *Projecting the Shadow: The Cyborg Hero in American Film*. Chicago: University of Chicago Press, 1995.

Schumacher, Michael. *Francis Ford Coppola: A Filmmaker's Life*. New York: Three Rivers Press, 1999.

Sterritt, David and Lucille Rhodes, ed. *Terry Gilliam: Interviews*. Jackson, Miss: University Press of Mississippi, 2004.

Steven Bach, *Final Cut: Art Money and Ego in the Making of Heaven's Gate, the Film That Sank United Artists*. New York: Newmarket Press, 1999.

Waxman, Sharon. *Rebels on the Backlot: Six Maverick Directors and How They Conquered the Hollywood Studio System*. New York: HarperCollins Publishers Inc., 2005.

Index